Color behind Bars

Recent Titles in
Racism in American Institutions
Brian D. Behnken, Series Editor

The Color of Politics: Racism in the American Political Arena Today
Chris Danielson

How Do Hurricane Katrina's Winds Blow?: Racism in 21st-Century
New Orleans
Liza Lugo, JD

Out of Bounds: Racism and the Black Athlete
Lori Latrice Martin, E

Color behind Bars

Racism in the U.S. Prison System

VOLUME 2: PUBLIC POLICY AND THE U.S. PRISON SYSTEM

SCOTT WM. BOWMAN, EDITOR

Racism in American Institutions
Brian D. Behnken, Series Editor

 PRAEGER

AN IMPRINT OF ABC-CLIO, LLC
Santa Barbara, California • Denver, Colorado • Oxford, England

Library of Congress Cataloging-in-Publication Data

Color behind bars : racism in the U.S. prison system / Scott William Bowman.
    volumes ; cm. — (Racism in American institutions)
Includes bibliographical references and index.
    ISBN 978–0–313–39903–9 (hardback : alk. paper) — ISBN 978–0–313–39904–6 (ebook)
    1. Prisons and race relations—United States. 2. Discrimination in criminal justice administration—United States. 3. Racism—United States. 4. Minorities—United States. I. Bowman, Scott Wm., editor.
HV9471.C645   2014
365′.608900973—dc23   2014000037

ISBN: 978–0–313–39903–9
EISBN: 978–0–313–39904–6

18 17 16 15 14   1 2 3 4 5

This book is also available on the World Wide Web as an eBook.
Visit www.abc-clio.com for details.

Praeger
An Imprint of ABC-CLIO, LLC

ABC-CLIO, LLC
130 Cremona Drive, P.O. Box 1911
Santa Barbara, California 93116-1911

This book is printed on acid-free paper ∞

Manufactured in the United States of America

Contents

Volume 2: Public Policy and the U.S. Prison System

Chapter 16

What Keeps Us Here?: Policies and Practices That Shape Minority Overrepresentation

Scott Wm. Bowman

Over the past 35 years, the United States has realized not only a massive expansion of the criminal justice system as a whole, but also unprecedented growth in the total numbers of individuals that are incarcerated. Research suggests that the most recent decades have demonstrated increases of approximately 300 percent for those that are incarcerated at various levels throughout the United States, with approximately 3 percent of the total population under some form of correctional supervision.[1] At face value, individuals concerned with the general overincarceration of the American population would be rightly justified, as these increases have reached most demographic groups and geographic regions. However, as has been the case for racial and ethnic minorities throughout the history of carceral systems, the growth has been exacerbated for people of color—particularly African Americans, Hispanics, and Native Americans. There are two statistics, one for African Americans and one for Hispanics, that demonstrate the contemporary issues associated with many minority groups. First, Walker, Spohn, and DeLone suggest that "African Americans comprise less than 15% of the U.S. population but nearly 40 percent of all incarcerated offenders,"[2] with an incarceration rate of 4,749 per 100,000 African American males in 2009 (compared to 708 per 100,000 white males).[3] Regarding Hispanics, Walker, Spohn, and DeLone indicate similar carceral growth:

> In recent years, Hispanics have been the fastest growing minority group being imprisoned. They were 10.5 percent of the prison population in 1985, 15.5 percent in 1995, 16.4 percent in 2000, and 20.6 percent in 2009. These

increases reflect a rate twice as high as in the increase for African American and white inmates.[4]

Additionally, it is suggested that Native Americans and Alaska Natives are incarcerated at rates that exceed their percentages of the total population.[5]

While the historical experiences of incarceration for various racial and ethnic minorities are directly pertinent to the current state of imprisonment, there are clear contemporary catalysts that have both implicitly and explicitly acted to further reinforce the attitudes and stereotypes that have either directly maintained or enhanced these disproportionalities. Whereas many of the former carceral activities were accomplished during a period of overt racism and discrimination, various contemporary activities have been directly rooted in institutional discrimination, political rhetoric, and race-neutral policies that produce disproportionate outcomes. The result for most racial and ethnic minorities in the United States has been (as Michelle Alexander so eloquently called it) "mass incarceration in the age of colorblindness."[6]

There are two major themes to the chapters in this volume: (1) the legislation that has directly shaped minority overrepresentation in jails and prisons throughout the United States and (2) the race- and ethnicity-based practices surrounding imprisonment that directly and indirectly influence racial/ethnic outcomes. The foundation of these themes was (and continues to be) rooted in the larger political rhetoric of being "universally" tough on crime. Starting with Richard Nixon (the *ironic* originator[7] of "law and order" and "the war on drugs") and continuing through the presidency of Barack Obama, presidents, legislators, judges (at both the state and federal level), and the larger citizenry have constructed and supported a social, political, and legal agenda of "getting tough on crime."[8] However, the written agenda and the implemented agenda have been resoundingly dissimilar. For many of the invisible racial and ethnic minorities in the United States—the overwhelming percentage of which come from poor, quasi-segregated neighborhoods—written policies have been enacted with the measure of swiftness and certainty that is consistent with the legislation, while their racial/ethnic and socioeconomic counterparts have held the privilege of seeing the outcomes play out in newspapers and television shows. Additionally, the racially/ethnically disproportionate outcomes have further established prison-based policies that have acted to aggravate many of the social, economic, and political interpretations of the systematic successes or failures of imprisonment. The criminal justice system, with its unprecedented economic footprint on state and federal budgets for the past three decades,[9] has sustained a consistent method of imprisonment at the expense of those most socially, economically, and politically vulnerable.

Regarding the first theme, comprehensive policies such as the original crack versus cocaine legislation, mandatory minimum legislation, "truth-in-sentencing" legislation, and three strikes legislation were each cloaked in the rhetoric of race neutrality, while individually producing outcomes that overwhelmingly affected African Americans and Hispanics (as well as Native Americans to a lesser degree). Within the post–civil rights era, political narratives have often been constructed according to a "postracial" ideology. This has been no different for the narratives associated with the criminal justice system and more specifically the policies directly associated with imprisonment, where racial and ethnic overrepresentation is often explained away as the sole fault of the individual or as "statistically unexplainable" nondiscrimination. Regardless, society has become seemingly comfortable with the current disproportionalities, supporting continued efforts to maintain punitive carceral outcomes.

Regarding the second theme, the manner in which policies and practices that are supplemental to imprisonment are implemented is also relevant to the overall examination of racial and ethnic overrepresentations. The personal and social factors associated with parole, reentry, treatment, and other community effects of imprisonment are generally challenging due to larger sociological, socioeconomic, and communal differences. These factors can include (1) trusting mental health treatment and having the family support necessary to seek and maintain services, (2) having family and community support (e.g., jobs, housing) during the reentry process after release from imprisonment, and (3) developing criminal justice–based support from corrections officers and parole officers that effectively prepare people for desistance from crime. Yet when considering the unique social and psychological experiences of blacks, Hispanics, and Native Americans—principally those of a lower socioeconomic status who are from disorganized and underdeveloped neighborhoods—the aforementioned issues become heightened. As a result, while the daily challenges that many black (25.8 percent poverty rate), Native American (27.0 percent poverty rate), and Hispanic (23.2 percent poverty rate) *nonfelons* face usually proves a challenge, weighting personal successes or failures by incorporating the carceral experiences of these minority groups indicates near-overwhelming challenges.[10]

As is discussed throughout this volume, particularly for racial and ethnic minorities, the current practices ineffectively address the larger carceral issues. Reiman describes this as a Pyrrhic defeat theory, stating, "I call this outrageous way of looking at criminal justice policy the *Pyrrhic defeat theory*. A 'pyrrhic victory' is a military victory purchased as such a cost in troops and treasure that it amounts to a defeat. The Pyrrhic defeat theory argues that the failure of the criminal justice system yields such benefits to those in positions of power that it amounts to success."[11] While Reiman is writing primarily about socioeconomic status and crime, the same can be said for poor racial and ethnic minorities in the criminal justice system and carceral expansion—"nothing succeeds like failure."[12]

Hopefully, we as Americans are attempting to redefine what is meant by criminal justice success through imprisonment. For example, drug courts and other specialty courts have proven to be effective alternatives to incarceration. Recently, U.S. attorney general Eric Holder has discussed finding alternatives to incarceration and alternative sentencing structures for those receiving a mandatory minimum sentence, suggesting that perhaps a Pyrrhic defeat is becoming an increasingly unacceptable outcome.[13] As the editor of this manuscript and a person whose basic livelihood is directly connected to these issues, it is my sincere hope that the subjects presented here *no longer* withstand the longevity of racial and ethnic overrepresentation in our jails and prisons.

Notes

1. Beckett and Sasson, 2000; Reiman, 2007.
2. Walker, Spohn, and DeLone, 2012, p. 406.
3. Walker, Spohn, and DeLone, 2012, p. 412.
4. Walker, Spohn, and DeLone, 2012, p. 406.
5. Walker, Spohn, and DeLone, 2012, p. 406.
6. Alexander, 2012.
7. The irony of Nixon voicing a need for law and order is directly related to his Watergate activities and subsequent resignation from the presidency.
8. Alexander, 2012; Beckett, and Sasson, 2000; O'Reilly, 1995; Reiman, 2007.
9. Wacquant, 2009.
10. Poverty rates from Macartney, Bishaw, and Fontenot, 2013.
11. Reiman, 2007, p. 5.
12. Reiman, 2007, p. 5.
13. Reiman, 2007.

References

Alexander, Michelle. *The New Jim Crow: Mass Incarceration in the Age of Colorblindness*. New York: New Press, 2012.

Beckett, Katherine, and Theodore Sasson. *The Politics of Injustice: Crime and Punishment in America*. Thousand Oaks, CA: Sage, 2000.

Engen, Rodney L., and Sara Steen. "The Power to Punish: Discretion and Sentencing Reform in the War on Drugs." *American Journal of Sociology* 105, no. 5 (2000): 1357–1395.

Macartney, Suzanne, Alemayehu Bishaw, and Kayla Fontenot. *Poverty Rates for Selected Detailed Race and Hispanic Groups by State and Place, 2007–2011*. Washington, DC: U.S. Department of Commerce, U.S. Census Bureau, 2013.

O'Reilly, Kenneth. *Nixon's Piano: Presidents and Racial Politics from Washington to Clinton*. New York: New Press, 1995.

Perez, Evan. "Holder Touts Benefits of Changes in Mandatory Minimum Sentences," November 6, 2013. Accessed February 16, 2014 from http://politicalticker.blogs.cnn.com/2013/11/05/holder-touts-benefits-of-changes-in-mandatory-minimum-sentences.

Reiman, Jeffrey H. *The Rich Get Richer and the Poor Get Prison: Ideology, Class, and Criminal Justice* (8th ed.). Boston: Pearson, 2007.

Wacquant, Loïc. *Punishing the Poor: The Neoliberal Government of Social Insecurity*. Durham, NC: Duke University Press, 2009.

Walker, Samuel, Cassia Spohn, and Miriam DeLone. *The Color of Justice: Race, Ethnicity, and Crime in America* (5th ed.). Belmont, CA: Wadsworth, 2012.

Ethno-Racial Factors in the U.S. Prison System: Forensic Psychological Realities of Correctional Officers

Ronn Johnson

This chapter discusses ethno-racial factors confronting correctional officers working in various types of U.S. prisons. Correctional officers are charged with maintaining safety in prisons, which today hold more than 2.3 million ethno-racially diverse inmates. The Bureau of Labor Statistics reports there are approximately 500,000 correctional officers (COs) in the United States, a number that is projected to rise.[1] Racial violence is a well-documented fact of life within prisons. An obvious question is whether the enclosed prison setting exacerbates ethno-racial tensions among incarcerated groups. It might be argued that prison somehow manufactures or exacerbates race-conscious behavior by prisoners or staff within various U.S. prisons settings (e.g., mental health, supermax, military, and juvenile). From a forensic psychological perspective, race-conscious behavior can be defined as a calculated action (or reaction) of inequality or exclusion that results in deliberate harm to a group or individual because of identifiable characteristics or observable traits (e.g., race or ethnicity).[2]

Race-conscious behavior includes prison policies that promulgate unfairness as well as actions of individual correctional and police officers.[3] Race-conscious behavior noticed on institutional and interpersonal levels can fuel ethno-racial conflicts (between inmates or between inmates and correctional officers).[4]

Some may illogically interpret that the election of a black president in the United States is a signal that racism no longer exists. Though in-your-face acts of racial discrimination have, for the most part, declined outside of prison,[5] this does not mean that there are no longer pockets of racism. Diversity may be on the lips, but there is a lynching rope in the pocket. It has been argued that today there are more brief incidents of denigrating but nonetheless psychosocially destructive microaggression toward various ethno-racial individuals.[6] There can also be what is sometimes referred to as "unconscious racism." However, Blanton and Jaccarard find little empirical support for this "unconscious" construct.[7] Concurrently, academic underachievement, comparatively lower college graduation but higher dropout rates, and underperforming schools in minority neighborhoods may function as signs that race-conscious behavior still occurs via institution. What is often called "institutional racism" refers to the policies and/or practices in prisons or other systems that create disparate treatment of a targeted inmate group.[8] Blacks, Native Americans, and Latinos are disproportionately represented within the U.S prison system. To the surprise of no one, some groups without sufficient educational backgrounds and/or inadequately treated mental disorders are incarcerated. The overrepresentation of blacks, Latinos, and Native Americans is a confluence of negative circumstances. One might also be able to argue that it is more difficult to separate race-conscious behavior from judicious implementation of necessary prison policy. Inmates of a particular skin color would have to make the case that enforcement of prison rules was substantially unequal based on race.

Trauma resulting from race-conscious behavior is often passed down to the next generation, expanding the stress and consequences of the psychological damage.[9] Psycho-culturally, previous exposure can prompt race-related stress responses that involve a heightened sensitivity or a healthy form of cross-cultural paranoia.[10] For example, it has been reported that past experiences with racism can result in a centralization or ethno-racial factor within a person's psychological disposition. As a result, even benign routine interactions between an inmate and correctional officer can function to reflexively elicit culturally conditioned responses.[11] U.S. prisons are racialized environments. The societal rules and privileges for civilians are not always applicable in a prison setting where safety trumps everything. The need for safety of both inmates and personnel within an environment full of ethno-racial tensions is the driving force for the operational decision made by some U.S. prisons to segregate inmates based on race and gang affiliation.

Is this race-conscious behavior or forensic psychological reality? Racial animosity or power struggles can be readily observed between prison gangs, which can spill over to correctional officers. Official California inmate demographic designations include "Hispanic," "black," "white," and "other," representing approximately 39, 29, 26, and 6 percent of inmates, respectively.[12] California, the birthplace of many of the most violent prison gangs, has one of the worst prison gang problems in the nation.[13] Gang affiliation and racial identification are used within the California Departments of Corrections and Rehabilitation (CDC) to separate inmates. The U.S. Supreme Court decided in *Johnson vs. California* (543 U.S. 499, 2005) that the California Department of Corrections' unwritten practice of racially segregating inmates is to be viewed through the legal prism of a constitutional review standard. The burden of proof was placed on California to provide evidence that its unwritten practice was circumscribed to a "compelling" government interest. The CDC began a mediated agreement with Johnson that avoided additional litigation in the lower courts on this issue. Correctional officers function as a vital cog in the ethno-racial reality of U.S. prisons. Correctional officers maintain professionalism in the face of ongoing demands from inmates, institutions, society, and other correctional personnel. In the U.S. prison system, correctional officers, or in some cases military personnel, are the most visible sources of authority in these institutions. The required duties of a correctional officer place the job among the most stressful in the world. Homicide is the fourth leading cause of occupational fatalities.[14] A Swedish investigation revealed a higher use of sick leave in prisons with lower CO job satisfaction and higher proportions of drug-related inmates.[15] Additionally, there is a nexus between police work and a wide range of chronic illnesses and conditions, including diabetes and heart disease, cancers, digestive disorders, and high cholesterol.[16]

Despite being affected by stress and pervasive ethno-racial tension, as a group, correctional officers are dedicated to providing a safe prison setting despite the psycho-historical context of U.S. prisons. Most correctional officers are aware that reflexive skin color reactions are potentially present in practically every interaction with an inmate. Job demands for a correctional officer in the 21st century have expanded to include participation in Homeland Security counterterrorism efforts (e.g., recognition of domestic terrorists and/or sleeper cells). Correctional academies must prepare correctional officer for the inevitable stressful cross-racial exchanges. The assumption is that a correctional officer has been psychologically screened and found to possess the ability and training to remain professional under job pressure. The informed correctional officer must immediately jump to his or her academy training while remaining aware of the ethno-racial aspects of each inmate interaction. The correctional officer's interactions with diverse inmates in U.S. prisons can be enhanced by the awareness of four ethno-racial maxims.

Ethno-Racial Maxim 1

The relational work with diverse groups is contingent upon the establishment and maintenance of ethno-racial credibility. Working for more than 30 years as a psychologist has resulted in my recognition that before crossing an ethno-racial boundary, one must establish cultural credibility and strengthen relational bonds.[17] For example, diverse inmates arrested by police report that they or others have become extremely aggressive with the arresting officer. Yet upon arrival to jail, the prisoners may become more cooperative or less combative largely because they recall being treated with respect by correctional officers.

Ethno-Racial Maxim 2

Each person in a cross-cultural situation brings historical trauma that affects behavior and disposition. Distinct psychological processes convert cross-racial interactions into personal and transgenerational recollections of racial memories.[18] *Residual ethno-racial stress can be reflexively reignited without regard to the intention of a peace officer.* Correctional or peace officers may have a pre-inmate encounter mindset that views race as a driving force in the behavior of prisoners. Inmates may anticipate that their race will be the primary factor in how they are treated by authorities, whether CO or probation office (PO).

Though correctional officers are not social workers or clinical mental health professionals, awareness and acceptance of an inmate's ethno-racial experiences are fundamental relational prerequisites for the respect required to achieve a desirable safety outcome.

Ethno-Racial Maxim 3

Peace officers bring their own ethno-racial history into every interaction, positively or negatively influencing each cross-cultural outcome. Correctional officers carry into every interaction their academy training, ability to assess self, management of boredom, and other psychological stress vulnerabilities (e.g., posttraumatic stress disorder [PTSD] or mild traumatic brain injury [MTBI]).

Ethno-Racial Maxim 4

Conflict is an inescapable part of the role of a peace officer. Every conflict has the potential for unwanted ethno-racial tensions. Not every or even a majority of conflicts result from an unwanted ethno-racial component. Correctional officers usually have full knowledge of the inmates they have to work with in prison. The inmates prison colors and other visible designations allow COs to appropriately assess whether an inmate has a history of being cooperative or resistant. Scene management situations (e.g., fights between inmates or supporting other officers) are enhanced by information before a potential conflict.

Psychological Screening of Correctional Officers for Diverse Prison Facilities

Ethno-racial demands require a correctional officer be psychologically stable and suitable for this stressful work. State and county laws often require that all background-approved correctional officer applicants undergo psychological screening. Most of these psychological evaluations are performed by licensed psychologists with well-documented training, appropriate professional associations, law enforcement affiliations, and ongoing supervision in correctional and police psychology.[19] Codes in some venues require a specific level of certification and/or experience. Some larger venues have permanent staff that perform these evaluations on an ongoing basis.[20] In general, the process requires a psychologist who meets the previously mentioned criteria to review all reasonably available records of a correctional officer applicant and conduct a job-relevant psychological interview using at least two appropriate psychological tests that are valid for correctional/probation officer purposes. Some examiners use only testing to screen and then elect to perform an interview only when they believe the testing raises issues. However, most states require a face-to-face interview, and one established practice is that testing should never be used as the sole basis for making an evaluation decision. In most venues, psychological testing is considered valid for 12 months. Departments vary as to whether and when a disqualified candidate can reapply. An applicant recycling through after a psychological disqualification must be able to provide clear and convincing evidence that he or she has done something substantial to address and correct the issues related to the original psychological bypass or disqualification. A waiting period of at least 18 months is recommended before an applicant is allowed to have a second preemployment psychological evaluation.[21]

California screening requires use of the POST (Peace Officer Standards of Training). Many venues and examiners outside the state also adhere to those standards. The POST was initially developed to achieve consistency in evaluating correctional officers. In 2006, the POST Commission approved the issuance of the "Psychological Screening Dimensions" for use in the preemployment psychological evaluation of peace officers. The new set of 10 validated peace officer psychological attributes was developed from an extensive job analysis. Each of the 10 psychological dimensions includes a behaviorally based definition and a list of associated positive and counterproductive correctional officer behaviors (e.g., adaptability/flexibility, avoidance of substance abuse, conscientiousness/dependability, integrity/ethics impulse control/attention to safety, stress tolerance, judgment). The use of POST psychological dimensions occurs after testing, review of documents, and a face-to-face interview as well as a second evaluation for those initially found psychologically not qualified. Some venues and examiners throughout the country elect to use the POST standards and process because they provide a degree of uniformity viewed as an acceptable standard of practice.[22]

Psychological screening is not performed for the purpose of screening in the best individuals; rather it is used to screen out those with psychological issues that would, over time, interfere with performance of the essential functions of their job. Corrections officers must be fit to deal with the predictable stresses of working with inmates from various ethno-racial groups found in U.S. prisons. The "rule-out" as opposed to "rule-in" approach is the standard of practice in the psychological screening of correctional officers.[23] The rule-out approach demonstrates that individuals with history of a behavior disorder are more likely than not to experience job performance difficulties or involve themselves in misconduct while trying to consistently fulfill the duties of a correctional officer.[24] The department chooses whom to screen in. In larger venues, this may be done by civil service exams, and the highest grades and legal preferences for special populations such as veterans and diverse candidates may result in an applicant pool that is not specifically selected to meet the job demands. In smaller venues, the advancing candidates may be simply the choice of the superintendent. In others, the initial selection is done by a board of municipal leaders and/or superior officers who guide the selection based on their experience and/or community needs. Some departments use standardized behavioral, nonmedical psychological screening questionnaires such as the Inwald Personality Inventory to guide the initial selection of correctional officer applicants who work in prisons throughout the United States.

Correctional Officers in Various Types of Facilities and Imprisonment Activities in the United States

Prisons maintain an irreplaceable role in the U.S. criminal justice system, a role that cuts ethno-racially across every international border. The United States has among the highest incarceration rates in the world. By the end of 2009, the rate was 743 adults incarcerated per 100,000 people. According to the U.S. Bureau of Justice Statistics (BJS), 2,266,800 adults were incarcerated in U.S. federal or state prisons and county jails at year-end 2010. This figure constitutes about 0.7 percent of adults in the U.S. resident population.

The U.S. prison system has come under considerable criticism. For example, in an article in the *New Yorker* titled "Why Do We Lock Up So Many People?," Celeste Fremon reflects thoughtfully about prisons.[25] She says, "A prison is a trap for catching time. Good reporting appears often about the inner life of the American prison, but the catch is that American prison life is mostly under-dramatic—the reported stories fail to grab us, because, for the most part, nothing happens." It has been estimated that about two-thirds of discharged inmates will be rearrested within three years.[26] Petersilia argues that a representative number of these released inmates "have been born with, or have developed, serious social, psychological, and physical problems" and "will be released to poor inner-city communities with few services."[27] U.S. prisons contain many of the same psychosocial problems seen on the outside. So, one might argue that meaningful imprisonment and reentry solutions should be tested by exploring various issues in the U.S. prison system. Kennedy points out, "The problem is that our response to the crime has become a part of what is sustaining it." He opines that "we are destroying the village in order to save it."[28]

Some of the most high-profile criminals in history were sent to prison. O. J. Simpson is incarcerated in a Nevada prison for crimes committed while attempting to secure what he identified as his personal property. Malcom X as well as boxers Ruben "Hurricane" Carter and Mike Tyson were sent to prison. Ted Kaczynski, who is better known as the Unabomber, is serving time for decades of terroristic bomb attacks. Khalid Shaikh Mohammed, better known as a self-described mastermind of the September 11, 2001, terrorist attacks, is held in the U.S. prison at Guantanamo Bay, Cuba. There is considerable diversity in the prison population. Some inmates are dangerous because they have severe mental disorders, are violent sex offenders, or are serving life sentences without the possibility of parole (LWOP). Other inmates are incarcerated for racially motivated hate crimes. Once placed in prison, some of these individuals join racially driven gangs (e.g., Nazis, skinheads, blacks, Mexicans).

The actions of some of the aforementioned inmates has fueled a tendency toward degrading or harsher forms of punishment. For example, Arizona sheriff Joe Arpaio is not a fan of rehabilitating inmates. He houses them in tents, feeds them dyed-green bologna, and clothes them in pink underwear. The facilities are army tents in the desert, and the work reminds one of the old chain gangs. It is certainly a controversial approach to penology, but it is seemingly done as a means of dissuading those released from ever returning to Sheriff's Arpaio's jurisdiction. U.S. attorney general Eric Holder has initiated legal challenges because of these practices, which have been called an unwanted form of race-conscious behavior. The philosophy of more punishment than rehabilitation stems from increased sex- and drug-related crimes, and can be observed in the rise of more restrictive supermax prisons.[29] Correctional officers are the backbone of the prison staff and are responsible for day-to-day operations with diverse inmates in various types of prisons within the U.S. system.

Correctional Officer Stress from Working in Various Types of Prisons

Prisons can be categorized by whether they are state or federal facilities. Duties within correctional officer classifications may overlap (e.g., counting, vigilance, checking, locking areas), but the classifications highlighted in this section illustrate the ethno-racial diversity of inmates and work requirements. Prisons may contain several different levels of security (low, medium, high). An inmate's assignment should be based on some type of risk assessment that is performed prior to his or her arrival at a correctional facility. A risk assessment is an evidence-based rating system used to anticipate the probability (low, medium, or high) that some particular behavioral variable might take place. For example, there is concern as to whether violent sexual offenders are likely to reoffend while incarcerated. A psychiatric inmate may have a high risk of suicidal behavior. Or an incarcerated terrorist may be more likely than other prisoners to attempt to radicalize other inmates. Or he or she may pose a threat because he or she is able to communicate to those outside of the prison. Risk assessment impacts correctional officer assignments, safety issues, and use of resources. Although there are several types of prisons, three will be emphasized here.

Supermax Prisons

It could be argued that Alcatraz was one of the nation's first supermax prisons. Located in the San Francisco Bay, it was once a federal prison known for strict confinement of the nation's most dangerous inmates. Today's correctional officers work with some of the most notorious inmates incarcerated in a supermax prison, which is designated as supermax because of its maximum level of security or confinement. The National Institute of Corrections classifies a supermax as a highly restrictive unit or facility "that isolates inmates from the general prison population and from each other due to grievous crimes, repetitive assaultive or violent institutional behavior, the threat of escape or actual escape from high-custody facilities, or inciting or threatening to incite disturbances in a correctional institution."[30] Supermax prisons are known for housing inmates pejoratively referred to as the "worst of the worst."[31] These are considered the most dangerous inmates (e.g., serial killers, murderers, terrorists) such as Theodore Kaczynski, Terry Nichols, and Zacarias Moussaoui, who was suspected of being part of Osama bin Laden's terror network. It is worth pointing out that lockup within these supermax prisons does not completely prevent inmates from facilitating criminal acts from behind bars. California and Texas have some of the largest populations of inmates located in these facilities. In 2000, Texas had 16 supermax prisons or supermax units with at least 10,000 racially diverse inmates. Correctional officers working in maximum security facilities are responsible for 24-hour surveillance of these inmates.[32]

The harsh level of control and deprivation experienced by inmates has resulted in a chorus of concerns about how inmates are chosen for placement in these institutions. Objections and litigation alleging Fourteenth Amendment violations are ongoing. Moreover, the UN Committee against

Torture has assessed supermax prisons as "excessively harsh regimes" that could represent a violation of the 1994 UN Convention against Torture and Other Cruel, Inhumane or Degrading Treatment or Punishment.[33] Despite the criticisms, no political consensus has emerged related to a viable alternative to deal with the diverse needs of inmates. Two especially challenging situations are presented by inmates with mental illness, some of whom have been determined to be criminally insane, as well as offenders associated with the U.S. military.

Ethno-Racial Issues, Prisoners, and the U.S. Military

The military is one of the most ethno-racially diverse institutions in the United States. A military prison is run by the military. These facilities have several functions and might house ethno-racially diverse enemy combatants, prisoners of war, and individuals considered to be a threat to national security. Sometimes a member of the military is found to be at fault in a major criminal act. The harsh treatment of prisoners of war resulted in the formation of Red Cross and Geneva Convention rules that spell out requirements designed to prevent abuses of diverse prisoners.

For example, in 1863 when the Union started using African-American troops, the parole and exchange (i.e., exchanging prisoners between warring factions) process broke down. While the Union insisted that all prisoners, black and white, be treated the same for exchange purposes, the Confederacy insisted that blacks be treated as runaway slaves and returned to their owners.[34] Generals Robert E. Lee and Ulysses Grant revisited this issue in October 1864 during the siege of Petersburg. Lee wrote to Grant that "negroes belonging to our citizens are not considered subjects of exchange." Grant answered, "I have to state the government is bound to secure to all persons received into her armies the rights due soldiers. This being denied by you in the persons of such men as have escaped from Southern masters induces me to decline making the exchanges you ask."[35] When the parole and exchange process broke down in 1863, the Confederacy was forced to move the multitude of Union prisoners it was holding in Richmond, Virginia, farther away from the battlefront. After examining several sites in southern Georgia, the Confederate military located a suitable spot at Andersonville Station for Camp Sumter.

Prisoner atrocities during both construction and use of Civil War prisons are well documented. For example, the original Andersonville Station became the notorious Andersonville Prison for Camp Sumter in Georgia, which was constructed 1864 by local black slaves. The original stockade was designed to hold 10,000 Union prisoners, but the population quickly swelled to over 30,000.

Andersonville has been compared to an American version of Auschwitz. Structurally, it was acres of open land surrounded by a stockade fence and earthworks barricades. There was barely enough room for a man to lie down. The death of prisoners was caused by exposure, malnutrition, and a variety of diseases that included smallpox, typhoid, dysentery, diarrhea, scurvy, and gangrene.

Later, even with the Geneva Convention guidelines, there was and continues to be wide variation in the treatment of prisoners in war. For example, during World War II, Americans and Filipinos surrendered to the Japanese on April 9, 1942. The Japanese decided to march about 76,000 prisoners (12,000 Americans, the remainder Filipinos) northward over horrible terrain in what is now referred to as the Bataan Death March. Only 54,000 already weakened prisoners reached the camp they were destined for. An estimated 7,000 to 10,000 died en route.[36]

Native Americans once populated what is now the lower 48 states. Under the Indian Removal Act (1830), which was signed by President Andrew Jackson, federal troops led by General Winfred Scott arrested and forcibly removed Native Americans from Georgia, Tennessee, North Carolina, and Alabama. During the winter of 1838, in what became remembered as the Trail of Tears, 15,000 Cherokee were rounded up in Georgia and marched to Oklahoma, some 1,200 miles away. The Treaty of New Echota was an "agreement" to give the Cherokee new land in Oklahoma so that Georgia land could be sold to new farmers in the state. Yet the Cherokee Nation never signed or agreed to the treaty. Also among those made to march were 2,000 black slaves owned by some of the wealthier Indians.[37]

U.S. Army soldiers functioned as correctional officers during this armed transport of Native Americans and black slaves. General Scott also ordered the murder of tribal leaders and their families. During the Trail of Tears,

> they were exposed to disease, food deprived, and physically depleted from the march. Over 4,000 of the 15,000 Cherokees died during this military prisoner action. During the removal, Indian homes were destroyed, clearing the way for a lottery that allowed white farmers to win the properties. Soldiers and others criticized these actions at the time of the emigration, which was later labeled a death march. The Indians and slaves were not properly

clothed for the harsh terrain or winter weather conditions. Many did not have shoes or moccasins. At one point, starved Indians were charged an exorbitant river ferry fee, at least 20 times higher than the regular rate. Even after paying the fee, they had wait for white ferry patrons to cross the river ahead of them. Many Indians were killed by local people or died while waiting to cross. Indians were shot if they tried to bury their dead loved ones. The killers sued the federal government, successfully securing a fee for burying the Indians they had killed.[38]

U.S. Military Prisons in War Zones and Rules for Enemy Combatants

All wars create the need for prisons, but each war has unique demands. The U.S. wars in Iraq and Afghanistan have generated legal decisions governing the trial and detention of prisoners. This has resulted in several types of facilities. Baghdad Central Prison, previously known as Abu Ghraib prison, lies about 22 miles from Baghdad. Both the U.S.-led coalition occupying Iraq and the Iraqi government detained prisoners in the facility, which was constructed in the 1950s. At least a decade ago, it was said to have house a high of around 15,000 inmates. The purpose of the Baghdad Central Prison is twofold. First, they house prisoners of war or individuals picked up as unlawful combatants who pose a threat to the security of the United States or our allies. Since about 2006, the Iraqi government has administratively managed the area in the facility that is known as "the hard site." This part of the prison was used to hold only convicted criminals. All other detainees—suspected criminals, insurgents, and those arrested and awaiting trial—are held in what is known as Camp Redemption. This facility separates detainees by specific security risk status.[39]

U.S. Juvenile Prisons and Correctional Officers

Correctional officers in diverse juvenile settings work with a shrinking but demanding population. Between 1997 and 2004, while the general prison population grew, the number of prisoners under the age of 18 fell 54 percent. Youth under the age of 18 accounted for 1 percent of new court commitments to state adult prisons in 2002. The Bureau of Justice Statistics reported numbers of inmates under age 18 held in custody in state and federal prisons by sex, for June 30, 2009 and 2010 can be seen in Table 17.1.

In contrast, the numbers for juveniles held in jails between 2000 and 2011 can be seen in Table 17.2.

TABLE 17.1   Juvenile Inmates in State and Federal Prisons By Gender (per 100,000)

2009		2010	
Males	Females	Males	Females
2,645	134	2,217	78
Total: 2,779		2,295	

The approach for juvenile correctional officers is theoretically focused on rehabilitation. As a result, juvenile correctional officers are charged with functioning as extensions of the state through the legal provision of *parens patriae*, meaning "the state as parent." In juvenile correctional practices, this is supposed to establish a relationship designed to promote juvenile growth or desired change.[40] However, Benekos and Merlo (2007) argue that elements of the juvenile justice system have become increasingly punitive as opposed to operating under principles of *restorative justice*, an approach that attempts to assuage the harm stemming from a crime. Restorative justice includes all stakeholders (offenders, victims, and communities) associated with crime in an effort to provide a constructive intervention for the juvenile offender. There are other legal protections for juveniles.

The Juvenile Justice and Delinquency Prevention Act (1974) restricts the assignment of juveniles within an adult correctional site to prevent contact between delinquent juveniles and adult inmates. In the case of *Eddings vs. Oklahoma*, the U.S. Supreme Court overturned the death sentence of a 16-year-old who had been tried as an adult. The decision indicated that a juvenile defendant's psychological and emotional issues could be considered as *mitigators* in determining whether the death penalty is applicable. Then in the case of *Thompson vs. Oklahoma*, the court was asked to decide if implementing the death penalty for a juvenile who was 15 years old at the time of the murder violated constitutional protections against cruel

TABLE 17.2   Juvenile Inmates in Jails, 2000–2011 (per 100,000)

Year	2000	2005	2006	2007	2008	2009	2010	2011
Held as Adults	6,126	5,750	4,835	5,649	6,410	5,846	5,647	4,600
Held as Juveniles	1,489	1,009	1,268	1,184	1,294	1,373	1,912	1,400
Total Youth Incarcerated	7,615	6,759	6,102	6,833	7,703	7,218	7,560	5,900

and unusual punishment. In 2005, the Supreme Court handed down a decision in *Roper vs. Simmons* prohibiting the death penalty for anyone younger than 18.[41]

Several Supreme Court decisions on rehabilitation approaches have spawned controversy among juvenile correctional officers. Part of this tension is because juvenile correctional officers tend to assume a mindset of enforcer, thinking, "After all, these juveniles committed a crime and must be punished."[42] On the other hand, rehabilitations programs where staff approach diverse offenders with what is therapeutically known as core relational conditions (i.e., warmth, empathy, genuineness, respect, flexibility) have been found to reduce recidivism. Conversations with correctional officers reveal an overriding need to err on the side of maintaining safety.[43] The culture of correctional officers promotes a more punitive and non-disclosing stance perceived to reduce opportunities for deception or taking advantage.[44]

The stressful work of juvenile correctional officers is additionally complicated by the unique developmental, sexual assault, and mental health issues presented by the diverse youth they encounter. For example, Grisso (2008) reported that youth with psychological disorders make up a substantial portion of the youth that appear in juvenile court. The challenge lingers—how to meet the unique needs presented by juveniles while securing public safety not only within the prison, but also in the community through reducing recidivism. Physical or learning disabilities function as obstacles in juvenile rehabilitation.[45] The overrepresentation of ethno-racial groups (e.g., African Americans and Hispanics) also challenges correctional officers who seek to remain culturally responsive to juveniles.

African Americans in the U.S. Prison System

Though African Americans currently compromise only 12.6 percent of the total U.S. population, they represent an alarmingly higher percentage of inmates within state, local, and federal prisons. Comparatively speaking, African Americans are a top ethno-racial group within the U.S prison system. According to the U.S. Bureau of Justice Statistics, blacks represented 39.4 percent of prison and jail inmates in 2009.[46] African Americans are at greater risk for involuntary mental health incarceration when compared to every other ethno-racial group. Lower socioeconomic status (SES) African Americans and Latinos have a higher probability of being referred for commitment by legal authorities.[47] The overrepresentation of African

Americans within the U.S. prison system raises questions about race-conscious behavior. Developmentally, the issue is whether this difference can be linked to bio-psychological factors operating within youth. But a more reasonable question seeks to identify factors that might contribute to this population being at higher risk for imprisonment than other ethno-racial groups. There are bio-psychosocial theories that suggested African Americans presenting at U.S. prisons have more undetected signs of mental disorders that worsen because of a lack of culturally tailored treatment and poverty.[48] Another example of race-conscious behavior or bias is reflected in decision makers who determine whether problem behavior requires mental health services rather than solely incarceration within the U.S. prison system.[49] Still others have concluded that differences in incarceration rate can be traced to treatment that is ineffective because it is not tailored to a specific ethno-racial group. At minimum, culturally tailored interventions require correctional staff to increase their awareness of the full range of mental health issues presented by African-American and white inmates.[50] Professionals should assess all inmates in advance of incarceration, using risk factors associated with African-American inmates. Empirically, there are risk factors associated with African-American inmates that all COs should be mindful of as they perform their duties. This knowledge will provide COs with the knowledge and awareness necessary to promote safety, improve rehabilitation, and reduce recidivism. Marmot (2006) reported that African Americans confront a series of barriers largely fueled by low socioeconomic status. SES coincides with low educational achievement, unfavorable unemployment, and an unwanted cognitive mindset dominated by the perception of an absence of locus of control. African-American families are more likely to be poor and have limited access to resources that treat psychosocial difficulties, leading to higher rates of depression, anxiety, and conduct disorders.[51] Poverty across generations contributes to poor psychosocial adjustment in parents, which results in ineffective parenting skills.[52] Criminal activity is more likely to occur in catchment areas dominated by socioeconomic stress. African Americans residing in these high-poverty areas have lower-performing schools and higher levels of unemployment, and they must continually deal with exposure to illegal drugs, gang activity, and recurring violence. In such situations, it is much easier to affiliate with crime/criminals or know people who have been incarcerated. Rehabilitation is challenged by the reality that former inmates are reentering the same distressed neighborhoods that probably contributed to their offense. Reentry into high-stress communities can lead to an increased risk for reoffending if planning for support is not taken into consideration with African-American inmates.[53]

U.S. prisons are saddled with warehousing the human consequences of a psychological chain that includes complex trauma, substance abuse, and violence. To little surprise, the impact of child abuse is significant for many clients of the correctional system. One investigation of African-American inmates on death row revealed that half had been sexually abused as a child, and nearly all were physically abused. Over 80 percent had experienced some form of verbal abuse, while 100 percent had encountered what they viewed as neglect.[54] The ethnic distribution of death row prisoners as of January 1, 2012, was 43.15 percent white, 41.83 percent African American, 12.52 percent Latino/Latina, 1.07 percent Native American, and 1.42 percent Asian.[55] African Americans are markedly overrepresented on death row (41.83 percent of death row inmates are black, and blacks make up 12.3 percent of the U.S. population). Previous exposure to abuse and neglect creates the nexus to violent behavior within U.S. prisons, and COs must work with and supervise African-American inmates.

Substance abuse represents a significant ethno-racial issue in the United States because of its association with homelessness, mental illness, crime across genders, and various cultural groups. For example, over half of all incarcerated violent criminals consumed alcohol prior to committing crimes.[56] It has been found that 60 percent of murderers were intoxicated when they committed homicide.[57] As for African Americans, the negative byproducts of drug use are substantially greater when contrasted with other ethno-racial groups. The symptoms for African-American drug abusers are observed through bio-psychosocial outcomes[58] as well as contact with legal authorities secondary to drug use.[59]

Substance abuse is often concomitant with mental health disorders. A study of the U.S prison system found that 45 percent of federal inmates and more than half of state prison (56 percent) and jail inmates (64 percent) acknowledged symptoms consistent with a diagnosable mental disorder in the prior 12 months.[60] The Centers for Disease Control and Prevention reported that African Americans are more likely to have mental disorders when compared to whites and are less inclined to secure mental health services. Correctional officers must remain aware that an African American entering the U.S. prison system is more likely than not to have an untreated mental disorder. This ethno-racial reality of disproportional representation reinforces the need for administrators of U.S. prisons to continually evaluate tools used as part of assessing risk in diverse inmates (e.g., black and Latino).

Latinos in U.S. Prisons

Latinos represent roughly 14 percent of the U.S. population, which makes them the largest ethno-racial minority group[61] in the country. Hispanic inmates make up an estimated 20 percent of all state and federal prisoners.[62] This percentage is higher than the last decade's overall incarceration increase,[63] that is, in federal, state, and local prison/jails, the percentage of Latino inmates rose from 16 percent in 2000 to 20 percent in 2008.[64] In contrast, the percentage of Latinos in the U.S. adult population rose only 2 percentage points—from 11 to 13 percent—over the same period.[65] A disproportionate number of Latinos are being incarcerated in state prisons. Mandracchia and Morgan found that black and Hispanic youth are not receiving mental health services that they need. More troubling, black and Hispanic youth responded to assessment items in a cognitive style consistent with criminal activity. These findings have important implications for correctional officers and criminal recidivism reduction. Mandracchia and Morgan (2012) found that recidivism is common among released offenders, with approximately 25 percent being reincarcerated within a three-year period following their release. Latinos are often released from prison without an adequate psychosocial safety net to prevent them from recidivating. McGovern and colleagues indicated that second language issues combine with a general distrust of the criminal justice system and a reluctance to cooperate with legal authorities out of concern that of family and friends may be deported.[66]

Court officials often assess Latino defendants as dangerous and likely to recidivate.[67] The pattern of criminal behavior starts early with Latino offenders. de Apodaca reported that Latinos are arrested at higher rates when they are in younger age brackets. Youthful Latino offenders (18 to 19 years old) made up 52 percent (438 out of 836) of the total number of arrests in California while whites contributed only 31 percent (257 out of 836).[68] The SAFER Latinos project[69] found several mediating elements related to youth violence for those between the ages of 10 and 24. These factors include family cohesion, school-related barriers, gang presence, and integration of violence norms along with community cohesion, efficacy, and alienation. Jennings and colleagues reported that "cumulative familial risks operationalized as neighborhood problems, financial strain, and maternal depression were negatively associated with the parenting practices and styles of low-income Hispanic mothers."[70] These same researchers noted the salience of parental psychopathology, specifically depression, as a key factor in determining parenting behaviors among Hispanic parents. Therefore, it appears that parental mental health has implications for the quality and the quantity of parenting. The use of educational programs and efforts to control gang activity are relevant interventions within many U.S. prisons.[71]

Hancock and Siu (2009) found that 70 percent of Latina immigrants were exposed to some interpersonal violence or a threat of violence within a 12-month period. Latino and Latina immigrants are sometimes subjected to general forms of physical and emotional abuse, as well as culturally specific forms such as "denial of women as persons, control of female sexuality, accusations of the female's inadequacies as a mother, and threats of taking away her children and deportation."[72] Cultural factors that may predispose Latinas to domestic violence include the negative aspects of machismo and the tendency of Latinos to confuse power with love in the family setting.[73]

These same researchers found that violent immigrant Latino men represent at least 60 percent of the men that had been victims of maltreatment and another 20 percent suffered from PTSD that was attributed to traumatic migratory experiences.[74] Lopez and Light found that 40 percent of offenders sentenced in federal courts were Latinos contrasted with 27 percent whites and 23 percent blacks.[75] In 2007, among Latino offenders, 37 percent were sentenced for drug offenses, and 48 percent were sentenced for immigration offenses. Seventy percent of Latinos sentenced during this period were not U.S. citizens.[76] Correctional officers serving this population must be aware of and understand cultural implications and risk assessment issues. Hancock and Sui found that domestically violent Latino immigrant men indicated the importance of family as a strong motivator to accept and use treatment in a court-ordered setting.[77] The risk factors that place these individuals within the prison system not only need to be researched further, but also controlled within our society. Correctional officers are confronted with the task of assessing these ethno-racial groups and thus they must remain mindful of the unique cultural factors associated with Latinos.

Conclusions and Implications for Future Research and Practice

Ethno-racial factors are a central part of the U.S. prison system. Interactions between various cultures (e.g., correctional officers, institutions, prison gangs, various ethno-racial groups) present significant challenges for correctional administrators and legislators as they attempt to shape prisons to meet 21st-century criminal justice needs. More research needs to explore these cultural interactions and the stressful work demands of correctional officers. More effective culturally crafted programs for U.S. inmates could result from such a research focus.

Notes

1. Bureau of Labor Statistics, 2014.
2. Crenshaw, 1988; Crenshaw and Peller, 1993; Haney López, 2000; Freeman, 1978.
3. Gee et al., 2009, p. 130.
4. Harrell, 2000; Krieger, 1999; Zárate, 2009.
5. Dovidio and Gaertner, 2000.
6. Sue and Sue, 2008.
7. Blanton and Jaccard, 2008.
8. Better, 2007; Gee et al., 2009; Griffith et al., 2007; Lea, 2000.
9. Gone, 2009.
10. Contrada et al., 2001; Cross, 1991; Helms, 1990; Sellers and Shelton, 2003.
11. Quintana, 2007; Sellers and Shelton, 2003.
12. California Department of Corrections and Rehabilitation, 2013.
13. Justice Scalia, dissenting, *Johnson vs. California*, 543 U.S. 499, at 524; Carlson, 2001; Hunt et al., 1993; Petersilia, 2006.
14. Johnson, 2011.
15. Härenstam, Palm, and Theorell, 1988.
16. Abdollahi, 2002; Vena et al., 1986; Violanti, Vena, and Marshall, 1996; Violanti et al., 2006; Violanti, Vena, and Petralia, 1998.
17. Grieder, Johnson, and Descanio, 2012.
18. Jung, 1981.
19. Johnson, 2013.
20. Dantzker, 2011.
21. Johnson, 2011.
22. Johnson, 2013.
23. Arcaya, 2011; Lowman, 1989.
24. Johnson and Marek, 2012.

25. Fremon, 2012.
26. Langan and Levin, 2002.
27. Petersilia, 2005.
28. Kennedy, 2011, p. 18.
29. Garland, 2002; Miller et al., 1996.
30. Riveland, 1999, p. 6.
31. Riveland, 1999, p. 6.
32. Richards, 2008; Ward and Werlich, 2003.
33. United Nations Committee on International Human Rights, 2011.
34. Pettijohn, 2006.
35. Pettijohn, 2006.
36. Norman and Norman, 2009; Tenney, 1995.
37. Miles, 2005.
38. Miles, 2005.
39. Martin, 2005; Strasser, 2004.
40. Blevins et al., 2007.
41. *Roper vs. Simmons*, 2005.
42. Farkas, 2000.
43. Pan, Chang, and Lin, 2007.
44. Ginsburg et al., 2002; Tracy, 2004.
45. Quinn et al., 2001.
46. U.S. Census Bureau, 2012.
47. Chow, Jaffee, and Snowden, 2003.
48. Geronimus et al., 2006.
49. Snowden, 2001.
50. Youman et al., 2010.
51. Dodge, Pettit, and Bates, 1994.
52. Brody et al., 2002.
53. Kubrin, Squires, and Stewart, 2007.
54. Lisak and Beszterczey, 2007.
55. NAACP Legal Defense Fund, 2013.
56. Johnson and Belfer, 1995.
57. Collins and Messerschmidt, 1993.
58. Strycker, Duncan, and Pickering, 2003.
59. Shillington and Clapp, 2003.
60. James and Glaze, 2006.
61. Mogro-Wilson, 2011.
62. Harris et al., 2009.
63. Stowell, Martinez, and Cancino, 2012.
64. West and Sabol, 2009.
65. López and Livingston, and Pew Hispanic Center, 2009.
66. McGovern, et al., 2009.

67. Harris et al., 2009.
68. de Apadocha, 2005.
69. Edberg et al., 2010.
70. Jennings et al., 2010, 316.
71. Jennings, 2010.
72. Kasturirangan et al., 2004.
73. Perilla, 1999.
74. Hancock and Sui, 2009
75. López and Light, 2009.
76. López and Light, 2009.
77. Hancock and Sui, 2009.

References

Abdollahi, M. Kathrine. "Understanding Police Stress Research." *Journal of Forensic Psychology Practice* 2, no. 2 (2002): 1–24.

de Apodaca, Roberto, Jack Schultz, Amy Anderson, and Martin McLennan. "Young, Unassimilated Hispanic Offenders: Absolutist vs. Relativist Cultural Assumptions." *Sexuality & Culture* 9, no. 3 (2005): 3–23.

Arcaya, Jose M. "Challenging the Police De-Selection Process during the Psychological Interview: How Gullibility Spells Hiring Doom for the Unwary." In *Handbook of Police Psychology*, edited by Jack Kitaeff, pp. 227–238. New York: Routledge, 2011.

Better, Shirley. *Institutional Racism: A Primer on Theory and Strategies for Social Change* (2nd ed.). Lanham, MD: Rowman & Littlefield, 2007.

Blanton, Hart, and James Jaccard. "Unconscious Racism: A Concept in Pursuit of a Measure." *Annual Review of Sociology* 34, no. 1 (2008): 277–297.

Blevins, Kristie A., Francis T. Cullen, and Jody L. Sundt. "The Correctional Orientation of 'Child Savers': Support for Rehabilitation and Custody Among Juvenile Correctional Workers." *Journal of Offender Rehabilitation* 45, no. 3–4 (2007): 47–83.

Brody, Gene H., Velma McBride Murry, Sooyeon Kim, and Anita C. Brown. "Longitudinal Pathways to Competence and Psychological Adjustment among African American Children Living in Rural Single-Parent Households." *Child Development* 73, no. 5 (2002): 1505–1516.

Bureau of Labor Statistics, Occupational Outlook Handbook, 2014–15 Edition, correctional officers. Accessed on February 19, 2014 at http://www.bls.gov/ooh/protective-service/correctional-officers.htm, 2014.

California Department of Corrections and Rehabilitation. *California Prisoners and Parolees*. Sacramento: California Department of Corrections and Rehabilitation, 2013.

Carlson, Peter. "Prison Interventions: Evolving Strategies to Control Security Threat Groups." *Corrections Management Quarterly* 5, no. 1 (2001): 10–22.

Chow, Julian Chun-Chung, Kim Jaffee, and Lonnie Snowden. "Racial/Ethnic Disparities in the Use of Mental Health Services in Poverty Areas." *American Journal of Public Health* 93, no. 5 (2003): 792–797.

Collins, James J., and Pamela M. Messerschmidt. "Epidemiology of Alcohol-Related Violence." *Alcohol Health & Research World* 17, no. 2 (1993): 93–100.

Contrada, Richard J., Richard D. Ashmore, Melvin L. Gary, Elliot Coups, Jill D. Egeth, Andrea Sewell, Kevin Ewell, Tanya M. Goyal, and Valerie Chasse. "Measures of Ethnicity-Related Stress: Psychometric Properties, Ethnic Group Differences, and Associations with Well-Being." *Journal of Applied Social Psychology* 31, no. 9 (2001): 1775–1820.

Crenshaw, Kimberele and G. Peller. "Reel Time/Real Justice." In *Reading Rodney King/Reading Urban Uprising*, edited by Robert Godding-Williams, pp. 56–70. New York: Routledge, 1993.

Crenshaw, Kimberlé Williams. "Race, Reform, and Retrenchment: Transformation and Legitimation in Antidiscrimination Law."*Harvard Law Review* 101, no. 7 (1988): 1331–1387.

Cross, William E. *Shades of Black: Diversity in African-American Identity.* Philadelphia: Temple University Press, 1991.

Dantzker, M. L. "Psychological Preemployment Screening for Police Candidates: Seeking Consistency if Not Standardization."*Professional Psychology: Research and Practice* 42, no. 3 (2011): 276–283.

Dodge, Kenneth A., Gregory S. Pettit, and John E. Bates. "Socialization Mediators of the Relation between Socioeconomic Status and Child Conduct Problems." *Child Development* 65, no. 2 (1994): 649–665.

Dovidio, John F., and Samuel L. Gaertner. "Aversive Racism and Selection Decisions: 1989 and 1999." *Psychological Science* 11 (2000): 315–319.

Edberg, Mark, Sean D. Cleary, Elizabeth Andrade, Rodrigo Leiva, Martha Bazurto, Maria Ivonne Rivera, Luisa Montero, and Melba Calderon. "SAFER Latinos: A Community Partnership to Address Contributing Factors for Latino Youth Violence." *Progress in Community Health Partnerships: Research, Education, and Action* 4, no. 3 (2010): 221–233.

Farkas, Mary Ann. "A Typology of Correctional Officers." *International Journal of Offender Therapy and Comparative Criminology* 44, no. 4 (2000): 431–449.

Freeman, Linton C. "Segregation in Social Networks." *Sociological Methods & Research* 6, no. 4 (1978): 411.

Fremon, Celeste. "The New Yorker: Why Do We Lock-Up So Many People? . . . & Other Must Reads." *Witness LA.* Accessed September 29, 2011, http://witnessla.com/prison/2012/admin/the-new-yorker-why-do-we-lock-up-so-many-people-other-must-reads/2012.

Garland, David. *The Culture of Control: Crime and Social Order in Contemporary Society.* Chicago: University of Chicago Press, 2002.

Gee, Gilbert C., Annie Ro, Salma Shariff-Marco, and David Chae. "Racial Discrimination and Health among Asian Americans: Evidence, Assessment, and Directions for Future Research." *Epidemiologic Reviews* 31, no. 1 (2009): 130–151.

Geronimus, Arline T., Margaret Hicken, Danya Keene, and John Bound. "Geronimus et al. Respond." *American Journal of Public Health* 96, no. 6 (2006): 955–956.

Ginsburg, Joel I. D., Ruth E. Mann, Frederick Rotgers, and John R. Weekes. "Motivational Interviewing with Criminal Justice Populations." In *Motivational Interviewing: Preparing People for Change* (2nd ed.), edited by William Miller and Stephen Rollnick, pp. 333–346. New York: Guilford, 2002.

Gone, Joseph P. "A Community-Based Treatment for Native American Historical Trauma: Prospects for Evidence-Based Practice."*Journal of Consulting & Clinical Psychology* 77 no. 4 (2009): 751–762.

Gopnik, Adam. "The Caging of America." *New Yorker*, 2012, January 30.

Grieder, Kristen, Ronn Johnson, and Kristen Descanio. "Forensic Role of Clinical Mental Health Professionals in On-Scene Risk Assessment Responses in Collaboration with Police." *Therapist* 24, no. 2 (2012): 61–63.

Griffith, Derek M., Erica L. Childs, Eugenia Eng, and Vanessa Jeffries. "Racism in Organizations: The Case of a County Public Health Department." *Journal of Community Psychology* 35, no. 3 (2007): 287–302.

Grisso, Thomas. "Adolescent Offenders with Mental Disorders." *Future of Children* 18, no. 2 (2008): 143–164.

Hancock, Tina, and Karla Siu. "A Culturally Sensitive Intervention with Domestically Violent Latino Immigrant Men." *Journal of Family Violence* 24, no. 2 (2009): 123–132.

Härenstam, Annika, Ulla-Britt Palm, and Töres Theorell. "Stress, Health and the Working Environment of Swedish Prison Staff."*Work & Stress* 2, no. 4 (1988): 281–290.

Harrell, Shelly P. "A Multidimensional Conceptualization of Racism-Related Stress: Implications for the Well-Being of People of Color." *American Journal of Orthopsychiatry* 70, no. 1 (2000): 42–57.

Harris, Casey, Darrell Steffensmeier, Jeffrey Ulmer, and Noah Painter-Davis. "Are Blacks and Hispanics Disproportionately Incarcerated Relative to their Arrests? Racial and Ethnic Disproportionality between Arrest and Incarceration." *Race and Social Problems* 1, no. 4 (2009): 187–199.

Helms, Janet E. *Black and White Racial Identity: Theory, Research, and Practice.* New York: Greenwood, 1990.

Hunt, Geoffrey, Stephanie Riegel, Tomas Morales, and Dan Waldorf. "Change in Prison Culture: Prison Gangs and the Case of the Pepsi Generation." *Social Problems* 40, no. 3 (1993): 398–409.

James, Doris J., and Lauren. E. Glaze. *Mental Health Problems of Prison and Jail Inmates*. Washington, DC: Bureau of Justice Statistics, 2006.

Jennings, Wesley G., Mildred M. Maldonado-Molina, Alex R. Piquero, and Glorisa Canino. "Parental Suicidality as a Risk Factor for Delinquency among Hispanic Youth." *Journal of Youth and Adolescence* 39, no. 3 (2010): 315–325.

Johnson, Elaine M., and Myron L. Belfer. "Substance Abuse and Violence: Cause and Consequence." *Journal of Health Care for the Poor and Underserved* 6, no. 2 (1995): 113–123.

Johnson, Ronn. "The Integration Section of Forensic Psychological Evaluation Reports in Law Enforcement: Culturally Responsive Ending Words." In *Handbook of Police Psychology*, edited by Jack Kitaeff, pp. 211–226. New York: Routledge/Taylor & Francis, 2011.

Johnson, Ronn. "Biopsychosociocultural Perspective on 'Operation Enduring Freedom/Operation Iraqi Freedom' Women Veterans as Civilian Police Officers: Mild Traumatic Brain Injury and Post-Traumatic Stress Disorder Challenges." *International Journal of Police Science & Management* 15, no. 1 (2013): 45–50.

Jung, Carl. G. *The Archetypes and The Collective Unconscious*. Trans. R. F. C. Hull (2nd ed.). Princeton, NJ: Princeton University Press, 1981.

Kasturirangan, Aarati, Sandhya Krishnan, and Stephanie Riger. "The Impact of Culture and Minority Status on Women's Experience of Domestic Violence." *Trauma, Violence, & Abuse* 5, no. 4 (2004): 318–332.

Kennedy, David M. *Don't Shoot: One Man, A Street Fellowship, and the End of Violence in Inner-City America*. New York: Bloomsbury USA, 2011.

Krieger, Nancy. "Embodying Inequality: A Review of Concepts, Measures, and Methods for Studying Health Consequences of Discrimination." *International Journal of Health Services: Planning, Administration, Evaluation* 29, no. 2 (1999): 295–352.

Kubrin, Charis E., Gregory Squires, and Eric Stewart. "Neighborhoods, Race, and Recidivism: The Community Reoffending Nexus and Its Implications for African Americans." *Sage Race Relations Abstracts* 32 (2007): 7–37.

Langan, Patrick A., and David J. Levin. *Bureau of Justice Statistics (BJS): Recidivism of Prisoners Released in 1994*. Washington, DC: Bureau of Justice Statistics, 2002.

Lea, John. "The Macpherson Report and the Question of Institutional Racism." *Howard Journal of Criminal Justice* 39, no. 3 (2000): 219–233.

Lisak, David, and Sara Beszterczey. "The Cycle of Violence: The Life Histories of 43 Death Row Inmates." *Psychology of Men & Masculinity* 8, no. 2 (2007): 118–128.

López, Ian F. Haney. "Institutional Racism: Judicial Conduct and a New Theory of Racial Discrimination." *Yale Law Journal* 109, no. 8 (2000): 1717–1884.

López, Mark Hugo, and Michael Light. *A Rising Share: Hispanics and Federal Crime*. Washington, DC: Pew Hispanic Center, 2009.

López, Mark Hugo, and Gretchen Livingston. *Hispanics and the Criminal Justice System: Low Confidence, High Exposure*. Washington, DC: Pew Hispanic Center, 2009.

Lowman, Rodney L. *Pre-Employment Screening for Psychopathology: A Guide to Professional Practice*. Vol. 15. Practitioner's Resource Series. Sarasota, FL: Professional Resource Exchange, 1989.

Mandracchia, Jon T., and Robert D. Morgan. "Predicting Offenders' Criminogenic Cognitions with Status Variables." *Criminal Justice and Behavior* 39, no. 1 (2012): 5–25.

Marmot, Michael. "WHO News: Tackling Social Factors to Improve Health." *Bulletin of the World Health Organization* 84, no. 4 (2006): 267–268.

Martin, Michael. *The Iraqi Prisoner Abuse Scandal*. Farmington Hills, MI: Lucent, 2005.

McGovern, Virginia, Stephen Demuth, and Joseph E. Jacoby. "Racial and Ethnic Recidivism Risks: A Comparison of Postincarceration Rearrest, Reconviction, and Reincarceration among White, Black, and Hispanic Releasees." *Prison Journal* 89, no. 3 (2009): 309–327.

Miles, Tiya. *Ties That Bind: The Story of an Afro-American Family in Slavery and Freedom*. Berkeley: University of California Press, 2005.

Miller, Ted R., Mark A. Cohen, and Brian Wiersema. *Victim Costs and Consequences: A New Look*. Washington, DC: National Institute of Justice, 1996.

Mogro-Wilson, Cristina. "Resilience in Vulnerable and At-Risk Latino Families." *Infants & Young Children* 24, no. 3 (2011): 267–279.

NAACP Legal Defense and Education Fund. *Death Row, USA: Spring 2013*. New York: NAACP Legal Defense and Education Fund, 2013.

New York City Bar. *Supermax Confinement in US Prisons*. New York: New York City Bar Association, 2011.

Norman, Michael, and Elizabeth Norman. *Tears in the Darkness: The Story of the Bataan Death March and Its Aftermath*. New York: Farrar, Straus and Giroux, 2009.

Pan, Peter Jen Der, Shih-Hua Chang, and Chi-Wei Lin. "Correctional Officers' Perceptions of the Competency-Based Counseling Training Program in Taiwan: A Preliminary Qualitative Research." *International Journal of Offender Therapy and Comparative Criminology* 51, no. 5 (2007): 523–540.

Perilla, Julia L. "Domestic Violence as a Human Rights Issue: The Case of Immigrant Latinos." *Hispanic Journal of Behavioral Sciences* 21, no. 2 (1999): 107–133.

Petersilia, Joan. "Hard Time: Ex-Offenders Returning Home after Prison." *Corrections Today* 67, no. 2 (2005): 66–71.

Petersilia, Joan. *Understanding California Corrections*. Berkeley: California Policy Research Center, 2006.

Pettijohn, Don. "African Americans at Andersonville." Accessed on February 21, 2014 from http://www.nps.gov/ande/historyculture/african_americans.htm, 2006.

Quinn, M. M., R. B. Rutherford, B. I. Wolford, P. E. Leone, and C. M. Nelson. *The Prevalence of Youth with Disabilities in Juvenile and Adult Corrections: Analysis of a National Survey*. Washington, DC: American Institutes for Research, National Center on Education, Disability, and Juvenile Justice, 2001.

Quintana, Stephen M. "Racial and Ethnic Identity: Developmental Perspectives and Research." *Journal of Counseling Psychology* 54, no. 3 (2007): 259–270.

Richards, Stephen C. "USP Marion: The First Federal Supermax." *Prison Journal* 88, no. 1 (2008): 6–22.

Riveland, Chase. *Supermax Prisons: Overview and General Considerations*. Washington, DC: National Institute of Corrections, 1999.

Sellers, Robert M. and J. Nicole Shelton. "The Role of Racial Identity in Perceived Racial Discrimination." *Journal of Personality and Social Psychology* 84, no. 5 (2003): 1079–1092.

Shillington, Audrey M., and John D. Clapp. "Adolescents in Public Substance Abuse Treatment Programs: The Impacts of Sex and Race on Referrals and Outcomes." *Journal of Child and Adolescent Substance Abuse* 12, no. 4 (2003): 69–91.

Snowden, Lonnie. "Barriers to Effective Mental Health Services for African Americans." *Mental Health Services Research* 3, no. 4 (2001): 181–187.

Southerland, Mittie D., Alida V. Merlo, Lynette Robinson, Peter J. Benekos, and Jay S. Albanese. "Ensuring Quality in Criminal Justice Education: Academic Standards and the Reemergence of Accreditation." *Journal of Criminal Justice Education* 18, no. 1 (2007): 87–105.

Stowell, Jacob, Ramiro Martinez, and Jeffrey Cancino. "Latino Crime and Latinos in the Criminal Justice System: Trends, Policy Implications, and Future Research Initiatives." *Race and Social Problems* 4, no. 1 (2012): 31–40.

Strasser, Steven. *The Abu Ghraib Investigations: The Official Reports of the Independent Panel and Pentagon on the Shocking Prisoner Abuse in Iraq*. New York: Public Affairs, 2004.

Strycker, Lisa A., Susan C. Duncan, and Michael A. Pickering. "The Social Context of Alcohol Initiation among African American and White Youth." *Journal of Ethnicity in Substance Abuse* 2, no. 1 (2003): 35–42.

Sue, Derald Wing, and David Sue. *Counseling the Culturally Diverse: Theory and Practice*. Hoboken, NJ: John Wiley & Sons, 2008.

Tenney, Lester I. *My Hitch in Hell: The Bataan Death March*. Dulles, VA: Brassey's, 1995.

Tracy, Sarah J. "The Construction of Correctional Officers: Layers of Emotionality Behind Bars." *Qualitative Inquiry* 10, no. 4 (2004): 509–533.

U.S. Census Bureau. "Census of Population and Housing." Washington, DC: U.S. Census Bureau, 2012.

Vena, John, John Violanti, James Marshall, and Roger. C. Fiedler. "Mortality of a Municipal Worker Cohort: III. Police Officers."*American Journal of Industrial Medicine* 10, no. 4 (1986): 383–397.

Violanti, John, John Vena, and James Marshall. "Suicides, Homicides, and Accidental Death: A Comparative Risk Assessment of Police Officers and Municipal Workers." *American Journal of Industrial Medicine* 30, no. 1 (1996): 99–104.

Violanti, John, John Vena, and Sandra Petralia. "Mortality of a Police Cohort, 1950–1990." *American Journal of Industrial Medicine* 33, no. 4 (1998): 366–373.

Violanti, John M., Cecil M. Burchfiel, Diane B. Miller, Michael E. Andrew, Joan Dorn, Jean Wactawski-Wende, Christopher M. Beighley, et al. "The Buffalo Cardio-Metabolic Occupational Police Stress (BCOPS) Plot Study: Methods and Participant Characteristics."*Annals of Epidemiology* 16, no. 2 (2006): 148–156.

Ward, David A., and Thomas G. Werlich. "Alcatraz and Marion: Evaluating Super-Maximum Custody." *Punishment & Society* 5, no. 1 (2003): 53–75.

West, Heather. C., and William J Sabol. *Prison Inmates at Midyear 2008: Statistical Tables*. Washington, DC: Bureau of Justice Statistics, 2009.

Youman, Kerstin, Amy Drapalski, Jeff Stuewig, Karen Bagley, and June Tangney. "Race Differences in Psychopathology and Disparities in Treatment Seeking: Community and Jail-Based Treatment Seeking Patterns." *Psychological Services* 7, no. 1 (2010): 11–26.

Zárate, Michael A. "Racism in the 21st Century." In *Handbook of Prejudice, Stereotyping, and Discrimination*, edited by Todd Nelson, pp. 387–406. New York: Psychology Press, 2009.

Cases Cited

Eddings vs. Oklahoma, 455 US 104. (1982)
Johnson vs. California, 543 US 499. (2005)
Roper vs. Simmons, 543 US 551. (2005)
Thompson vs. Oklahoma, 487 US 815. (1988)

Chapter 18

Counseling, Treatment, and Culture in Prison: One Size Fits All?

Leonard Steverson

Introduction

In this chapter, we will examine the relationship between race/ethnicity, culture, and counseling in the American correctional system. The correctional system emphasized in this chapter will be primarily prisons instead of jails or other short-term holding institutions and will evaluate adult, rather than juvenile, programs; although those are equally relevant, an analysis of this type goes beyond the scope of this chapter. Also, most of the examination will focus on general populations, rather than special inmate populations such as sex offenders, violent criminals, and inmates with developmental disabilities. Also, specialized jargon regarding psychotherapy treatment modalities will be limited. A critical perspective will be the guiding criminological theoretical approach in this approach.

Criminological Theory and Race and Ethnicity

Prior to a discussion on crime and race and the treatment of offenders in the prison system, it would be beneficial to examine crime theory and how it has evolved. "Theory" basically refers to a set of assumptions that serves as a guide for understanding some type of phenomena, in this case, crime. Criminological theory, then, seeks to provide some explanations as to why people commit criminal acts and to better understand the measures taken by social control agents to contain these behaviors. A brief overview of key ideas in criminological thought, from the earliest ideas up to the prevalent critical theories of today, will be reviewed. The theoretical perspectives listed here are but a few of many criminological theories, but these are considered particularly germane to the issue of race and ethnicity.

The earliest explanations of crime probably attributed acts of aberrant behavior, which would later be seen as acts of deviance and more formally, crime, to spiritual or supernatural causes; in an era before scientific knowledge, earlier humans accepted that external evil forces were the culprits. During the Enlightenment period of the 18th century, what is now known as the classical school of criminology developed and focused on the commission of crimes being driven by free will; according to this perspective, an individual makes a conscious choice after weighing the benefits and consequences of the activity. This philosophical approach to criminal behavior was not scientific but was an advance over the earlier perception of crime as merely being caused by supernatural forces. Cesare Beccaria, Jeremy Bentham, Robert Peel, and others were key thinkers in this classical criminology.[1]

A more systematic approach to the study of crime took place in the early and mid-19th century as European statisticians gathered crime data to analyze crime trends. In 19th-century America, crime was associated with sin and immorality and was considered in the same vein as other disreputable behavior such as indigence and sloth. Social conditions related to industrialization and immigration were observed as cities grew, and sociology developed from this need to understand changing social conditions.[2] The great increase in the number of people emigrating from other countries, with different languages, traditions, and beliefs, led many to believe in an inherent propensity toward criminal behavior in "foreigners" of different racial and ethnic backgrounds.

Biological/constitutional theorists of crime in Europe in the 19th century attempted to use the scientific method to understand crime and to find biological manifestations connecting individuals to crime. Italian physician Cesare Lombroso spelled out ways that certain racial groups are inherently prone to criminality and ranked them in a hierarchal manner. He believed that African Americans held a disregard for others and that murder and savage sexuality were part of their biological make up. In his work, Lombroso sometimes referred to people of Jewish ethnicity as being a racial grouping, and he believed that Jewish criminality was based more on environmental than biological reasons. The fact that Lombroso himself was Jewish might have led him to that conclusion. Lombroso inspired many other biologically based criminologists that followed him, but was also met with a wave of criticism by scholars of race and crime. In time, Lombroso began to change his rigid ideas about biology as the primary determinant of criminality and to consider the role of socialization as a factor as well. Biological/constitutional theories continued, and scholars with this perspective investigated other factors related to criminality such as innate intelligence.[3] Ideas of inferior intelligence had major ramifications in the form of the eugenics movement in which forced sterilization was used to guarantee that "inferior" people would not continue to populate the earth and victimize others. Although influenced by the so-called positive criminology of the Europeans, American scholars of crime continued to approach crime sociologically and to focus on the ecological, or social, factors that contribute to crime and delinquency.[4] Delinquency was a salient area of study in America during the first half of the 20th century.

A sociologically based criminology continued in the United States as theorists focused on environmental explanations of crime. The idea of social disorganization implicit in many sociological theories of deviance and crime borrows the idea of human ecology from biology in which animal and plant life are involved in an elaborate interconnected environment; to sustain life, these organisms must depend on others in some instances and compete with them in others. Concerned that ecosystems (such as cities) produce certain negative effects by changes to that system, for example, the problems related to mass waves of immigration, the Chicago school theorists (notably Robert Park and other faculty members at the University of Chicago) and others noted the role of crime in neighborhoods as it related to race and ethnicity. Park, a former newspaper writer, noticed that human groups tend to assimilate in communities (as are found in racial/ethnic areas such as Little Chinatown or Little Italy), in a similar manner as plant groups found in nature. The interdependence of human groupings is enhanced in democratic, free market societies as groups compete in a Darwinian struggle for survival of the fittest. Dominant human groups (analogous to species of plant life) often enter an area and take over, as can be seen by the example of the European colonization of Native American groups that lead to the near extinction of these groups. The Chicago school theorists also noted how human groups tend to start at geographic centers of areas and expand outward, creating social consequences of this migration.[5]

More recent social disorganization theorists have focused on the role of community economics, joblessness, race, and crime. Following the same theoretical perspective, W. Julius Wilson commented on urban

African-American communities, making the point that when neighborhoods and communities reach a saturation point of poverty and other
social maladies, the middle-class residents move away, leaving abandoned
communities with no role models showing how to conform to rules in the
greater society. Wilson's ideas have been revised to include groups other
than African Americans (i.e., Latin Americans and Native Americans)
and communities other than those in urban areas.[6]

Labeling theories also have a long history as theoretical explanations for
crime and other behavior. Theorists of this type posit that a label (e.g.,
criminal, ex-con, drug addict, thief) can affect a person's self-image and
actually contribute to criminal behavior. When people treat others differently because of the labels attached to them, stigma is said to occur, and it
often causes the labeled person to rebel against social norms, thereby exac-
erbating the problem.[7] The concept of the looking-glass self explains how
people develop a concept of self based on the reactions of others—if the
perception is negative, the person's self-concept and potential reactions to
others sometimes manifest in deviance and crime.[8] The concept of the
self-fulfilling prophecy is applicable here because if people see themselves
as deviant or criminal, they are more likely to act out the part society has
created for them, even if they did not initially possess a deviant orientation.[9] More specifically related to the issue of racial/ethnic labeling is
W. E. B. Du Bois's concept of double consciousness in which law-abiding
people of minority groups feel looked down upon by people of the majority
even though they are following society's rules—this creates a sort of internal double bind situation regarding self-perception.[10] Obviously, stereotyping and other forms of labeling play a large role in the processing of
offenders through the criminal justice system in the forms of racial and ethnic profiling, sentencing disparities, and correctional treatment inequities.

Critical Theory and Race/Ethnicity

Critical theories appeared that have forced people to take a different view of
the crime phenomenon. There are many different varieties of what is
known as critical criminology; however, a general description is a theoretical way of viewing crime that focuses on inequality in racial/ethnic, class,
and gender relations and how the powerful in society control criminal
activity.[11] Critical theory has its roots in the work of Karl Marx, though
Marx focused primarily on the economic conditions that created inequities
in society and never gave much attention in his writings to crime. Using the

idea of an oppressive control by the elites in society, Marxist thought was applied to criminology and found its way into the works of many crime scholars in Great Britain and the United States. The approach took root in what was called the new criminology of the early 1970s. Marxist criminology, often called radical or conflict criminology, has some adherents, though most have adopted other strains of the perspective, including feminist, masculinity, peacemaking, left realist, cultural, postmodern, and convict perspectives.

The idea of criminal justice practitioners (i.e., the police, criminal prosecutors, corrections personnel) as the "good guys" and criminal offenders as the "bad guys" is prevalent in our perspectives on the actors in the criminal justice system, and this view is often seen in depictions of these two groups in television and movies. A critical approach attempts to provide further investigation into the bigger picture of the American crime situation. The prison system has long been a system that creates a power differential between the keeper and the kept. The power differential that has been a significant part of American history (and which has existed in most of the world) has melded into the history of the treatment of criminal offenders. The concepts of race and ethnicity are key elements in this issue of power and control.

As mentioned previously, a critical perspective in criminology examines the power relations involved in the social control of criminal behavior that are often left unexamined. Of course, race, class, and gender are primary factors in understanding power relations in the criminal justice system— and indeed, in all societal structures.[12] In this chapter, the primary focus will be on race and the closely related issue of ethnicity, and how these elements are important in adopting a critical examination of correctional counseling, which is treatment in the U.S. prison establishment. Also examined will be how these factors fit into the overall rehabilitative culture of incarceration.

Race and Ethnicity in American Society

Today, the term "race" is not as easy to define as it used to be, when the traditional definition designated differences in human physical/biological makeup such as skin color, eye texture and color, and variations in bodily features. This conceptualization is extremely insufficient due to the fact that these rigid categories, originally anthropologically defined as Caucasian, Negroid, and Mongoloid, and more recently as white (or Caucasian),

African American (or black), Hispanic (or Latino/Latina), Native American, and Asian/Pacific Islander. The idea of these strictly delineated racial categories is known as racialism, and a belief in these concrete categories is a fallacy because no one is of any discrete racial groupings due to the long history of racial mixing throughout human history. Social scientists today see the concept of race as a social construct in which these categories are not biologically distinct. However, many groups of people receive differential treatment due to the fact that some people believe strongly in these racial distinctions. In addition, because the closely related concept of social class is enmeshed in race relations, the issue of power, which includes practices involving domination and submission, becomes a major part of the concept of race.

The concept of ethnicity is different than race, even though these two terms are commonly intermingled in conversations about race. If the traditional idea of race relies on biological distinctions (even though, as just noted, these distinctions are more socially than biologically based), ethnicity refers to social or cultural distinctions that are based on customs and traditions into which a person is socialized. Therefore, differences in religious beliefs, language, and cultural practices create distinctions in ethnicity. For example, people in the racial grouping of white, or Caucasian, might have the ethnic designation of Italian American or Jewish American and adopt cultural aspects particular to those cultural distinctions. The terms "race" and "ethnicity" are often intermingled in that people who consider themselves to be members of a certain racial group have certain culturally transmitted beliefs and practices they have adopted as well.

Social class is highly relevant to this discussion as it refers to the placement of people and groups into different strata, or levels, based on their socioeconomic status (often referred to as SES). People in minority groups (those who not only have lower numbers in the population, but who also have less power, control, and advantage socially than the majority) are often people at lower levels of the social class system. It has therefore been easy in the past to equate race with lesser abilities and intellectual aptitude, an idea that has permeated American society and its different social structures, including the prison system, and that has been the rationale behind differential treatment.

The ambiguous distinction of race and ethnicity creates difficulties in describing people. For example, Latin Americans, or Hispanics, are often lumped into the same racial category even though they might self-identify as white, black, or Native American. Other problems with racial and ethnic identity come because this group does not have a common place of ancestry. Instead, they have ancestors who recently immigrated from Mexico, Cuba, Puerto Rico, or other areas in Central and South America. To assume that all of these groups have a common racial or ethnic heritage and cultural belief system would be an inaccuracy.

The labels of race are important, and the meanings and implications of these labels change over time. The term "negro," for example, was acceptable in the literature on race in past decades but now has taken on a pejorative meaning. Likewise, referring to anyone who appears to have Hispanic ancestry as "Mexican" would be egregious. Labels define who we are and contribute to self-concept; therefore, cultural sensitivity should be considered as we choose terms to describe people of different groups. In this chapter, certain terms such as white/Caucasian, black/African American, and Hispanic/Latino/Latina, will be used interchangeably to reduce redundancy. Still, their use will be dictated by sensitivity and respect.

The American System of Punishment and Racism/Ethnocentrism

Punishment policies in the United States are set apart from those of other nations in that America claims the highest rates of incarceration in the world, the only use of the death penalty among Western countries, the most severe punishments in the Western world, and a long history of destructive policies that have adversely affected African Americans. The differential treatment of blacks in the American criminal justice system results primarily from racial differences in types of offenses but to a lesser degree from racial and ethnic prejudices and discriminatory practices based on these prejudices, some of which were intended and some of which were not. The drug policies of the 1980s and 1990s are a case in point. These policies, which will be discussed soon, have disproportionately affected African Americans and have caused a swell of black inmates into state and federal penal institutions.

It might be tempting to ascertain that it was unadulterated racism that created this racial disparity in the U.S. prison system, but this conveys an incomplete analysis of race and prison. It is therefore better to observe three major social processes that have played a role in the current situation. Three processes—politics, sociology, and the social psychology of race and crime—are useful in more completely analyzing the disparity.

The political aspects as they relate to the American dilemma of race and incarceration point to a long history of racial tension and discord as well as the use of this tension to generate votes for political candidates and their parties. Political schemes to attract voters often use crime to promote an agenda of fear to motivate citizens to vote in a particular way, as in the case of the so called "Southern strategy" dating back to the 1940s but emerging more forcefully in the 1960s. This strategy accomplished, among other things, white fear of criminal victimization by blacks. A "get tough on crime" policy ensued that promoted racial profiling, the targeting of certain offenses, inequitable treatment in sentencing, and the notable "war on drugs" that resulted in law enforcement (e.g., zero tolerance policing) strategies in predominately black neighborhoods. An example of how racial fear affected African Americans disproportionately can be found in the so-called 100 to one law of 1986 that punished crack cocaine sales much more severely than powder cocaine sales. Both involve the same illegal substance, but crack cocaine offenses are generally committed by blacks and powder cocaine offenses by whites.

The sociological approach to race and crime observes the American social structure that, since the country's existence, has developed a system of racial dominance by whites that has maintained the system through a series of discriminatory processes, not all of them intended, that have sustained the culture. Until the American Civil War, white dominance in the South was maintained by slavery. Afterward, it depended on Jim Crow laws, which resulted in a massive migration of blacks from the South to northern cities. When opportunities for employment moved from urban to suburban areas as a national war on drugs began, many blacks found themselves in urban ghettos with many social maladies such as poverty, housing and educational problems, crime, and substance abuse.

The third category—the social psychology of race and crime—involves the stereotyping that is pervasive in American society. Blacks are more likely to be associated with crime, as the findings of many social psychology studies have suggested. An implicit bias exists in media depictions that represent blacks as criminals and whites as victims. Even many African Americans are guilty of "colorism," in which African Americans with darker skin or more pronounced physiological features are more likely to be considered criminal offenders.

Other conditions that have created the present disparity involving race and criminal justice include the polarization of crime control policies that support either victims or offenders. This can also be seen in the rehabilitation and correctional philosophies mentioned in this chapter. Another factor is the idea—based on religious precepts—that crime is equated with sin, and criminals (sinners) should receive strict punishment. Finally, one must consider the structure of the U.S. government, which is quite different from other Western nations. It has elected or politically appointed judges and prosecutors and a built-in complication of sentencing and prosecuting people based on the passions of the communities they serve with the hope of winning reelection.[13]

Historical Patterns of Offender Rehabilitation

Some historical patterns in the development of offender rehabilitation have been observed in four models—the penitentiary, therapeutic, social-learning, and offender rights approaches. The penitentiary model took its form in either the earlier Jacksonian style, which consisted of the Pennsylvania and Auburn systems, or an array of progressive schemes, including the Maconuchie system, indeterminate sentencing, and the Elmira prison system. Incarceration was a key ingredient in these models.[14] Prior to the penitentiary system, many of the ways of dealing with criminal behavior in the early American colonies were borrowed from punishment practices in Europe and are similar in three ways—capital punishment, corporal punishment, and institutionalization.[15] Capital punishment, that is, the death penalty, was used for the most severe offenses, but these offenses did not involve only homicide and violent injury, but also crimes of moral turpitude such as adultery. The usual means of imposing the death penalty were hanging, burning, and pressing/crushing the offender until dead. Corporal punishments, such as placement into stocks and the pillory (in which perpetrators were affixed in wooden devices with the head and hands available for observers to view and through rotten food or other items at them), branding, public dunking, and other torturous activities were also heavily utilized. The early institutions were punitive houses of correction, which were reserved for those considered immoral, and almshouses and workhouses, which were provided as part of the poor relief system.

England attempted to deal with the problem of how to handle offenders with the strategies noted earlier in this chapter, which are often seen now as inhumane and even barbaric. In its infancy, the United States borrowed many of these strategies but did not accept all Britain's punishment schemes.[16] Prior to the first police force, the social control measures in Britain were exerted by the elite class to maintain order. Capital punishment was not working and banishment, in which offenders were sent to serve their sentences in America and later Australia, were also ineffective.

In postrevolutionary America, the new country refused to continue to accept these banished offenders. Many British prisons of the 18th century housed people with mental health disorders because there was no other place to accommodate them.

In the early American colonies, penal institutions—jails, houses of correction, and workhouses—were hardly adequate for punishing or reforming offenders. Thus, the penitentiary system was born of the need for a better system of punishment. The Walnut Street Jail in Philadelphia was transformed into a state prison known as the Eastern Penitentiary in 1790. The states of New York, New Jersey, Virginia, Kentucky, and Massachusetts followed Pennsylvania's lead and established state systems in the coming years. Pennsylvania's Eastern Penitentiary and New York's Auburn Penitentiary systems used the idea of penitence (seeking and asking for forgiveness of indiscretions) as a focal point of their punishment strategy, and the name penitentiary comes from this idea. The idea of penitence implies that an individual can become reformed. This idea, which later surfaces in the concept of rehabilitation, made the early American system of corrections unique.

As noted, the American penitentiary system presented an innovative way of dealing with colonial crime, generating great interest in Europe. Two French observers, Alexis de Tocqueville and Gustave de Beaumont, came to America in 1831 to study this new form of imprisonment, which at the time consisted of the Eastern and Auburn systems.[17] The idea of reforming offenders in the U.S. prison system, although still in its infancy, was a far cry from corporal punishment, branding, and other torture activities.

The second approach, the therapeutic model of the 19th and 20th centuries, saw the criminal offender as a sick individual in need of a cure, and used the medical model as a basic foundation of the strategy to find that cure. Cesare Lombroso's conception of the "born criminal" and other theories of biological determinism found their way into criminology as the foundation for the treatment models that would be used. Earlier forms of criminological theory failed to focus on the individual characteristics of the criminal and simply lumped them together in a collective deviant unit.

Influenced by the burgeoning field of social psychology, the field of corrections in the early 20th century began to focus on the offender not as a born deviant, but as a person who was incorrectly socialized. In other words, the socialization process, which begins at a very early age in a person's life and guides the person into learning and following social norms, was not correctly inculcated by the individual. Therefore, another perspective developed about the offender, one that perceived him or her as an immature actor who had received improper social training from the agents of socialization in her or her life, that is, family, school, religious institutions, and community. The idea of social therapy developed and consisted of therapists working with their clients in an effort to change the person's social environment. Specific strategies appeared in correctional treatment, such as the therapeutic community in which the hierarchal prison structure between inmates and correctional staff is changed through the direct involvement of inmates in their own situations. This was, of course, in marked contrast to the traditional authoritarian structure of domination/subordination found in the correctional milieu.

The final approach, the rights model, takes into account the democratic ideal of individual rights. Rehabilitation can be seen as a threat to individual liberty. And at a time when more evasive treatment strategies were being used on mental patients, a focus emerged regarding the rights of offenders. The prisoners' rights movements of the mid-20th century came about as a result of this new focus. In addition, since imprisonment often causes a great deal of distress due to the oppressive and sometimes violent nature of prison life and the necessary life adjustments that must be made, the state, according to the prisoners' rights movement, is therefore obligated to provide psychosocial services to offenders.[18]

The Rehabilitation Ideal versus the Punishment Paradigm

America therefore has a serious struggle with the dialectic problem of offender treatment versus public security. The focus on treatment is what has become known as the rehabilitative ideal. A major event in the nation's history of rehabilitation came in 1974 when a group of researchers produced a study whose dominant message came to be known as "nothing works." In other words, strategic attempts to change offender behavior are futile. The famous Martinson report, named after the lead researcher, consisted of a meta-analysis of rehabilitation programs and implied that rehabilitation attempts are futile. Politicians seized the report to focus on a shift to more punitive models in corrections and, incidentally, to gather votes from citizens who were concerned about crime and the lax treatment of offenders.

Cullen takes aim at the "punishment paradigm" of the past few decades that was fueled by Martin's "nothing works" message. Cullen feels that rehabilitative ideal should be the guiding force in corrections rather than a philosophy that has spawned such ineffective punitive strategies as book camp programs, scared straight initiatives, and intensive supervision. He provides five reasons the treatment paradigm should replace the punitive approach: (1) the current rejection of rehabilitation was an error, and shifts in the conservative get tough agenda in the past few decades have made things worse; 2) punishment in the current form does not work because the theory guiding the paradigm—rational choice—is highly limited and does not account for or target other factors in reoffending; 3) rehabilitation, despite the current political environment, does work, and scholars are now producing studies that show promise in corrections using rehabilitation strategies; 4) despite the political climate, American citizens support the idea of offender rehabilitation; and 5) there are moral reasons for providing treatment resources to offenders—a rehabilitation focus acknowledges that racial/ethnic, gender, and other factors play a role in the etiology of criminal behavior, that rehabilitation is a collaborative effort between offenders and the state, and that rehabilitation reaffirms, rather than degrades, human dignity.[19]

The Multicultural Term in Counseling

Multicultural counseling refers to a counseling approach that values and celebrates pluralism and diversity in regards to race, ethnicity, class, and sexual orientation and illustrates a willingness to develop counseling skills that work within a culturally relative framework. It also seeks to support practices that ensure social justice goals. It adopts postmodern and social constructionist ideologies in that it accepts that reality is socially constructed and can be viewed from different perspectives.[20] It is also closely connected to critical theory in that it takes into consideration the power differential that has long existed between different cultural groups, and it pointedly rejects a Eurocentric approach to counseling.

Currently, many clinicians who are engaged in counseling clients, whether institutional or "free world," are trained with a perspective that values multicultural competencies. This was not the case prior to the 1960s when, influenced by the civil rights movement, an emphasis was placed on the mental health concerns of racial and ethnic minorities, especially African Americans. Professional organizations such as the American Counseling Association (previously known as the American Personnel and Guidance Association) and the American Psychological Association (APA) had members who focused on the need for a research agenda related to racial and ethnic clients and a better understanding of the role of diversity in mental health counseling. Segregation efforts on a macro level in American society created a situation where Euro-American counselors were in contact with people of different racial and ethnic groups. However, they were not adequately trained in working with racial and ethnic minorities. College coursework began to address the issue, but clinical training efforts lagged. In the 1970s, research on Latin Americans, American Indians, and Asian Americans was introduced in scholarly journals.[21] Many journals published articles on counseling the "culturally different" and on counseling techniques from a "cross-cultural" perspective. The following decades continued the progressive trend, and a focus on culture, diversity, and racial and ethnic identity was found in scholarly publications. In addition, multicultural competence was required in counselor program accreditation and counselor credentialing.

Due to the various racial and ethnic groups that make up the American correctional system, a multicultural approach includes an understanding of cultural differences and a systematic program that addresses these cultural differences. The following text considers treatment concerns and strategies for the racial and ethnic categories that are the focus of this examination.

African Americans

The most recent data on race/ethnicity in the prison system shows that in 2010, African-American males (classified in official prison statistics as black, non-Hispanic males) had an imprisonment rate that was almost seven times higher than those of white non-Hispanic males. Black non-Hispanic females had an imprisonment rate nearly tripling that of white, non-Hispanic females.[22] In addition, in comparison with other racial categories, African Americans have high levels of physical health problems such as diabetes, heart disease, cancer, and HIV/AIDS. There are also very high levels of infant mortality with this group. Many African Americans are geographically located in urban areas and are exposed to many of the deleterious effects of urban life. They also suffer from low occupational wages, low educational levels, and low socioeconomic status. African Americans' residence in substandard housing in high-crime areas can also contribute to increased levels of psychological stress.

It is a given that the enslavement of Africans is an ugly mark on American history. The treatment of slaves includes forced family separations and disruptions. Despite this history of instability, African-American families have been at the core of group unity and individual member support. There is little in the literature that deals with African-American cultural adaption processes. Most blacks have been in the United States for many generations, so it is commonly thought that acculturation issues in treatment are not relevant to the conversation. Due to the history of treatment of black Americans, even after slavery, there often exists a lack of trust in relationships, including therapeutic ones, with white therapists or counselors. This obviously has major implications in many court-ordered treatment strategies, as are found in correctional programs.

As with all minority populations, African Americans have special needs that have to be considered if treatment strategies are to be effective. Key treatment issues with this population include understanding the role of spirituality in the healing process, understanding the client's perception of mental health, acknowledging that race and culture are not the same, and understanding the role of healer in the therapeutic process.[23]

Latin Americans

The United States has experienced a surge of Latin American prisoners. Latin males have the second highest imprisonment rate among males, and Latinas have the third highest among females. As mentioned earlier in this chapter, to categorize Latin Americans into one single homogeneous cultural group is inappropriate because there are many diverse areas of origin, traditions, cultural practices, and histories. In the United States, Latinos from Mexico comprise the largest grouping, followed by those from Puerto Rico and then from Cuba; smaller numbers hail from the Dominican Republic, Central America, and South America. A common trait is that these people have long histories of being oppressed and conquered in their areas of origin. They also have long histories of intermarriage, creating a racially and ethnically mixed group.[24] Therefore, counseling is more effective with an understanding of the differences in these groups. It is also important to realize the similarities.

Regarding race and ethnic treatment issues, Latin Americans have some similarities to African Americans. The racial fear and media stereotyping of this group has resulted in large numbers of Latinos and Latinas entering the system. They have had to endure de jure segregation and recently a significant amount of de facto segregation. A major difference is the issue of immigration status. Closely related to immigration status are racial profiling and the show your papers laws of some states that single out Latinos and Latinas because they might be in the country illegally. The issue has become political as many legal Hispanic residents have been subjected to racial profiling.

Many Latin American groups have a strong family orientation, called *familismo*, which can be traced to Spanish colonial-era journals.[25] A failure to understand the family dynamics of *la famiia* would make many Hispanic families appear to be psychopathological to mainstream counselors, particularly in regards to enmeshment and co-dependency, when culturally, this is normal.

Spirituality and strong religious traditions are also common to many Latin Americans. The Roman Catholic religion is the most common. Religious traditions sometimes contain a mixture of Catholicism, American Indian traditions, and, in some cases, African elements. These issues of faith also extend to health, as traditional remedies and healers are often more valued than mainstream medical care.[26] Treatment attempts should consider the role of these spiritual factors.

The issue of gender is also important when working with Latin American populations. The gender socialization process is often quite rigid. Males are expected to adhere to traditional masculine traits (i.e., strength, the protection of women and children, community loyalty, sexual aggressiveness), while women are expected to be virtuous, nurturing, sexually chaste, and more spiritual (a reference to the qualities of the Virgin Mary). *Machismo* reflects the masculine ideal, and *marianismo* illustrates the feminine ideal in this gender role socialization.[27] The fact that prisons are segregated by sex and that homosexual behavior is not uncommon creates situations that require culturally competent treatment strategies.

An additional concern is that of the lack of English proficiency of some members of this group. Immigration variations and different degrees of acculturation make these levels quite diverse. Since most counselors speak just English, this can be a barrier to treatment. Miscommunication can have serious consequences if inaccurate diagnoses and subsequent treatment efforts result from misinterpretations.

Latin Americans, like many other groups, are often reluctant to engage with mental health professionals who are not of a similar background. Due to cultural traditions, many Hispanics are more likely to desire to converse with a priest or other person who deals in spiritual work than someone in the clinical mental health field.[28]

American Indians

As with other racial groups, American Indians suffer from low socioeconomic status, addictions, poverty, family issues, and violence at high rates. Suicide rates are especially high. Some scholars report that native groups have experienced a type of historical trauma or the intergenerational trauma that started with the genocide and removal of their ancestors. Also seen as a "soul wound," this needs to be acknowledged in a treatment context.[29] The issue of colonization is important in the context of historical trauma. Colonization refers to oppressive strategies used to disconnect people from their traditions and force them to assimilate into the dominant culture. Another important concept is that of imperialism, which is an ideology that validates the oppression of minority groups in an effort to promote feelings of entitlement in the majority group. Indigenous decolonization refers to attempts to reconnect Native Americans to their traditions and cultural belief systems. Strategies to connect social problems of indigenous populations in order to reduce the effects of colonization are called structural frameworks and are recommended by some scholars.[30]

In therapeutic work with native peoples, the following factors should be observed: the degree of assimilation, the persistent problem of alcohol abuse, the prevalence of suicide (which is twice the national average), counseling relationship issues and methods, initial contact and ongoing rapport with the therapist, the source of issues, and treatment strategies that are specific to the particular tribe with which a person identifies.[31]

The idea of mental health counseling is not attractive to many Native Americans, as they often see it as a consequence of human weakness.[32] Traditional Indian healers are often able to use spiritual wisdom to promote healing. Stories and other traditional ways of interjecting narratives in certain problems are common, and Western mental health practices that deviate from these narratives are often not accepted by native peoples. Also, traditions such as the sweat lodge ceremony, peyote ceremonies, spiritual dances, and others that are not part of mainstream counseling are more likely to be seen as therapeutic by Native Americans than are Western psychotherapeutic methods.

Asian Americans/Pacific Islanders

It might be tempting to categorize people of Asian descent into one homogenous category, but like Latin Americans and American Indians, this group is much more heterogeneous than is often thought. There are over 30 nations of origin of Asian Americans along with many distinct cultural groups.[33] Asian Americans come from China, Japan, Korea, Vietnam, the Philippines, and India, and just looking at these countries illustrates the level of cultural diversity in this racial category.[34] As with the other cultural groups, factors such as age, level of acculturation, socioeconomic status, education, foreign-born versus American born, and immigrant status are important in understanding treatment concerns.

Many Asian American and Pacific Island groups are fundamentally different in their perceptions of health issues. For example, in contrast to the Western world's concepts of mind-body dualism, many Asian Americans see balance as primary to good health. Traditional Japanese culture seeks symptom relief rather than a cure, including for psychological issues.[35]

Another issue to be considered regarding cultural variation is that many Asian Americans focus on group rather than individual concerns, which is in marked contrast to Western culture. The concepts of group welfare ahead of individual welfare, group decision making versus individual decision making, and a belief in the natural and inevitable process of illness that should be quietly accepted as opposed to something to be aggressively fought are difficult for many Western trained clinicians to understand and can easily be considered by them as evidence of psychopathology.[36]

Asian Americans represent a small racial group in American prisons. In Western society, they are often described as a "model minority" with higher levels of socioeconomic status, occupational professionalism, and prestige. This is an incomplete picture, however, as many Asians do not possess the characteristics of the model minority ideal. Many also find themselves incarcerated and, due to the existence of possible cultural differences, correctional counselors should be knowledgeable and mindful of these differences.

Should One Size Fit All in Correctional Treatment?

Prisons are obviously very different from mental hospitals, though both have the purpose of assisting those in the system with problems in living while being confined in an institutional setting. Termed "total institutions," programs such as these function to rehabilitate people—to restore something that is lacking in that person's socialization process. The person in either institution is normally still deemed "salvageable." A difference between these programs is that there is more concern about safety in prisons, whose task is twofold—to balance both the needs of the offender and the protection of the public (the treatment versus security dualism). The latter issue is the salient function of correctional institutions. Therefore, the question is how to adequately treat offenders—to both better themselves and develop skills to adequately function in society—in as effective a manner as possible, given the constraints of imprisonment.

According to the most recent statistics, counseling programs, including life skills training, substance abuse counseling, community adjustment, and HIV/AIDS counseling, are offered in almost all public state and federal prisons and three out of four privately run facilities. Other counseling programs that are operating in many prison systems are mental health counseling, personal finance management, conflict resolution, employment counseling, parenting classes, and sex offender treatment.[37] Although the amount of treatment activity taking place in correctional institutions is commendable, a lack of culture-centered counseling is not.

A "one size fits all" approach to correctional treatment is currently used in American corrections. A specific example of this can be found in group counseling, a staple in prison programming in which offenders work out problems "in group" led by a prison counselor. Although individual psychotherapy and psychopharmacology are used in institutional settings, group work is the most common form of treatment to address issues, and there are benefits to group therapy. Some studies suggest that it provides a safe place to resolve conflict and to develop trust among inmates and that it can improve personal insight and communication skills. Other studies have failed to produce these results.[38]

But to be truly effective, should treatment programs focus on racial and ethnic differences? This would involve a more macro level approach to treating offenders that takes into account factors such as the effects of colonialism, domination, and oppression that have led to different worldviews. A historical rehabilitation process that looks at intergenerational posttraumatic stress that has caused generations of racial and ethnic minorities to maintain dysfunctional adaptations could be highly beneficial to correctional rehabilitation strategies.[39]

Security measures in prisons will surely become an issue with this culture-focused treatment agenda. Allowing ceremonies and rituals such as sweat lodges for Native American populations, which already exist in some prisons, requires resources to be utilized, including time and money for correctional staff oversight and possible security problems.

Another concern is the segregation of racial and ethnic groups based on these common treatment concerns. Compartmentalizing all African

Americans, Latin Americans, Native Americans, and Asian Americans together (regardless of security classification levels) could enhance the problems that already exist in prisons that encourage gang membership and increased racial and ethnic divisions, even violence.

The question, therefore, is: Due to a continuous dearth of funds allotted to correctional systems, should scarce resources be spent enhancing treatment programs, specifically with a multicultural counseling focus? Cullen, as noted earlier, implores the correctional system to make rehabilitative counseling the dominant paradigm.[40] A specific strategy would be to adopt a culture-centered approach. Major shifts in counseling have been made in this area over the past few decades, and many counselors have been—and are continuing to be—trained in this modality.

A percentage of the public will continue to believe that rehabilitation strategies simply mollycoddle offenders. A focus on multicultural treatment will certainly seem inappropriate to this group. In a post-9/11 society where people with different cultural beliefs and practices are increasingly seen as "other," convincing politicians and the voting public that this focus is beneficial will be a challenge. Theorists, researchers, and activists should be diligent in discovering effective strategies and communicating their findings.

Critical theory and multicultural counseling are a wonderful "fit," as both promote—from ideological and practical standpoints—a challenge to Eurocentric world views that one size (that of the dominant culture) fits all cultures. The public should not again buy into a "nothing works" philosophy, and individuals in the field should engage politicians and citizens in this discussion. Trying to fit a square peg into a round hole does not work. Neither does trying to fit a diverse population into a single treatment framework.

Notes

1. Quinney, 2000, pp. 5–7.
2. Quinney, 2000, pp. 7–13.
3. Gabbidon, 2010, pp. 9–11.
4. Quinney, 2000, pp. 15–27.
5. Vold, Bernard, and Snipes, 2002.
6. Wilson, 1987.
7. Goffman, 1963.
8. Cooley, 1922.
9. Merton, 1948, pp. 193–210.

10. Du Bois, 1903, p. 9.
11. DeKeseredy, 2011, p. 7.
12. Sheldon, 2008, p. 3.
13. Clare and Kramer, 1976, pp. 28–30.
14. Rotman, 1990, pp. 59–76.
15. Clare and Kramer, 1976, pp. 28–30.
16. Irwin, 2005, pp. 15–16.
17. Western, 2006, p. 1.
18. Rotman, 1990, pp. 59–76.
19. Cullen, 2007, pp. 717–728.
20. Sue et al., 1998, p. 1.
21. Santiago-Rivera, Arrendondo, and Gallardo-Cooper, 2002, pp. 5–6.
22. Guerino, Harrison, and Sabol, 2012.
23. Parham and Brown, 2003, pp. 81–98.
24. Santiago-Rivera, Arrendondo, and Gallardo-Cooper, 2002, p. 21.
25. Santiago-Rivera, Arrendondo, and Gallardo-Cooper, 2002, pp. 42–43.
26. Santiago-Rivera, Arrendondo, and Gallardo-Cooper, 2002, pp. 5–6.
27. Santiago-Rivera, Arrendondo, and Gallardo-Cooper, 2002, pp. 49–51.
28. Echeverry, 1997, pp. 72–107.
29. Duran, 2006, p. 7.
30. Chenault, 2011, pp. 19–22.
31. Duran, 2006, p. 4.
32. Atkinson, Morten, and Wing Sue, 1998, p. 147.
33. Kagawa-Singer and Chung, 2002, pp. 47–66.
34. Organista, Marin, and Chun, 2010, p. 14.
35. Kagawa-Singer and Chung, 2002, pp. 58–59.
36. Kagawa-Singer and Chung, 2002, p. 6.
37. Stephan, 2005.
38. Maier and Fulton, 1998, pp. 152–153.
39. Yellow Horse Brave Heart, 2004, pp. 13–16.
40. Cullen, 2007, pp. 717–728.

References

Atkinson, Donald R., George Morten, and Derald Wing Sue. *Counseling American Minorities* (5th ed.). Boston: McGraw Hill, 1998.

Chenault, Vernida S. *Weaving Strength, Weaving Power*. Durham, NC: Carolina Academic Press, 2011.

Clare, Paul K., and John H. Kramer *Introduction to American Corrections*. Boston: Holbrook, 1976.

Cooley, Charles H. *Human Nature and the Social Order* (rev. ed.). New York: Charles Scribner's Sons, 1922.

Cullen, Frances T. "Making Rehabilitation Corrections' Guiding Paradigm." *Criminology and Public Policy* 6 (2007): 717–728.

DeKeseredy, Walter S. *Contemporary Critical Criminology*. London and New York: Routledge, 2011.

Du Bois, W. E. B. *Souls of Black Folk: Essays and Sketches*. Chicago: A. C. McClurg and Co., 1903.

Duran, Eduardo. *Healing the Soul Wound: Counseling with American Indians and Other Native Peoples*. New York and London: Teachers College Press, 2006.

Echeverry, John J. "Treatment Barriers: Accessing and Accepting Professional Help." In *Psychological Interventions and Research with Latino Populations*, edited by Jorge Garcia and Marca Cecilia Zea, pp. 94–107. Needham Heights, MA: Allyn and Bacon, 1997.

Gabbidon, Shaun L. *Criminological Perspectives on Race and Crime* (2nd ed.). New York: Routledge, 2010.

Goffman, Erving. *Stigma: Notes on a Spoiled Identity*. Englewood Cliffs, NJ: Prentice Hall, 1963.

Guerino, Paul, Paige M. Harrison, and William J. Sabol. *Prisoners in 2010*. Washington, DC: Bureau of Justice Statistics, 2012.

Irwin, John. *The Warehouse Prison: Disposal of the New Dangerous Class*. Los Angeles: Roxbury, 2005.

Kagawa-Singer, Majorie, and Rita Chi-Ying Chung. "Toward a New Paradigm: A Cultural System Approach." In *Asian American Mental Health*, edited by Karen S. Karasaki, Sumie Okazaki, and Stanley Sue, pp. 47–66. New York: Kluwer Academic/Plenum, 2002.

Maier, Gary J., and Louis Fulton. "Inpatient Treatment of Offenders with Mental Disorders." In *Treatment of Offenders with Mental Disorders*, edited by Robert W. Wittstein, pp. 152–153. New York and London: Guilford, 1998.

Merton, Robert K. "The Self-Fulfilling Prophecy." *Antioch Review* 8 (1948): 193–210.

Organista, Pamela B., Gerardo Marin, and Kevin M. Chun. *The Psychology of Ethnic Groups in the United States*. Los Angeles: Sage, 2010.

Parham, Thomas, and Sherlon Brown. "Therapeutic Approaches with African-American Populations." In *Culture and Counseling: New Approaches*, edited by Frederek D. Harper and John McFadden, pp. 81–98. Boston: Pearson Education, 2003.

Quinney, Richard. *Bearing Witness to Crime and Social Justice*. New York: State University of New York Press, 2000.

Rotman, Edgardo. *Beyond Punishment: A New View on the Rehabilitation of Criminal Offenders*. New York: Greenwood, 1990.

Santiago-Rivera, Azara, Patricia Arrendondo, and Maritza Gallardo-Cooper. *Counseling Latinos and La Familia: A Practical Guide*. Thousand Oaks, CA: Sage, 2002.

Sheldon, Randall G. *Controlling the Dangerous Classes: A History of Criminal Justice in America* (2nd ed.). Boston: Pearson, 2008.

Stephan, James J. *Census of State and Federal Correctional Facilities, 2005.* Washington, DC: Bureau of Justice Statistics, 2005.

Sue, Derald Wing, Robert T. Carter, J. Manuel Casas, Nadya A. Fouad, Allen E. Ivey, Margaret Jensen, Teresa LaFromboise, Jeanne E. Manese, Joseph G. Ponterotto, and Ena Vazquez-Nutall. *Multicultural Counseling Competencies: Individual and Organizational Development.* Thousand Oaks, CA: Sage, 1998.

Tonry, Michael. *Punishing Race: A Continuing American Dilemma.* London: Oxford University Press, 2011.

Vold, George B., Thomas J. Bernard, and Jeffery B. Snipes. *Theoretical Criminology* (5th ed.). New York and Oxford: Oxford University Press, 2002.

Western, Bruce. *Punishment and Inequality in America.* New York: Russell Sage Foundation, 2006.

Wilson, W. Julius. *The Truly Disadvantaged.* Chicago: University of Chicago Press, 1987.

Yellow Horse Brave Heart, Maria. "The Historical Trauma Response among Natives and Its Relationship to Substance Abuse." In *Healing and Mental Health of Native Americans: Speaking in Red*, edited by Ethan Nebelkopf and Mary Phillips, pp. 13–16. Walnut Creek, CA: Altamira, 2004.

Chapter 19

Prison Privatization: The Political Economy of Race

Laurie A. Gould and Matthew Pate

Introduction

Over the past three decades, the issue of privatized corrections has attracted a great deal of scholarly attention. Reisig and Pratt characterize the topic of full-scale privatization as "a topic of ardent debate."[1] There are innumerable ethical, political, and practical questions surrounding the introduction of private financial interests into the correctional setting. Of these, cost, programming, and recidivism are among the more important issues, but questions of racial and ethnic inequity also have emerged as an especially consequent area of concern.

While privatization in corrections can take myriad forms, the focus of this chapter is limited to the full-scale privatization of correctional facilities (i.e., those institutions that are built, owned, and operated by a private corporation).[2] With full-scale privatization, "the public functions of punishment, detention, rehabilitation, and general interests of public safety are performed largely by for-profit corporations."[3]

Private correctional companies claim that by following the profit motive, they "can perform most services cheaper and more effectively than can the public sector, which is considered to be unmotivated, ineffective, and unresponsive to the public's needs and demands."[4] Proponents of privatized corrections argue that private companies are so effective that they can offer the same level of security and programming as state-run facilities and still earn a profit for shareholders.[5] As will be discussed, these assertions are neither universally shared, confirmed, nor lauded by correctional scholars.

History of Privatization

Privatization of correctional services is certainly not a new idea in the United States, as jails in the colonial era were largely privately owned. These jails would charge prisoners, their families, and the government a fee to cover the cost of imprisonment.[6] The use of private companies continued well into the 1800s, and "the origins of special facilities for juvenile offenders . . . depended in large measure on what today would be called privatization."[7] However, notable concerns over inmate health emerged in many of these early facilities. For example, in one facility, prisoners were contracted out to farmers and other businessmen for a few dollars per day, but inmates were forced to work so hard that the majority of them died within seven years.[8] The conditions were so bad that self-mutilation and suicide among inmates was commonplace.[9]

Convict leasing was a fairly common practice in southern correctional systems, especially when labor demand skyrocketed after the civil war during the reconstruction effort. Convict leasing took on a variety of forms:

> Some companies outside the prison provided raw materials that were refined in prison workshops and later sold by private companies. At others, prisons leased their inmates out to private farms or other businesses if they could not produce salable items within the prison. In a number of states, contractors paid the prison a fee or a percentage of the profits for the right to employ convicts. . . . Even when prisons were not operated entirely by private entrepreneurs, inmates were used as a cheap source of labor. Prisoners often worked on farms, railroads, and mines, in addition to other public work programs.[10]

Of the Tennessee convict leasing system, Cable notes that inmate deaths were common while they were on work details at farms and various mines (referred to in his text as "branch prisons"). Despite assurances from the warden that sick inmates were always transferred back to the penitentiary and never forced to continue working, it appears that death rates of branch prisoners were unusually high. According to Cable, convicts in branch prisons

> are worked in gangs surrounded by armed guards, and the largest company, at least three hundred and twenty-fivequartered in a mere stockade. As the eye runs down the table of deaths, it finds opposite the names, among other mortal causes, the following: Found dead. Killed. Drowned. Not Given.

Blank. Blank. Blank. Killed. Blank. Shot. . . . the report shows heavy rates of mortality at these branch prisons, resulting largely from such lingering complaints as dropsy, scrofula, etc., and more numerously by consumption than by any one thing except violence; rates of mortality [are] startlingly large compared to the usual rates of well-ordered prisons, and low only in comparison with those of other prisons worked under the hands of lessees.[11]

Issues of racial disparity were notable under the convict leasing system, as the majority of southern inmates were black. In Georgia, for example, 90 percent of the inmates were black, and most were serving long sentences.[12]

In the end, the "opportunity for profit led to such widespread prisoner abuse and corruption, which violated our institutionalized beliefs about the humane treatment of citizens, that the government was forced to heed public outcry" and do away with private jails. Corruption, abuse, and a lack of profit all contributed to the collapse of privatized correctional services, yet they remerged in the 1980s. An important difference between past efforts at privatization and the current movement is the issue of responsibility. Specifically, the government now acknowledges that it is ultimately responsible for the care of inmates incarcerated in privately run facilities.[13]

Contemporary Privatization

In the present era, almost all existing correctional institutions outsource at least some of their basic operations to private companies. White notes that an entirely public prison is a near impossibility, except in cases where the institution is a fully self-contained society.[14] Typical privatized functions inside public facilities include food service, medical care, and programs for special populations.[15] Full-scale privatization is certainly not the norm in contemporary corrections; however, the number of privatized institutions has grown markedly over the past decade.

Contemporary private prisons date back to 1984, when the Federal Bureau of Prisons contracted with Eclectic Communications, Inc. to house young (18- to 26-year-olds) offenders at a private ranch in La Honda, California. Also in 1984, Corrections Corporation of America (CCA) became the first private company to manage a jail (Hamilton County Jail in Tennessee).[16] Currently, CCA runs 60 private prisons and houses 75,000 inmates (the total bed capacity is 80,000), making it the single largest provider of private prison services.[17] The GEO group (formerly

Wackenhut), which merged with the Cornell Company in a $685 million merger in 2010,[18] has emerged as the second largest provider of private prison services. Wackenhut received its first contract from the Bureau of Immigration and Processing in 1987 to provide secure custody for 150 illegal detainees. The company has grown substantially and now owns and/or manages 114 correctional, mental health, and community facilities and also has a bed capacity of 80,000.[19]

There are a variety of reasons for the increased use of private prisons, but blooming prison populations and overcrowding are typically cited in the literature. Incarceration data reveal that from "1925 to 1973 . . . there was virtually no change in the rate of imprisonment, with the rate hovering around 100 prisoners per 100,000 people."[20] After 1973, however, the ratio dramatically increased to 446 prisoners per 100,000. While the rate of crime remained relatively unchanged, public policy toward certain crimes became more punitive. Tougher sanctions for drug violators, minimum mandatory sentencing, truth in sentencing laws, and a general shift from rehabilitation to retribution have caused prison populations to expand since the 1970s.[21] Increases in prison populations continued between 2003 and 2013, and only modest decreases have occurred in the years since. As of December 2010, the Bureau of Justice Statistics reported that state and federal correctional institutions housed 1,612,395 prisoners.[22]

Much of the U.S. prison population is housed in publically run facilities, but there have been increases in the private prisoner population. In 2000, there were approximately 1.3 million adult offenders held in state and federal institutions, of which 5.8 percent of state prisoners and 10.7 percent of federal prisoners (or 6.3 percent of all prisoners combined) were housed in private prisons.[23] In 2010, approximately 8.0 percent of state and federal inmates were being held in private prison facilities. While those numbers may appear insignificant, it is important to note that the number of federal inmates held in private facilities doubled between 2000 and 2010, from 15,524 to 33,830.[24]

Given that private prisons house such a small number of U.S. prisoners, many might ask why this topic is worthy of attention. Hallett responds to this by noting that the private prison industry represents the fourth largest prison system in the United States. He goes on to note that "the federal system has recently surpassed all of the individual states in terms of size, only Texas and California today have a higher inmate population than the American prison industry."[25] As the United States has the highest incarceration rates in the world, the fourth largest prison system in this country clearly merits examination.

The Advantages of Prison Privatization

Ostensibly, there are three principle advantages of full-scale privatization: the ability to rapidly increase prison bed space, a reduction in prison operating costs, and an increase in service quality for inmates.[26] Prison privatization has flourished due to expanding prison populations over the past two decades. As previously stated, numerous "get tough" policies and more punitive sentencing practices have led to unprecedented prison populations and exacerbated prison overcrowding. Simply put, many states could not accommodate rising prison populations and turned to private companies to house excess prisoners. As the Bureau of Justice Assistance (BJA) notes, "the dramatic increase in prison and jail populations and the associated need to construct prison and jail facilities quickly and cheaply have often been cited as a major impetus behind the move toward privatization."[27] It takes an estimated five to six years for governments to construct new prisons, whereas private corporations can build a new prison in less than two or three years, thus providing states much faster overcrowding relief. Private corporations can build prisons in half the time because they are not under the same constraints as governments (e.g., they can eschew competitive bidding, and they are not subject to pressure from constituents).

Economic savings in day-to-day operational costs is another purported benefit of private prisons. Reductions associated with labor costs are the primary savings mechanism employed, since 65–70 percent of prison operating costs are tied to employee salaries and benefits.[28] A report issued by the Sentencing Project (an advocacy group for sentencing and prison reform) estimated that private prisons pay new employees approximately $5,327 less per year than their public counterparts.[29] Additionally, correctional staff in privately run facilities are given, on average, 58 fewer training hours compared to public prison staff.[30] Private prison firms acknowledge that staff costs are lower in their facilities, compared to government-run prisons, but maintain that they are simply more efficient at managing costs.[31] However, the cost savings associated with private prisons may be minimal at best. A recent meta-analysis of private prison studies from Lundahl, Kunz, Brownell, Harris, and Van Vleet, revealed no significant cost savings associated with private prisons. The researchers concluded that private prisons offer no clear economic benefit over their public counterparts, and "neither cost savings nor improvements in quality of confinement are guaranteed through privatization."[32]

Improved service delivery for inmates is another advantage of privatization lauded by proponents. Lack of quality care in publicly run facilities was brought to the forefront by a number of inmate lawsuits and riots in publicly run facilities. Private prison corporations maintain that high standards in service delivery and staffing are necessary because contract renewals are dependent on a job well done. Further, proponents argue that sufficient oversight mechanisms are currently in place (e.g., judicial activism, court mandates) to ensure that abuses will not occur in private facilities.[33]

The Disadvantages of Prison Privatization

Owing to the nature of the institution, whether one views a given bureaucratic organization as a success or failure resides largely in the definition of one's terms. Nowhere is this more readily apparent than in the debate as to whether privatized corrections "work." As noted earlier in this chapter, several researchers conclude that privatized corrections can provide services at the same or improved levels and at lower costs.[34] In contrast, many scholars argue that privatized management is mired in inescapable conflicts of interest,[35] that the apparent savings represent a false economy and unsustainable development,[36] and that they weaken the moral bond between citizen and state while simultaneously evading core governmental responsibilities.[37] Others argue that privatized corrections are not really private, as contractors are effectively proxy agents of the state and are therefore bound by the same laws and obligations.[38]

From even this brief review, one sees that concerns over prison privatization are myriad and include issues of accountability, quality/effectiveness, cost effectiveness, and fundamental ethical problems. In the past, punishment was seen as the exclusive domain of the state because the government wanted to "limit if not eliminate the influence of private interests over the detection, trial, and sanctioning of lawbreakers—in short, to ensure that all individuals are treated equally before the law."[39] When private interests enter the realm of punishment, one must question how accountable private corporations are to taxpayers, community residents, and inmates.[40]

Because private corporations exist to produce profit for their ownership, innovation, economy, and efficiency—all conditioned by free market forces—become institutional focal concerns. At least facially, this is how supporters of privatization construct their argument. Some economists, such as Krugman, contend that participants in the industry of privatized corrections tout free market influences while at the same time benefiting from a system that is both closed and strongly imbalanced to the advantage of the corporations—to the great detriment of taxpayers. As Krugman argues, "They [the corporations] are, instead, living off government contracts. There isn't any market here, and there is, therefore, no reason to expect any magical gains in efficiency."[41] This position appears to be supported by a Bureau of Justice Assistance study that concludes that the promised savings from privatization "have simply not materialized."[42]

Beyond dubious promises of financial savings, privatized corrections often fall short in other realms of accountability as well. When private corporations enter into agreements with government, they are obliged (at least in theory) to fulfill the expectations of the government.[43] Whether privatized corrections meet this expectation is equally debatable.

To this point, Feeley offers an incisive critique: "Ironically, in the name of shrinking government, privatization—at least in criminal justice—has expanded both the functions of the state and the costs of government. Moreover, it has done so in ways that make these functions less accountable and the costs less visible."[44] What makes Feeley's observation more poignant is his further contention that "This development has taken place largely unnoticed, or if noticed, with little self-consciousness reflection."[45]

While it is likely naive to expect a vast decentralized collection of public bureaucracies to engage in unitary existential reflection (a point Feely acknowledges), this is an area where privatization has done a particular disservice to American corrections. As Feeley states, "No agency, no office, no official is charged with thinking about the system as a whole or developing new and improved ways to do things."[46]

This observation gets to a crucial point about the process through which corrections management becomes privatized. Without centralized oversight, there are innumerable points at which the best interests and voice of the public may be subordinated to other concerns. In particular, the consent of voters can be bypassed during the prison construction process because private corporations fund the construction costs of new prisons, meaning that legislators do not need to get voter approval on bond issues.[47] In bypassing voter approval, taxpayers are removed from this critical process and are unable to voice their approval or disapproval of new prison construction.

Accountability to community residents can also be problematic with private prisons. For some economically depressed communities, private prisons can bring a much-needed economic base. Indeed, areas with extremely high unemployment rates often support the construction of prisons (both public and private) in their towns because they bring jobs and boost the local economy.[48] However, for some, these benefits may be short lived because "a private firm can elect not to renew its contract after fulfilling its obligations. Residents may rely on the prison as an employer and taxpayer, yet the firm can quickly and carelessly exit their community."[49]

Lastly, accountability to inmates is surely suspect in private correctional facilities. In terms of inmates' safety, there have been several high-profile incidents detailed in the news. In a Walensburg, Colorado, facility, two guards repeatedly beat a prisoner while he was handcuffed and shackled.[50] The Northeast Ohio Correctional Center in Youngstown experienced similar problems. As a Bureau of Justice Assistance report on privatization concludes, "The problems associated with the CCA-operated Northeast Ohio Correction Center in Youngstown, Ohio, have dramatized how badly a privatized prison can be operated."[51] During the first 10 months after the facility opened, 20 inmates were stabbed, two of whom died. Shortly afterward, six inmates (including four murderers) managed to abscond from the institution.[52] More recently, "a CCA prison psychiatrist in Florida was accused of asking female inmates to give him lap dances and to expose themselves. It is also alleged that he was offering to trade medication for sex."[53]

At a CCA-run facility in Idaho, guards are accused of running a "gladiator school." Video footage purportedly shows "guards standing by as one inmate beat another into a coma. It was alleged that staff members used violence and the threat of violence to gain leverage over inmates."[54] The aforementioned cases are extreme examples of inmate abuse and likely not indicative of all privately run facilities. However, in their meta-analysis of private prison studies, Lundahl and colleagues noted that publicly run facilities outperform private facilities in the areas of prison order and the inmate grievance process.

In addition to inmate safety, efforts at inmate release are also suspect. Private correctional corporations exist for one reason, to make money. Because the very existence of private correctional corporations is dependent on filling available bed space, their primary goal can only be to incarcerate inmates for as long as possible. Schlosser goes so far as to analogize privatized corrections to the lodging industry: "An inmate at a private prison is like a guest at a hotel—a guest whose bill is being paid and whose check-out date is set by someone else. A hotel has a strong economic incentive to book every available room and encourage every guest to stay as long as possible. A private prison has exactly the same incentive."[55]

Even so, we must reconcile this logic with the fact that privatized correctional facilities often run at lower than maximum rates of capacity. In something of a paradox, private prisons, on average, operate at less than their maximum capacity.[56] In their 2004 comparison of public and private corrections, Blakely and Bumphus observe that "the private sector operated at 82% capacity while public sector prisons operated on average at 113% capacity. Thus, private prisons were operating at 18% below their capacity levels while public prisons were operating at 13% above their designed capacity levels."[57] As Chang and Thompkins suggest, operating a for-profit correctional facility at less than full capacity may seem counterintuitive, but as Scheinder attests, private corporations have the resources to build greater capacity more quickly than governments.[58] Both Donahue and Hallett and Lee concur with the clarification that governments have the additional fetters of public bidding for contracts and the obligation to weather opposition to privatized corrections.[59] Chang and Thompkins proffer another functional aspect of subcapacity operation, in that the availability of open bed space may permit its use for "more lucrative emergency contracts."[60]

Whatever the capacity status of a given institution may be, there is an inherent dilemma in reconciling the conflicting operational mandates of capacity and rehabilitation. Genders outlines the issue thusly:

> [The] underlying force of rehabilitation, as traditionally conceived, is reductionist. The profit motive would disappear in a shrinking market. By providing rehabilitative regimes, prisons would be in the business of putting themselves out of business. This would be at odds with the core values of commercialism. Hence, privately operated institutions . . . which have the declared aim of rehabilitation, are left in the theoretical position where they have conflicting goals depending on whether success is defined in terms of penal policy values or commercial market interests.[61]

Indeed, CCA's annual report in 2010 speaks to the perilous dilemma: "The demand for our facilities and services could be adversely affected by the relaxation of enforcement efforts, leniency in conviction or parole standards and sentencing practices or through the decriminalization of certain activities that are currently proscribed by our criminal laws."[62] Given the inherently political nature of corrections, "it would be naïve to believe that private prison corporations are not involved in lobbying, and it would be equally naïve to expect that they are only interested in capturing a larger market share from the public-sector prisons."[63]

Because private correctional corporations exist to make money, it is reasonable to examine the potential for cost cutting, especially in the area of staff (both hiring and training), programing, and security. The 2004 riot at Crowley Correctional Facility in Colorado (a CCA facility) has emerged as the most notable example of the deleterious effects of cost cutting in the correctional environment. In their examination of the riot, the Colorado Department of Corrections (DOC) acknowledges that prison riots, whether they occur in public or private facilities, are extremely complex, and warning signs can often be missed. Those difficulties notwithstanding, the Colorado DOC noted that the facility was not prepared to handle inmate disturbances. In particular, the facility was understaffed and key personnel were untrained, both of which impacted the ability to quell the inmate disturbance once it was underway. The Colorado DOC also noted the following issues:

- New employees had been on the job for less than two days when the riot began.
- The facility did not have an emergency plan in place.
- The facility did not have enough emergency response team members.
- The facility did not have compliance in armory management.
- Emergency drills were rarely conducted.

To be fair, public correctional facilities are not without their own problems related to corruption and abuse, but the problems seem somewhat magnified in the private system because the party involved is not a governmental institution, but rather a money-making corporation. Even if private prisons were free of abuses and there were substantial safeguards to prevent abuse of inmates, it is impossible to escape the fundamental ethical problem with privatized corrections. It is not "proper to delegate the administration of punishment—which involves state representatives deliberately causing suffering (i.e., punishment) of lawbreakers—to its private citizens."[64]

Race and Privatization

While the issue of privatization is an important topic within the general correctional literature, the intersection of race and privatization is especially consequent. Hallett notes that 66 percent of inmates housed in private facilities are racial minorities, with blacks making up the largest group (nearly 44 percent).[65] To be sure, issues of racial disparity exist within the publically run system as well, but it is argued herein that disparity in the private system is more problematic given the nature of incarceration for profit.

The present imbalanced nexus of race and punishment (both in public and privately managed correctional institutions) is brought most clearly into focus when the relationship is located in the wider scheme of economic and social power relations. Across all racial groups, the U.S. inmate population is drawn most heavily from the poorest members of society.[66] In a now dated—but revelatory—statistic, Rosenblatt (1996) as well as Chang and Thompkins (2002) note that a vast majority of the American correctional population was unemployed at the time of arrest.[67] In 1990, of all those incarcerated, 58.2 percent were unemployed at the time of their arrest.[68] Of those who were employed, their income levels were disproportionately near or below the poverty level.

If one takes as the starting point an observation that the underclass (and by extension, overrepresented ethnic and racial minority populations) constitute the bulk of the U.S. correctional population, we are then obliged to interrogate the nature and mechanics of the social function undergirding this phenomena. Moreover, we must ask what forces come to bear that offer privatization of corrections as a solution to the problems of society.

With little fear of overstatement, it is now widely held by many on both ends of the political spectrum that the present correctional apparatus of the United States has become an insatiable leviathan. For better or worse, the untenable beast of U.S. corrections nonetheless receives perennial support from the all levels of government. Much as sharks are symbiotically groomed by cleaner wrasses, U.S. corrections has become a self-reinforcing matrix, or "iron triangle," of "subgovernmental" relationships. As Lilly and Knepper state:

> The key participants in the national corrections-commercial complex are (a) private corporations devoted to profiting from imprisonment, (b) government agencies anxious to maintain their continued existence, and (c) professional organizations that sew together an otherwise fragmented group into a powerful alliance. These national-level players are in turn linked to corrections subgovernments within states to form a massive policy-making alliance.[69]

Even while remaining cognizant that the percentage of the U.S. correctional population managed by private entities is relatively low, the influence exerted by the industry is quite high.

As Lilly and Knepper suggest, the flow of capital and personnel between realms ensures that mutually beneficial relationships endure. Ripley and Franklin help confirm this tendency toward self-perpetuation with their observation that the disintegration of interlocked subgovernmental entities is rare.[70] As several sources conclude, over time, both governmental policy-makers and corollary private interests (i.e., those of corporations, lobbyists, or nongovernmental organizations [NGOs]) adopt the assumption that they are not only acting in their own interests, but also in those of the general public.

From these three dimensions (overrepresentation of certain groups, the mounting costs of maintaining a large correctional population, and sub-governmental influence), a sprawling debate has developed around what might be called the political economy of punishment. Necessarily, this debate is multifaceted, multilayered, and far too great to be adequately explored within the confines of this format. Even so, there are a number of accessible perspectives that evocatively enrich consideration of the topic. While often ending at irreconcilable conclusions, the most defined positions typically revolve around considerations of race, class, economics, and political power.

Among the most enduring memes of modern correctional culture is the idea of the "prison industrial complex." The term itself is a turn on the farewell address of President Dwight D. Eisenhower on January 17, 1961. Mired in the furor of the Cold War with the Soviet Union, Eisenhower admonished the American people about excesses associated with further propagation of the dispute, saying, "we must guard against the acquisition of unwarranted influence, whether sought or unsought, by the *military-industrial complex*. ... The potential for the disastrous rise of misplaced power exists and will persist."[71]

Thirty years later, the academic community analogized the burgeoning American correctional industry as a prison industrial complex.[72] Driven by politically prompted fear of crime, an impoverished rural America desperate for economic stability, and the avarice of private corporations, privatized corrections emerged as a self-reinforcing growth industry. As Schlosser states, the rise of the prison-industrial complex may be characterized as:

> A set of bureaucratic, political, and economic interests that encourage increased spending on imprisonment, regardless of the actual need. The prison-industrial complex is not a conspiracy, guiding the nation's

criminal-justice policy behind closed doors. It is a confluence of special interests that has given prison construction in the United States a seemingly unstoppable momentum.[73]

This momentum was initiated by a confluence of political aspirations and social uprisings beginning with Senator Barry Goldwater's effective rattling of the middle class in the early 1960s. Fear of crime helped close the ranks of a new conservatism. Richard Nixon would pick up these themes in the early 1970s. While these national-level figures shaped the broader debate, it was New York governor Nelson Rockefeller who arguably had the most influence. Chastened by a hostile reception at the 1964 Republican Convention, Rockefeller, a liberal Republican with national aspirations, sought to reassert his law and order credentials. He did so by first crushing the 1971 Attica prison riot and subsequently with a series of laws aimed at drug-related offenses. As America simultaneously declared a "war on crime" and a "war on drugs," the place of the prison industry was solidified.

Of course, all industrial revolutions require a steady flow of raw materials to fuel the enterprise. Prompted by political rhetoric and bristled by the memories of late 1960s unrest in urban centers, fear of crime was easily distilled into fear of the sprawling untamed ghetto. For the recalcitrant classes, those who would not or could not quietly assimilate, a new use was found. The American *Lumpenproletariat*—the homeless, drug addicts, the mentally ill, alcoholics, beggars, petty criminals, along with the sociopathic and truly violent—ensure few vacancies in the nation's legal catch basin.[74]

To this point, several researchers conclude that increases in poverty, unemployment, income inequality, conservative political beliefs, and inter-race conflict help spur the incarceration rate, independent of the crime rate.[75] These findings accord with the assumptions of critical theory regarding interclass dynamics. More specifically, dominant classes (be they economic, racial, or socio-political) use incarceration as a means to preserve their power and social control over the recalcitrant and "dangerous classes," that is, persons who are unemployed, poor, mentally ill, dissident, as well as racial, ethnic and socially marginal.[76] As Parenti (1999) suggests, class struggle manifests as crime control and imprisonment.

Perhaps the most evocative pronouncements regarding the modern carceral state are made by Wacquant (2007). His central contention is that modern corrections exist as an apparatus to fulfill multiple social functions: regulation of the lower sections of the labor market, as an analog to ghettos for preservation of ethno-racial order and segregation, and as a mechanism to reassert "panoptic" surveillance of the poor (both inside the institution and outside).

Magnifying these points, Wacquant attempts to disabuse readers of what he terms the "demonic myth of the prison industrial complex." Without explicitly stating it as such, Wacquant nonetheless reconciles the "myth" of the prison industrial complex to the status of a naive instrumental Marxist allegory. As he further states, "Anchored in a conspiratorial vision of history, this thesis suffers from . . . major lacunae that undercut its analytical import and ruin its practical pertinence."[77]

Wacquant bases his pronouncement on four main premises. First, he argues that the increasing scale of American corrections cannot be solely tied to the "industrialization" of corrections. Specifically, he asserts that neither racism nor capitalism "provide the necessary and sufficient conditions for America's unprecedented and unrivaled carceral experiment." Rather, the expansion is better constructed within the frame of the transition from "welfare" to "workfare."[78]

In the second instance, Wacquant challenges the causal order motivating phenomena such as the rise of privatized corrections. As he states, "Profiteering from corrections is not a primary cause but an incidental and secondary consequence of the hypertrophic development of the penal apparatus."[79] He further characterizes the expansion of corrections as primarily "a political logic and project, namely, the construction of a post-Keynesian, 'liberal-paternalistic' state suited to institute desocialized wage labor and propagate the renewed ethic of work and 'individual responsibility' that buttress it."[80] In this contention, one sees discernible Foucauldian influences with regard to the deeper function of the carceral state. The expanse of the subgovernmental surveillance-correctional apparatus resurges as *magnus ab integro sæclorum nascitur ordo* ("the great is born anew").

Perhaps the most stinging of Wacquant's critiques emanates from an inescapable point of correctional administration, that is, "this activist vision is premised on a flawed parallelism between the state functions of national defense and penal administration, which overlooks this crucial difference: military policy is highly centralized and coordinated at the federal level, whereas crime control is widely decentralized and dispersed."[81]

Again, as Wacquant observes, "Even if some far-sighted ruling group had somehow concocted a nightmarish plan designed to turn the carceral system into a lucrative industry using the bodies of the dark-skinned poor as 'raw materials,' there is no single lever that it could have seized and used to ensure their delivery."[82]

Attenuating a bit, if one were to paradigmatically "switch horses" from an instrumental to a more conservative structuralist perspective, an argument might be made that overtly coordinated function of the overall correctional apparatus is not necessary to derive similar system outputs. As Schlosser argues, "The prison-industrial complex is not only a set of interest groups and institutions. It is also a state of mind." Therefore, it is sufficient that parallel institutions having the same operational mandates and emerging from similar psycho-emotive origins serve the same masters. While reasonable, this construction obviously lacks the conspiratorial romance of the more instrumental thesis.

To this point, an argument has been proffered that the modern carceral state disproportionately impacts the lower echelons of the economic order, which also includes many racial and ethnic minorities. As cited previously, members of racial and ethnic minority groups comprise two-thirds of the private correctional population.[83] Therefore, it is incumbent to interrogate the nature of the relationship between economic status, race, and privatized corrections.

The bulk of scholarship studying this relationship tends to treat overrepresentation of racial and ethnic minorities in privatized corrections as a mechanism of capitalist economies' reconciliation of surplus labor. Perhaps the two most notable examples of this are Rusche and Kirchheimer and Melossi and Pavarini.[84] Their arguments are premised on the idea that punishment is a function of the labor market. They contend that prisons operate as retention for surpluses in the labor market. Collaterally, they argue that changes in punishment reflect changing requirements in the labor market.

Smith and Hattery build upon Wright's theory that modern prisons are a morally acceptable alternative to genocide (of the slavery era) in that they perform a similar cordoning off of functions with regard to race and class.[85] Moreover, they argue that this cordoning off reinforces a competitive advantage for white males in the labor market.

Wacquant concurs with this perspective in his observation that the modern carceral state functionally perpetuates the goals of slavery and segregation—the economic advantage of the socially powerful is maintained, while at the same time a pool of readily exploitable labor is created.[86]

Where privatized prisons share all of the aforementioned putative functions with publicly run prisons, they also affect the labor market more directly with regard to staffing. Where one might expect opposition to privatization from parties interested in inmates' rights, some of the most strident rebuke has come from organized labor.

As Chang and Thompkins observe, "Historically, organized labor emphasizes the adverse impact of prison labor on free workers' job security, wages, and working conditions, as well as the deprivation of prisoners' work rights, benefits, and working conditions."[87] The labor thesis rests on the fact that inmate workers provide labor at rates vastly lower than what is possible in the free world. For those that remain employed (by Federal Prison Industries/UNICOR), their pay ranges from $0.23 to $1.15 per hour.[88] While certainly true, this line of argument suffers on a number of frontiers.

Kling and Krueger (1999) conclude that the overall impact of prison labor—even if every inmate were made to work—would increase the U.S. gross domestic product only 0.2 to 0.4 percent. Moreover, between 2008 and 2010, over 7,000 federal inmates were dropped from work roles as the Bureau of Prisons began shuttering manufacturing operations nationwide. The most recent data suggests that the number of inmate workers in the federal system is approximately 14,200.[89]

Scott Paul of the Alliance for American Manufacturing, a coalition of business and unions, argues, "It's bad enough that our companies have to compete with exploited and forced labor in China. They shouldn't have to compete against prison labor here at home. The goal should be for other nations to aspire to the quality of life that Americans enjoy, not to discard our efforts through a downward competitive spiral."[90] The weakness in this reasoning (with specific regard to jobs outsourced to foreign countries) rests in the fact that many of the jobs done by U.S. prison workers are labor intensive, low skill and therefore unattractive to the bulk of the American workforce. As such, inmate labor is more directly in competition with labor from workers in less developed nations than in the United States.[91] As Wacquant (2007) instructs, "no [domestic] economic sector relies even marginally on convict laborers."[92] In view of these facts, the argument that inmate labor poses a meaningful threat to American livelihoods is tenuous at best.

There is, however, one place in the debate over privatized corrections where labor interests are correct to express concern. That place concerns not only inmate laborers, but also correctional staff. Several scholars have expressed concerns that privatized corrections will be so driven by profit motive that the fair or ethical treatment of both inmates and staff is in peril. Many argue that profit maximization will be achieved through cuts in staffing, training, and ancillary services.[93] Because labor costs account for approximately 70 percent of all prison expenses, some researchers maintain that correctional staffing numbers are the inevitable first line of budgetary defense.[94]

Blakely and Bumphus analyze a set of conjoined concerns with regard to the systemic implications of privatization. With regard to staff salary, they observe that "the private sector paid new officers approximately $5,327 less than did the public sector while offering less advancement in salary, with the difference in maximum salaries being $14,901."[95] With regard to correctional officer training, they note similar discrepancies: "the public sector required 58 additional hours of pre-service training above that provided by the private sector." In their analysis of employee turnover, they found that private sector correctional officers were almost three times as likely to leave their job than an officer in the public sector (43 percent versus 15 percent). Moreover, they calculate that inmate-on-inmate violence occurs at a rate in the private sector that is twice that of the public sector. As they rather succinctly state, "the private sector is a more dangerous place to be incarcerated."[96]

While the differences between private and public correctional facilities—both in terms of work and living environment—are measurable, the two spheres share a common feeder in that correctional officers as well as inmates tend to come from lower ranks of the socioeconomic strata. The chief difference between them is that 91 percent of U.S. correctional officers are white,[97] whereas black and Hispanic inmates together make up 62 percent of the U.S. prison population.[98]

Given that less than 9 percent of all correctional officers are nonwhite and/or Hispanic, it bears considering whether the experience of these minority officers in privately run institutions is significantly different than that of their white co-workers. The scholarly literature with regard to corrections as a whole provides mixed results on the impact of race on job satisfaction.

The literature reflects variation with regard to region of the country. For instance, researchers examining correctional facilities in the western part of the country found no significant relationships between job satisfaction and race of correctional staff.[99] Nor have researchers studying Midwestern facilities.[100] In their national surveys of wardens, neither Cullen and colleagues (1993) nor Flanagan and colleagues (1996) found a relationship between race and job satisfaction.

Examinations of southern and northern institutions yield more mixed results. Blau and colleagues (1986) reported lower white correctional officer satisfaction in New York, but the difference disappeared once location was used as a control. Cullen and colleagues (1985) as well as Van Voorhis and colleagues (1991) report higher job satisfaction among white correctional officers working in the southern part of the country. Conversely, in their study of Kentucky prisons, Grossi and Berg (1991) found no statistically significant association between race and job satisfaction.

Studies of federal prisons yield a similar array of findings. In some instances, black officers reported lower levels of job satisfaction compared to whites, but other studies have found no significant association between race and job satisfaction. Nor do Wright and Saylor (1991) find any statistically significant relationship between race and job satisfaction, even when controlling for the percentage of minority staff and inmate racial composition.

At least one study focuses solely on job satisfaction in privately managed facilities. These researchers, likewise, conclude there is no statistically significant relationship between a correctional officer's race and job satisfaction:

> [Characteristics such as gender and race] are not important in shaping job satisfaction or organizational commitment of private prison employees . . . results of this study tend to support the viewpoint that the work environment is more important in influencing . . . job satisfaction . . . than are personal characteristics, at least for private prison employees.[101]

It is difficult to sufficiently circumscribe the relationship between privatized corrections and race in America. On the one hand, there is often a qualitative difference between private and public correctional facilities. On the other, there is little empirical literature to substantiate that privatized corrections is *eo ipso* disproportionately more harsh on ethnic and racial minorities. By way of inference, one might assume that because privatized corrections tend to have more negative consequences for inmates generally, minorities would suffer in greater stead. That, however, to this point an unsubstantiated inference. The canons of history dictate that the plight of minorities is likely no better in the private sector.

Looking to the other side of the bars, one does see evidence that minority correctional officers seem to assess their own situations as positively as do their white counterparts. Whether that translates back across to inmate experiences is, again, unknown. What is more certain is that private prisons exist as both savior and pariah. They are at once a fount of local revenue and a source of ire for organized labor. Most certainly, they are big business with deep connections to the seats of political power. Whether they will endure in their present configuration is a matter yet to be determined.

Notes

1. Reisig and Pratt, 2000.
2. Pratt and Maahs, 1999.
3. Gran and Henry, 2007.
4. Shichor and Sechrest, 1995.
5. Pratt and Maahs, 1999.
6. Vardalis and Becker, 2000.
7. Lippke, 1997.
8. Ogle, 1999.
9. Lanza-Kaduce, Parker, and Thomas, 1999.
10. DiIulio, 1988, p. 13.
11. Cable, 1885, pp. 128–129.
12. Mulch, 2009.
13. Ogle, 1999.
14. White, 2001.
15. Lanza-Kaduce, Parker, and Thomas, 1999.
16. Mulch, 2009.
17. Corrections Corporation of America, n.d.
18. Business Wire, 2010.
19. GEO Group, n.d.
20. Schneider, 1999, p. 199.
21. Shichor and Sechrest, 1995.
22. Schneider, 1999.
23. Bureau of Labor Statistics, 2012.
24. Bureau of Justice Statistics, 2001.
25. Hallett, 2006, p. 12.
26. Bureau of Justice Assistance, 2001.
27. Bureau of Justice Assistance, 2001, p. 15.
28. Bureau of Justice Assistance, 2001.
29. Mason, 2012.
30. Mason, 2012.
31. Bureau of Justice Assistance, 2001.
32. Lundahl, Kunz, Brownell, Harris, and Van Vleet, 2009.
33. Bureau of Justice Assistance, 2001.
34. Savas, 1987.
35. MacDonald, 1990.
36. MacDonald, 1992.
37. Logan, 1996.

38. Thomas, 1997.
39. Lippke, 1997, pp. 26–27.
40. Gran and Henry, 2007.
41. Krugman, 2012.
42. Bureau of Justice Assistance, 2001, p. 58.
43. Gran and Henry, 1999.
44. Feeley, 2004, p. 322.
45. Feeley, 2004, p. 322.
46. Feeley, 2004, p. 324.
47. Gran and Henry, 2007.
48. Gran and Henry, 2007.
49. Gran and Henry, 2007, p. 176.
50. Green, 2001.
51. Bureau of Justice Assistance, 2001, p. 58.
52. Masci, 1999.
53. Mason, 2012.
54. Bureau of Justice Assistance, 2001.
55. Lundahl, Kunz, Brownell, Harris, and Van Vleet, 2009, p. 392.
56. Hallett, 2002.
57. Blakely and Bumphus, 2004, p. 29.
58. Chang and Thompkins, 2002; Schneider, 1999.
59. Donahue, 1989; Hallett and Lee, 2001.
60. Chang and Thompkins, 2002, p. 50.
61. Genders, 2002, p. 288.
62. Corrections Corporation of American, 2010, p. 19.
63. Schneider, 1999, p. 211.
64. Shichor and Sechrest, 1995, p. 452.
65. Hallett, 2006.
66. Rosenblatt, 2006.
67. Rosenblatt, 1996; Chang and Thompkins, 2002.
68. Chang and Thompkins, 2002.
69. Lilly and Knepper, 1993, p. 154.
70. Ripley and Franklin, 1984.
71. Eisenhower, 2012, p. 1038.
72. Adams, 1984.
73. Schlosser, 1998.
74. Schlosser, 1998.
75. Jacobs and Helms, 1996.
76. Sheldon, 2001.
77. Wacquant, 2007, p. 84.
78. Wacquant, 2007, p. 30.
79. Wacquant, 2007, p. 84.

80. Wacquant, 2007, p. 84.
81. Wacquant, 2007, p. 85.
82. Wacquant, 2007, p. 85.
83. Hallett, 2002.
84. Rusche and Kirchheimer, 1968; Melossi and Pavarini, 1981.
85. Smith and Hattery, 2008; Wright, 1997.
86. Wacquant, 2001.
87. Chang and Thompkins, 2002, p. 61.
88. UNICOR, n.d.
89. UNICOR, n.d.
90. Elk and Sloan, n.d.
91. Chang and Thompkins, 2002.
92. Wacquant, 2007, p. 85.
93. Misrahi, 1996.
94. Weiss, 2001.
95. Blakely and Bumphus, 2004, p. 29.
96. Blakely and Bumphus, 2004, p. 30.
97. Jurik and Musheno, 1986.
98. Jurik and Winn, 1987.
99. Jacobs and Kraft, 1978.
100. Walters, 1993.
101. Hogan, Lambert, Jenkins, and Hall, 2009, p. 160.

References

Adams, Gordon. "The Department of Defense and the Military-Industrial Establishment: The Politics of the Iron Triangle." In *Critical Studies in Organization and Bureaucracy*, edited by Frank Fischer and Carment Siranni, pp. 371–385, Philadelphia: Temple University Press, 1984.

American Correctional Association. "Offender Population." Accessed December 10, 2013, via http://www.aca.org/government/population.asp#incarcerated.

Austin, James, and Coventry, Garry. *National Council on Crime and Delinquency.* As cited in Mulch, Matthew. "Crime and Punishment in Private Prisons." *National Lawyers Guild Review* 66, no. 2 (2009): 70–94.

Barlow, David E., and W. Wesley Johnson. "The Political Economy of Criminal Justice Policy: A Time-Series Analysis of Economic Conditions, Crime, and Federal Criminal Justice Legislation, 1948–1987." *Justice Quarterly* 13 (1996): 223–241.

Blakely, Curtis and Bumphus, Vic. "Private and Public Sector Prisons: A Comparison of Select Characteristics." *Federal Probation* 68, no. 1 (2004): 27–31.

Blau, Judith, Stephen Light, and Mitchell Chamlin. "Individual and Contextual Effects on Stress and Job Satisfaction: A Study of Prison Staff." *Work and Occupations* 13 (1986): 131–156.

Brister, Richard. "Changing of the Guard: A Case for Privatization of Texas Prisons." *Prison Journal* 76 (1996): 310–330.

Bureau of Justice Assistance. *Emerging Issues on Privatized Prisons*. Washington, DC: U.S. Department of Justice, 2001.

Bureau of Justice Statistics. *Prisoners in 2010*. Washington, DC: U.S. Department of Justice, 2011.

Bureau of Justice Statistics. *Prisoners in 2000*. Washington, DC: U.S. Department of Justice, 2001.

Bureau of Labor Statistics. "Household Data Annual Averages: Table 11. Employed Persons by Detailed Occupation, Sex, Race, and Hispanic or Latino ethnicity." Washington, DC: Bureau of Labor Statistics, 2012.

Business Wire. "The GEO Group and Cornell Companies Announce $685 Million Merger," 2010. Accessed on December 4, 2013, via http://www.business wire.com/news/home/20100419006086/en/GEO-Group-Cornell-Companies -Announce-685-Million.

Cable, George. *The Silent South: Together with the Freedman's Case in Equity and the Convict Lease System*. New York: C. Scribner's Sons, 1885.

Camp, Scott, and Steiger, Thomas. "Gender and Racial Differences in Perceptions of Career Opportunities and the Work Environment in a Traditionally White, Male Occupation." In *Shaping Tomorrow's System: Contemporary Issues in Criminal Justice*, edited by Nikki Jackson, pp. 258–290. New York: McGraw-Hill, 1995.

Chang, Tracy, and Thompkins, Douglas. "Corporations Go to Prisons: The Expansion of Corporate Power in the Correctional Industry."*Labor Studies Journal* 27, no. 1 (2002): 45–69.

Chasin, Barbara. *Inequality & Violence in the United States: Casualties of Capitalism*. Amherst, NY: Humanity Books, 2004.

Cheung, Amy. *Prison Privatization and the Use of Incarceration*. Washington, DC: Sentencing Project, 2004.

Corrections Corporation of America. "2010 Annual Report on Form 10-K." Accessed on November 16, 2013, from http://ir.correctionscorp.com/phoenix .zhtml?c=117983&p=irol-reportsannual.

Corrections Corporation of America. "CCA at a Glance," n.d. Accessed November 15, 2013, via http://cca.com/Media/Default/documents/CCA-Resource -Center/CCA_At-a-Glance.pdf.

Criminal Justice Institute. *The Corrections Yearbook*. Middletown, CT: Criminal Justice Institute, 2000.

Cullen, Francis, Edward Latessa, Renee Kopache, Lucien Lombardo, and Velmer Burton. "Prison Wardens' Job Satisfaction." *Prison Journal* 73 (1993): 141–161.

Cullen, Francis, Bruce Link, Nancy Wolfe, and Frank, James. "The Social Dimensions of Correctional Officer Stress." *Justice Quarterly* 2 (1985): 505–533.

DiIulio, John. "What's Wrong with Private Prisons." *Public Interest* 92 (1988): 66–83.

Donahue, John. *The Privatization Decision*. New York: Basic Books, 1989.

Elk, Mike, and Bob Sloan. "The Hidden History of ALEC and Prison Labor." *Nation*, n.d. Accessed October 27, 2013, via http://www.thenation.com/article/162478/hidden-history-alec-and-prison-labor#.

Feeley, Malcolm M. "Entrepreneurs of Punishment: The Legacy of Privatization." *Punishment & Society* 4, no. 3 (2004): 321–344.

Flanagan, Timothy, Wesley Johnson, and Katherine Bennett. "Job Satisfaction among Correctional Executives: A Contemporary Portrait of Wardens of State Prisons for Adults." *Prison Journal* 76 (1996), 385–397.

Genders, Elaine. "Legitimacy, Accountability and Private Prisons." *Punishment & Society* 4 (2002): 288.

GEO Group. "About Us." Accessed November 15, 2013, via http://www.geogroup.com/about_us., n.d.

Gran, Brian, and William Henry. "Holding Private Prisons Accountable: A Socio-Legal Analysis of 'Contracting Out' Prisons." *Social Justice* 34, no. 3–4 (2007): 173–194.

Green, Judith "Bailing out Private Jails." *American Prospect* 12 (2001): 23–28.

Grossi, Elizabeth, and Bruce Berg. "Stress and Job Dissatisfaction among Correctional Officers: An Unexpected Finding." *International Journal of Offender Therapy and Comparative Criminology* 35 (1991): 73–81.

Hallett, Michael. *Private Prisons in America: A Critical Race Perspective*. Urbana: University of Illinois Press, 2006.

Hallett, Michael. "Race, Crime, and For Profit Imprisonment: Social Disorganization as Market Opportunity." *Punishment & Society* 4 (2002): 369–393.

Hallett, Michael, and J. Frank Lee. "Public Money, Private Interests: The Grassroots Battle Against CCA in Tennessee." In *Privatization in Criminal Justice: Past Present and Future*, edited by David Shichor and Michael Gilbert, pp. 224–247. Cincinnati, OH: Anderson, 2001.

Hochstetler, Andrew L., and Neal Shover. "Street Crime, Labor Surplus, and Criminal Punishment, 1980–1990." *Social Problems* 44 (1997): 358–368.

Hogan, Nancy, Eric Lambert, Morris Jenkins, and Daniel Hall. "The Impact of Job Characteristics on Private Prison Staff: Why Management Should Care." *American Journal of Criminal Justice* 34 (2009): 151–165.

Jacobs, David, and Ronald E. Helms. "Toward a Political Model of Incarceration: A Time-Series Examination of Multiple Explanations for Prison Admission Rates." *American Journal of Sociology* 102 (1996): 323–357.

Jacobs, James, and Lawrence Kraft. "Integrating the Keepers: A Comparison of Black and White Prison Guards in Illinois." *Social Problems* 25 (1978): 304–318.

Jurik, Nancy, and Gregory Halemba. "Gender Working Conditions and the Job Satisfaction of Women in a Non-Traditional Occupation: Female Correctional Officers in Men's Prisons." *Sociological Quarterly* 25 (1984): 551–566.

Jurik, Nancy, and Michael Musheno. "The Internal Crisis of Corrections: Professionalization and the Work Environment." *Justice Quarterly* 3 (1986): 457–480.

Jurik, Nancy C., and Russell Winn. "Describing Correctional-Security Dropouts and Rejects An Individual or Organizational Profile?" *Criminal Justice and Behavior* 14, no. 1 (1987): 5–25.

Kling, Jeffrey, and Alan Krueger. "Cost, Benefits, and Distributional Consequences of Inmate Labor." National Symposium on the Economics of Inmate Labor Force Participation. Washington, DC: George Washington University, 1999.

Krugman, Paul. "Prisons, Privatization, Patronage." *New York Times*, June, 22, 2012.

Lanza-Kaduce, Lonn, Karen Parker, and Charles Thomas. "A Comparative Recidivism Analysis of Releasees from Private and Public Prisons." *Crime and Delinquency* 45 (1999): 28–48.

Lilly, J. Robert, and Paul Knepper. "The Corrections-Commercial Complex." *Crime & Delinquency* 39, no. 2 (1993): 150–166.

Lippke, Richard. "Thinking about Private Prisons." *Criminal Justice Ethics* 16 (1997): 26–39.

Logan, Charles. *Private Prisons: Cons and Pros.* New York: Oxford University Press, 1996.

Lundahl, Brad, Chelsea Kunz, Cyndi Brownell, Norma Harris, and Russ Van Vleet. "Prison Privatization: A Meta-Analysis of Cost and Quality of Confinement Indicators." *Research on Social Work Practice* 19 (2009): 383–94.

MacDonald, Douglas. *Prisons for Profits: The Privatization of Corrections.* New Brunswick, NJ: Rutgers University Press, 1990.

MacDonald, Douglas. "Private Penal Institutions." In *Crime and Justice: A Review of Research*, edited by Michael Tonry, pp. 132–158. Chicago: University of Chicago Press, 1992.

Masci, David. "Prison-Building Boom." *CQ Researcher* 9, no. 35 (1999): 801–824.

Mason, Cody. *Too Good to Be True: Private Prisons in America.* Washington, DC: Sentencing Project, 2012.

Mauer, Marc. *The Race to Incarcerate.* New York: New Press, 1999.

Melossi, Dario, and Massimo Pavarini. *The Prison and the Factory: The Origins of the Prison.* London: Polity, 1981.

Misrahi, James. "Factories with Fences: An Analysis of the Prison Industry Enhancement Certification Program in Historical Perspective." *American Criminal Law Review* 33 (1996): 411–429.

Mobley, Alan, and Gilbert Geis. "The Corrections Corporation of America, aka 'The Prison Realty Trust, Inc.'" In *Privatization in Criminal Justice*, edited by David Shichor and Micahel J. Gilbert, pp. 207–226. Cincinnati, OH: Anderson, 2001.

Mulch, Matthew. "Crime and Punishment in Private Prisons." *National Lawyers Guild Review* 66, no. 2 (2009): 70–94.

Ogle, Robbin. "Prison Privatization: An Environmental Catch-22." *Justice Quarterly* 16 (1999): 579–600.

Pager, Devah. "The Mark of a Criminal Record." *American Journal of Sociology* 108 (2003): 937–975.

Parenti, Christian. *Lockdown America.* New York: Verso, 1999.

Pratt, Travis, and Jeff Maahs. "Are Private Prisons More Cost-Effective Than Public Prisons? A Meta-Analysis of Evaluation Research Studies." *Crime and Delinquency* 45 (1999): 358–372.

Reisig, Michael, and Travis Pratt. "The Ethics of Correctional Privatization: A Critical Examination of the Delegation of Coercive Authority." *Prison Journal* 80 (2000): 210–222.

Ripley, Randall, and Grace Franklin. *Congress, the Bureaucracy, and Public Policy.* Homewood, IL: Dorsey, 1984.

Robbins, Ira. *Legal Dimensions of Private Incarceration.* Washington, DC: American Bar Association, 1988.

Rosenblatt, Elihu. *Criminal Injustice: Confronting the Prison Crisis.* Boston: South End Press, 1996.

Rusche, Georg, and Otto Kirchheimer. *Punishment and Social Structure.* New York: Columbia University Press, 1968 [1939].

Savas, E. S. "Privatization and Prisons." *Vanderbilt Law Review* 40, no. 4 (1987): 868–899.

Schlosser, Eric. "The Prison-Industrial Complex." *Atlantic Monthly*, December 1, 1998.

Schneider, Anne. "Public-Private Partnerships in the U.S. Prison System," In *Public-Private Policy Partnerships*, edited by Pauline Rosenau, pp. 199–216. Cambridge, MA: MIT Press, 1999.

Sheldon, Randall G. *Controlling the Dangerous Classes.* Boston: Allyn and Bacon, 2001.

Shichor, David, and Dale Sechrest. "Quick Fixes in Corrections: Reconsidering Private and Public For-Profit Facilities." *Prison Journal* 75 (1995): 457–478.

Smith, Earl, and Angela Hattery. "Incarceration: A Tool for Racial Segregation and Labor Exploitation." *Race and Gender* 15, no. 2 (2008): 79–97.

Thomas, Charles. *Comparing the Cost and Performance of Public and Private Prisons in Arizona.* Phoenix: Arizona Department of Corrections, 1997.

Uggen, Christopher, and Jeff Manza. "Democratic Contraction? Political Consequences of Felon Disenfranchisement in the United States." *American Sociological Review* 67 (2002): 777–803.

UNICOR. "FPI General Overview/ FAQs," n.d. Accessed October 27, 2013, via http://www.unicor.gov/about/faqs/faqsgeneral.cfm.

Van Voorhis, Patricia, Francis Cullen, Bruce Link, and Nancy Wolfe. "The Impact of Race and Gender on Correctional Officers' Orientation to the Integrated

Environment." *Journal of Research in Crime and Delinquency* 28 (1991): 472–500.

Vardalis, James, and Becker, Fred. "Legislative Opinions Concerning the Private Operation of State Prisons: The Case of Florida."*Criminal Justice Policy Review* 11 (2000): 136–148.

Wacquant, Loïc. *Prisons of Poverty*. Minneapolis: University of Minnesota Press, 2007.

Wacquant, Loïc. "Deadly Symbiosis: Rethinking Race and Imprisonment in Twenty-First-Century America." *Punishment & Society* 3 (2001): 95–134.

Walters, Stephen. "Gender, Job Satisfaction, and Correctional Officers: A Comparative Analysis." *Justice Professional* 7 (1993): 23–33.

Weiss, Robert P. "Political Economy of Prison Labor Reprivatization in the Postindustrial United States." *Criminology* 39 (2001): 253–291.

Welch, Michael. *Ironies of Imprisonment*. Thousand Oaks, CA: Sage, 2000.

White, Ahmed. "Rule of Law and the Limits of Sovereignty: The Private Prison in Jurisprudential Perspective." *American Criminal Law Review* 38, no. 1 (2001): 111–147.

Wright, Erik. *Class Counts: Comparative Studies in Class Analysis*. New York: Cambridge University Press, 1997.

Wright, Kevin, and William Saylor. "Male and Female Employees' Perceptions of Prison Work: Is There a Difference?" *Justice Quarterly* 8 (1991): 505–524.

Chapter 20

The Zero Point of Mass Incarceration: Mandatory Minimums and the Enfleshment of Determinate Sentencing

Nicholas Brady

Knock. Knock. A familiar sound fills Albert Watson's apartment. Not a light tap, but a decisive bang against the door. This was a clear signal to him that the authorities were coming in with or without permission. Sergeant Didone, along with two other officers, broke down the door and approached Albert, who was sprawled out on the bed. Didone knew he had drugs on him somewhere, so he ordered him to empty out all his pockets. There was an assortment of different objects, but the most important one was a cream-colored envelope. No stamp or address on it, but it contained 13 capsules of white powder. Heroin. Albert was taken away in handcuffs to await his charge and trial. This was one of many times he had been arrested and would be his third time being charged and convicted of drug possession. The other sentences had been served mostly in rehabilitative hospitals, but this sentence would hurt. This drug possession charge was for intent to traffic and came with a mandatory minimum of five years in prison. He, unlike many others, decided to take his chances with a jury. His defense was insanity with testimony from his psychiatrist. Albert had first encountered dope as a prescription to help relieve the pain of his war injuries. The doctor had felt so sorry for him that she prescribed him more after he was deployed back home. The prescription ended far sooner than his addiction did. It was this desire that drove him down a road that could not lead anywhere other than a courtroom. His defense fell on deaf ears. The jury convicted him of possession with intent to traffic, and he was sentenced to serve his time with no chance of parole. This story is wholly his own, yet is also familiar—a drug addict convicted as a dealer by the law and receives a harsh sentence with no possibility of parole. Same story, different body. Saidiya Hartman warns us of the danger of circulating stories of the black's "ravaged body": "Rather than inciting indignation, too often they immure us to pain by virtue of their familiarity."[1] But perhaps the familiarity is immuring us to something else. How familiar is this story?

Albert's story does not end with him serving his sentence in prison. Instead, the U.S. Supreme Court ruled that it was "cruel and unusual" for a drug addict to receive a mandatory minimum sentence and vacated the sentence in 1970. This is not an example of the judiciary being slow, for the court cites the Narcotics Addict Rehabilitation Act of 1966 in its decision to vacate the sentence. Also at this time, the same man that would become synonymous with mandatory minimums and the war on drugs, Republican governor Nelson Rockefeller, would veto one of the first bills introducing mandatory minimums to the state of New York in 1969.[2] Rockefeller and Attorney General Robert Kennedy had, as late as 1962, been working together on a comprehensive approach to fighting narcotics that would treat addiction as a medical issue outside the criminal punishment system.[3] Their consensus was reinforced by an overwhelming majority (75 percent) of federal judges, wardens, probation officers, and attorneys who felt mandatory minimum sentencing was too harsh and too inflexible to help the fight against narcotics.[4]

This bipartisan consensus would continue into the 1970s when Congress repealed the Boggs Act of 1952, declaring its experiment with mandatory minimum sentencing and cannabis a failure. Despite this setback, four years from the date of the aforementioned veto, the Rockefeller administration introduced bills assigning a 15-year mandatory minimum sentence to the possession of four ounces of a hard drug.[5] This change of opinion percolated in more places than New York. Both at the state and federal level, the rehabilitative model that had dominated political wisdom regarding corrections was losing out to demands for determinate sentencing. This drama of debate and contestation between the two schools of ideas regarding punishment (rehabilitative and retribution) played itself out most poignantly on the national stage, where the swings of opinions and the coalitions formed were simultaneously more extreme, yet also more obscure. In between the turbulent 1960s and Reagan 1980s, the 1970s were an interstitial time where oppositional forces collided to form a quiet storm of consensus for mass incarceration.[6]

Intellectual giants such as Angela Davis and Ruth Wilson Gilmore have eloquently and powerfully articulated the fact that prisons are an industry.[7] The "prison industrial complex" has become the catchall term for the phenomenon of mass incarceration. This term pushes the profit motive to the forefront of our analysis for understanding the constant growth of the prison population. While neither Davis nor Gilmore deemphasize the role of racism in mass incarceration, there remains a slippage in the term. The term "prison industrial complex" points us to the workings of the political economy of prisons, yet this focus does not easily answer why the shift to mass incarceration took place in the first place. There are factors that are mystified or obfuscated when our focus is simply on the "industrial complex." The epigraph of this paper points us to the fact that something precedes and brings into existence the prison industrial complex: the "desire to see black flesh in chains." Farley's focus is on a libidinal economy instead of a political economy. Economies are not necessarily about—but are often treated as synonymous with—the exchange of capital. Instead, an economy is the accumulation, exchange, and distribution of certain objects of analysis. Economies can be the exchange of capital, ideas, or desire. Jared Sexton defines the libidinal economy as "the economy, or distribution and arrangement, of desire and identification . . . a dispensation of energies, concerns, points of attention, anxieties, pleasures, appetites, revulsions, and phobias capable of both great mobility and tenacious fixation."[8] Before the profit motive became a major concern, politicians, academics, judges, attorneys, and others were debating about and uniting around their feelings on a particular phobic object: black crime (the redundancy of such a term notwithstanding). The energy produced by this crisis created the momentum surrounding the shift from indeterminate sentencing to determinate sentencing. This chapter will argue that the libidinal economy of antiblackness precedes and creates the conditions of possibility for the political economy of the prison industrial complex. In particular, this chapter will explore the libidinal economy of the politics surrounding mandatory minimums in the 1970s and show that antiblackness is the node through which disparate parties united.

Ramsey Clark, the attorney general for the Johnson administration, stated very poignantly in 1970 that "fear in turn seeks repressiveness as a source of safety."[9] This chapter will wade through the many layers of repression that politicians, intellectuals, reporters, and other elites of civil society have knowingly and unknowingly constructed to clarify the flows of fear and desire that give birth to our contemporary system of safety and justice. Yet this raises the question of methodology. How does one tell the story of a hidden economy of desire and identification? How does one elucidate the mystified phobias of partisan battles and explore the intimacies of domination at the heart of political bargaining? If the archive is "the system that governs the appearance of statements and generates social meaning," then these enunciations ". . . cannot appear without the thought of the 'elite.' "[10] So, how does one make the terror of blackness and pleasure of domination explicit from an archive of sources with a vested interest in legitimizing the state's monopoly on pain and punishment? In her now classic text on the relationship between slavery and subject-formation, *Scenes of Subjection*, Saidiya Hartman describes her method as an attempt "to read [the archive] against the grain in order to write a different account of the past."[11] Hartman goes on to write, "read[ing] against the grain is perhaps best understood as a combination of foraging and disfiguration—raiding for fragments upon which other narratives can be spun and misshaping and deforming the testimony through selective quotation and the amplification of issues germane to the study."[12] Such a project might be described as bad history, yet such a pejorative misses the impetus for her method. Conventional wisdom tells the writer "to be still and listen to what his subject has to tell him."[13] Yet the sources speak from the dominant paradigm, so "to be still" is the same as acquiescing to epistemic violence. The work it takes to spin new narratives and excavate hidden desires demands that the sources be read against the intentions of their author. This chapter is not an attempt to find some mythical space of refuge outside or above the fray to judge and criticize. Instead, this chapter can be read as an attempt to get into the trenches, so to speak, and go to war against the archive itself.[14] The chapter is "a struggle within and against the constraints and silences imposed by the nature of the archive" by reading the sources against each other and themselves.[15] If Hartman's methodology is a personal war expressed on the written page, the victory is not the recovery of something lost, but the uncovering of that which was formerly covered up and repressed. Thus, this chapter's methodology will not assert anything as pretentious as a new theory, but instead will be the "challenge . . . for theory to face itself," to "occasion anxiety of thought," to put "theory in jeopardy," or, to say it more succinctly, to theorize in black. To read against the grain reveals what is implicit in the documents with the ultimate aim of making the screaming vacuum of the archive heard and felt. With that said, let us jump into the abyss of the turbulent 1960s to disinter the anxiety around black politics.

I

Coming into the 20th century, the federal government generally stayed out of the politics of crime, especially sentencing. This authority was deferred to the judiciary, and the states were allowed wide discretion in building their own sentencing practices. The exception to this was the Parole Act of 1910 because it set up a national standard for indeterminate sentencing. The law established a parole board in each prison that could, within the guidelines stipulated in a convict's sentence, let a prisoner go if it was determined that the prisoner was properly rehabilitated.[16] This, in effect, made all sentences indeterminate and represented the federal government's focus on rehabilitation as the model for punishment. For those that subscribed to the rehabilitative school of punishment, prisons were not created for warehousing or doling out "just desserts." Instead, penologists, politicians, and corrections bureaucrats understood prisons as a space to heal the prisoner and refashion him back into a law-abiding citizen.[17] It is a common fallacy to see rehabilitation as oppositional to punishment. Instead, it is simply a different, perhaps softer, model of punishment on a continuum of penal ideologies. It is important to note that no matter the model, the issue at hand is always punishment. Rehabilitative and retributive models of punishment are not separated by an unbridgeable gulf, but instead can be viewed as two sides of the same coin. With a little bit of force, the coin can easily be flipped to the other side.

As late as 1962, there was very little focus on crime at the federal level, in spite of the crime rate rising significantly in the 1950s.[18] In 1962, J. Edgar Hoover believed that "law enforcement ha[d] not yet attained the measure of public support it deserve[d]."[19] In spite of this, from the beginning of the 1960s and onward, the anxiety around black empowerment and black crime were so intertwined that one hardly talked about one without mentioning the other. Senator Richard Russell's statement in 1960 is indicative of this: "I say that the extremely high incidence of crimes of violence among members of the Negro race is one of the major reasons why the great majority of the white people of the South are irrevocably opposed to efforts to bring about enforced association of the races."[20] The obvious response would be that whites were the central agents for creating a state of terror in the South, yet this was a main argument repeated by the coalition of southern Democrats and conservative Republicans. Russell was far from a rogue senator, for his fear was representative of a general sentiment regarding black liberation.

The connection between black freedom and criminality is as old as the republic itself. The law recognized slaves only insofar as they were property of the master until they resisted the master; then they were criminals.[21] The issue of black criminality has since been a constant, in both the North and South.[22] The urban North's relationship to antiblackness was obscured—both in the past and in the contemporary moment—because these cities were seen as beacons of racial harmony. For many, this obfuscation helped prove the ontological relationship between blacks and crime. "This exodus of Negroes from the South and their influx into the great metropolitan centers of other areas of the Nation has been accompanied by a wave of crime."[23] Representative John Bell would go on to criticize civil rights for its inability to solve the "negro crime" problem and ended by saying that "segregation is the only answer as most Americans—not the politicians—have realized for hundreds of years."[24] Bell's quote exhibits the frustration around civil rights for conservatives because no matter how long they filibustered and resisted, they could not stop the Civil Rights Act of 1964 from passing. In spite of the loss, there was a nerve of fear and revulsion of black protest that the conservatives were figuring out how to push. The turbulent 1960s produced an explosion of energy and nausea around the issue of black protest and urban unrest. Sit-ins, boycotts, freedom rides, and marches were met with police hostility as well as political hostility: "as to the so-called freedom riders . . . instead of being encouraged by groups, and cast into the political arena to be made a political issue, they should be made a violation of the criminal statutes."[25] Senator John Stennis cast the nonviolent strategy of the freedom riders as a strategy to ignite violence. Contemporary discussion of the 1960s bifurcates political strategies into nonviolent and violent forms of protest, yet at that time, all forms of black protest were seen as violent insofar as they violated the stability of segregation. This association of black politics with violence *enfleshed* black agency as crime in itself. This was much bigger than the opinion of a few politicians. This coupling of black politics to crime was a major accumulation of energy that flowed under the surface of the political. In theory, the general public agreed with the vague idea of equality, but in reality, felt uncomfortable about the tactics of the movement. This anxiety and latent hostility were a powder keg hidden from sight awaiting the proper event and leader to ignite its fury.

Barry Goldwater was perhaps the first major charismatic leader to recognize, and know how to manipulate, the antiblack fear of the civil rights movement. In spite of the fact that Goldwater would lose the presidential election to Johnson in a historic landslide, his strategy formed the conservative blueprint for how to strategically stoke antiblack flames to win elections.[26] Goldwater tied the civil rights victories to several of the riots of 1964: "choose the way of this present administration and you have the way of mobs in the street."[27] In this same speech, he would cast civil rights activists as boogeymen who could make riots appear and disappear at will. Adding more fuel to the fires, Goldwater's campaign released several ads making allusions to the riots. One began with words: "Graft! Swindle! Juvenile Delinquency! Crime! Riots!"[28] The structure of this ad is interesting. The first three terms are petty types of crime (murder and rape were not mentioned), and the text ended with the general concept of "crime" as a point of emphasis. Yet "riots" seems out of place, for it is not a type of crime but an event with criminal implications. Even if we are to view it as a type of crime, its placement after the word "crime" seems to simultaneously disconnect it from the established narrative of petty crimes yet merges it to a larger fear of crime itself. This has the effect of making the first three terms fall out of emphasis. Instead, what becomes emphasized and interlocked is *crime* and *riots* as the ultimate objects of mania and disorientation.

America's fixation on riots naturally led into a fear of urban (specifically black) crime, and Goldwater exploited the obvious connection. Taking a jab at the civil rights movement, Goldwater stated, "When men seek political advantage by turning their eyes away from riots and violence, we can well understand why lawlessness grows even while we pass more laws."[29] Again, civil rights activists are characterized as inciting, or ignoring, riots for political purposes (contrary to the fact that many of the leaders were denouncing riots and other violent acts). The connection between riots and lawlessness in general is made more explicit in this speech. The point is clear: the passage of civil rights legislation rewarded lawbreakers. In a different speech, Goldwater mentions that "our women" fear the streets because of riots.[30] The use of the term "our" creates an "us versus them" dichotomy, but who is either included or excluded within the "us" and "them" is incredibly obvious. The "them" are the criminals dominating the streets and terrorizing the homeland. The "us" is more ambiguous with the aim of reaching the most general audience possible, yet it resonated strongest with white voters. So the underlying demand was to protect the white socius, the federal government had to stop rewarding black protesters and instead punish black lawbreakers. In one sweeping motion, Goldwater intensifies fear of urban unrest and demands a harder police force to protect the helpless woman/homeland from the urban monsters.

What gets lost in focusing on Goldwater is that Democrats were at the forefront of connecting black protest to crime and calling for law and order as the solution. Senator John McClellan from Arkansas stated that "the Civil Rights law is calculated to provoke . . ."[31] McClellan repeats the word "provoke" throughout his discourse, but the question remained: Provoke what? His argument is that tactics that force people to change will hurt harmony and cause greater amounts of disorder and lawlessness. Senator Russell took the argument further in 1962, saying, "if our highest officials continue to applaud sit-ins, lie-ins, stand-ins, and all other violations of property rights, it can lead us into a state of anarchy."[32] The argument that nonviolent tactics are violent themselves and lead to greater states of violence was repeated at all levels of government, whether it was Supreme Court justices, state governors, or the usual suspect J. Edgar Hoover: "[The Civil Rights] attitude breeds disrespect for the law and even civil disorder and rioting."[33] The underlying consensus between the different parties and levels of government was that the difference between nonviolent and "violent" tactics collapsed into simple tautologies: blackness is violent, blackness is chaos, blackness is crime.

Less than a year after Goldwater lost and Johnson began his Great Society program, "a state of anarchy" exploded in Watts, California. The Watts riot was one of the more devastating riots in recent history, with 36 people dead and over 1,000 people injured (as well as nearly 1,000 buildings damaged). The significance of the Watts riot cannot be understated, but this chapter will analyze it (along with the long hot summer of 1967) as an essential event for bringing urban unrest into the general consciousness. The impact of Watts on the general conversation regarding crime and punishment is expressed by the headline in a *U.S. News and World* report article, "Race Friction: Now a Crime Problem?"[34] After Watts, nearly half of all major cities experienced a riot (most of these cities had multiple riots) between 1965 and 1969.[35] In response to these events and the subsequent public outcry for a federal response, Johnson ordered the creation of the Kerner Commission (the National Advisory Commission on Civil Disorders) to get to the bottom of how to stop a future explosion. The report called for an increase in policing budgets and programs to help low-income households in cities.[36] The Kerner Commission fell on deaf ears. As Democratic senator Byrd argued, "poverty neither provides license for laziness nor for lawlessness. We can take the people out of the slums, but we cannot take the slums out of the people . . . all the housing and all the welfare programs conceivable will not stop the riots."[37] The coin had flipped. While his opinion is nothing new—black people have been described as both lazy and sly criminals before—the anxiety of riots/crime had shifted the conversation toward a harder stance against urban protest/unrest. The energy had been diverted and flowed toward law and order.

The opposition toward civil rights now shifted into an affirmation of stronger law enforcement to control riots/crime. Foreshadowing his future administration's focus on law and order, Nixon famously stated that the "first civil right" was "the right to be free from domestic violence."[38] More than 100 bills criminalizing riots were introduced between 1965 and 1969, including some that barred those who were charged with a riot felony from receiving federal dollars or employment.[39] Recognizing their inability to resist the passage of civil rights bills, another strategy of resistance was to attach antiriot amendments to the bills to ensure their passage, for example, the Civil Rights Act of 1968 and the "Rap Brown" Federal Anti-Riot act (1968) bill was attached to the Fair Housing Act of 1968. Going into the last year of the Johnson administration, crime had been transformed into the number one issue in the mind of the public. While many on the left recognized the strategy of criminalizing black politics, the strategy was effective at moving the framework of the discussion away from whether segregation was bad or good to how one would deal with (black) crime.[40] These strategies allowed critics to go on the offensive and push the Johnson administration for being soft on crime.

As the election of 1968 neared, the clamor around riots and crime was swallowing the Johnson administration into the abyss of antiblackness. In the final months of his presidency, Johnson decided to jump into the issue of crime and put forth the most ambitious federal bill on law enforcement. The bill was nicknamed the Safe Streets Act, and it focused on increasing police budgets, rehabilitating within prisons, and further supporting anti-poverty efforts as a supplement. The bill came out of committee relatively untouched, but once on the floor, it was dramatically changed by a coalition of Republicans and southern Democrats. "These revisions gave extra

funds with the 'highest priority' of funds earmarked for riots and civil disorders, reassigned control of funds from the Attorney General to state governors, and expanded the power of electronic surveillance."[41] Another
revision was to exclude this bill from the new civil rights requirements,
including the requirement that departments (such as police) receiving
federal funds must be racially balanced. Strom Thurmond effectively controlled the debate on the floor by interrupting several speakers and imply-
ing that advocating for racial balance was tantamount to being weak on
crime.[42] On the floor, the liberals were ultimately defeated by the tidal wave
of public anxiety over black violence. Even vocal opponents to the bill, such
as John Dox from New York, reluctantly voted for it. He said, "I regret
exceedingly, and will only vote for it because of the widespread desire of
all our people to curb crime and prevent continuation of violence in our
land."[43] The grammar of this sentence is interesting, particularly the use
of possessives: "our people" and "violence in our land." Given the rampant
fearmongering around blackness and the antiriot law enforcement that
would help to stamp out many black political organizations across the
country, who is "our people" that liberals and conservatives are uniting to
protect from the black "violence in our land"?

The libidinal economy that connects blackness to crime is much larger
than one politician, one political party, or even one end of the political
spectrum. Ultimately, both parties and both sides of the ideological spectrum can resolve their consensual dramas to satiate their mutual desire to
be free from the terror of blackness. The energy that criminalizes black
protest is the flip side of the flow of energy that desires it. The sensuality
of the phobic object connects these seemingly opposite flows of fixation.
As Oscar Wilde put it, "the basis of optimism is sheer terror." The energy
that allowed the civil rights movement to flourish is what produces the
energy criminalizing black agency. This anxiety around black protest and
urban unrest fused to become the mystified psychosocial flow that
stimulated a fixation on crime and galvanized people to fight crime with
different, harsher sentencing styles.

II

"Criminals seem to be everywhere except in jail working off their debts to
society."[44] So begins the *Wall Street Journal*'s article on the most expansive
reform of sentencing in the 1980s: The Comprehensive Crime Control Act
of 1984 (hereafter called CCCA). Within it were two large acts (the

Sentencing Reform Act and the Armed Career Criminal Act) that signaled a definitive shift from indeterminate sentencing to determinate sentencing. The CCCA established a sentencing commission and a mandatory minimum sentence for repeat offenders with a firearm. The CCCA also introduced the drug user as a specific category for determinate sentencing and abolished federal parole. Public memory of "law and order" initiatives cites conservatives—in particular Nixon and Reagan—as the forces behind shifting public, political, and intellectual will toward these "hard-line" stances against drugs and crime. Yet the actual legislative history reveals not only that Democrats were at the forefront of this issue, but most of the parts of this crucial piece of legislation were already put in place in 1975 by a coalition of powerful Democrats and Republicans. Unlike in the 1960s, the primary coalition-builders in the Democratic party were northern liberals such as Ted Kennedy of Massachusetts (and later Joseph Biden of Delaware) working with highly conservative Democrats such as Strom Thurmond and Robert Byrd.[45] While much separated the parties—punitive ideology, arguments on the root cause, and so on—their coalition was formed around a specific anxiety: the specter of black riots and the terror of black criminality.

The story of the CCCA begins where part one of this chapter left off: the haphazard attempt by the Johnson administration to get tough on crime that was co-opted by an anti–civil rights/antiriots coalition of southern Democrats and conservative Republicans. Begun by the administration in 1968, the Judiciary Committees of the House and the Senate were debating efforts to recodify and reorganize criminal statutes. These debates concerned a bill named S.1 (its Senate docket number). The new coalition set up several new conservative statutes, including criminalizing the disclosure of top-secret information, abolishing the insanity defense, and implementing broad antiriot provisions that included naming a scuffle involving three people at a protest site a "riot."[46] S.1 remained a conservative measure vilified by those on the left, including Ted Kennedy, who called it an "unwise and unnecessary encroachment upon civil liberties and lawful political dissent."[47] Other than his clear disagreement with S.1, what is important is the differentiation of "encroachment[s] upon civil liberties" and "encroachment[s] upon . . . lawful political dissent." The latter part is an allusion to the antiriot portion of the bill, and Kennedy's separation of that particular aspect from the other encroachment on civil liberties is peculiar. In spite of his stated dissent, Kennedy would later say to Senator McClellan (chair of the Judiciary Committee) that he could get liberal votes for S.1 as long as some of the "repressive" measures were removed.[48] McClellan reluctantly agreed to water down the bill because he was planning to retire soon and wanted sentencing reform to be his legacy as chairman of the Judiciary.

What seemed like an unbridgeable gulf between two sides was being fleshed out, and points of consensus were being reached by 1976. One key point of consensus between the liberal senator and his conservative counterparts was a fear of the "career criminal." According to Kennedy, this wily, trickster criminal "successfully play[s] the odds" because "his chances of actually being caught, tried, convicted, and jailed are too slim to be taken seriously."[49] Kennedy criticized both sides for being ideological, but he came down especially hard on liberals: "it is futile to counter the law-and-order fallacy with the opposite fallacy that crime cannot be controlled unless we demolish city slums and eliminate poverty and discrimination . . . we can no longer afford the luxury of confusing social progress with progress in the war on crime."[50] While he calls the "law-and-order" approach a fallacy, he not only uses their language ("the war on crime"), but also replicates their solution: "we can require courts to impose a mandatory minimum sentence . . . in such *street crimes* as in murder, rape, aggravated assault and burglary . . . [emphasis mine]."[51] Apparently, murder, rape, aggravated assault, and burglary do not happen in suburban neighborhoods and small towns. The focus on urban streets is a consistent motif in war on crime/drug speeches, and its libidinal economy can be traced to the fear of urban unrest we analyzed in part one of this chapter. Kennedy's *modus operandi* with the war on crime was sentencing reform, primarily mandatory minimum sentencing for repeat offenders and a sentencing commission to create a uniform point system for judges to follow. His coalition with Senator McClellan watered down the repressive aspects of S.1 and combined it with the formation of a sentencing commission to create a new bill: S.1437. Kennedy was still worried about the bill, so he had Professor Dershowitz from Harvard Law School look it over. Dershowitz claimed it was "a net gain for civil liberties," so Kennedy introduced it to the floor.[52] However, the "net gain for civil liberties" did not include taking out the encroachment(s) upon lawful political dissent or the anti-riot provisions. In the cost-benefit analysis that went through two different leftist authorities, the specifically anti-black statuette was thought to be worth it in order to establish sentencing reform that would lead to the disproportionate incarceration of black bodies. In the tug-of-war between the left and the right, the easy bargaining chip was the fungible black body. Whether ripped apart or re-formed, the black body was a mere object—like clay—in the hands of the political order.

Ultimately, "black lives are still imperiled and de-valued by a racial calculus and a political arithmetic that were entrenched centuries ago."[53]

The antiriot measures were a strong node of consensus to get the coalition of anti–civil rights senators on board. Strom Thurmon and Robert Byrd became key allies to make sure S.1437 could pass without major debate or mark-up.[54] S.1437 passed the Senate in 1978, five months before Senator McClellan died.[55] There was no such coalition in the House, and the leadership purposefully held up the process until the measure was rejected. The House Democrats were sticking to the rehabilitative ideology "because judicial discretion is the cornerstone of the criminal justice system, assigning the task of developing guidelines to the Judicial Conference is only logical."[56] By the next Congress, Kennedy replaced McClellan as the chair of the Judiciary Committee, and Thurmond became the ranking Republican. Their partnership over S.1347 would continue into a new version of the bill that was passed in the Senate in 1980 with an additional statute that severely limited federal parole.[57] The House continued to filibuster the Senate's version of the bill while affirming its own version of sentencing reform that focused on a sentencing commission led by the Judiciary. This consistent resistance from the House was only delaying the inevitable, for public anxiety over crime and drugs was being properly stoked into large electoral victories for the Republican Party and, in the end, the Senate's version would not only win over the House, but would win without conceding anything to the other side.

With the election of Ronald Reagan and the electoral sweep by the Republican Party, the Judiciary Committee switched leadership, and Strom Thurmond became the chair. Joseph Biden emerged as the ranking Democrat on the committee, but Kennedy remained an important entity within the coalition. Under Thurmond, the antiblack energy flowed from a fear of riots and unrest to a specifically anticrime bill that included statutes to allow the seizure of assets in drug-related cases, limit the means for reviewing state court convictions by federal habeas corpus, increase penalties for narcotics violations, and provide a mandatory minimum sentence for crimes involving a firearm or repeat offenders.[58] Many of the statutes from S.1347 carried over, including limiting the insanity defense and federal parole, as well as Kennedy's sentencing commission. The result of all this was the Comprehensive Crime Control Act. With the coalition of Democratic leadership and a Republican-dominated Senate, the CCCA passed through with even more ease than the bills that preceded it. The House still posed a problem, but in a slick parliamentary procedure, the Senate bill was attached to an urgent funding bill at the last second and passed through the House.[59] The bill was resolved with the leadership of Thurmond and was signed into law in 1984 by Ronald Reagan.

The impact of the CCCA cannot be overstated, for it established the climate for numerous other bills focusing on determinate sentencing (primarily mandatory minimums) to flourish in the 98th, 99th, and 100th Congresses. Yet these bills are often attributed to the Reagan era, which disconnects the antiblack fear of drug users and pushers from the antiblack fear of the civil rights protesters and riots. This disconnection robs our ability to recognize the "changing same" nature of the paradigm of antiblackness. This economy of fixation, anxiety, paranoia, and terror around the phobic object flows through the ebb and flow of electoral politics and political leadership. The White House and Congress may vacillate between two political parties, but the libidinal economy flows underneath these shifting poles like water. In this way, the "tough on crime" tactics (mandatory minimum sentencing and the abolition of parole) and antiblack bonding of crime to urban "streets" attributed to Reagan (or even Nixonian) Republicans began with the liberal senator from Massachusetts, Ted Kennedy. Mandatory minimum sentencing represented a shift of ideology from rehabilitative justice to retributive justice, but what is the meaning of such a shift within the "changing same" paradigm of antiblackness?

III

At the time of its passage, the Comprehensive Crime Control Act had its fair share of critics. Trial lawyers criticized how attorney fees could be confiscated along with other property if a narcotics criminal was convicted.[60] They felt that this was not only an attack on every citizen's constitutional right to representation, but also criminalized their jobs as defense attorneys. Many of the critics stated that the law was "schizophrenic" given that its stated intent was to not increase the prison population while all its provisions knowingly led to an increased prison population.[61] One defense attorney stated that "they seem to be saying we really don't want to fill the jails up, but . . . they suggest that punishment is the main interest, not rehabilitation."[62] The potentially hypocritical nature of the bill can be partially attributed to the numerous interests within the coalition that put it together, for even the sentencing commission would later comment that the CCCA had language to fit all different ideologies of punishment (deterrence, rehabilitation, and retribution).[63] Yet a close reading of the CCCA reveals the contradictory language does little more than pay lip service to rehabilitation while focusing on retributive punishment and increasing the prison population.

The mandate on prison capacity that is at the root of the supposed confusion was put in by Senator Mathias before the bill was passed. This reflected a consistent debate around prison capacity and whether this measure would overburden the judicial and prison infrastructure that was already stretched.[64] The Mathias-Thurmond amendment read, "the sentencing guidelines prescribed under this chapter shall be formulated to minimize the likelihood that the federal prison population will exceed the capacity of the federal prisons."[65] The amendment was not a mandate against overcapacity because it only called for the sentencing commission to "minimize the likelihood" of exceeding the limits. In a clause supposedly mandating that prisons should be kept at capacity, the congressional representatives already recognized that to keep prisons at capacity, an "expansion" would be necessary. Thurmond and Mathias were not the first to recognize that their laws would increase the prison population. Ted Kennedy wrote about it in an editorial titled "Punishing the Offenders" in 1975. When he demanded that mandatory minimum sentences deal with the "plague" of "street crime," he also called for more money to expand judicial and corrections infrastructure.[66] The schizoid nature of the law was really no confusion at all. The consensus around harsher punishment and more prisons had been reached in the 1970s—amendments like those provided by Mathias and Thurmond represented congressional representatives paying lip service with no teeth.

Other critics of the CCCA were federal judges who were not fond of a law that effectively dismantled judicial discretion. Another thorn was the perception that judges were not consulted in the writing of the law, nor would they be on the sentencing commission itself.[67] The first issue missed the fact that Senator Kennedy called Judge Frankel the father of sentencing reform.[68] According to Kennedy, at a dinner, Judge Marvin Frankel effectively convinced him that determinate sentencing was the only way to effectively fight the war on crime. This is most likely an exaggeration, but what could not be exaggerated was the influence Judge Frankel had on Kennedy and other liberal congressional representatives. Unlike many judges, Frankel criticized indeterminate sentencing for making every judge a "law unto himself" and outlined the structure of a sentencing commission Kennedy would later advocate for in his book *Criminal Sentences: Law without Order.*[69] His views on sentencing and punishment were complicated, for he also criticized the Nixon administration's law and order initiatives as "official cruelties unlikely to accomplish anything beneficial."[70] Frankel believed the law could work as a proper deterrent only if sentencing was equal and fair. These models—deterrence and retribution along with rehabilitation—are often posed as different ideologies of punishment that are mutually exclusive. This view was part of the argument for why the CCCA was schizophrenic, for the law seemed to take no particular position on which ideology of punishment was its foundation. Yet the CCCA did not arise out of a fundamental confusion. The differences between these ideologies were resolved by a shared economy of identification and anxiety: the fear of black criminality.

In the aforementioned Kennedy editorial, he describes three impetuses for (black) criminality: the criminal as effect of societal inequality, the criminal as trickster careerist, and the criminal as plague. The first impetus for crime is described in the Johnson administration's Kerner Report as the primary cause of riots, thus demanding more Great Society social welfare programs. Kennedy admits that "perhaps the social policies we initiate in the 1970s will reduce the crime rate in the 1980s. But that is too long to wait."[71] The reason is because "we face the crime menace now." This menace is the career criminal, a slick figure who understands that "the hours are short, no professional qualifications are required, taxes are nonexistent, and the risks are minimal."[72] Because the courts and prosecutors are overworked, the career criminal "successfully plays the odds time and time again" and, if she is caught, " 'cop[s] a plea' and return[s] to circulation."[73] The trickster figure is a trope that is deeply embedded in both black folklore and antiblack views on slaves in such a way that the trickster, in many ways, is another metonym for the black: a lazy yet crafty figure who uses his wits to get out of work and embarrass the master.[74] The trickster criminal figure is an outgrowth from this trope. The fear of this trickster is what prompts Kennedy to assert the urgency of the crime problem. According to him, while at one point career criminals were a small group of people, this blatant disrespect for the rule of law had spread through the urban streets like a disease. In fact, he begins his editorial with these words: "Violent crime is spreading like a national plague."[75] This repeats the language Republicans like Byrd and Democrats like McClellan used to describe the civil rights protests and urban riots. Same phobia, different topic and time. As Frantz Fanon once wrote, "The negro always symbolizes the biological danger."[76] Seemingly, blackness is always spreading and infecting the cleanliness of the socius, so its movement must be isolated and sealed off. The idea of the time was, if rehabilitation cannot work, then deter it. If deterrence cannot work, then attempt to contain blackness for as long as possible. This leaves one option—since there is no magic formula for reducing the crime rate, we must try them all. Crime must be controlled comprehensively. The coalition of supporters for CCCA was not confused; instead, it understood these forms of punishment as a continuum of techniques to discipline and obliterate a particularly phobic object.

There is still a minor point of contradiction to wallow in. If Frankel was against Nixon's law and order strategy, then why did he and Kennedy support mandatory minimums? How were mandatory minimums—a law ruled "cruel and unusual" in 1970 by the U.S. Supreme Court—not an example of "official cruelties"? Kennedy writes on this issue, "A mandatory minimum sentence is not based on a vindictive desire to punish. It arises out of the belief that certainty of punishment is the most effective deterrent to criminal conduct."[77] Yet there is a slippage here. What is the mechanism of the deterrent? Perhaps a set of harsher penalties and using the career criminal to exhibit the power of the state to inflict pain? If deterrence is still the "desire to punish," then the only thing separating the two sides is the issue of "vindictiveness." Vindictiveness means the desire for revenge and implies that this desire is personalized—that the punished and punisher share an intimate relationship that warrants vengeance. This distinction rings hollow when the "certainty of punishment" can be proven only by showcasing the pain that awaits a transgression. What is more intimate than a theatre of pain? Instead of the scaffold where the flesh decomposes out in the open, the ravaged body was hidden from view behind walls and bars. The language of his editorial undoes the hollow language he uses to legitimize his violence. Crime was a plague. The plague prayed on our weakness, our indeterminacy. Order was the only response to the chaos of protest, urban unrest, and crime. Order is built on certainty. Certainty could be obtained only with elimination of indeterminate sentencing. The only solution to solve the problem of "revolving door justice" was to shove the criminal through the bloodstained gate and shut the door tight. Two years minimum, five years minimum, 15 years minimum—there are never too many years. The message must be delivered that the certainty of pain of the highest order awaits every infraction of "street crime."

If punishment is always an economy of pain, then determinate sentencing was to make sure criminals—specifically the phobic object of the black—felt the strongest amount of pain possible. Whether liberal or conservative, believer in deterrence or believer in retribution, all were connected by the desire to liquidate the criminal into pure flesh to be held, divided, and/or ripped apart.[78] For this reason, a liberal judge like Marvin Frankel and conservative intellectuals like Norborne Robinson III and Andrew von Hirsch can come together in agreement.[79] All could agree that a criminal "deserves [punishment] because he has engaged in wrongful conduct—conduct that does or threatens injury and that is prohibited by the law."[80] Because the criminal causes pain, he must receive pain in return. von Hirsch goes on to say that doling out pain is ethical because "fewer innocent persons will be victimized by crimes, while those less deserving will be made to suffer instead."[81] The immunity from pain for the subject is fortified through the subjection of "those less deserving." von Hirsch considers only one situation where this arrangement would not be ethical: "Consider, for example, a society in which most persons were literally slaves . . . and most punishments were for acts of disobedience by slaves to their masters: that system of punishment could hardly be defended as deserved—for most punishable acts would in no sense be blameworthy."[82] The only time punishment would be unethical is in a slave society. Yet von Hirsch cannot even contemplate the relationship between the criminal and the black/slave. It is unthinkable to von Hirsch that America could be such a society, yet as Frank Wilderson wrote, "The onus is not on one who posits the Master/Slave dichotomy, but on one who argues there is a distinction between Slaveness and Blackness. How, when, and where did such a split occur?"[83] Given not only the constitutional fact that the prisoner is a slave, but also that the black body has been at the center of all debates investigated in this chapter regarding determinate sentencing, then the question remains for von Hirsch, as well as all others advocating for punishment as an ethical institution: How, when, and where did the history of this country split from slavery?

One last thing to consider is an ironic prophecy from Ted Kennedy. In the 1970s, he predicted that if budgets for prosecutorial offices were not increased, then plea bargains would increase due to an increased amount of traffic of arrested bodies.[84] What Kennedy did not seem to fully grasp was that erasing judicial discretion would only shift that discretion over to the prosecutor: the discretion to pick a charge, to include or not include a found weapon, to over- or underestimate the amount of drugs found, and so on. Given that trials cost money—and the court system literally cannot handle the number of arrests that are made[85]—prosecutors are not only evaluated on their conviction rate, but also on their efficiency rate (how many plea bargains they can force).[86] The bureaucratic emphasis on efficiency and cost-effectiveness shifts the focus from getting the facts straight to how fast can we finish this case and get to the next one. The fastest way to finish is to get the arrested individual to forgo the trial and plead guilty. This is why Paul Butler, a former prosecutor who was charged and almost found guilty, calls the prosecutorial process a "meat grinder."[87] This is an apt metaphor. Discretion means the freedom to make a decision, but its Latin root—*discernere*—is also connected to the term "discern," which means to separate things. Discerning often connotes using one's gaze to separate things. Thus, the freedom to make a decision is based on the ability of one's look to separate, divide, or rip something apart. As Fanon described in the beginning of his chapter titled "The Fact of Blackness," even the look of a white child can rip apart his subjectivity and put the fragments back together.[88] The gaze of the prosecutor, who has the destiny of the arrested in her hands, cannot help but be more devastating. The subjectivity of the prosecutor is directly parasitic on the subjection of the flesh of the criminal. Determinate sentencing slides discretion down to the prosecutor, but mandatory minimums empower him with a useful weapon: the illusion of choice. Do you take the plea bargain or take your chances in court against the mandatory minimum? It is a game worse than Russian roulette, for every pull of the trigger shoots out a bullet. But, of course, any game involving blackness is not really a game at all because it always involves death (in its myriad of forms) as its constituent element. Thus, the libidinal economy of the anti-black gaze produces the conditions of possibility for a process that cannot stop increasing the prison population, even as crime rates decrease.

Thus, not only do the debates around determinate sentencing historically precede the phenomenon of mass incarceration, but they also are the zero point for its development of momentum. The anxiety around black protest and urban unrest reanimated the position of mandatory minimums from its short-lived slumber, and negrophobia sustained the debate for the decades preceding the Comprehensive Crime Control Act. The different ideologies of punishment that were clashing in these debates around mandatory minimums were not mutually exclusive, but were different flows of energy colliding at the black body to form a perfect storm of pain and perverse enjoyment that produced mass incarceration. Mandatory minimums provided a substantive solution to debate and were the condition of possibility for transforming the prosecutor's office into a "meat grinder" that efficiently pushed arrested bodies from cuffs to bars.

To conclude, blacks have gone by many names—nigger, vagrant, addict, criminal—yet the paradigm remains the same: fear it and control it, desire it and confine it. The absence of—or the fleeing away from—consideration of the historical connection between prisons and slavery represents the dark abyss of the left, the unconscious of its political imagination, or as Saidiya Hartman put it, "the position of the unthought."[89] The gulf is not seen but is felt and thus must be resolved with popular culture, academic texts, and policy proposals. Mandatory minimums were yet another of these policy proposals that came into existence through coalitions formed around nodes of antiblack insecurity. If "crime" is just another term for blackness, then mandatory minimums represented a change from attempting to rehabilitate blackness to a desire to make blackness feel the pain it deserved for violating the social order. Mass incarceration—a historical quadrupling of the prison population—is the effect of such a change in attitude and policy. Mandatory minimums were a policy proposal that signaled an epochal change to mass incarceration, yet change does not mean a shift in the paradigm. A shift would be the end of slavery and the return of black subjectivity. Instead, mandatory minimums are simply another type of sentence in the grammar of black suffering and the story of black subjection.

Notes

1. Hartman, 1997, p. 3.
2. "Governor Vetoes 2 Criminal Bills," 1969.
3. This term was coined by Ray Winbush, director of the Institute of Urban Research at Morgan State University, at a symposium on mass incarceration at Coppin State University on June 16, 2012. I use this term in place of "criminal justice" to highlight that our system's relationship to criminality is not as wide or ambiguous as a term like "justice" might connote. Instead, penologists, lawmakers, and other academics are very frank in their discussions that whether it is "rehabilitation, deterrence, or retribution," it is all punishment. von Hirsch, 1985, pp. 30–31.
4. "Congress to Get Wide Narcotics Bill," 1962, p. 23.
5. Thompson, 2010, pp. 703–4.
6. I am using a definition of the word "interstice" inspired by Spillers, 1987, pp. 73–100.
7. See Davis, 1998, and Gilmore, 2007.
8. Sexton, 2008, pp. 192–93.
9. Quoted in Weaver, 2007.
10. Quoted in Weaver, 2007, p. 11; Spivak, 1988, pp. 11–12.
11. Hartman, 1997, p. 10.
12. Hartman, 1997, p. 12.

13. Reeves, 2010.

14. The motif of internal wars with the dominant order is a trope within black theory. See Dubois, 1997; Fanon, 1967.

15. Hartman, 1997, p. 11.

16. Parole Act of June 10, 1910, ch. 387, 36 state. 819.

17. The clarity of the rising crime statistics is another issue altogether. The many alternative causes for the spike in crime rates at this time is discussed in in great detail in Stith and Koh, 1993, pp. 226–27.

18. Weaver, 2007, pp. 244–47.

19. Hoover, 1955, p. 43.

20. Quoted in Weaver, 2007, p. 241.

21. Hartman, 1997.

22. For works on the North, read Muhammad, 2010, and McLennan, 2008. For works on the South, read Adamson, 1983, and Curtin, 2000.

23. U.S. House, 1960, pp. 5062–63.

24. U.S. House, 1960, p. 5063.

25. Stennis, 1961, p. 8738.

26. Goldwater, 1964.

27. Goldwater, 1964, p. 744.

28. American Museum of the Moving Image, n.d.

29. Goldwater, 1964, p. 746

30. *Congressional Quarterly Almanac*, 1960, pp. 701–2.

31. McClellan, 1964, pp. 23–40, 28.

32. Russell, quoted In Weaver, 2007, p. 247.

33. For more information on this antiblack consensus, see Hoover, 1955, p.72; Whittaker, 1967, p. 324; and Weaver, 2007.

34. "Race Friction," 1965, pp. 21–24, 21.

35. Weaver, 2007, pp. 244–45.

36. U.S. National Advisory Commission on Civil Disorders, 1968.

37. "Poverty: Phony Excuse for Riots?" 1967, p. 14.

38. Nixon, 1968 ("domestic" referring to national and not family violence).

39. See discussion on "Riots and Federal Workers" in Weaver, 2007.

40. White, 1968.

41. Weaver, 2007, p. 255.

42. U.S. Senate, 1967.

43. John G. Dow (D–NY) quoted in Weaver, 2007, p. 257.

44. "How to Lock Them Away," 1987.

45. Ibid.

46. Stith and Koh, 1993.

47. Kennedy, 1976.

48. Lewis, 1977, p. A33.

49. Kennedy, 1975, p. 29.

50. Kennedy, 1975, p. 29.

51. Kennedy, 1975, p. 29.

52. Stith and Koh, 1993, pp. 232–33.

53. Hartman, 2008, p. 17.

54. Stith and Koh, 1993, p. 234.

55. Stith and Koh, 1993, p. 234.

56. H.R. Rep. No. 1396, 96th Congress, 2nd session. 487–500.

57. S. 1722, 96th Congress, 1st session (1980).

58. See *Forfeiture in Drug Cases*, 1981–1982; *Federal Criminal Law Review*, 1981–1982; Comprehensive Drug Penalty Act of 1982.

59. Stith and Koh, 1993, pp. 260–61.

60. Tofani, 1984, p. A1.

61. Possley, 1984, p. D1.

62. Possley, 1984, p. D1.

63. Stith and Koh, 1993, p. 230.

64. Kennedy, 1975.

65. Austin et al., 1996.

66. Kennedy, 1975.

67. Possley, 1984.

68. Goldstein, 1977, p. D14.

69. Greenhouse, 2002, p. C15.

70. Greenhouse, 2002, p. C15.

71. Kennedy, 1975.

72. Kennedy, 1975.

73. Kennedy, 1975.

74. For a discussion on the trickster figure within black folklore and antiblack views on slavery, read Gates, 1989. In literary criticism, the black trickster figure has been affirmed as a method of resistance against the dominant order by using the master's tools (like language or the legal system itself) against him in unexpected ways. The trickster criminal figure is a trope throughout the speeches and editorials written on the necessity of determinate sentencing. The fear of this trickster figure triggers calls for harsher punishment, longer prison sentences, and more prisons. The reality of the trickster is not important here. What is important to note is there is no outwitting the blunt force of antiblackness. Henry Louis Gates would later learn this when he was arrested for *signifyin'* or "loud talking." The social death of the prison cell awaits the trickster. The tragic nature of this history reminds one of an old cliché, "A smart nigger is a dead nigger."

75. Kennedy, 1975.

76. Fanon, 1967, p. 127.

77. Kennedy, 1975.

78. Spillers, 1987, p. 67.

79. Raspberry, 1973, p. A27.

80. von Hirsch, 1985, p. 51.
81. von Hirsch, 1985, p. 51.
82. von Hirsch, 1985, p. 51.
83. Wilderson, 2010, p. 14.
84. Kennedy, 1975.
85. Alexander, 2012.
86. Butler, 2010, p. 23.
87. Butler, 2010, p. 7.
88. Fanon, 1967, p. 82.
89. Hartman, 2003.

References

Adamson, Christopher R. "Punishment after Slavery: Southern State Penal Systems, 1865–1890." *Social Problems* 30 (1983): 555–569.

Alexander, Michelle. "Go to Trial: Crash the Justice System," *New York Times*, March 10, 2012.

American Museum of the Moving Image. "The Living Room Candidate, Presidential Campaign Commercials, 1952–2004," n.d. Accessed on November 15, 2013, http://livingroomcandidate.movingimage.us/index.php.

Austin, James, Charles Jones, John Kramer, and Phil Renninger. *National Assessment of Structured Sentencing*. Darby, PA; Diane Publishing, 1996.

Butler, Paul. *Let's Get Free: A Hip Hop Theory of Justice*. New York: New Press, 2010.

Congressional Quarterly Almanac. Washington, DC: Congressional Quarterly News Features, 1960, 701–702.

"Congress to Get Wide Narcotics Bill," *New York Times*, September 29, 1962.

Curtin, Mary Ellen. "Black Prisoners and Their World: Alabama, 1865–1900." *Alabama Review* 55, no. 4 (2002): 285.

Davis, Angela. *Masked Racism: Reflections on the Prison Industrial Complex*. Accessed February 14, 2014 from http://colorlines.com/archives/1998/09/masked_racism_reflections_on_the_prison_industrial_complex.html, 1998.

Dubois, W. E. B. *Souls of Black Folk*. Boston: Bedford, 1997 [1903].

Fanon, Frantz, *Black Skin, White Masks*. New York: Grove, 1967.

Federal Criminal Law Review, 97th Congress, 1st and 2nd session, pt. III, 1981–1982.

Forfeiture in Drug Cases, 97th Congress, 1st and 2nd session, 1981–1982.

Gates, Henry Louis. *The Signifying Monkey*. New York: Oxford University Press, 1989.

Gilmore, Ruth W. *Golden Gulag: Prisons, Surplus, Crisis, and Opposition in Globalizing California*. Berkeley: University of California Press, 2007.

Goldstein, Tom. "Judicial Discretion Faces Curb in Senate Bill on Sentencing Methods." *New York Times*, June 16, 1977.

Goldwater, Barry. "Peace through Strength," address September 3, 1964. *Vital Speeches of the Day* 30 (1964): 744.

"Governor Vetoes 2 Criminal Bills: Mandatory Sentencing and Barring of Bail Rejected." *New York Times*, May 24, 1969.

Greenhouse, Steven. "Marvin Frankel, Federal Judge and Pioneer of Sentencing Guidelines, Dies at 81." *New York Times*, March 5, 2002.

Hartman, Saidiya. *Lose Your Mother: A Journey along the Atlantic Slave Route*. New York: Farrar, Straus and Giroux, 2008.

Hartman, Saidiya. *Scenes of Subjection: Terror, Slavery, and Self-Making in Nineteenth-Century America*. New York: Oxford University Press, 1997.

Hartman, Saidiya, and Frank B. Wilderson, III. "The Position of the Unthought." *Qui Parle* 13, no. 2 (2003): 183–201.

Hoover, Edgar. "Our Common Task: When Crime Occurs, There Has Been a Failure Somewhere," address October 3, 1955. *Vital Speeches of the Day* 22 (1955): 43.

"How to Lock Them Away." *Wall Street Journal*, January 5, 1987. Accessed May 15, 2014, from http://search.proquest.com/docview/135266872?accountid=5683.

Kennedy, Edward. "Reforming the Federal Criminal Code: A Congressional Response," *North Carolina Center Law Journal*.1, no. 8 (1976): 8–9.

Kennedy, Edward M. "Punishing the Offenders." *New York Times*, December 6, 1975.

Lewis, Anthony. "Politics of the Possible." *New York Times*, November 14, 1977.

McClellan, John L. in "Crisis in Race Relations: How Will It Be Met? Interviews with Congressmen around the Nation." *US News & World Report*, August 10, 1964.

McLennan, Rebecca M. *The Crisis of Imprisonment: Protest, Politics, and the Making of the American Penal State, 1776–1941*. New York: Cambridge University Press, 2008.

Muhammad, Khalil Gibran. *The Condemnation of Blackness: Race, Crime, and the Making of Modern Urban America*. Cambridge, MA: Harvard University Press, 2010.

Nixon, Richard M. "Address Accepting the Presidential Nomination at the Republican National Convention in Miami Beach, Florida" Accessed March 26, 2014 from http://www.presidency.ucsb.edu/ws/?pid=25968, August, 1968.

Parole Act of June 10, 1910, ch. 387, 36 state. 819.

Possley Maurice. "Justice: Crime-Control Package Big Surprise to Some." *Chicago Tribune*, November 25, 1984.

"Poverty: Phony Excuse for Riots? 'Yes,' Says a Key Senator." *U.S. News and World Report*, July 31, 1967.

"Race Friction: Now a Crime Problem?" *U.S. News and World Report*, August 30, 1965.

Raspberry, William. "Crime and Punishment." *Washington Post, Times Herald*, September 19, 1973.

Reeves, Judy. *A Writer's Book of Days: A Spirited Companion and Lively Muse for the Writing Life*. Novato, CA: New World Library, 2010.

Sexton, Jared. *Amalgamation Schemes*. Minneapolis: University of Minnesota Press, 2008.

Spillers, Hortense. "Mama's Baby, Papa's Maybe: An American Grammar Book," *Diacritics* 17, no. 2 (1987): 67.

Spivak, Gayatri. "Subaltern Studies: Deconstructing Historiography." In *Selected Subaltern Studies*, edited by Ranajit Guha and Chakravorty Spivak, pp. 3–34. New York: Oxford University Press, 1988.

Stennis, John C. "Proscription of Travel in Interstate and Foreign Commerce for Purposes of Inciting a Riot." Washington, DC: 1st Session, *Congressional Record* 107, pt. 2, 1961.

Stith, Kate, and Steve Y. Koh, "The Politics of Sentencing Reform: The Legislative History of the Federal Sentencing Guidelines."*Faculty Scholarship Series*, Paper 1273 (1993): 226–227.

Thompson, Heather Ann. "Why Mass Incarceration Matters: Rethinking Crisis, Decline, and Transformation in Postwar American Society." *Journal of American History* 97, no. 3 (2010): 703–734.

Tofani, Loretta. "The Harder Line on Federal Crime: New Law's Effect Debated." *Washington Post*, December 28, 1984.

U.S. Congress. Comprehensive Drug Penalty Act of 1981. 97th Congress, H.R. 5371, 1982.

U.S. House. "Northern Congressmen Want Civil Rights but their Constituents Do Not Want Negroes." *Congressional Record*, 86th Congress, 2nd Session, 106 (4) 5062–5063, 1960.

U.S. National Advisory Commission on Civil Disorders. *Report of the National Advisory Commission on Civil Disorders*. Washington, DC: Government Printing Office, 1968.

U.S. Senate. "Controlling Crime through More Effective Law Enforcement." Hearings before the Subcommittee on Criminal Laws and Procedures of the Senate Committee on the Judiciary, 90th Cong., 1st sess., 1967.

von Hirsch, Andrew. *Doing Justice: The Choice of Punishments*. New York: Northeastern, 1985.

Weaver, Vesla M. "Frontlash: Race and the Development of Punitive Crime Policy." *Studies in American Political Development* 21 (2007): 230–265.

White, Jean M. " 'Crime in Streets' Is Called Slogan to Curb Negroes." *Washington Post*, January 23, 1968.

Whittaker, Charles E. "Planned, Mass Violations of Our Laws: The Causes and the Effects upon Public Order," address February 14, 1967. *Vital Speeches of the Day* 33 (1967): 324

Wilderson, Frank. *Red, White, & Black: Cinema and the Structure of U.S. Antagonisms*. Durham, NC: Duke University Press, 2010.

Williams, John Bell, "Northern Congressmen Want Civil Rights but Their Constituents Do Not Want Negroes." 86th Cong., 2nd sess., *Congressional Record* 106, pt. 4, March 9, 1960, 5062–5063.

Wilson Gilmore, Ruth. *Golden Gulag: Prisons, Surplus, Crisis, and Opposition in Globalizing California*. Berkeley: University of California Press, 2007.

Chapter 21

Race and the Three Strikes Law

Brian Chad Starks and Alana Van Gundy

Three strikes laws originated from a general societal unrest and concern primarily as a result of two particularly egregious criminal cases. First, in 1988, Diane Ballasiotes was kidnapped and killed by an escaped work release inmate from a Seattle, Washington, work release facility. Second, in California in 1993, 12-year-old Polly Klass was abducted at knifepoint in her home during a children's slumber party and killed by a repeat violent offender. Each case involved a young, white, female victim and a repeat, violent, sexual offender. While states already had legislation in place to address and incarcerate repeat offenders, these cases (among others) struck fear in many that violent and repeat offenders were being released too early. Alternatively, people saw these cases as proof that such prisoners should not be released at all. As a result, California and Washington led the charge for what we know as the "three strikes laws," with Washington passing the first three strikes and you're out law by voter initiative in 1993. Between 1993 and 1995, the federal government and 24 states enhanced their current legislation directed at repeat offenders by adding three strikes legislation or creating new policy that applied to repeat and violent offenders.[1]

Three strikes laws were originally enacted to address perceptions that serious offenders are released from prison too early and that they are not prepared to successfully reintegrate into society. The intended consequences of this form of legislation were to protect the public from violent offenders, ally public fears that surrounded the aforementioned cases, harshly punish those that had previously been given chances at nonrecidivism (yet failed), and deter others from becoming repeat offenders. Yet in the original time period in which these laws were enacted, some states extended the three strikes legislation for those who are repeat and *nonviolent* offenders. In other words, while three strikes laws were intended for repeat violent offenders, they vary greatly in their definition of a "strike," how many strikes it takes to be "out," and what it means to be "out." These variations have ostensibly offered an uneven application across states, amongst individual cases, and through the overall functioning of the justice system.

The 1994 Violent Crime Control and Law Enforcement Act

In addition to the kidnapping, rapes, and murder of Ballisiotes and Klass, social unrest and concern drastically increased following a few high-profile violent crimes that resulted in mass victimization. One prolific incident that caused general alarm was the 1993 siege of Waco. Following an undercover operation, the Bureau of Alcohol, Tobacco, and Firearms attempted to serve a warrant to search the Branch Davidian complex in Waco, Texas, in February 1993. The Davidians were speculated to be in violation of the Firearm Owners Protection Act of 1986 and had reportedly stockpiled multiple forms of weapons, including M-16s and AR-15 machine guns. The attempt at executing the search warrant failed and culminated in a two-hour shootout between the Davidians and federal agents that resulted in the deaths of four federal agents and six Davidians.

The standoff with the Davidians lasted until April 1993. After being notified by the FBI that child abuse and molestation was occurring within the compound, Attorney General Janet Reno presented a case to President Bill Clinton that conditions were deteriorating, children were at risk, and a mass suicide could be imminent. Reno and Clinton approved a tank and tear gas raid on the compound. Despite live broadcast of the raid, information on the chronology and what occurred throughout this raid is inconsistent, but it was reported that three fires simultaneously started throughout the Davidian compound. The fires trapped the remaining Davidians in the compound, and 50 adults and 20 children under the age of 15 were killed. All that remained were buried alive, suffocated by the gas, or killed by the fire. Of the Davidians who managed to leave the compound prior to the fire, 12 were criminally charged with unlawful possession of firearms, conspiracy, or aiding and abetting to kill federal officers.

Shortly following the incident at Waco, in July 1993, a mass shooting occurred in San Francisco. Gian Luigi Ferri entered the building at 101 California Street, a glass high-rise that housed a law firm with which Ferri had had previous dealings. Ferri was armed with two handguns and one pistol, and he opened fire on multiple floors of the office building and continued his massacre into the stairwells. Ferri killed nine people and injured six, and then he turned the gun on himself. To no avail, multiple victims and family members of the victims of this massacre sued the makers of the handguns and pistol that Ferri was carrying. However, this shooting spree ignited fear and anger in general society, with many calling for tighter gun control.

As a means of addressing this social unrest, generalized fear, and anger related to the massive loss of life, in 1994, the 103rd Congress passed HR 3355, The Violent Crime Control and Law Enforcement Act. The bill focused on addressing crime and created an unprecedented slew of funding for additional law enforcement officers, for prisons and new prison construction, and for prevention programs designed and implemented primarily by law enforcement. HR 3355 was originally written by Senator Joe Biden and was signed into legislation by Clinton.

The provision of interest within this Bill is Title VII, Mandatory Life Imprisonment for Persons Convicted of Certain Felonies. In subsection one of Title VII, the new federal three strikes law emerged. It states:

> Notwithstanding any other provision of law, a person who is convicted in a court of the United States of a serious violent felony shall be sentenced to life imprisonment if (A) the person has been convicted (and those convictions have become final) on separate prior occasions in a court of the United States or of a State of – (i) 2 or more serious violent felonies; or (ii) one or more serious violent felonies and one or more serious drug offenses; and (B) each serious violent felony or serious drug offense used as a basis for sentencing under this subsection, other than the first, was committed after the defendant's conviction of the preceding serious violent felony or serious drug offense.[2]

The federal provision is followed with a list of what crimes may be considered as strikes, and they include assault with intent to commit rape, arson, extortion, firearms use, kidnapping, murder, manslaughter other than involuntary, assault with intent to commit murder or rape, aggravated sexual abuse or abusive sexual contact, aircraft piracy, robbery, carjacking, conspiracy or solicitation to commit any of the aforementioned offenses, any offense punishable by a maximum term of imprisonment of 10 years or more that has an element of force, and serious drug offenses that are punishable under the Controlled Substances Act. Felonies that do not qualify for the three strikes law include robbery at the state level if no firearm or threat of firearm was used and if the event did not result in death or serious injury and arson if the offense posed no threat to human life. There are special provisions for the three stikes law regarding Native Americans residing on semisovereign reservations/lands and for those that have had prior convictions overturned.[3]

Within one year of the federal enactment of the three strikes law, Thomas Farmer was given the first life sentence for his third strike under this new legislation. The *New York Times* published an article titled "In For Life: The Three Strikes Law; A Special Report, First Federal Three Strikes Conviction Ends a Criminal's 25 Year Career." It read:

> Tommy Lee Farmer had never heard of the new Federal Three Strikes law until sheriff's deputies brought him into court last October.
>
> That was when his lawyer gave him the bad news. Mr. Farmer had expected to face state charges for his role in a botched holdup of a supermarket here. But three weeks earlier, President Clinton had signed a law intended to put incorrigible career criminals behind bars for life.
>
> Mr. Farmer, the son of a minister and brother of a college professor, had spent most of his 43 years in prison for crimes that included murder, conspiracy to murder and armed robbery. Now he was learning that he was to be the first person in the nation charged under the law.
>
> Last month—in a sentence that so pleased President Clinton that he interrupted his vacation to herald it as a milestone in American justice— Mr. Farmer was sent to prison for life.
>
> "Tommy Farmer is the perfect poster child, or man, for the Three Strikes law," said Stephen J. Rapp, the United States Attorney for the Northern District of Iowa in Cedar Rapids, who prosecuted the case. "He has been through the criminal justice system repeatedly and didn't learn his lesson."[4]

After its creation and implementation, the federal three strikes law was widely touted as legislation that worked to end the careers of violent, long-term offenders. The bill eased the fear and concern surrounding violent offenders, drug use, and drug abuse, and it extended the time individuals spent behind bars. Capitalizing on the available social support, states began enacting their own forms of this law, some even implementing two strikes legislation, for example, in Arkansas, California, Georgia, Montana, North Dakota, Pennsylvania, South Carolina, and Tennessee. Table 21.1 is

TABLE 21.1 Three Strikes Legislation by State

State	Year Implemented	What Constitutes a Strike?	How Many?	Punishment	People Incarcerated (Percentage Nonwhite)
Arkansas	1995	Murder, kidnapping, robbery, rape, terrorist act	Two	Not less than 40 years in prison; no parole	74 (82 percent)
		First-degree battery, firing a gun from a vehicle, use of a prohibited weapon, conspiracy to commit murder, kidnapping, robbery, rape, first degree battery or first degree sexual abuse	Three	Range of no-parole sentences, depending on the offense	
California	1994	Any felony if there is one prior felony conviction from a list of strikeable offenses as denoted by the state	Two	Mandatory sentence of twice the term for the offense involved	32,508 (76 percent) 8,828 (76 percent)
		Any felony if there are two prior felony convictions from list of strikeable offenses	Three	Mandatory indeterminate life sentence, with no parole eligibility for 25 years	
Colorado	1994	Any Class 1 or 2 felony or any Class 3 felony that is violent	Three	Mandatory life in prison with no parole eligibility for 40 years	681 (60 percent)
Connecticut	1994	Murder, attempted murder, assault with attempt to kill, manslaughter, arson, kidnapping, aggravated sexual assault, robbery, and first-degree assault	Three	Up to life in prison	57 (67 percent)

(continued)

TABLE 21.1 (Continued)

State	Year Implemented	What Constitutes a Strike?	How Many?	Punishment	People Incarcerated (Percentage Nonwhite)
Georgia	1995	Murder, armed robbery, kidnapping, rape, aggravated child molestation, aggravated sodomy, aggravated sexual battery Any felony	Two Four	Mandatory life without parole Mandatory maximum sentence for the charge	15,891 (75 percent)
Indiana	1994	Murder, rape, sexual battery with a weapon, child molestation, arson, robbery, burglary with a weapon or that results in a serious injury, drug dealing	Three	Mandatory life without the possibility of parole	2,111 (44 percent)
Louisiana	1994	Murder, attempted murder, manslaughter, rape, armed robbery, kidnapping, any drug offense punishable by more than five years, any felony offense punishable by more than 12 years Any four felony convictions if at least one was on the preceding list	Three/Four	Mandatory life in prison with no parole eligibility Mandatory life in prison with no parole eligibility	12,218 (73 percent)
Maryland	1994	Murder, rape, robbery, first- or second-degree sexual offense, arson, burglary, kidnapping, carjacking, manslaughter, use of a firearm in a felony, assault with intent to murder, rape, rob, or commit sexual offense	Four, with separate prison terms service for first Three Strikes	Mandatory life in prison with no parole eligibility	262 (88 percent)

State	Year	Offenses	Strikes	Sentence	Number (percent)
Montana	1995	Deliberate homicide, aggravated kidnapping, sexual intercourse without consent, ritual abuse of a minor	Two	Mandatory life in prison with no parole eligibility	0
		Mitigated deliberate homicide, aggravated assault, kidnapping, robbery	Three	Mandatory life in prison with no parole eligibility	
Nevada	1995	Murder, robbery, kidnapping, battery, abuse of children, arson, home invasion	Three	Life in prison without parole; with parole possible after 10 years; or 25 years with parole possible after 10 years	310 (53 percent)
New Jersey	1995	Murder, robbery, carjacking	Three	Mandatory life in prison with no parole eligibility	17 (94 percent)
New Mexico	1994	Murder, shooting at or from a vehicle and causing harm, kidnapping, criminal sexual penetration, armed robbery resulting in harm	Three	Mandatory life in prison with parole eligibility after 30 years	0
North Carolina	1994	47 violent felonies; separate indictment required finding that offender is a violent habitual offender	Three	Mandatory life in prison with no parole eligibility	5,119 (73 percent)

(continued)

TABLE 21.1 (Continued)

State	Year Implemented	What Constitutes a Strike?	How Many?	Punishment	People Incarcerated (Percentage Nonwhite)
North Dakota	1995	Any Class A, B, or C felony	Two	If second strike was for Class A felony, court may impose an extended sentence of up to life; if Class B felony, up to 20 years; if Class C felony, up to 10 years	24 (41 percent)
South Carolina	1995	Murder, voluntary manslaughter, homicide by child abuse, rape, kidnapping, armed robbery, drug trafficking, embezzlement, bribery, certain accessory and attempt offenses	Two	Mandatory life in prison with no parole eligibility	395 (67 percent)
Utah	1995	Violent felonies	Three	Ranges from additional three years to life without parole, with judicial discretion	14 (29 percent)

| Washington | 1993 | Any Class A felony or conspiracy to commit any Class A felony, assault, child molestation, controlled substance homicide, extortion, incest against child under 14, indecent liberties, kidnapping, organized crime, manslaughter, promoting prostitution, vehicular assault or homicide when caused by impaired or reckless driver, any Class B felony with sexual motivation, and any other felony with a deadly weapon | Three | Mandatory life in prison with no parole eligibility | 323 (52 percent) |
| Wisconsin | 1994 | Murder, manslaughter, vehicular homicide, aggravated battery, abuse of children, robbery, sexual assault, taking hostages, kidnapping, arson, burglary | Three | Mandatory life in prison with no parole eligibility | 24 (25 percent) |

*Table was reproduced and amended from Vincent Schiraldi, Jason Colburn, and Eric Lotke, *3 Strikes and You're Out: An Examination of the Impact of Strikes Laws 10 Years after Their Enactment*, Washington, DC: Justice Policy Institute. .

*Note: Florida, Pennsylvania, Tennessee, Vermont, and Virginia did not provide data for inclusion and thus are not included in this table.

an amended table as provided by Schiraldi, Colburn, and Lotke (Justice Policy Institute Brief) and presents information on the states that implemented a two or three strike rule since the passage of HR 3355, what constitutes a strike in that state, how many strikes one may amass prior to striking out, the punishment, and the people currently affected by it. Importantly, the current strike legislation that exists within these states was implemented within two years of the federal legislation being enacted.

Table 21.1 shows that state three strikes legislation was initially developed in 1994 and 1995, very close to the time of the crimes that sparked such outrage and public fear. Societal pressure was placed on federal and state legislators to quickly respond to these fears of egregious crimes, habitual offenders, and violent offenders. And the government clearly listened. Importantly, even though the legislation was quickly enacted, both public support for and widespread criticism of the policy existed.

Support for Three Strikes Legislation

Three strikes legislation was essentially a societal backlash against an increased fear of crime, previous offenders, and violent offenders. Many people argue that the regulations have decreased the rates of offending and significantly decreased criminal careers. When examining the bills enacted at both the federal and state levels, the clear goal is to ensure long prison sentences for offenders and harsher punishment for those who commit repeat offenses. The intended consequence of this goal is to reduce public fear, ensure public safety, and incarcerate people with histories of or who are at risk of criminality.

Naomi Harlin Goodno argues that there are three reasons why three strikes laws are effective.[5] Her arguments are based on California's three strikes model but may translate to other states and the federal model. First, she states that supporters of the law believed it would have an incapacitation effect as well as a deterrent effect. Her evidence is that in California, the number of sentenced second and third strikers declined every year (incapacitation effect) and that the state crime rate has dropped since the law was enacted (deterrence effect). Therefore, the goal of the law has been met. Second, she argues that the initial concerns of implementing the law have not come to fruition. Goodno states that the cost of enforcing the law is lower than originally predicted, so it has not overrun state budgets or overcrowded prisons. Third, the three strikes law provides built-in safeguards to ensure that the law's intent is met. For example, she states that concerns that the law is unduly harsh because a minor violation can trigger the third strike is essentially invalid because the intent of the law is to address recidivism, which it does simply by incarcerating individuals at risk for recidivating. The safeguards that she refers to consist of drug treatment programming and judicial and prosecutorial discretion (she argues that 25 to 45 percent of third strikers will have a previous strike thrown out by a judge or prosecutor due to these forms of discretion), which address the goals of decreasing recidivism rates.[6]

In a 10-year retrospective report titled "Prosecutors' Perspective on California's Three Strikes Law," additional support for Goodno's argument was provided.[7] The authors spent a considerable amount of time addressing what they termed misinformation and fallacies surrounding three strikes legislation. They argued that the U.S. Supreme Court found three strikes legislation to be constitutional and not cruel and unusual despite the punishment possibly being disproportionate to the current level of culpability.[8] They also show support for the legislation by arguing that 10 years after implementation, the law has garnered only 4.6 percent of inmates a third strike sentence; the law has not caused prison costs to bankrupt the state; it has not resulted in a decrease in funding for education; it has not overcrowded prisons; California has not had to open numerous prisons; and it has not created a backlog in the court system. Therefore, the law's goal of targeting the small portion of individuals who are violent repeat offenders has been met.

Rackauckas, Feccia, and Gurwitz provide additional support for the use of three strikes legislation.[9] They analyzed 13 years worth of three strike cases prosecuted in Orange County, California, and found that supporters of three strikes legislation have valid viewpoints. Their data showed that only 11.9 percent of all defendants subject to a life sentence under the three strikes provision were actually sentenced to a life term, which they point out is evidence that the statute is not overused or abused. Of those who were given life sentences, 55 percent of the offenses were serious or violent felonies. The researchers argued that individuals in the court system who received life sentences are not minor criminals that pose little threat to society. Rather, they represent a threat to public safety.[10]

Support for three strikes legislation rests on its ability to fuel the public need to punish individuals that routinely violate the law. The intent of the law is to protect the general public by targeting a population that victimizes others and is at risk for recidivating upon release from a penal institution. An incapacitation effect will clearly be seen when increased numbers of individuals are incarcerated, and some support is provided that those con-victed of a first or second strike may be deterred from further crime. Research has shown that prosecutorial and judicial discretion may still be enacted via omitting or throwing out a previous conviction, but because most of these data come from studies conducted in California, there is some concern about whether support would be found in other states as well as at the federal level.

Criticism and Resistance

Despite widespread public support, three strikes legislation has been criticized and resisted on many grounds. It is important to note that while 24 states quickly enacted three strikes laws (or enhanced existing ones), more than half of our nation's states did not. Criticism for what some con-sidered a knee-jerk response to criminal activity was rampant. As discussed earlier in this chapter, individuals and society questioned the law's intent, cost, impact, and effect. While few would argue that violent repeat offend-ers should be allowed to reintegrate into society prior to being prepared to do so, many people were concerned about offenders that may fall through the cracks of the criminal justice system, in other words, nonviolent offend-ers, those who would "age out" of crime, and those the prosecution or judicial system felt should not be impacted by this form of legislation.

One of the biggest criticisms of three strikes legislation is clearly the cost of funding it. Implementation of the law costs a state or federal government greatly through substantial and additional funding for preconviction jail time, case processing, trials, building jail and prison facilities, incarcerating individuals for greater lengths of time, and housing long-term and geriatric offenders. The criminal justice system is already overburdened, processing time is longer than it should be in many instances, prison facilities are anti-quated and over capacity, and programs for successful reintegration are scarce. New legislation that convicts more individuals for a longer time does nothing but add to this burden.

Another criticism is the uneven application and unintended consequen-ces of the laws themselves. The wide variation and implementation in the legal definition of what a strike is, when one is sought, and what happens when an individual has run out of them has resulted in long prison terms for those convicted of nonviolent or less serious charges. The laws also affect prosecutorial discretion because prosecutors are now expected to charge individuals with their last strike, uphold three strikes laws, and reduce opportunities for plea-bargaining. By proxy, prosecutors have learned how to circumvent these restrictions, leading to inconsistencies in implementing three strikes legislation.[11] Similarly, it has limited judicial discretion by requiring a mandatory sentence for the last strike and/or particular offenses. Limiting prosecutorial and judicial discretion is of the utmost concern to law enforcement and the courts.

Initial resistance to three strikes legislation also revolved around impact. Would this type of program work? Would the legislation allow for law enforcement, the courts, and corrections to protect society by incarcerating the most serious violent offenders while not overburdening an already troubled system? Many were concerned that the political nature of the passage and implementation of this law would not allow for a fair and unbiased assessment of the true impact of the program. Reports were scarce for the first few years, but five- and 10-year assessments of legislation (primarily assessing the impact of the laws in California, Florida, and Georgia) did evidence concern for who was being incarcerated, how long they were being incarcerated, and if crime rates were declining as a result of the laws.[12]

Analysis on the legislation's impact on crime rates is mixed, with multiple states showing no decrease in crime but some showing a slight decrease in crime.[13] However, criminal justice practitioners and academics agree that while crime rate may be a variable of interest, there are many other things to examine related to impact and consequences. For example, in 2008, Radha Iynengar found that even while many would argue the three strikes law does show impact in the form of a decreasing crime rate, it offers two unintended consequences: third strike–eligible offenders are more likely to commit violent crimes, and because some laws are so harsh (in this instance, California), offenders with second and third strike eligibility migrated to neighboring states to commit criminal offenses. Findings such as these concern individuals who question whether the cost of the legislation outweighs its benefits.[14]

An additional criticism surrounds the demographics of who is being sentenced under the this type of legislation. Of particular concern are older offenders and minorities. Males and Macallair showed that in California, the average age of offenders sentenced for a second strike was 32.9 and for a third strike was 36.1 (two thirds of the third strikers were between the ages of 30 and 45).[15] They argue that felony offenders in their thirties and forties have had more time to commit offenses and are therefore eight to 10 times more likely to be sentenced under three strikes legislation.

This is important because of their possibility of aging out (research would argue this is the population least affected by the legislation, but in fact, they are the most affected), and they are less likely to commit a violent offense in comparison to a young offender.[16]

The last criticism, and the focus of this chapter, is that three strikes legislation disproportionately affects minorities. In 1999, Dickey and Hollenhurst argued that one of the unintended impacts of three strikes legislation in California was that blacks are incarcerated at higher rates and for longer periods of time: "African-Americans comprise 31% of inmates in the state's prison, but 37% of offenders convicted under two strikes and 44% percent of Three Strikes offenders."[17] Later, they argue that according to a 1997 report, "in California, Blacks make up 7% of the state's population but account for 20% of felony arrests, 31% of state prisoners, and 43% of those imprisoned for a third strike."[18]

Ehlers, Schiraldi, and Lotke conducted a study in 2004 that focused on how California's three strikes law had been applied to blacks and Latinos on both a statewide and county-by-county basis.[19] They found that while racial inequity existed in the criminal justice system prior to enactment of this legislation, implementation of it simply accelerated racial disparity. Blacks and Latinos are incarcerated at higher rates than Caucasians. The researchers provide the following facts:

- In California, Blacks make up 6.5% of the population, 30% of the prison population, 36% of second strikers, and 45% of third strikers.
- The proportion of Latinos in the general population and the prison population is fairly similar. 32.6% of the population is Latino, 36% of the prison population is Latino, and 32.6% of the strikers are Latino.
- Caucasians in California make up 47% of the general population, 29% of the prison population, 26% of second strikers, and 25.4% of third strikers.
- Felony arrests among Blacks were 4.4 times higher than for whites, but Blacks' rate of incarceration was 7.5 times higher, their rate of incarceration for second strikes was 10 times higher and for third strikers, 13 times higher.
- The arrest rate for Latinos was 50% higher than for Caucasians, their incarceration rate was 81% higher, and their rate of incarceration as a striker was 82% higher.[20]

Their study found that while the aforementioned statistics represented the state level, the county levels mirror the state trends. In other words, across the board in California, blacks receive the harshest punishments, followed by Latinos and then Caucasians. These findings held regardless of size of the county, levels of use or harshness of the three strikes law, and the location of the offender.

Ehlers, Schiraldi, and Ziedenberg presented an additional report on the California three strikes law titled "Still Striking Out: Ten Years of California's Three Strikes" in which they created what they termed a three strikes rate.[21] This rate calculates the number of strikers in the prison population per 100,000 residents in California (11). They state that:

- The Black incarceration rate for third strikes is 12 times higher than the third strike incarceration for Whites.
- The Latino incarceration rate for a third strike is 45% higher than the third strike incarceration rate for Whites.
- For second and third strike sentences combined, the Black rate is over 10 times higher than the White incarceration rate.
- For second and third strike sentences combined, the Latino incarceration rate is over 78% higher than the White incarceration rate.[22]

The aforementioned studies were conducted between 10 and 20 years ago. Despite support showing that three strikes legislation disproportionately impacts minorities, changes have not been made to remedy the situation. Table 21.1 shows, for example, that 12 states currently report more than 50 percent of those that are incarcerated are of minority status. Arkansas, Maryland, and New Jersey report that over 80 percent of those that are incarcerated for third-strike offenses are blacks or Latino. Only Indiana (44 percent), North Dakota (41 percent), Utah (29 percent), and Wisconsin (25 percent) report that less than 50 percent of their current third strikers are minorities. These statistics evidence the nationwide lack of concern for the disproportionate impact of three strikes legislation on minorities.

Discussion

The relationship between racial and ethnic minorities and the current system of criminal justice has been well documented and—at best—is a contentious issue. The response to and treatment of minorities by law enforcement, courts, and corrections is the basis of a large body of literature that offers rigorous and multiple debates on how to address or change this relationship. Within our discussion, we present a brief overview of the criminal justice system and minorities, discuss the development and consequences of the war on drugs, and base our argument on the premise that the three strikes legislation is an extension of policies such as the war on drugs. We argue from the viewpoint of critical race theory and provide suggestions for amending current three strikes legislation as a means of addressing the resultant racial disparities.

Critical Race Theory

Critical race theory emerged in the mid-1970s from black intellectuals who feared that the work done by both black and white activists fighting for the legal rights of blacks could be oppressed and undermined by the white power structure. These intellectuals—namely Richard Delgado, Alan P. Freeman, and Derrick Bell—were critical of the legal system that historically ignored the rights of blacks and discriminated against them. The theory's main point of contention is that whites created the legal system and will do anything to maintain control of its power, in particular, utilizing it as a tool of oppression. Despite appearances that racial rights have been acknowledged and granted in the courtroom, critical race theory argues it is still in the best interest of the white community to oppress minority populations, either through policy or through practice.

For example, according to Derrick Bell, the 1954 Supreme Court ruling of *Brown vs. Board of Education* was passed to desegregate schools so that blacks could have an equal opportunity at receiving a good education. However, most of the literature fails to share with readers that the threat of international relations was deemed the major reasoning behind the integration of schools. The United States feared the Soviet Union would find issues with the treatment of blacks within the United States, so *Brown* was offered up as a way to diffuse the negativity surrounding the treatment of blacks.

Critical race, from a theoretical perspective, is in some sense a product of conflict theory, which is often used to provide a plausible explanation for racial discrimination in the criminal justice system. Walker and colleagues (2011) explain the premise of conflict theory: "The law is used to maintain the power of the dominant group in society and to control the behavior of individuals who threaten that power."[23] It is from this framework that we argue that the relationship between minorities and the criminal justice system is a form of oppression that occurs through the creation of policies that intentionally or unintentionally target those of minority status.

The Criminal Justice System and Minorities

The disproportionate representation of minorities in the criminal justice system is evidenced in arrest rates, conviction rates, and harsher sentencing practices.

For example, approximately 32 percent of black men will be in a state or federal correctional facility in their lifetime, compared to 17 percent of Hispanic men and 5.9 percent of white men (these are estimated rates of first incarceration). The statistics for jail inmates show a continuation of these racial trends. In 2002, sixty percent of inmates in local jails were of ethnic/racial minorities. Approximately 40 percent were black, 19 percent were Hispanic, 1 percent were American Indian, 1 percent were Asian, and 3 percent were of more than one race/ethnicity.[24]

The War on Drugs

One contribution to the soaring population of minorities within incarceration facilities (both racial/ethnic minorities and women) is the war on drugs. The war on drugs was launched in 1982 by President Ronald Reagan in response to the rampant use of crack cocaine in inner-city neighborhoods. The government created a drug task force, took federal funds earmarked for white-collar crimes, and directed them toward addressing drug use and the related violence that seemed to be taking over the country. The amount of funding and attention giving to this crack epidemic was highly influenced and widely supported by the media, which depicted blacks as crack heads, crack whores and crack dealers. The media essentially targeted blacks and made this group the focus of the war on drugs. These attacks contributed to the racial stereotypes of blacks as criminal, which inspired a public outcry to address black drug addicts and drug dealers. As a result of the war on drugs, blacks were arrested for drug crimes at rates that contributed to their mass incarceration.

Creating and implementing the war on drugs sent many young black men to prison for life for nonviolent offenses such as possession of drug charges. The policy was implemented to address what society viewed as a perceived threat and as a result, black men are more likely to be arrested for these forms of nonviolent offenses. This idea of perceived threat has allowed decision makers to racialize crime in multiple instances, which places blacks at a strong disadvantage in society but more specifically, within the criminal justice system.

This racialization of crime has a historical and political component that must be acknowledged when examining policies such as the war on drugs and three strikes legislation. Prior to winning the 1968 presidential election, President Richard Nixon publicly announced that blacks are at fault for crime in our nation.[25] The president's endorsement legitimized society, politicians, criminal justice practitioners, and scholars as they equated blacks with criminal activity. This induced fear in citizens and made the black man a target in the eyes of many, especially whites. The fact that many whites are afraid of young black men makes it easier to support targeting them as dangerous criminals that should be put away for life. Crawford and colleagues (1998) cite James Q. Wilson in a 1992 *Wall Street Journal* article: "It is not racism that makes white uneasy about blacks . . . it is fear. Fear of crime, of gangs and violence."[26]

Policies such as three strikes legislation and the war on drugs have been a means of dealing with that fear. Even though the original intent may not have been to target minorities, their overrepresentation in each phase of the criminal justice system as a result of these policies serves as support for institutionalized discrimination. Drugs are used and sold in white suburbs, yet the faces that society sees as most clearly representing the drug problem are young black men from the inner city. The notion is, "Wherever you shine the brightest light, you will find the most dirt." This crime light is shone more frequently and much brighter on the black community.

Three Strikes Legislation

The war on drugs had a clear and intended goal—to reduce drug use and related violence in inner cities. Reaching this goal has resulted in the mass incarceration of blacks. One must understand that legislation often has both intended and unintended (or unrecognized) consequences, and one must further consider whether the war on drugs covertly intended to target minorities. Critical race theory would argue that three strikes legislation was presented under the purview of terms such as "color-blindness" or the rule of law, but the legislation has targeted those of minority status. Many egregious crimes that have sparked public outrage have involved white perpetrators and white victims, yet the three strikes policy has resulted in increased minority incarceration rates.

Three strikes legislation intended to address the social disorder caused by violent recidivists, yet the actual effects of the legislation are different. Those most affected are minorities who have committed nonviolent offenses. This was not a population targeted by three strikes legislation when it was first proposed. The fact that this policy has resulted in a dispro-portionate number of blacks and Hispanics sentenced to long prison terms (primarily life without the possibility of parole) should lead legislators to question the results of the policy. The fact that the war on drugs happened to be the cause of such a disproportionate representation of blacks sentenced under a later policy targeting those with three strikes legislation, calls for a redirection and new understanding of the intent, implementation, and result of legislation and policy that has resulted in the mass incarceration of black and Hispanic males.

Three strikes legislation also has a clear and intentional purpose—to protect the general public by incarcerating the most serious, violent, repeat offenders that endanger public safety. While it may be the case that incarcerating many individuals will decrease the crime rate, it is the unintended consequences that are of concern to scholars focused on the relationship between race and oppression. Table 21.1, for example, shows that in one state, 94 percent of those incarcerated under three strikes legislation are of minority status. In many states, that number is between 70 and 80 percent, a clear statistical majority of the total imprisoned population. So while the main purpose of the legislation may be to protect society, one would be remiss to not recognize and address that one of the unintended consequences of this legislation is clearly to disproportionately incarcerate those of color.

The intended purpose of the three strikes legislation of removing violent recidivists from the community is one the authors of this chapter are in agreement with. The idea of career violent offenders being incarcerated for long periods of time makes most citizens sleep better at night and feel more confident in their general safety. Making our communities safer must be the primary focus of criminal justice legislation, so using policy to specifically deter crime is understandable. However, it is our argument that, while the intended goals of legislation such as the war on drugs and three strikes policy is appropriate, the manner in which the policy is implemented has resulted in a form of mass oppression of minorities that is highly concerning.

As evidenced throughout this chapter, three strikes legislation has contributed to the mass incarceration of nonviolent offenders, a significant number of whom are minorities. The disproportionate representation of minorities in all phases of the criminal justice system has long been a major topic of discussion, even before the mid-1990s. Blacks are and have been disproportionately arrested, denied pretrial bail, prone to take plea bargains, found guilty at trial, and given harsher sentencing in comparison to whites. Three strikes legislation has only increased these numbers. This situation must not be ignored. Was this the real intention of three strikes? Was there a hidden agenda? Were minorities again the target of criminal justice policy? We are merely suggesting that evidence of race-based disparities should at least be a part of the conversation on the unintended consequences of the legislation. On its face, the policy appears to target a certain type of criminal; yet based on real outcomes, one can see that black nonviolent offenders are most often targeted. With that in mind, we would like to offer a few suggestions that might concurrently allay public fear of violent recidivists and address racial disparities in the incarcerated population.

First, the intended purpose of this policy—removing violent recidivists—should remain its focal point. Yet we caution policy makers to adhere to outcome-based data that provides evidence that these criminal offenders were already subjected to harsh sentencing guidelines. Second, we must consider redefining the class of felonies that qualify defendants for such extreme punishment. For example, in the state of Georgia, if a defendant commits armed robbery (a class A felony), serves his or her sentence, and once released commits a class B drug felony, the judiciary has the legal discretion of applying the two strikes law. This situation must be critically examined.

Third, federal legislation encouraging state statutes to be more punitive deserves a second look. The definition of three strikes must be more clearly defined. Some states have taken the three strikes model and upped the ante to two strikes. In Georgia, if a defendant commits a violent offense such as armed robbery, serves his or her time, gets released, and commits another violent felony such as rape, the judiciary can recommend and sentence the defendant to life without parole. The federal policy should offer more equal and consistent application of the law for all states. It should not be used to circumvent get tough on crime rhetoric based on a geographical location (some regions are more punitive than others, for example, the South). We feel that the three strikes influence has allowed some jurisdictions to justify the overuse and abuse of judicial authority to incarcerate.

It is the authors' intention to make suggestions related to alleviating some of the miscarriages of justice for the minority population. We also hope that our suggestions will improve the legislation as it relates to community protection. We hope that any amendments to three strikes legislation achieve both of these goals.

Notes

1. Austin, Clark, Hardyman, and Henry, 1998.
2. Violent Crime Control and Law Enforcement Act, 1994.
3. Violent Crime Control and Law Enforcement Act, 1994.
4. Butterfield, 1995.

5. Goodno, 2007.

6. Goodno, 2007.

7. Otero and LaBahn, 2004.

8. *Ewing v. California*, 2003.

9. Rackauckas, Feccia, and Gurwitz, 2007.

10. Rackauckas, Feccia, and Gurwitz, 2007.

11. Bjerk, 2005.

12. Austin, Clark, Hardyman, and Henry, 1998; Macallair and Males, 1999; Schiraldi, Colburn, and Lotke, 2004; Stolzenberg and D'Alessio, 1997.

13. Helland and Tabarrok, 2007; Shepherd, 2002.

14. Iyengar, 2008.

15. Males, Macallair, and Taqi-Eddin, 1999.

16. Males, Macallair, and Taqi-Eddin, 1999, p. 4.

17. Dickey and Hollunhurst, 1999, p. 3.

18. Dickey and Hollunhurst, 1999, p. 14.

19. Ehlers, Schiraldi, and Lotke, 2004.

20. Ehlers, Schiraldi, and Lotke, 2004, pp. 2, 5.

21. Ehlers, Schiraldi, and Ziedenberg, 2004, p. 11.

22. Ehlers, Schiraldi, and Ziedenberg, 2004, p. 11.

23. Walker et al., 2011, p. 31.

24. Bureau of Justice Statistics, 2003.

25. Alexander, 2012.

26. Crawford et al., 1998.

References

Alexander, Michelle. *The New Jim Crow: Mass Incarceration in the Age of Colorblindness.* New York: New Press, 2012.

Austin, James, John Clark, Patricia Hardyman, and D. Alan Henry. *Three Strikes and You're Out: The Implementation and Impact of Strike Laws.* Washington, DC: National Institute of Justice, 1998.

Beck, Allan J., and Paige Harrison. *Prison and Jail Inmates at Midyear 2002.* Washington, DC: U.S. Department of Justice, Office of Justice Programs, 2003.

Bjerk, David James. "Making the Crime Fit the Penalty: The Role of Prosecutorial Discretion under Mandatory Minimum Sentencing." *Journal of Law and Economics* 48 (2005): 591–625.

Butterfield, Fox. "In for Life: The Three Strikes Law: A Special Report; First Federal 3-Strikes Conviction Ends a Criminal's 25-Year Career." *New York Times,* September 11, 1995.

Clark, John, James Austin, and D. Alan Henry. "Three Strikes and You're Out: A Review of State Legislation." Washington, DC: National Institute of Justice, 1997.

Crawford, Charles, Ted Chiricos, and Gary Kleck. "Race, Racial Threat, and Sentencing of Habitual Offenders." *Criminology* 36, no. 3 (1998): 481–512.

Dickey, Walter J., and Pam Hollenhurst. "Three Strikes Laws: Five Years Later." *Corrections Management Quarterly* 3 (1999): 1–18.

Ehlers, Scott, Vincent Schiraldi, and Eric Lotke. *Racial Divide: An Examination of the Impact of California's Three Strikes Law on African Americans and Latinos.* Washington, DC: Justice Policy Institute, 2004.

Ehlers, Scott, Vincent Schiralde, and Jason Ziedenberg. *Still Striking Out: Ten Years of California's Three Strikes.* Washington, DC: Justice Policy Institute, 2004.

Goodno, Naomi Harlin. "Career Criminals Targeted: The Verdict Is In; California's Three Strikes Law Proves Effective." *Golden Gate University Law Review* 37, no. 2 (2007): 1–25.

Hellend, Eric, and Alexander Tabarrok. "Does Three Strikes Deter? A Non-Parametric Estimation." *Journal of Human Resources* 22 (2007): 309–330.

Iyengar, Radha. "'I'd Rather Be Hanged for a Sheep Than a Lamb: The Unintended Consequences of 'Three Strikes Laws.'" National Bureau of Economic Research Working Paper 13784. Accessed on February 16, 2014, at http://www.nber.org/papers/w13784.pdf?new_window=1., 2008.

Males, Mike, Dan Macallair, and Khaled Taqi-Eddin. *Striking Out: The Failure of California's "Three Strikes and You're Out" Law.* Washington, DC: Justice Policy Institute, 1999.

Otero, Gilbert, and David LaBahn. "Prosecutors' Perspective on California's Three Strikes Law: A Ten-Year Retrospective." Sacramento: California District Attorney's Association, 2004.

Rackauckas, Tony, Bill Feccia, and Brian Gurwitz. "Has the Three Strikes Law Been Properly Implemented since Its Enactment, or Has It Been Abused? Who is Right: Its Critics or Its Supporters? What Do the *Facts* Say?" *Journal of the Institute for the Advancement of Criminal Justice* 1, no. 1 (2007): 22–27.

Schiraldi, Vincent, Jason Colburn, and Eric Lotke. *An Examination of the Impact of 3-Strike Laws 10 Years after Their Enactment.* Washington, DC: Justice Policy Institute, 2004.

Shepherd, Joanna M. "Fear of the First Strike: The Full Deterrent Effect of California's Two and Three Strikes Legislation."*Journal of Legal Studies* 31, no. 1 (2002): 159–201.

Stolzenberg, Lisa, and Stewart J. D'Alessio. "Three Strikes and You're Out: The Impact of California's New Mandatory Sentencing Law on Serious Crime Rates." *Journal of Crime and Delinquency* 43 (1997): 457–469.

Violent Crime Control and Law Enforcement Act of 1994, HR 3355, 103rd Cong. 2nd sess., Congressional Record 155, January 12, 1994.

Walker, Samuel, Cassia Spohn, and Miriam DeLone. *The Color of Justice: Race, Ethnicity, and Crime in America* (5th ed.). Belmont, CA: Cengage Learning, 2011.

Chapter 22

How Prisons Became Dystopias of Color and Poverty: Prison Abolition Lessons from the War on Drugs[1]

Michael J. Coyle

Introduction

After decades of contentious debate regarding the federal sentencing disparities between crack cocaine and powder cocaine, it is important to ask what this history teaches us about the drug war and especially the single greatest issue impacting the so-called criminal justice system: the problem of race/ethnicity. Also, given that more people are in prison for drugs than any other "crime" (and in deep disproportion people of color), it is important to ask what this history teaches us about using prison to build our ideal society.

My goal in this chapter is to review the rise of public rhetoric and policy as crack cocaine emerged on the national scene and became a matter of concern in American life. I also examine how in time, responses to crack cocaine have both shifted and remained the same. I argue that while responses to the perceived social problem of crack cocaine reflect the innate racism that defines criminal justice in the United States, they do so not in terms of any deliberate attempt by individuals and institutions to produce a racist society, but rather because these responses reflect the perpetuation of underlying racist thinking and entrenched racist practices of U.S. society. This does not mean we are living in a society that is not bathed in an underlying racism; it only means that—for example, in our justice system—we have learned to not overtly express racism. We now face the double task of distinguishing racism that has gone underground and eliminating it. Finally, my goal is to use these realities to argue for the end of prison use in the war on drugs.

The Emergence of Crack Cocaine

Crack cocaine became prevalent in the mid-1980s and received massive media attention due, in part, to its exponential growth in the drug market. The explosive popularity of crack cocaine was associated with its cheap price, which for the first time made cocaine available to a wider economic class. In the wake of widespread media attention, crack was portrayed as a violence-inducing, highly addictive drug that created a plague of social problems, especially in inner-city communities.

With the media spotlight focusing on crack, Congress quickly passed federal sentencing legislation in both 1986 and 1988. This included mandatory sentencing laws based on the premise that crack cocaine was 50 times more addictive than powder cocaine. For good measure, Congress doubled that number and came up with a sentencing policy based on the weight of the drug an individual was convicted of selling. Thus, federal sentences for crack were constructed to relate to sentences for powder cocaine in a 100:1 quantity ratio. The result was that while a conviction for the sale of 500 grams of powder cocaine triggered a five-year mandatory sentence, only five grams of crack cocaine were required to trigger the same five-year mandatory sentence. Similarly, while sale of 5,000 grams of powder lead to a 10-year sentence, only 50 grams of crack triggered the same 10-year sentence.

The Differences between Crack Cocaine and Powder Cocaine

Powder cocaine is made from coca paste, which is derived from the leaves of the coca plant. Crack cocaine is made by taking powder cocaine and simply cooking it with baking soda and water until it forms a hard rocky substance. These "rocks" are then broken into pieces and sold in small quantities.[2]

Initially, crack cocaine was widely viewed as a social menace that was categorically different from powder cocaine in its physiological and psychotropic effects. However, these assumptions were more reflective of the prevalent panic and fear that arose out of the explosive growth of the crack market than conclusions of scientific investigation. While federal law constructed a penalty structure that reflected these assumptions, by the end of the 1990s, only 14 states had adopted laws that distinguished in their penalty schemes between powder cocaine and crack cocaine, and only one state (Iowa) utilized the 100:1 quantity ratio of the federal system.

Over time, numerous studies have shown that the physiological and psychotropic effects of crack and powder are the same, and they are now widely acknowledged as pharmacologically identical. For example, a study published in the *Journal of the American Medical Association* finds analogous effects on the body for both crack cocaine and powder cocaine.[3] Similarly, Charles Schuster, former director of the National Institute on Drug Abuse and Professor of Psychiatry and Behavioral Sciences, testified to Congress that once cocaine is absorbed into the bloodstream and reaches the brain, its effects on brain chemistry are identical regardless of whether it is crack or powder.[4]

Crack Myths: Crack Violence and the Crack Baby

While politicians in the capital debated policy, crack cocaine, like all illicit drugs, found its niche on the street. When crack emerged in the drug market in the 1980s, it arrived as a technological innovation that made the "pleasures" of cocaine available to people who could not previously afford it in the expensive powder form. Initially, crack cocaine, as an innovation, produced vigorous competition in the drug market.[5] As with all illegal markets, crack distribution rights and boundaries were apportioned amongst competitors with the use of violence. In time, the dust has settled, the "markets" have matured, and the associated violence has significantly decreased.

Initially, the high violence associated with the "maturation process" of the crack market fostered a perception that the ingestion of crack instigated violent behavior in the individual user. However, studies have since shown otherwise. Prolonged use of high doses of crack or powder can produce a form of paranoid toxic psychosis in which aggressive acts are more likely; there is "no evidence, however, that this is more likely to occur after the use of crack as opposed to powder cocaine."[6]

In its May 2002 recommendations to Congress, the United States Sentencing Commission (hereon, the Commission) argued that the 100:1 penalties on crack were based on beliefs about the association of crack offenses with violence that have been shown to be inaccurate.

The Commission concluded that the violence associated with crack was primarily related to the drug trade and not to the effects of the drug itself, and further, that both powder and crack cocaine cause distribution-related violence. In a study of thousands of federally prosecuted cocaine cases, the Commission reported that for fiscal year (FY) 2000, weapon involvement for powder cocaine offenses was 25.4 percent and for crack cocaine offenses, 35.2 percent. The frequency with which weapons were actually used is much lower. For powder offenders, the use rate was 1.2 percent, and for crack offenders, it was 2.3 percent, not a difference, the Commission argued, that justifies a 100:1 quantity disparity.[7]

The Commission also argued that the solution to crack-related violence was not to encapsulate offenders in lengthy mandatory sentences that assume all crack offenders are violent. Rather, the commissioners suggested federal law should begin by assuming crack offenders are nonviolent and then apply new guidelines for increased punishment for violent offenses.

Crack cocaine was also initially widely viewed as a menace that was ravaging not only inner-city adults, but also innocent babies. The notion of the "crack baby" became common and was associated with the weak, shivering, and inconsolable newborn (most often African American) infant, experiencing immediate and long-term effects of withdrawal from crack. Over time, these descriptions have been interpreted in the medical field as the result of hysteria and not fact. For example, in her testimony before the Commission, Deborah A. Frank, a medical doctor and professor of pediatrics at Boston University, described the notion of a crack baby as "a grotesque media stereotype [and] not a scientific diagnosis."[8] She also reported finding that in pregnant crack users, the effects on the fetus are no different than for those who are pregnant and in poverty, or those using tobacco or alcohol, or those having poor prenatal care or poor nutrition. Finally, from her studies, she reported concluding that there is no evidence of increased risk of birth defects for women using crack during pregnancy and that newborns of crack-addicted mothers have no withdrawal symptoms.

The crack baby, it turns out, like the supposed origins of crack-related violence, was a ghost.

Drug Quantities and Crack Cocaine Penalties

The federal sentencing laws Congress passed in 1986 and 1988 were designed in part to hinder the crack cocaine drug trade. The intent of Congress was to impose a minimum 10-year prison sentence on a major

TABLE 22.1   Median Street-Level Dealer Drug Quantities and Mandatory Minimums

Drug	Median Drug Weight	Applicable Mandatory Minimum
Crack cocaine	52 grams	10 years
Powder cocaine	340 grams	none

trafficker (e.g., a manufacturer or a head of organization distributing large drug quantities) and a minimum five-year sentence on a serious trafficker (e.g., a manager of a substantial drug trade business).[9] As such, the laws were constructed to respond to the quantity of drugs involved in the offense.

However, the drug weight numbers attached to the sentences via the Anti-Drug Abuse Act of 1986 failed to capture the different roles associated with the crack trade. As can be seen in Table 22.1, research from the Commission shows that the five grams of crack set by Congress as the trigger for a five-year mandatory sentence is not a quantity associated with mid-level street dealers (much less serious traffickers).[10] The median crack cocaine street-level dealer (comprising two-thirds of federal crack defendants) charged in federal court was arrested holding 52 grams of the substance— enough to trigger a 10-year mandatory sentence. For powder cocaine, the median street level dealer was charged with holding 340 grams of drugs, which is not enough to even trigger the five-year sentence.

The results of these erroneous calculations were dual. First, they resulted in extremely severe prison terms for low-level crack offenders, who formed two out of every three crack offenders. Second, with mandatory minimum sentences focusing solely on quantities, offenders with different levels of culpability were often lumped together. As the Commission's May 2002 report to Congress stipulates, "Contrary to the intent of Congress, the five and ten year minimum penalties most often apply to low level crack cocaine traffickers, rather than to serious or major traffickers."[11] Indeed, an examination of cocaine sentences for 25 grams or less at the time showed that the average sentence was 14 months for powder cocaine but 65 months for crack cocaine.[12]

Some experts believe crack is more likely to be abused because of its brief high and low price. Charles Schuster, former director of the National Institute on Drug Abuse and professor of psychiatry and behavioral sciences, attempted to convince the Senate Judiciary Committee that while research illustrates smoked crack and intravenous powder offer the same high, and the 100:1 ratio is indefensible, a ratio of disparity should be kept.[13] He gave three reasons why a much lower ratio of 3:1 should be kept: (1) crack cocaine has adverse public health and social consequences that are potentially greater than those for powder because of the ease with which crack can be smoked repeatedly, (2) this makes crack cocaine appealing to many, and (3) "although individual risk may not vary between smoked crack and injected powder the numbers (of people) at risk of becoming addicted to crack may be significantly greater."[14]

Critics of the sentencing disparities between crack cocaine and powder cocaine have drawn other arguments. For example, Los Angeles federal judge Terry Hatter argues that contrary to what is in place currently, penalties for powder should be higher than those for crack because crack cocaine is made from powder cocaine.[15] Others have argued that powder sentences should be higher than crack sentences because powder trafficking has more offenders above the street level than crack trafficking.[16]

But the sentencing disparity between the two types of cocaine in the initial criminalization phase of crack went beyond the 100:1 quantity ratio. Crack was the only drug that carried a mandatory prison sentence for first offense possession. For example, a person convicted in federal court of possessing five grams of crack automatically received a five-year prison term, while a person convicted of possessing five grams of powder would probably receive probation. In fact, at the time, the maximum sentence for simple possession of any other drug, be it powder cocaine or heroin, was one year in prison.

For most people, the 100:1 sentencing ratio between crack and powder appeared inexplicably extreme. Even many intimately involved with enforcing crack penalties found federal law overly punitive and asserted it inappropriately targeted a drug population that consisted primarily of addicts who possessed or sold crack to support their own habit.[17]

Evolution of the Sentencing Disparity between Crack Cocaine and Powder Cocaine

The United States Sentencing Commission was created in 1984 by Congress to develop federal sentencing guidelines that would, among other goals, reduce unwarranted sentencing disparities. In 1994, as part of the Omnibus Violent Crime Control and Law Enforcement Act, the

Commission was directed to study the differing penalties for powder and crack. After a yearlong study, the Commission recommended to Congress a revision of the crack/powder 100:1 sentencing disparity, finding it to be unjustified by the small differences between the two forms of cocaine. After consulting the data at hand as well as field experts, the Commission advised Congress to immediately equalize the crack cocaine to powder cocaine sentencing ratio (1:1) that would trigger the mandatory sentences. The Commission also counseled that the federal sentencing guidelines should provide criteria other than drug type to determine sentence lengths so that, for example, offenders engaging in violence receive longer sentences than offenders who do not.

However, Congress rejected the recommendations and refused to change the law, which marked the first time it had gone against recommendations in the Commission's history. Two years later, in April 1997, the Commission once more recommended that the disparity between crack and powder cocaine be reduced, again by weight, this time providing Congress a range of 2:1 to 15:1 to choose from. The new recommendation was based on both raising the quantity of crack and lowering the quantity of powder required to trigger mandatory minimum sentences. However, Congress again did not act on the recommendation. By the end of the year, the Clinton administration, which throughout the "tough on crime" political climate of the 1990s had supported Congress's rejections of the Commission's recommendations, signaled some agreement with the call for reform. Though not until the last year of his second term, President Clinton did finally endorse a 10:1 ratio—to be arrived at by raising crack weight minimums and lowering powder ones. Congress, however, again made no revisions.

In the first years of the new millennium, a variety of efforts continued the battle against what widely came to be known as the "crack cocaine disparities." While various bills were proposed and discussed, such as the Drug Sentencing Reform Act of 2001, nothing moved Congress to actually act. As evinced in its 2002 *Report to Congress*, which again called for reducing sentencing disparities, the Commission conducted extensive studies and held three public hearings at which it received testimony from the medical and scientific communities, federal and local law enforcement officials, criminal justice practitioners, academics, and civil rights organizations.[18] In this same report, the Commission unveiled a study of thousands of federally prosecuted cocaine cases sentenced between 1995 and 2000, expert testimony gathered from a series of public hearings, and a survey of U.S. district and appellate judges, all in support of the argument that the disparity of the 100:1 ratio was not appropriate.

While the crack disparities continued into the first decade of the new millennium to garner the attention of the Commission, civil rights and community activists (especially the organization Families against Mandatory Minimums), progressive criminologists, and a modicum of the political field, real change was slow to come. After the first bipartisan legislation of the previously mentioned Drug Sentencing Reform Act of 2001was raised, a slow but steady stream of activity followed. Occasionally, U.S. district court decisions worked to weaken the sentencing structure, and—more importantly—two U.S. Supreme Court cases allowed lower courts some discretion in determining sentencing penalties.

A serious discourse shift occurred with the 110th Congress of 2007, which alone saw the introduction of seven disparate crack cocaine reform bills. In 2009, a promising bill that would have entirely eliminated the sentencing disparities, the Fairness in Cocaine Sentencing Act, passed the U.S. House Committee on the Judiciary along with more than 50 co-sponsors from the House of Representatives, but in the end, only a compromise bill was passed. The compromise bill is known as the Fair Sentencing Act, but despite its name, it only reduces the 100:1 ratio disparity to an 18:1 ration. It requires 28 grams to trigger a five-year mandatory sentence and 280 grams or more to trigger the 10-year sentence (as compared to the older five grams and 50 grams respectively for the same sentence). The act leaves penalties for powder offenses unchanged and eliminates a mandatory minimum sentence for simple possession.

In the summer of 2010, almost 30 years after the launch of the crack cocaine war, President Obama signed the Fair Sentencing Act into law, marking the first significant step away from the harsh punishments facing low-level crack cocaine offenders. While the act amended the toughest drug law Congress had ever enacted, the current ratio of 18:1 is a far cry from what reason, science, justice, and decades of study demonstrate is appropriate for the logic of modern criminal justice policy.

Race and Class in Crack Cocaine and Powder Cocaine Law and Enforcement

The failure of Congress to amend the sentencing disparities between crack cocaine and powder cocaine reflects a culture-wide set of misconceptions about crack—who uses it, who sells it, and what the consequences of its trade, such as violence, have been. But the failure to bring the crack to powder ratio to 1:1 illustrates something much more disturbing, namely, a deeply embedded racist and classist undertone to our society's political, legal, and law enforcement structure.

Throughout the years, the disproportionate sentencing ratio in the federal system has been legally challenged as unconstitutional on the grounds that it denies equal protection and due process, and because the penalties constitute cruel and unusual punishment. However, courts have generally not responded positively to such claims, not least because a "discriminatory intent" on behalf of lawmakers cannot be proven. Human Rights Watch, on the other hand, has not hesitated to describe federal crack sentencing policy as "an indefensible sentencing differential [that is] unconscionable in light of its racial impact."[19] Ethan Nadelmann of the Drug Policy Alliance, a New York group that promotes alternatives to the war on drugs, argues that the government claims to be protecting minority communities while its harsher enforcement of crack has never worked out that way.[20] As one district attorney sums it up, "[T]he simple fact is that although both populations have similar rates of drug abuse, minority drug defendants are serving substantially longer prison sentences than non-minority defendants."[21]

The class implications of crack cocaine federal sentencing are deeply disturbing. Since the two forms of cocaine are pharmacologically indistinguishable, by dictating harsher sentences for possession of crack than for possession of powder, the law is more severely punishing the poor, who obtain the affordable form of cocaine (crack), than the affluent, who obtain the more expensive form of the same drug (powder). Were alcohol illegal, this would be the equivalent of imposing a higher punishment for the sale of a cheap jug of wine than for an expensive French wine.

The race implications of crack cocaine federal sentencing are even more disturbing. In testimony before the U.S. Sentencing Commission, the Leadership Conference on Civil Rights reported that despite similar drug use rates between minorities and whites, minorities are disproportionately subject to the penalties for both types of cocaine (Congress has never lacked this information, as the Commission has been reporting it for decades).[22] Research on patterns of drug purchase and use demonstrates that overall, drug users report their main drug providers are sellers of the same racial or ethnic background as they are.[23] The implication here is that if we were designing and building a nonracist justice system, we would expect to find proportionate representation of minorities in the crack cocaine drug war. Yet as the Commission has been telling Congress for more than a decade, while African Americans constitute less than 20 percent of the U.S. population, federal crack defendants are more than 80 percent African American.[24] How can this be?

Criminal justice analysts widely argue that racial disparities in arrest and imprisonment relate to demographics. Crack is usually sold in small quantities in open-air markets. Powder is more expensive and is usually sold in larger quantities behind closed doors in locations that are inherently private. In urban areas, the "fronts" of crack use and sales are large metropolitan centers that gather the greater emphasis of law enforcement. Since minorities and lower-income persons are most likely to inhabit these areas, they are therefore at greater risk of arrest for crack cocaine possession than are white and higher-income powder offenders. The latter inhabit working-class and upper-class neighborhoods where drug sales are more likely to occur indoors instead of the street sales of the urban neighborhoods that receive disproportionate (greater) attention from law enforcement.

While it is true that open-air drug sales are easier to observe than indoor drug sales, the current allocation of law enforcement resources results in a policing structure that is race and class imbalanced. Coupled with the harshly unequal penalties between the two cocaine drugs, the result can only be described as a race- and class-oriented drug policy.[25] Understandably, such law enforcement has also been seen as evidence of racial profiling.[26]

While responses to the perceived social problem of crack cocaine reflect the innate racism that defines criminal justice in the United States, they do so not in terms of any deliberate attempt by individuals and institutions to produce a racist society, but rather because these responses reflect the perpetuation of underlying racist thinking and entrenched racist practices of U.S. society. While in the three-decade saga of crack cocaine legislation and enforcement no one ever took the podium to declare it a war on African Americans, it is hard to look at its impacts and call it anything else. After warnings of its racist design and decades of evidence about its racist effects once implemented, what else can we call the failure to displace crack law? It is racist.

Perhaps the easiest way to comprehend how such profound racism can stay in place in our justice system year after year is to understand how the everyday functioning of our institutions depends not on a rigorous discourse to design just—or redesign unjust—institutions and practices, but on the continuous work of bureaucratic functionaries, each of whom carries forth only one small part of the work. For example, in Any City, USA, the police officer on her beat must carry forth her patrol assignment as directed by her lieutenant, who must assign the officers under his command according to how the police chief directed him. The chief, in turn, has designed the station's limited drug war policing efforts according to the budget the mayor laid out. And the mayor receives such moneys from a governor with expectations that this year's total drug weight busts will at least match last year's tonnage. In turn, the governor feels pressure from her electorate to fight and win the war on drugs. In this fashion, the racism of the drug war is the responsibility of everyone and absolutely no one.

If law enforcement is to produce visible results in the drug war (both number of arrests and drug quantities seized), it cannot use its limited resources to police downtown board rooms and suburban living rooms for powder cocaine, as such work would require immense hours of labor and produce few measurable results. Meanwhile, one officer in an unmarked vehicle can make dozens of observations and numerous arrests a day on one inner-city street corner where crack cocaine is being sold. A city prosecutor, worried about her own conviction rate and facing different chances of victory with richer or poorer defendants—ones that can also differentially be coerced into plea bargains—will choose what cases to prosecute accordingly. The judge and jury adjudicate only the cases brought before them, and the jailer holds only those delivered by the court.

This is Hannah Arendt's *banality of evil*, where human atrocities are often committed not by fanatics and sociopaths, not by deranged and powerful leaders, but by ordinary people doing their jobs.[27] Few are trying to make the crack drug war a perfect expression of racism, but few are doing much of anything to stop it. What must be grasped is that just because the argument of an absence of intent to produce such racist policy can be made does not mean the enterprise is not thoroughly racist. Nor does it mean that just because everyone can point to someone else that nobody is responsible.

The current 18:1 sentencing ratio communicates to racial minorities and the poor a message of inherit inequity in the law, the courts, and—in reality—the entire justice system. This message breeds discontent and creates cynicism about law enforcement, and it is becoming a social fact of great consequence. As Wade Henderson of the Leadership Conference on Civil Rights argues, "The drug war will continue to lack credibility in minority communities until these sentencing laws are changed."[28] Even the perception of racial disparity is problematic because it fosters disrespect for and lack of confidence in the justice system among the very groups Congress intended would benefit from the heightened penalties for crack cocaine offenses.

The consequences are palpable. As Charles J. Hynes, district attorney for New York's Kings County disclosed in his testimony to a hearing of the Senate Judiciary Committee, in selecting jurists, he and his prosecutorial colleagues are faced with the "fact [that] minorities believe overall that law is unfair towards minorities."[29] Such beliefs translate into juries with no representation of peers (prosecutors seeking to avoid jury members of color) and null juries (juries that refuse to convict defendants no matter what the evidence because they know that the law and its systems can be entirely biased against certain defendants).

Prison Abolition Lessons from the Crack Cocaine Drug War

The several decades of the war on crack cocaine have taught us what several centuries of prisons have: Their application is profoundly and inherently racist. As all the data in these volumes illustrate time and time again, despite the many efforts, despite the countless recounting of the profound racism of what we call the criminal justice system, prison and the various "crime wars" that feed it never change. But the crack cocaine drug war, like all the drug wars, is not just any war. Collectively, they have become the greatest feeders into U.S. prisons, which have surpassed the size of any prison system that has previously existed. And the harm that begins with the drug war is only extended in the prison.

Contrary to common assumptions, the historicity of the penal project demonstrates a construction that is more closely determined by paradigmatic thinking about society—that importantly sorts, values, and treats humans according to indices of difference, (e.g., race/ethnicity, gender, class)—than it is driven by efforts to build livable human communities, such as drug-free spaces. In fact, analysis of linguistic distinctions used in the everyday functioning of the penal system reveals a collection of shifting serial myths. These myths, which base their claims in "human nature," and "human intentionality," characterize human conflict as being reducible to originating "crime" events creating categories of people as "offenders" and "victims." These myths obscure the constructed nature of penality and facilitate the transformation of claims—about "good" versus "bad" people, about "criminals" and the like, such as the crack violence and crack baby myths examined earlier in this chapter.

Empirical data demonstrate that with the exception of a small number of outliers at either end of the spectrum who either never commit "crimes" or who regularly and repeatedly commit them, the vast majority of persons commit a variety of violent and nonviolent crimes throughout their life span (consider the ubiquity of illicit drug use and the sexual assault of one out of four women in the United States during their life span). In other words, if everyone were to be held equally accountable for breaking the law, few would be without a prison experience. Therefore, it is more accurate to say that the penal project is less a response to crime than it is a selection process for who will be made subject to the criminal justice system. What logic does a drug war campaign that entails incarceration have before such data?

As a project reflecting the anxieties and social paradigmatic thinking of its age, the penal project has always been and always will be designed by one group that is threatened by another group according to its tally of "differences." As the examination of how crack cocaine law was designed and is maintained, how police resources enforce it, how courts certify it, and who is in prison or on probation/parole for it, as all these demonstrate, those most feared by the dominant group today are predominantly poor male persons of color.

In addition, we must not forget the influential threads that maintain and grow the penal system. For example, *penality as capitalism* (profiteering in the carceral project through political lobbies, private police, lawyering, private prisons, or what has been called the prison industrial complex); *penality as entertainment* (the use and sale of penal products in an endless looping of media, entertainment, and consumer conglomerates); *penality as power* (for career politicians and other moral entrepreneurs); *penality as profession/career* (numerous jobs in policing, lawyering, guarding, and academics); and *penality as a complex cultural system* (disseminating social control, addressing conflict and harm in relationships, and so on).

In the end, the so-called criminal justice system in the United States is one of the three most expensive government programs globally and historically, and one that is mostly recognized as failing in its mission. It has failed to provide a reasonable "public safety" program, is internationally recognized as "criminogenic," and is regularly in violation of national and international treaties and laws protecting human rights and civil liberties. In turn, the majority of people employed in criminal justice institutions report significant lack of faith in the system's capacity to deliver on the work it attempts. These failures are also demonstrated by institutions' own measurements of their work, for example, high recidivism rates (above 30 percent in many states) or the failure of courts to accomplish even 10 percent of their work (more than 90 percent of cases never go to trial, as a culture promoting "pleading out" has been developed to manage the courts' incapacity to dispose of their cases in proper trials).

The overabundance of available empirical data demonstrates that the penal project and what we call the criminal justice system have little to do with the ideology of crime, safety, or justice. Rather, we have a system occupied with the tasks discussed earlier in this discussion. A desire for penal abolition is therefore not based on naive or romantic perceptions of human beings, disregard for human taste for social control and community-building work, disregard for public safety, or a pretense that human beings in community are not accountable to each other. Rather, to speak of these is only to begin to be honest about the penal project's immense inhumanity, racism, and operational failures that advise us to leave it in the dustbowls of historicity. Departing from there, the real work begins.

Conclusion

The principles that guided the first acts of Congress related to crack cocaine were at best uninformed and typical of a justice culture that acts without taking responsibility for the class and race implications of its legislating. While dramatic hyperbole has defined much of the history of crack cocaine, a sober and impartial assessment of its—and other drugs'—sentencing is needed. Recent state voting patterns legalizing cannabis for personal use and cultivation show a change in the mood of the American public about the war on drugs. Perhaps the day when we look at drug use the way we do alcohol or nicotine use, that is, as a health concern, is not too far away. Perhaps the day we demand that the millions of nonviolent drug users be treated with something other than the outrageously damaging and expensive prison is also not too far away. Finally, perhaps the day when a courageous political voice will emerge to lead us in such ways is also not too far away.

Notes

1. Large parts of the early historical analysis of this chapter previously appeared as a work product of the author in "Race and Class Penalties in Crack Cocaine Sentencing," a 2002 publication of the Sentencing Project, a nonprofit organization bringing national attention to inequities in the criminal justice system through research, media campaigns, and strategic advocacy.

2. U.S. Sentencing Commission, 2002.

3. Hatsukami and Fischman, 1996.

4. Testimony of Charles Schuster before the Subcommittee on Crime and Drugs of the Senate Judiciary Committee, May 22, 2002.

5. Testimony of Alfred Blumstein, Carnegie Mellon University, before the United States Sentencing Commission, February 21, 2002.

6. Testimony of Charles Schuster, op. cit.

7. U.S. Sentencing Commission, 2002.

8. Testimony of Deborah A. Frank, M.D., before the United States Sentencing Commission, February 21, 2002.

9. Testimony of Commissioner John R. Steer before the Subcommittee on Criminal Justice, Drug Policy and Human Resources, May 11, 2000.

10. U.S. Sentencing Commission, 2002, p. 45, Figure 10.

11. U.S. Sentencing Commission, 2002.

12. U.S. Department of Justice, 2002.

13. Testimony of Charles Schuster, op. cit.

14. U.S. Department of Justice, 2002.

15. Lewis, 2002.

16. Testimony of Alfred Blumstein, op. cit.

17. Testimony of Charles J. Hynes before the Subcommittee on Crime and Drugs of the Senate Judiciary Committee, May 22, 2002.

18. U.S. Sentencing Commission, 2002.

19. Testimony of Human Rights Watch before the United States Sentencing Commission, February 25, 2002 (see http://www.hrw.org).

20. Lewis, 2002.

21. Testimony of Charles J. Hynes, op. cit.

22. Testimony of Wade Henderson before the U.S. Sentencing Commission, February 25, 2002 (see http://www.civilrights.org).

23. Lockwood, Pottieger, and Inciardi, 1995, p. 21.

24. U.S. Sentencing Commission, 2002.

25. Musto, 1999. See also Tonry, 1995.

26. Testimony of National Council of La Raza before the U.S. Sentencing Commission, February 25, 2002.

27. Arendt, 1963.

28. Leadership Conference on Civil Rights, 2002.

29. Testimony of Charles J. Hynes, op. cit.

References

Arendt, Hannah. *Eichmann in Jerusalem: A Report on the Banality of Evil.* New York: Viking, 1963.

Hatsukami, Dorothy K., and Marian W. Fischman. "Crack Cocaine and Cocaine Hydrochloride: Are the Differences Myth or Reality?" *Journal of the American Medical Association* 276, no. 19 (1996): 1580–1588.

Leadership Conference on Civil Rights, "Leadership Conference on Civil Rights Urges Congress to Improve Fairness of Crack/Cocaine Sentencing Laws" (press release), May 22, 2002.

Lewis, Neil A. "Justice Department Opposes Lower Jail Terms for Crack." *New York Times*, March 20, 2002.

Lockwood, Dorothy, Anne E. Pottieger, and James A. Inciardi. "Crack Use, Crime by Crack Users, and Ethnicity." In *Ethnicity, Race and Crime: Perspectives Across Time and Place*, edited by Darnell F. Hawkins, pp. 212–234. New York: State University of New York Press, 1995.

Musto, David S. *The American Disease: Origins of Narcotic Control*. New York: Oxford University Press, 1999.

Testimony of Alfred Blumstein, Carnegie Mellon University, before the United States Sentencing Commission, February 21, 2002.

Testimony of Charles J. Hynes before the Subcommittee on Crime and Drugs of the Senate Judiciary Committee, May 22, 2002.

Testimony of Charles Schuster before the Subcommittee on Crime and Drugs of the Senate Judiciary Committee, May 22, 2002.

Testimony of Commissioner John R. Steer before the Subcommittee on Criminal Justice, Drug Policy and Human Resources, May 11, 2000.

Testimony of Deborah A. Frank, M.D., before the United States Sentencing Commission, February 21, 2002.

Testimony of Human Rights Watch before the United States Sentencing Commission, February 25, 2002.

Testimony of National Council of La Raza before the U.S. Sentencing Commission, February 25, 2002.

Testimony of Wade Henderson before the U.S. Sentencing Commission, February 25, 2002.

Tonry, Michael. *Malign Neglect: Race, Crime and Punishment*. New York: Oxford University Press, 1995.

U.S. Department of Justice. *Federal Cocaine Offenses: An Analysis of Crack and Powder Penalties*. Washington, DC: U.S. Department of Justice, 2002.

U.S. Sentencing Commission, *Report to Congress: Cocaine and Federal Sentencing Policy*. Washington, DC: U.S. Sentencing Commission, 2002.

Chapter 23

Return to the Rez: Native American Parolees' Transitions to Community Life

Joseph S. Masters and Timothy P. Hilton

Reintegration encompasses much more than reentry or the transition from prison to outside communities. As Visher and Travis suggest, too much past research has focused on prisoner reentry and success based on whether they reoffended and return to prison, a phenomena commonly known as recidivism.[1] They argue that more emphasis should be placed on reintegration or ex-prisoners' abilities to acquire meaningful roles within their families and communities, which depend on a host of personal and environmental factors, including a community's ability to address the challenges faced by those transitioning from prison.

Native American reservations are unique. Most are in rural areas and are often far from large population centers and abundant job opportunities. These communities tend to be close-knit, which may create both opportunities and challenges for those returning after a prison sentence. Public policies, including the Major Crimes Act (1885), which places jurisdiction for on-reservation crimes considered particularly serious in the hands of the federal government, may also create unique dynamics for Native Americans transitioning from prison. Further, because a high percentage of the residents on most reservations live in Housing and Urban Development (HUD)–funded housing, HUD policies that restrict some ex-offenders from occupying units can create additional complications as they attempt to return home. These restrictions apply to persons convicted of drug or sexual offenses and make it difficult for many Native Americans to return to their families.[2]

Native Americans in the Upper Peninsula

Michigan's Upper Peninsula (UP) is a geographically isolated and largely rural region in the upper Midwest. The region comprises nearly 30 percent of Michigan's land area but is home to roughly 3 percent of its population. The vast majority of communities in the UP have lost population in recent decades. The area is also aging, as many young people have left, and older adults have returned to retire in the UP.[3] Many communities are economically depressed, and unemployment rates in some counties, including Baraga County—which is home to the Keweenaw Bay Indian Community— have been as high as 25 percent since 2013. Policy experts have long criticized unemployment rates because they exclude many who are not working and are no longer looking for formal work. While there are few recent empirical studies of unemployment within Native American reservations, past estimates of the number of nonworking adults on reservations in the United States have been as high as 80 percent.[4]

There are five tribes in the UP: (1) Bay Mills Indian Community, (2) Hannahville Indian Community, (3) Keweenaw Bay Indian Community, (4) Lac Vieux Desert Band of Chippewa, and (5) Sault Ste. Marie Tribe of Chippewa Indians. These tribes have populations ranging from a couple hundred to over 40,000, and a majority live on or near one of the reservations.

Native Americans and Criminal Justice Systems

Native Americans are overrepresented among prisoners and parolees in the United States. Native Americans are 1.5 times more likely than whites to be arrested, four times as likely to go prison, and more than twice as likely to be on parole.[5]

Tribal courts have limited jurisdiction and frequently operate under the guidelines of the federal government. The Major Crimes Act (passed in 1885) gives the federal government jurisdiction in cases involving murder, manslaughter, rape, assault, arson, burglary, or larceny that occur on reservations and involve native-on-native crime. Native Americans are subject to federal sentencing guidelines for these crimes and, if found guilty, are held in federal prisons, often out of state and far from offenders' homes and families.[6]

In addition to disadvantages created by the Major Crimes Act, Native Americans are often also disadvantaged by a long history of unfair treatment by law enforcement and other criminal justice officials. Strongly distrusting judicial systems, many Native Americans refuse to plea bargain and as a result, receive harsher sentences than they would have received otherwise.[7]

According to the Bureau of Justice Statistics (BJS), approximately 650,000 prisoners in the United States are released each year, and at any given time, there are approximately 750,000 individuals receiving court-ordered supervision. The average parolee is 33 years old and has less than a high school education.[8] In March 2007,

> Michigan's prison population reached an all-time high of 51,554. Less than three years later, the state [had] reduced its population by more than 6,000 inmates to 45,478. This reduction [came] about largely by reducing the number of inmates who serve[d] more than 100% of their minimum sentence, decreasing parole revocation rates, and enhanced reentry planning and supervision through the Michigan Prisoner Reentry Initiative.[9]

However, as stated earlier in this discussion, many Native American offenders serve federal as opposed to state sentences and are not eligible for these services.

Resources and Barriers to Reentry

According to the Bureau of Justice Statistics (BJS), 93 percent of all prisoners will eventually be released, and most return to the communities from which they came.[10] For many Native Americans, this means returning to a socially isolated and economically depressed area. Hampered with a felony, securing stable employment, adequate housing, health care, substance abuse treatment services, and educational opportunities is extremely difficult, especially in areas with high unemployment and tight labor markets.

For Native Americans, reintegration often means reconnecting with other tribal members. Tribal membership can create access to a wide support network of extended family and other tribal members who may provide tangible resources while also offering spiritual and psychological support. Having a strong cultural identity may also give some ex-offenders comfort as they begin to re-create a life for themselves outside prison. For some, however, tight networks among tribal members may be seen as threatening, especially for those who committed a crime on the reservation and/or against another tribal member. In the following discussion, we present several dimensions of reintegration and identify potential barriers and resources Native Americans may face in these areas as they leave prison to return to Native communities in the UP.

Housing

One of the first priorities for any parolee is determining where to reside.[11] In 1999, of all the parolees in the United States, 49 percent reported spending their first night after release with a family member and, after two months, 80 percent stated they were living with family members.[12] While parolees' social networks are critical to easing the transition from prison, parole stipulations sometimes prevent released offenders from returning home. This is common when the victim of a crime was a family member and in cases where a sex offender is restricted from residing with minor children. Having another family member who is also on parole may hinder a parolee from returning to his or her home since felons are often prohibited from living with other felons.[13]

As mentioned earlier, ex-felons returning from prison for a drug or sexually related crime are typically restricted from HUD-funded housing, and many are ineligible for food stamps (because of drug-related offenses), which may place Native Americans at a substantial disadvantage given that many homes on reservations are HUD subsidized. Some veterans' benefits and Temporary Assistance for Needy Families (TANF) are also restricted for many ex-offenders, further complicating and limiting their housing options.

Employment

There is a strong correlation between ex-offenders' employment status and rates of recidivism. Sampson and Laub noted that higher levels of job instability lead to higher arrest rates.[14] Lipsey's meta-analysis of nearly 400 studies from 1950 to 1990 found that the single most effective factor in reducing recidivism was employment.[15] In addition, as earnings increase, crime rates decrease.[16]

Research shows most parolees are eager to work. However, in most cases, parolees do not have jobs waiting for them on release, and the ones that do typically get low-paying jobs.[17] Employment in the UP is tenuous for many people, especially those with limited skills, experience, and education as well as for those with criminal histories. Jobs are scarce in the UP, and unemployment is very high in some areas. In April 2012, the unemployment rate in the

UP was 10.5 percent as compared to 8.2 percent for the state of Michigan and 8.1 percent for the United States as whole.[18]

UP communities with high numbers of Native Americans are among the most economically depressed. Baraga County, for example, where the Keweenaw Bay Indian Community is located, had an unemployment rate of over 22 percent in January 2011. In that same month, Chippewa County, where the Sault Ste. Marie Tribe of Chippewa Indians and Bay Mills Indian Communities are located, had an unemployment rate of nearly 14 percent.[19]

Education

Limited education is often a barrier to employment for ex-offenders. Among adult prisoners, 19 percent are completely illiterate, and 75 percent are functionally illiterate, compared to 4 percent and 21 percent, respectively, of the nonincarcerated public.[20] Three-quarters (75 percent) of state prisoners and 59 percent of federal prisoners do not have a high school diploma or GED.[21] Since 1994, felons have been restricted from receiving Pell grants, effectively shutting many out of higher education.[22]

The Michigan Indian Tuition Waiver (MITW), which provides free tuition to any of Michigan's public universities, is the result of an agreement between the state and area tribes. MITW is an invaluable benefit for many Native Americans in the state. However, eligibility is restricted to members of federally recognized tribes who have been in Michigan for at least one year, which makes many recent parolees who served time outside of Michigan (including federal parolees) ineligible.

Family

Research has shown that family contact during incarceration is associated with lower recidivism rates.[23] Garland, Spohl, and Wodahl found that relationships with family members are often strained as a result of separations during incarceration, which may increase recidivism risks.[24] Native Americans who serve federal sentences out of state are especially at risk of having limited contact with family during incarceration.

An Urban Institute study found that family support services, including counseling and more tangible supports like housing and financial assistance, were associated with increased rates of employment, reduced substance use, and reduced recidivism among parolees.[25] HUD regulations, which often prevent Native American parolees from living with their families, may limit the value of these family supports in reintegration processes.

Health, Mental Health, and Substance Use

The Urban Institute found that at the time of release, one-half of the men and two-thirds of the woman being paroled reported having been diagnosed with a chronic physical health condition requiring long-term management. The study also found that available treatments were typically insufficient to address health care needs. Lack of health insurance was found to be a common barrier to health care. The study also found that those leaving prison were far more likely than the average citizen to have a mental health issue (including psychiatric disorders). Many parolees were unable to access mental health care, and lack of health insurance was seen as a major barrier to successful reintegration.[26]

While many tribal members can access health care services through tribal health care clinics funded by the Indian Health Service or through contracted health service providers based on individual funding allotments, services provided are often limited, and Native Americans are often overcharged for the services they receive.[27]

Substance use not only increases the likelihood of reoffending, but it may also hinder returning prisoners' abilities to secure and maintain jobs and reestablish relationships with family members.[28] High rates of substance use and abuse on reservations are a pervasive problem. A study conducted by the Bureau of Justice Statistics (BJS) reported that Native Americans have a rate of arrest for alcohol violations more than double the national rate. Arrests of Native Americans under the age of 18 for alcohol-related violations are also twice the national average.[29]

Community, Culture, and Spirituality

Although the cultural independence of Native Americans has often been described as a major obstacle to economic development in tribal areas, positive relationships between adhering to cultural and religious traditions and institutions and successful reentry are well documented.[30] Cultural traditions and institutions may be an important coping strategy for tribal members who have been marginalized. Engaging in cultural and spiritual activities may help strengthen family and community networks, creating a crucial safety net that could help returning tribal members cope with many uncertainties, including those associated with low-skilled work in poor job markets.[31]

Native American culture and spirituality, often rooted in strong and long-standing tribal and family ties emphasizing both acceptance and mutual accountabilities, have increasingly been integrated into social services delivery. For example, staff at New Day Treatment Center, a substance abuse rehabilitation facility in the Keweenaw Bay Indian Community, often incorporate tribal spiritual and cultural activities like drumming, sweat lodges, and powwows into clients' individual treatment plans (at clients' requests).

Culture and spirituality have also been linked to successful transition from prison to community life. Involvement in religious organizations, for example, has been shown to be associated with decreased recidivism.[32] This association has yet to be documented for Native Americans returning to reservations, however.

In-depth, semistructured interviews were completed with 15 Native Americans living in areas throughout the UP. Our goal was to include at least one member of each of the five federally recognized tribes within the UP, target participants living on and off reservations, and at least one women. We also hoped to achieve some variation with respect to age and time since leaving prison. Staff from Northern Michigan University's Center for Native American Studies helped us identify tribal members who could distribute information about our study to potential participants. We also asked some participants for help recruiting additional participants (i.e., snowball sampling).

Our sample consisted of six members of the Keweenaw Bay Indian Community, six from the Sault Ste. Marie Tribe of Chippewas, one from the Lac Vieux Desert Band of Chippewa, one from Bay Mills Indian Community, and from one from the Hannahville Indian Community. Of the 15 participants, five had served their most recent sentences in state prisons and 10 in federal prisons. Thirteen participants were men, and two were woman. Participants' ages ranged from 24 to 64, with the average age being 42. The time since the subjects had left prison ranged from 1 month to just over 30 years, with a majority ($n = 12$) being out for five years or less.

Interviews covered a variety of topics related to reintegration, including housing, employment, health, social relationships (including family, other tribal relationships, and other friends), use of human services, education, use of time (and daily routines), and interactions with law enforcement and criminal justice systems. The following text summarizes the most prominent findings from these interviews.

Housing

Thirteen of the 15 participants (87 percent), all men, reported that obtaining stable housing was very difficult in the early stages of community reentry (postprison) due in large part to HUD regulations banning housing for ex-offenders who had been convicted of certain drug-related or sexual crimes. One man described his relationship with HUD, saying, "Ever since I been home they don't like me being in housing at all. They don't want me staying in housing even if it's just for a night." He later explained that staff from the tribal housing agency, which is also expected to enforce HUD regulations, were less threatening: "I think they kind of know . . . I mean I think they know I got places I can stay, but they just really don't say nothing." He also explained that he gets by "couch hopping" from house to house to avoid detection by HUD staff, parole officers, and even Federal Bureau of Investigation (FBI) agents who monitor parolees. When asked how he reported his address to his parole officer, he explained that he gave them one address and makes sure he stops there from time to time to get his mail.

Four participants were sex offenders and faced additional difficulties securing housing. Housing was even more difficult to find off the reservation for many participants because of residency restrictions for sex offenders. One participant explained he was not able to stay with family on the reservation because of HUD restrictions and had trouble getting housing in the surrounding community:

> I had an apartment all set up and ready and I had the first month's rent and the security deposit. And come to find out my PO says I can't live there cuz it was within 1,000 feet of a schoolyard . . . I had a lease signed and everything and then he said I couldn't stay there. Most apartments they have for rent are near the school . . .

Four participants reported they felt unwelcome to return to their families, at least initially, because their being home might put their families in jeopardy of losing their HUD housing. Despite policy restrictions and risks, several of the participants were residing with family members either full time or part time in HUD-subsidized housing units. Several participants openly discussed risks associated with returning to the reservation, where many of those with whom they might be welcome to stay reside in HUD units from which they are banned. One participant who had been living with his mother for approximately one month after being released from prison explained that he was putting her in jeopardy by staying there: "My mom and them got a letter saying they really don't want me in the house. They give her an eviction letter if I am not out in seven days."

One participant explained that he moved from house to house on the reservation to avoid detection by federal officials who monitor where ex-felons reside on the reservation. Despite staying with family or friends most nights and living on the reservation where he grew up, he considers himself homeless. As he explained, "I am really homeless right now. I just kind of bounce around back and forth from place to place until I can find my apartment."

We met with one participant at a home owned by his uncle. This young man explained that he had been informed by the tribe (through a formal letter) that he was not welcome to stay in any HUD-subsidized unit on the reservation. When the young man's uncle returned to the home during the research interview, he explained the tribe's position and the need to comply with HUD guidelines or risk sanctioning. This man (the uncle) was also a member of the tribal council that oversaw tribal compliance with federal mandates. Fully aware that taking in his nephew was a HUD violation, he simply said, "We do what we have to do to care for our own." He later explained that he would like to see the tribal council begin to develop ex-felon housing that was exempt from HUD regulations (i.e., housing that is not federally funded).

The two women in our study described having a much easier time accessing housing after their release. Both had children (one had four and the other five), and both stated that they had to request special permission from the tribe to live in HUD-subsidized tribal housing. Each was able to secure tribal housing within 30 days of these requests. Neither had been convicted of a drug- or sex-related crime, which at least partially explains the ease with which they were able to access housing.

While both of these women were relieved to have secured housing, each also explained that "living on the rez" had advantages and disadvantages. Close access to family and friends was seen as a major advantage, as it allowed them to secure childcare more easily as well as other social supports. Still, both also admitted that living amongst some people who remembered them from long ago and could recall their criminal past was sometimes problematic. Access to jobs was seen as a major disadvantage, as the reservations on which these women lived were geographically and economically isolated. Getting to work, they explained, meant driving at least an hour each way.

When asked whether they would choose to be on the reservation if they had a choice to live elsewhere, both of these women said they would because of the importance of tribal resources, both formal services like health care and housing, and informal social supports. Both also explained that living on the reservation allowed them to stay connected to Native American culture and spirituality, and to raise their children within these traditions.

Employment

Employment was described as a major issue for all participants, and the majority explained that finding steady work had been difficult. While more than half of the participants ($n = 8$) were working at the time of the interviews, all 15 participants reported that having a criminal record made finding a job difficult. One ex-offender described having to report his criminal background:

> Having to tell the truth, that's the deal breaker. I mean, I been to a couple places and it usually looks good. You know everything looks good until that. They say, "Well, ya know, this is not gonna stop you from getting the job," but then they say they're gonna give it to the guy without the felony—or as politely as they can put it. Sometimes it's just the look they give you. You know they're not gonna give you the job.

None of the participants admitted to hiding their criminal history when applying for a job, but many explained they had been tempted to do so.

Others believed their criminal past was an obstacle to getting a job but not the only barrier. All 15 participants reported facing racial discrimination, especially when applying to jobs located off the reservation. One ex-offender described difficulties with his job search and troubles with his probation officer before he moved back to his reservation:

> My parole officer in [city] was not on a good basis with me ... He just did not want my type there ... I have a record dating back to when I was 11 years old. A lengthy record. A very troubled past. And I was in kind of like the Yankee area where they didn't look too highly on Natives in that area.

Racial discrimination, several participants explained, contributed to their decision to move back to reservations.

Several participants explained that limited skills and experience also made finding a job tough, especially within a tight labor market and in remote areas with few employers. Combined with a felony conviction, a good job was often seen as entirely out of reach. One participant explained that employers will not hire people like him when there are others wanting the job, "For me not to get hired on gave me the impression that they overlooked me for someone that wasn't an ex-convict or felon, because they had that choice. So why pick me?" He later explained that the one job opportunity he did receive postrelease was given to him by another ex-offender:

> I understand recidivism and I understand that people who hire ex-cons can get their business ripped off, but dammit, give us a chance . . . Give us a chance . . . I had a chance with a tree service and I proved myself. I started at $8 an hour just a scrub lawn mower dude, throwing wood around. I moved myself up to lead ground man to the head of the landscaping crew and my departing salary of $12.50 an hour. You don't get those chances being an ex-convict. The reason I got that chance was because my boss was an ex-convict. He could relate to me, he was in my shoes.

The sentiment that outcompeting other applicants for a job was very unlikely was common among participants, which explains why several wanted to become self-employed or sought employment through less competitive channels.

Many participants viewed their tribal affiliation as the surest pathway to securing a job. While the tribes of the UP maintain hiring policies that give preference to members of federally recognized tribes, there is competition for many tribal jobs, especially in tight labor markets when numbers of natives and nonnatives applying for these positions increase. In recent years, changes to gaming policies restricting felons from working in many positions have also limited job opportunities for Native American ex-offenders. (Each of the tribes in the UP operates at least one gambling casino.)

Increasingly, tribal jobs that are available to ex-offenders are low wage, are less than full time, and do not offer health benefits other than tribal health care. For some, not being able to access good tribal jobs was viewed as a loss of status and in some cases was equated with an inability to fully live as a tribal member. The tribe, several explained, was viewed much like a family, and even the act of applying for a tribal job was fraught with emotion. One participant described the process of applying for tribal jobs and ultimately successfully landing a position:

> When I applied for positions, just the application itself was resurfacing of the wounds. You could pay your debt to society, yet they still judge you for it. I was very lucky that the tribe was willing to overlook [his crime] . . . As you know with a tribe, we are all related, it's more of a family than a business.

Family

All 15 of the participants in to study stated that family was important in their transition from prison to life outside, and all reported receiving some type of assistance from family members after their prison release. Several participants explained that their family was their greatest resource. One man described the help he received from his family, even after committing a heinous crime against another family member:

> I come from a big family and they stood beside me, they never disowned me. When you hear about how a family disowns [someone who committed a crime], it doesn't happen in Anishinabek [referring to Native American culture in the Great Lakes region], we don't do that. In fact it makes us stronger, we connect even more, and we try harder to help those ones that need help.

Like many participants, this man equated family with culture and explained that Native American family members do not turn their backs on one another, especially those who have had difficulty. This man, along with several other participants, also described lines between family and community as being transparent. In several interviews, we heard participants explain that it was often difficult to distinguish close blood relatives from other tribal members, who are very often considered extended family.

While families were always described as important, family members were not always able to support participants, especially during incarceration. Twelve participants (75 percent) had served federal as opposed to state sentences and therefore spent several years hundreds, and in some cases thousands, of miles from home. All 12 explained that the only family contact they had during their sentences was via emails, letters, and phone calls because their families lacked the financial resources to visit. One woman explained she was unable to see her children for several years:

"I was far away from family and friends. I would write to the children and my aunt would take my phone calls because she is the one that had the kids and that was about twice a month that I talked to the kids. My only priority was getting out and getting my children back." One man explained that when he returned from prison, he was excited to see his children, but that it was strange at first because he had not seen them in 18 months:

> My initial return, I was happy to be back . . . It was kind of awkward at first. I got there in the middle of the night, the kids got up the next morning and I was just there. It was good to see them again, they grew up so much in the 18 months that I was gone.

As already explained, family contact during incarceration has been shown to help offenders maintain a support system they can rely on following release. Lack of personal contact with those living outside prison can jeopardize offenders' perceptions of support, if not the actual support available. Many also often wondered what, if any, help they would receive after their release.

A few participants described how they isolated themselves from both their family and community for several months after being released because of shame related to crimes committed and apprehension of facing those who they feared they had let down. Feelings of shame and guilt were common among the participants, especially those whose offenses had involved family members. An inability to mend relationships during prison sentences, some explained, exacerbated these feelings.

Family-related anxieties were especially common for parents, who in addition to being separated from parents, siblings, and partners, often felt a sense of angst related to being unable to maintain a parental role while in prison. In some cases, incarceration meant losing custody of children. This was true for both women in the study, who explained they could not rely on their children's fathers to care for the children while they were in prison, so their children entered Michigan's child protection service (CPS) system. When possible, Native American children in CPS are placed with other Native Americans as per the Indian Child Welfare Act (ICWA). Three of the 15 participants (20 percent) explained they had benefitted from ICWA because their children were placed with Native American families during their incarceration (and in some cases placed with extended family members). Placement with Native American families is not always possible, however. One woman explained her frustration with both losing custody of her daughter after her arrest and her fear that her daughter will lose her cultural identify before they are reunited:

> I had not seen anyone from my family for almost six years, and it was pretty hard. Two of my kids are currently with family, one is incarcerated and my oldest is in a Caucasian home, a white home. She is off the reservation. I don't like it, it takes away from the way that we live, they don't have stuff for her the we have here and it's going to be a different transition for her coming back (to the reservation). She still goes to powwow's and ceremonies, but she don't ask questions when it's over because she just goes right back to that house.

At the time of the interviews, neither woman had yet regained custody of their children; however, both were hopeful that reunification would happen soon. Still, both feared that they would not be able to reestablish the bonds they had had with their children prior to incarceration, especially with children who had been living off the reservation for an extended period. For them, family and tribe were intricately connected.

Community

All 15 participants listed tribal membership as the single most important factor in their community reintegration. One ex-offender described his "tribal number," or the identification number on tribal membership cards, as his "greatest asset." Loss of community, several participants explained, was the most difficult part of being in prison. All participants reported having lived on a reservation prior to their imprisonment, and all—even those who were sometimes unable to access these benefits—explained that help from the tribe in the form of access to housing, jobs, and employment was critical.

In many cases, tribal assistance and resources came through informal tribal channels. Reports of receiving help from other tribal members in the form of transportation, money, housing, and spiritual and other counseling were common. One participant described his relationship to other tribal members:

> When you're a tribal member you're related. Somewhere you go back far enough you're related to everyone in that tribe, it's more of a family. It is more so a family than a business. If you apply for a job outside the tribe you're going to stand less of a chance of getting a job. As soon as they see that

box checked that you have a felony they are probably going to just throw it in the trash can. So yes, being in the tribe obviously has its advantages.

Being part of a small and intricately tied community has advantages and disadvantages for ex-offenders returning to reservations. Many are returning to communities where they committed crimes and to family and friends against whom crimes were committed. For some, this resulted in intense feelings of shame and guilt. At the same time, most also reported that family and community members welcomed them, even when they were attempting to isolate themselves for a period.

One man explained the shame he felt when he returned home. He had been sentenced for sex offenses against family members. He isolated himself from his family. He even missed his father's funeral, which is considered the most sacred ceremony in his tribe. Instead of shunning him, however, his friends and family expressed great concern:

It took a while because my family was still mad and upset at me for what I did and of course I kind of isolated myself too. My sister and my dad were the only ones who contacted me. I kind of knew what my family was doing and I just stayed to myself out at my home. I didn't get to start seeing my brothers and sister until after my dad had died. My brother wanted everybody over at the house, but I didn't show up. That shocked everybody I guess, then family started showing up at my house saying, what's the matter. They wanted me back in their lives but it took a long time for me because I was ashamed for what I have done. I still have a hard time with that. All I can do is go on from here and try to be the best that I can.

Being a tribal member gave many participants a sense that there was help available no matter what difficulties they faced, even when assistance was limited by resource availability and policy constraints (e.g., HUD housing policies, gaming-related employment practices, and MITW residency requirements). One participant had been prevented from returning to his reservation after this prison release. He described his postprison life as a "new sentence." A federal judge, he explained, had banished him from his reservation for 18 months, which disqualified him from tribal housing assistance, tribal employment, and Indian health services. At the time of the interview, he was homeless and living outdoors, 15 miles away from his reservation. He described the difficulties he faced being away from the reservation and the injustice of not being able to go home:

It's really hard for me cause I never lived off our reservation on my own in my life. I never did. I have always had people around me that would help me if I needed to. Place of employment and background checks and everything else. When I found out it was really, really hard. The federal government when they sentenced me to the four months and the three months in the halfway house, they also sentenced me to be banished from my rez for 18 months. I'm still 9 months outside of that, so that is pretty hard.

For this man and for several other participants, living off the reservation was seen as unimaginable. Despite few jobs, and often limited housing prospects, reservation life is almost universally viewed as preferable to living outside the tribal area.

Cultural and spiritual connectedness to others in the community partially explains some participants' preference for living on the reservation. One participant described the importance of community to Native Americans while explaining that those who follow Anishinabek (culture of Native Americans in the Great Lakes region) ways of helping other individuals help the whole community, which in turn makes you stronger. More than half ($n = 8$) of the participants described participating in Native American spiritual and religious events (including sweat lodges, drum circles, powwows, and other ceremonies) and attributed their spirituality with their abilities to reacquire meaningful and fulfilling roles within their families and communities. As one man explains his initial reunion with his community after leaving prison:

Friends came up with the drum right away. And they came over and we had sweat lodges . . . I would probably be lost without it [culture]. I was very proud of my culture, cause I kind of grew up with it—my mother, dad, grandfather. Most of the cultural ways. Of course, mom wanted us to have spirituality somehow so she also took us to the Catholic Church. Of course, when I went up for services she'd say, "Don't forget who you are."

Human Services and Education

As stated previously, the majority of participants' most recent prison sentences were in federal as opposed to state prisons. (Eleven served federal and four served state prison sentences.) Interview data suggest that federal and state ex-offenders' experiences with postprison reentry services varied substantially. Those who served state sentences reported having a much wider array of service options than those who served federal sentences.

The four former state inmates were all enrolled in Michigan Prisoner Reentry Initiative (MPRI) services, which included an array of services, including housing assistance (in one case more than six months of fully funded housing), substance abuse treatment, transportation assistance (including bus tokens and occasional taxi vouchers), mental health counseling, job training and placement services, and general case management.

MPRI was very much appreciated by the four former state inmates. One former MPRI client described how fortunate he felt to be able to access these services:

> Before living here [where he currently resides] I stayed at the hotel across the road for six months. I have been in this one for over a year. I have no complaints about how the MPRI has treated me; they have helped me out a lot. Like I said they pay for me to stay here, provide me with bus tickets to get to my AA meetings and $50 Walmart cards to go shopping every month. When I first got out it was $100 for food and clothing. Because of my disabilities the MPRI paid for my prescriptions for a year. They been helping us the best they can you know, if it wasn't for them I'd have no place to go.

Those who had served federal sentences reported having a more meager array of postrelease services, typically consisting of no more than a bus ticket and a few dollars for lunch and dinner on the long ride home. One participant described his postrelease services: "They just released me. I was basically on my own. When you leave the federal prison they give you a couple dollars and a bus ticket. For the ride home they gave me $35 and it was a 25-hour bus ride to Lower Michigan to a halfway house."

Several participants ($n = 10$) were enrolled in substance abuse treatment and/or were attending Alcoholics Anonymous meetings at the time of the interviews. MPRI clients often had access to both inpatient and outpatient substance abuse treatment services after their release. Federal parolees' access to services varied by tribe. (None reported that they were able to access services through federal probation.) Some tribes provided extensive recovery-oriented services to members, and others offered relatively little in the way of treatment options.

Recovery was difficult for many participants returning to reservations, especially in the early stages of reintegration. One participant described the challenge of returning to the community where he had had difficulty with substance use in the past:

I have become depressed over all this. Being sober means I have lost family and friends. Much of my family and childhood friends are actively addicted and they really choose not to be around me, even my siblings. We really don't have much to talk about, I don't know if it's whether they are afraid of me or because I have been through all of this. I don't know, maybe it might be out of respect [because he is not using substances] . . . In order for me to get involved with them again would be for me to get involved in that whole circle again. To be trusted by them in that aspect you almost have to be right alongside them. It's just an awkward feeling for me to be around them and be sober.

In many cases, avoiding friends and family with whom ex-offenders had previously been close is not only an adaptive behavior, it is law. As many participants explained, their parole officers mandate that they not share a home or fraternize with other ex-offenders. For some participants, this law was a mixed blessing. It provided several participants with additional incentive to stay clear of those with whom they might be tempted to reoffend, but it is also severely limited social circles in some cases. As one participant explained:

Ever since treatment and everything else it's been so hard. It's been emotionally draining. Being locked up is easier than going through this. Just to get back to nothing, which is where I am at right now, basically homeless, is a lot for me to handle . . . I am grateful for my sobriety, but I am not even able to go on my reservation. I can't even get counseling for my depression from the tribe.

All 10 participants who reported being in recovery for substance abuse explained that their culture was an invaluable asset in their recovery efforts. Spirituality and recovery from addiction were viewed as intricately connected. For some, recovery offered an opportunity to begin to understand and appreciate Native American spiritual beliefs. For others, recovery offered a chance to revisit spiritual beliefs and religious practices of their past. One participant explained the personal and spiritual meaning of his recovery, which incorporates the Native American concept of the "red road," the right path:

Walking the Red Road is what I rely on, it keeps me sober and . . . away from drugs, it's what saved my life literally. It's a hard thing to put into words because it's so personal to everyone. It's what I am trying to teach my grandchildren, they are out there in that circle dancing and I have never been more proud to be a Native American. There were times growing up being Native American was not too cool and now without that spirituality and the family of the tribe I wouldn't have pride. I do now . . . All I need in my life is my family and my people. A lot of times the courts mandate you to AA or other programs and they don't fit everybody. Some of the programs meant nothing to me. The spirituality just felt right you know, I started going to sweats, started going to ceremonies, started being proud of being Native American. That spirituality is every day. I was lucky to have that choice where I did not have to attend mandated programs where they are a lot more ridged with the steps . . . to go back into society to be a productive person. For native people we understand it that this way of life is here for you when you are ready.

In addition to fewer human services, several federal parolees were also disadvantaged in their access to education. MITW is the result of a long-standing treaty between the state and federally recognized tribes that guarantees tuition at state universities at no charge to tribal members. Those who serve federal sentences out of state do not qualify when they are released, however, because MITW has a one-year minimum state residency requirement.

Several participants enrolled in community colleges or universities shortly after their release because they saw education as one means of compensating for the disadvantages of a criminal record and gaps in work histories. Many reported that having to wait a year to enroll was difficult, especially when faced with limited access to jobs. One participant described his decision to self-finance enrollment at a private university:

Going to school was one of my priorities. I started going right away . . .
I started to go to school for business management online through Phoenix, that was very expensive. None of my education could be paid for [by the state] because I didn't live in the area for the past year. I was like, "Wow, there goes $21,000." If I would have been sentenced in a state prison I would have been eligible for the Michigan Indian Tuition Wavier. After this summer I would have resided in the state of Michigan for a year and now when I go to school I can use all my overages [student loan money in excess of tuition] to pay off those loans.

The interview data presented in this discussion suggest that social ecological theory, which focuses on interactions between individuals and their social environments and interactions between social systems and how these create unique opportunities and constraints for individuals, may be a helpful framework in explaining Native American parolees' experiences transitioning from prisons to communities in rural and remote areas.

Urie Bronfenbrenner's social ecological framework, the process-person-context model, divides social environments into levels or system types.[33] Microsystems refer to individuals' immediate surroundings. Families, friends, other tribal members, and relationships with law enforcement personnel (including parole officers) are relevant microsystems in this analysis. Mesosystems refer to interactions between microsystems. In this analysis, relevant mesosystems include family and law enforcement personnel, family and tribes, and friends and law enforcement personnel. Exosystems include social institutions operating locally and for this analysis include HUD, law enforcement agencies, and federal, state, and tribal governments (and the programs they offer). Because of political inequities, these systems create many systematic disadvantages for Native Americans leaving prison. Macrosystems are what Bronfenbrenner refers to as the cultural blueprints that shape social institutions. Relevant macrosystems in this analysis include attitudes toward ex-offenders and racism.[34]

The most important microsystems relevant to our participants' reintegration were relationships with family and friends, especially other tribal members. Many saw family and friends as even more important than employment and housing because close relationships were see as integral to "mino-bimaadiziwin," living a good, balanced life. Family almost always provided tangible resources, including housing, food and money, to those returning from prison. Some participants explained that they were sometimes estranged from family members while in prison—both because of shame they felt for crimes committed and irregularity of contact (often because they served sentences far from home). Most, however, also explained that families were very receptive to them when they returned home and offered critical help, including emotional support. In some cases, extended family members also cared for prisoners' children during incarceration.

The perceived roles of friends in community reintegration experiences were mixed. Some saw them as positive, offering emotional and tangible supports, while others viewed them negatively, especially when friends use drugs and alcohol or commit crimes that could jeopardize the ex-offender's parole. Other tribal members were viewed positively, and almost all participants stressed the importance of belonging to a tight-knit community and accessing tangible and emotional supports throughout the tribe. In some cases, nonfamily tribal members cared for prisoners' children during incarceration, which was important to many prisoners who wanted their children to develop an understanding of and appreciation for Native American culture. Relationships with tribal members, many explained, were also a vehicle for engaging in cultural and spiritual aspects of the community, which many believed were critical to their reintegration.

It was clear that participants' microsystems often interacted in unique ways and that these interactions or mesosystems were also important in understanding reintegration experiences. Parolees' relationships with family and law enforcement agents, especially parole officers, interacted in ways that created unique dilemmas. As discussed earlier, family was seen as critical to successfully transitioning from prison to communities, and participants relied heavily on family, especially immediately after their release. Many participants also explained that family help sometimes put them at risk of a parole violation, as parole officers often enforced both HUD policies (which do not allow ex-felons to reside in HUD-subsidized units, even when staying with family members) and parole restrictions that do not allow parolees to fraternize with other felons, including those within the family. There were several cases in which participants returned to reservations and were staying with family members but kept a separate mailing address to avoid detection by law enforcement agents. Several spoke of the need to live "under the radar" and having to sometimes "couch surf" to avoid parole violations. Many were also concerned with putting their families at risk, as families who violate HUD policies may lose their housing.

Tribes themselves are often the first enforcers of HUD policies, as they have an interest in avoiding violations on reservations, which could compromise relationships with federal agencies. Taking in family members returning from prison and violating HUD policies may put families at risk of tribal sanction. For the returning ex-offender, navigating these relationships requires foresight and care.

Prior studies have shown that the goals of parole officers and the expectations and goals of Native American parolees often differ. Parole officers typically stress the importance of searching for a job, securing employment, and obtaining permanent housing. Native American parolees are often less focused on attaining formal employment and an independent address than on establishing or reestablishing meaningful roles within their families and communities.[35] Tribal communities and traditional families often expect those returning from prison to contribute to and engage in cultural and spiritual activities, offer help to those in need, and become a strong presence in community and family life. Formal employment and independent housing are important but secondary to community and family responsibilities.

As with family, parolees' relationships with friends were also often at odds with their relationships with law enforcement agents. While most participants stated they looked forward to reengaging with friends after prison, especially fellow tribal members, they were fearful of comprising relationships with parole agents. The incarceration rate for Native Americans is more than twice that of whites, and parole conditions restricting fraternization with other convicted felons make it difficult for parolees to reengage with many in their communities.[36] Some participants viewed their parole conditions as an opportunity to avoid those who might lead them to using drugs and alcohol, and ultimately crime. Some ignored this condition (and interacted with other ex-felons despite parole conditions). More common were situations in which parolees interacted with other ex-felons on a limited basis while being careful to avoid detection.

Tribal traditions often include more senior tribal members serving as role models for junior members with whom they share common life histories. It is not uncommon for ex-felons who have successfully reentered society to mentor others returning from prison. This is a norm and has become an expectation for both mentors and new parolees. While mentorship itself is generally viewed favorably across society, law enforcement agencies rarely allow it to occur between ex-felons.

For many Native American parolees, interacting with other tribal members—even engaging in simple activities like hunting, fishing, gathering foods, and spending time outdoors—is important in the process of reconnecting with the community. These are often viewed as spiritual and/or cultural activities and are often associated with mino-bimaadiziwin (a good, balanced life). They may also reduce risks of recidivism. These acts are also often viewed as tribal rights, and preventing parolees from engaging in them can be seen as a threat to sovereignty.

At times, the most important systems in understanding our participants' reintegration experiences were those outside their immediate social circles. In social ecology, these systems are known as exosystems. Legal systems and government programs that create disadvantages for Native Americans leaving prison are important exosystems in understanding participants' reintegration experiences. The Major Crimes Act, for example, strips tribal courts of jurisdiction in many cases that involve crimes on reservations.

This creates systematic disadvantages for many Native Americans, who often serve sentences far from home, sometimes thousands of miles away. Those serving federal sentences are also ineligible for state-funded program like MPRI that are aimed at assisting those transitioning from prison. The federal government offers very few services for those leaving prison to help in their transition. Similarly, while tribes are sovereign governments and enter agreements with the federal government to create HUD-subsidized housing on reservations, HUD policies that restrict housing for many ex-offenders essentially take away tribes' (and families') abilities to help those transitioning from prison, especially on reservations where the percentages of households in HUD-funded housing is high.

Several socio-cultural factors or macrosystems were critical to understanding reintegration of Native Americans from prison to their home communities. All participants reported, for example, that negative attitudes toward ex-offenders, especially by employers, made the transition from prison more difficult. Punitive policies that embody these attitudes often restricted ex-offenders' access to housing, education, and even entire reservations. Racism toward Native Americans was a common experience, and some participants viewed living on reservations as an attractive option because it allowed them to escape these attitudes. At the same time, participants universally viewed being Native American positively and expressed that being a tribal member was a benefit rather than a detriment in their transition from prison.

Implications

Policies like the Major Crimes Act, HUD housing restrictions, residency requirements for the MITW, and parole conditions restricting parolees from fraternizing with other ex-felons create disadvantages for Native American parolees. In Michigan, Native American parolees are typically ineligible for reentry services through MPRI because they served federal as opposed to state sentences. The federal government offers almost no reentry assistance services.

In addition to creating disadvantages at an individual level, these policies also limit tribal sovereignty by placing severe limits on tribes' abilities to help members returning to their communities. Whereas nonnatives leaving prison typically return to their families and home communities, many Native Americans do so at great risk to themselves, their families, and their tribes. In addition, the yearlong residency requirement of the MITW, created by treaty between the state of Michigan and federally recognized tribes, essentially allows the state to deny ex-offenders a tribal right.

Federal, state, and tribal governments should critically evaluate these policies and remove those that create systematic disadvantages for Native Americans. If Native Americans are subject to the provisions of the Major Crimes Act and receive federal sentences for crimes for which others would receive a sentence in a state prison, efforts should be made to allow prisoners to serve time closer to family, in the nearest federal prisons. Tribal and criminal justice system resources should be devoted to helping families remain connected to members serving prison sentences, especially those in prisons far from home. Native Americans who become federal as opposed to state parolees because of the Major Crimes Act should be made eligible for state prisoner reentry services. The yearlong residency requirement for the MITW should be removed for those who left the state to serve a federal prison sentence. Requirements that restrict parolees from associating with other ex-felons should be removed on reservations to allow Native American parolees to live fully as tribal members, participating in tribal events and mentoring others facing similar difficulties.

Federal, state, and tribal government agencies should collaborate in creating programs for returning parolees to address their housing, employment, education, and other service needs. Developing housing on reservations for those exiting prison should be created to house those without other housing resources. Programs should also be created to help those in prison maintain contacts with family and other tribal members during incarceration. This will help make the transition home an easier one following release. Additional resources should be created for families with members serving prison sentences to allow children to remain with other family members or at least remain in the tribe. This may require outreach to create more foster care options within tribes.

Whatever programs are created to assist Native Americans transitioning from prisons to communities, services should respect Native American cultures and build on, rather than compromise, traditional methods of helping by tribes and families. Policies that prevent families from taking in other family members after being released from prison and restrict ex-felons who successfully reintegrated into tribal communities from mentoring new parolees should be reconsidered. These policies not only make community reintegration difficult, they also undermine traditional values and basic tribal sovereignty.

Finally, reentry programs should be designed to foster reintegration in every sense of the word. Existing programs designed around reducing recidivism and promoting employment and housing stability are valuable, but they do not fully reflect communities'—nor parolees'—interests and values. The concept of reintegration encompasses more than just having formal employment, having an official residence, and staying out of prison. It is also includes reestablishing meaningful roles within communities and families, contributing to community and family life, and becoming immersed in cultural and spiritual aspects of an area. For many Native Americans, reintegration is as much or more about living as a member of a tribe, giving to others in the community, and engaging in cultural and spiritual activities than having formal employment and an official residence.

Definitions of successful reintegration should be reconsidered to fully reflect cultural variations discussed in this chapter. For many Native Americans, formal definitions of reentry success as defined by parole officers and reentry program staff are foreign. For them, the Anishinabek concept of "nnmino-yaa," which encompasses tribal affiliation, community engagement, giving to others, and living in harmony and balance with natural, spiritual, and social environments is a more meaningful version of success. Achieving this requires active engagement with families and other tribal members, participating in ceremonies and traditions, and self-reflection. Having a job and permanent residence may or may not be necessary, but alone they are insufficient for achieving a personal and culturally relevant sense of success.

Notes

1. Visher and Travis, 2003.
2. U.S. Department of Housing and Urban Development, 2012.
3. Upper Peninsula Economic Development Alliance, 2009.
4. Kleinfeld and Kruse, 1977.
5. Hartney and Vuong, 2009.
6. Cobb and Mullins, 2010.
7. Hagan and Peterson, 1995.
8. Petersilia, 2003.
9. Pew Center on the States, 2010.
10. Petersilia, 2003.
11. Petersilia, 2003.
12. Nelson, Deess, and Allen, 2011.

13. Rhine, Smith, and Jackson, 1991.

14. Sampson and Laub, 1993.

15. Lipsey, 1995.

16. Bernstein and Houston, 2000.

17. Petersilia, 2003.

18. State of Michigan, Department of Technology, 2012.

19. U.S. Department of Labor: Bureau of Labor Statistics, 2012.

20. Mentor and Wilkinson, n.d.

21. Alliance for Excellent Education, 2006.

22. Taylor, 2008, p. 55.

23. Klein, Bartholomew, and Hibbert, 2002.

24. Garland, Spohl, and Wodahl, 2008, p. 7.

25. Visher et al., 2004.

26. Visher et al., 2004.

27. U.S. Department of Health and Human Services, Office of the Inspector General, 2009.

28. Urban Institute, n.d.

29. Greenfield and Smith, 1999.

30. O'Connor, Duncan, and Quillard, 2006.

31. Pickering, 2000.

32. O'Connor, Duncan, and Quillard, 2006.

33. Bronfenbrenner, 1993.

34. Bronfenbrenner, 1993, p. 39.

35. Nielsen, 1993.

36. Hartney and Vuong, 2009.

References

Alliance for Excellent Education. *Issue Brief: Saving Futures, Saving Dollars; The Impact of Education on Crime Reduction and Earnings*. Washington, DC: Alliance for Excellent Education, 2006.

Bernstein, Jared and Ellen Houston. *Crime and Work: What We Can Learn from the Low-Wage Labor Market*. Washington, DC: Economic Policy Institute, 2000.

Bronfenbrenner, Urie. Ecological Models of Human Development. In *Readings on the Development of Children* (2nd ed.), edited by Mary Gauvain and Michael Cole, 37–43. New York: Freeman, 1993.

Cobb, Kimberly, and Tracy G. Mullins. *Tribal Probation: An Overview for Tribal Court Judges*. Washington, DC: Bureau of Justice Assistance, U.S. Department of Justice, 2010.

Garland, Brett, Cassia Spohn, and Eric Wodahl. "Racial Disproportionality in the American Prison Population: Using the Blumstein Method to Address the

Critical Race and Justice Issue of the 21st Century." *Justice Policy Journal* 5, no. 2 (2008): 4–42.

Greenfield, Lawrence, and Steven Smith. *American Indians and Crime*. Washington, DC: U.S. Department of Justice, Bureau of Justice Statistics, 1999.

Hagan, John, and Ruth D. Peterson. *Crime and Inequality*. Stanford, CA: Stanford University Press, 1995.

Hartney, Christopher, and Linh Vuong. *Created Equal: Racial and Economic Disparities in the U.S. Criminal Justice System*. Oakland, CA: National Council of Crime and Delinquency, 2009.

Klein, Shirley, Geannina Bartholomew, and Jeff Hibbert. "Inmate Family Functioning." *International Journal of Offender Therapy and Comparative Criminology* 46, no. 1 (2002): 95–111.

Kleinfeld, Judith, and Jack Kruse. *High School: Views of North Slope Borough Students*. Fairbanks: University of Alaska: Institute of Social and Economic Research, 1977.

Lipsey, Mark. "What Do We Learn from 400 Research Studies on the Effectiveness of Treatment with Juvenile Delinquents?" In *What Works: Reducing Reoffending: Guidelines from Research and Practice*, edited by James MacGuire, pp. 63–78. Oxford: John Wiley and Sons, 1995.

Mentor, Kenneth W., and Mary Wilkinson. "Literacy in Corrections." *Ken Mentor Papers*, n.d. Accessed June 3, 2012, http://kenmentor.com/papers/literacy.htm.

Nelson, Marta, Perry Deess, and Charlotte Allen. "The First Night Out: Post-Incarceration Experiences in New York City." *Federal Sentencing Reporter* 24, no. 1 (2011): 72–75.

Nielsen, Marianne. *Surviving in Between: A Case Study of a Canadian Aboriginal-Operated Criminal Justice Organization*. Alberta: University of Alberta, 1993.

O'Connor, Thomas, Jeff Duncan, and Frank Quillard. "Criminology and Religion: The Shape of an Authentic Dialogue." *Criminology and Public Policy* 5, no. 3 (2006): 559–570.

Petersilia, Joan. *When Prisoners Come Home: Parole and Prisoner Reentry*. New York: Oxford University Press, 2003.

Pew Center on the States. *Prison Count, 2010*. Washington, DC: Pew Charitable Trusts, 2010.

Pickering, Kathleen Ann. *Lakota Culture, World Economy*. Lincoln: University of Nebraska Press, 2000.

Rhine, Edward, William Smith, and Ronald Jackson. *Paroling Authorities: Recent History and Current Practices*. Alexandria, VA: American Correctional Association, 1991.

Sampson, Robert, and John Laub. *Crime in the Making: Pathways and Turning Points through Life*. Cambridge, MA: Harvard University Press, 1993.

State of Michigan, Department of Technology. *Michigan's Unemployment Rate Declines again in April.* Lansing: Michigan Department of Technology, 2012.

Taylor, Jon Marc. "Pell Grants for Prisoners: Why Should We Care?" *Straight Low Magazine* 9, no. 2 (2008): 55.

Upper Peninsula Economic Development Alliance. *An Economic Opportunity Study for the Michigan Upper Peninsula/Wisconsin Border Region,* Escanaba, MI: Upper Peninsula Economic Development Alliance, 2009.

Urban Institute. Recent Findings from the Urban Institute on Substance Use and Reentry. *Urban Institute Research of Record,* n.d. Accessed June 23, 2012, http://www.urban.org/projects/reentry-portfolio/substance-use.cfm.

U.S. Department of Health and Human Services, Office of the Inspector General. *HIS Contract Health Services Program: Overpayments and Potential Saving.* Washington, DC: DHHS, 2009.

U.S. Department of Housing and Urban Development. *Code of Federal Regulations, Title 24,* 2012. Accessed July 10, 2012, http://cfr.vlex.com/vid/960-204-denial-admission-household-19929862.

U.S. Department of Labor: Bureau of Labor Statistics. *Local Area Unemployment Statistics Map.* http://data.bls.gov/map/MapToolServlet, Accessed July 7, 2012.

Visher, Christy, et al. *Baltimore Prisoners' Experiences Returning Home.* Washington, DC: Urban Institute, 2004.

Visher, Christy A., and Jeremy Travis. "Transitions from Prison to Community: Understanding Individual Pathways." *Annual Review of Sociology* 29 (2003): 89–113.

Chapter 24

Race and the Death Penalty in America

Danielle Dirks[1] and Emma Zack

The death penalty survives not as the ultimate punishment, but because it was primarily a form of punishment against the black flesh and black freedom.[2]

Introduction

"This may as well be 1921, a lynching just happened in Georgia, and nobody could do a thing to stop it."[3] The date, in fact, was 90 years later, on September 21, 2011. And there was not just one execution on this particular evening in America, but two. The first, an African-American man named Troy Anthony Davis, who had served more than 20 years on Georgia's death row for the killing of a white police officer, Mark MacPhail. The second, a white man named Lawrence Brewer, who had served over 10 years on Texas's death row for the killing of an African-American man named James Byrd. While Davis's execution garnered international attention for the long-standing claims surrounding his innocence, the juxtaposition and racial implications of his execution alongside Brewer's were addressed by only a few commentators. These cases beg further attention together as they help to illustrate the way that the modern death penalty in America operates in the post–civil rights era.

September 21, 2011, was Troy Davis's fourth set execution date. His case was said to be unique for a number of reasons. First, no physical evidence linked him to the death of Officer Mark Allen MacPhail. Second, seven of the nine original eyewitnesses had recanted their testimony, revealing over the years that the police who had interrogated them had coerced and threatened them with worsening their own standings within the criminal justice system. Of the two witnesses who had not recanted their testimony, one man was the individual thought to be the actual murderer, Samuel "Redd" Coles, who a few witnesses reported had admitted to—even bragged about—the killing. He has since passed away. The question of Davis's innocence plagued his case and his supporters for decades. On the night of his execution, the world watched and waited as any last chances for a halt to his execution lost out. He was pronounced dead by lethal injection at 11:08 p.m.[4]

Meanwhile, in Texas, Lawrence Brewer was making "a mockery out of the process" by refusing to eat a single morsel of his "elaborate" final meal before his execution.[5] His case was unique for an entirely different set of reasons. He and John William King had been sentenced to death in the lynching death of James Byrd, a 67-year-old African-American man whom they beat before dragging him behind a truck, mutilating and dismembering his body over the course of several miles.[6] Byrd, according to his autopsy, was likely conscious for the entire event, prior to his arm and head being severed.[7] There was no question that the men were known white supremacists within the area.[8] The crime shook not only the small town of Jasper where the lynching took place, but the entire nation. While Texas has a long and active death penalty record, what made this case unique was that it was the first time in the state's illustrious history that a white defendant was sentenced to death for killing a black victim. The year was 1999.

Viewed together, these two cases paint a picture of an America that places equal value on citizens' lives when it comes to reserving state killing for the "worst of the worst." An eye for an eye, a life for a life—no matter the race, ethnicity, or backgrounds of the individuals unfortunately involved. Absent from this picture, though, is the long and troubling racial history of America's death penalty that helped to shape these cases from their beginnings. Discussions of these two cases distanced them from this highly racialized history, creating the appearance of a colorblind justice system in the administration of death.

In the case of Troy Davis, proponents of his "long-awaited" execution argued racism could not be a factor in his case because not only was he sentenced to death by a "jury of his peers" (seven out of 12 jurors were also African American), but that the witnesses who had testified against him were also his peers. It was also argued that the lengthy appeals process and even the extraordinary nature of the U.S. Supreme Court's role in his case meant the system was working and that Davis's claims were about a "fair shake" as a death row inmate could get in Georgia, a state plagued by racial discrimination in its death sentencing. In the case of Lawrence

Brewer (and his co-defendant, Bill King), prosecutors could affirm their commitment to "equal" treatment under the law, political figures could demonstrate a collective outrage over the brutal lynching, and death penalty proponents could now point to their cases to dismiss any claims of a racist administration of justice in Texas. This, in a state where despite white-on-black racial violence permeating every facet of social life, whites used lynching and state-sanctioned executions to target African-American men, women, and children for most of its history.[9] Some may point to the details of these cases and argue that the death penalty has progressed to the point where executions are fairly applied. Whereas a century prior, Troy Davis most certainly would have been lynched for being accused of killing a white man (as were thousands of other African Americans) and Lawrence Brewer (and his accomplices) most certainly would have lynched a black man with impunity, today people can look to the juxtaposition of these cases and argue that the death penalty is applied fairly and equitably.

Except it is not. For anyone with knowledge of American racial relations or history, it should come as no surprise that racial bias and discrimination plague American capital punishment. Racial and ethnic bias, discrimination, and disparities are found in every area of American life and institutions, including housing, education, employment, politics, health, and wealth. It would somehow be freakish if the ultimate penal sanction, deeply tied to the undeniably racist contemporary administration of the American criminal justice and legal systems, were free of racial and ethnic discrimination.

Rather than a progressive, or even "modern," capital punishment system, we argue that the death penalty looks no different than it did in other eras of our history when racial bias and antipathy drove death sentencing and the killing of black bodies and black flesh. In this chapter, we begin with a brief overview of the American death penalty before demonstrating how racial bias mars every stage and facet of the capital system, from arrest to the postconviction period. In doing so, we hope to demonstrate that far from having an equitable system of justice today, race illegitimately plays a significant extralegal factor that continues to unfairly determine who lives and who dies in America today.

The American Death Penalty

The American death penalty dates back to the colonial era when thousands of individuals were executed for a range of death-eligible crimes that were far expanded beyond that of capital murder today.[10] In the early South, in addition to executions, whites carried out thousands of lynchings and "legal lynchings" of African-American men, women, and children.[11] To spread a message of white supremacy and racial and gender domination, whites targeted individuals who threatened the current social order and the institution of slavery both during and after its end.[12] Over 85 percent of the persons lynched during this time were African Americans accused of committing any number of minor offenses involving property or alleged crimes against white people.[13] This unequal justice was codified into law as states developed several death-eligible crimes for African Americans but few or none for whites.[14] For example, in Mississippi, African Americans could be executed for 38 crimes, but not a single crime committed by whites warranted an execution.[15] Despite some revisions, little has changed in terms of the racial dynamics of death sentencing today. African Americans are still disproportionately sentenced to death and are executed. This is particularly true if they are defendants in cases involving white victims. This pattern holds true for persons of Latino and Hispanic descent as well.[16] When looking at the bulk of evidence on racial disparities in sentences and executions, the racial patterns that held true then continue to hold true today.[17] This has led many legal scholars, including as Stephen B. Bright (2006) to conclude, "The death penalty is a direct descendent of lynching and other forms racial violence and racial oppression in America."[18] It is within this vein that many scholars argue that state-sanctioned executions simply came to replace lynchings as they became increasingly viewed as illegitimate forms of racial violence.[19]

This continued use of executions has earned the United States the distinction of being a world leader for the death penalty, alongside nations with abysmal human rights records such as China, Iran, Iraq, and Saudi Arabia.[20] Currently, 33 U.S. states use the death penalty as a criminal punishment, and 3,170 people await death on America's death rows.[21] Each year over the past decade, execution teams have strapped roughly 40 to 50 human beings to gurneys and then have pumped lethal drugs into their veins with the explicit goal of killing them. It is indeed odd that a Western democracy would still be engaged in the practice of killing its own citizens when the rest of the Western industrialized world abandoned the practice—formally or in practice—decades ago.[22] Yet capital punishment is not the only aspect of the American penal system that has placed the United States in stark contrast with other democracies.

The American penal system has come to serve as the largest racialized mass incapacitation program the world has ever known. In the past 30 years, the penal population in America has exploded from roughly 300,000 to more than 2 million people.[23] Today, the United States incarcerates 1 in 100 of its citizens, which is the highest rate of incarceration per capita in the world.[24] In addition to the massive size of this program, American jails and prisons are overwhelmingly and disproportionately filled with citizens of color. One in three African-American men will serve time in a prison over the course of their lives.[25] Latino men comprise the fastest growing population of prisoners today, and women's rates of incarceration have skyrocketed since the early 1980s.[26] This negative impact is further compounded by tough on crime policies that establish lengthy and mandatory sentencing schemas such as three strikes and truth in sentencing legislation. The racial disproportionality can be seen on America's death rows as well. African Americans make up approximately 12 percent of the American population, yet comprise 42 percent of those on death row.[27] In this context, America's retention of executions as a form of criminal punishment aligns closely with the broader racialized form of contemporary penal control that is characterized by an imprisonment binge.

Post-Furman Era

The United States, however, has not always used the death penalty. After a powerful civil rights movement in this country exposed the illegitimacy of racial sentencing and execution disparities, the U.S. Supreme Court ruled it unconstitutional in 1972 with the landmark *Furman vs. Georgia* decision. After a decade without a single execution, the decision invalidated all states' death penalty statutes on the grounds that the death penalty—as it was practiced—was capricious and arbitrary in its application and was thus unconstitutional.

In the wake of *Furman*, states rushed to develop new death penalty statutes.[28] In 1976, the U.S. Supreme Court ruled on five cases that would shape the future of the American death penalty. Under *Gregg vs. Georgia*, states' "new and improved" death penalty statutes would establish a bifurcated trial system through which guilt and sentencing would be decided separately and would provide clearer sentencing guidelines for capital crimes. The goal was to reduce the racial discrimination apparent in death sentencing, particularly in light of evidence that race was the most significant driving force for determining who would be executed.[29]

In the years following the reinstatement of the death penalty in the United States, the rates of death sentences and executions increased slowly. However, in the 1980s and 1990s, the death penalty experienced what can only be referred to as a renaissance. Death sentences soared as hundreds of people were sentenced to death each year, expanding the death row population to a record 3,593 prisoners. Executions reached an all-time high, with 98 individuals executed in 1999 alone.[30] Rather than abandon what Western democracies had come to view as an archaic and cruel human rights violation, the United States embraced state killing in a way that appeared to be a return to pre-*Furman* fervor. However, this time around, the death penalty was argued to be free of the racial biases that had once plagued the practice in the United States.

Fair Administration of the Death Penalty?

But is the death penalty fairly administered? More than half of Americans believe it is, and there are certainly death penalty proponents who forward such a claim.[31] Some of these claims acknowledge past problems, such as proponent Dudley Sharp, who says, "No evidence of system wide discrimination in the imposition of the death penalty exists beyond the 1950s."[32] Similarly, scholar Ernest van den Haag argued, "Many abolitionists contend that the death penalty is distributed unfairly, that Blacks and the poor are likely be executed for murders which are punished less severely when committed by whites. This was quite true at one time but recent data indicated it no longer is."[33] These arguments run counter to numerous assertions that the American capital punishment system has always been, and continues to be, plagued by racism.

Others more adamantly deny the existence of racial bias, either by pointing to single cases where whites are executed (e.g., Lawrence Brewer) to demonstrate equal treatment under the law or by looking to factors that demonstrate a lack of racial bias in cases with defendants of color. In the case of Troy Davis, claims of racial bias and his innocence were summarily dismissed by death penalty proponents as a result of the "media lying about innocent people." One proponent said, "Davis [is] the media's current baby seal of death row."[34] While these individual cases are important, they fail to represent well-documented empirical evidence of the racial bias that continues to demonstrate discrimination at every stage of the American capital punishment system.

Finally, some death penalty proponents believe that racial bias is merely a myth, that is, a "vile strategy" concocted by death penalty abolitionists.[35] Research on pro–death penalty Internet discourse reveals additional telling examples of this sentiment. One website of a death penalty supporter parodies racism in an "Abolitionist's Dictionary" entry: " 'racism' \'ras-sis-im\ n: 1: the sole reason why blacks and latinos [sic] can be found on death row."[36] This sort of continued denial of discrimination related to the American death penalty, coupled with the U.S. Supreme Court decision in *McCleskey vs. Kemp (1987)* that racial disparities in death sentencing are "inevitable," have culminated in a system in which discrimination is not only is tolerated, but authorized.

Though the United States no longer relies on minute-long trials with all-white juries while lynch mobs wait outside the courtroom, overwhelming evidence clearly establishes that the racial disparities that once character-ized executions and "legal lynchings" still exist today. Despite the fact that in any given year, roughly half of all murder victims in the United States are black, 75 percent of people who have been executed since 1976 were sentenced to death for killing white victims.[37] A U.S. General Accounting Office (1990) meta-analysis of 28 death penalty cases found a consistent pattern of racial disparities throughout the United States. The post-*Furman* era has seen significant racial disparities in death penalty sentencing, with an execution system that continues to disadvantage black and Latino defendants while privileging the lives of white victims. Simply put, argu-ments that contemporary death penalty practices are free of racial bias crumble under clear and substantial evidence that racial bias and discrimi-nation continue to plague every step of the American capital system.

Bias, Discrimination, and Disparities at Every Stage

The American capital punishment system involves many interdependent factors and is a process governed by multiple actors who make decisions at every stage. These processes are predominantly—and in some jurisdic-tions, exclusively—governed by white actors. Racial biases, intentional or not, may enter at any stage within the many questions and decisions that arise in the prosecution of a death-eligible crime. Bias or discrimination at one stage may precede bias or discrimination at additional stages within the process. The effect is cumulative in creating racial and ethnic disparities within the capital system. If we are to begin at looking at where disparities may enter the death penalty system, it is essential to look at the nature of death-eligible crimes.

Race, Homicide, and Police Investigations

The risk of being sentenced to death requires one to be accused of committing an aggravated murder within a state that has a death penalty statute. Capital punishment is driven by death-eligible crimes that involve aggravated homicide.[38] Murder in the United States is a racialized crime, with rates of fatal violence so high among African Americans in urban centers they have been called a form of genocide.[39] While black Americans comprise just 13.1 percent of the American population,[40] they account for nearly half of all homicide victims in the United States each year.[41] Homicide in the United States is largely intraracial. In about 90 percent of all cases, both the victims and offenders are from the same racial and/or ethnic group. Despite this fact, executions in the United States have overwhelming involved the small percentage of interracial homicides, particularly those involving defendants of color and white victims.[42] Seventy-five percent of people who have been executed since 1977 have been convicted of killing white victims, despite the fact that whites comprise roughly half of all murder victims each year.[43] To understand this disparity, one must first look to the treatment of homicide victims and police investigations.

Racial disparities in executions begin with the low rate of arrests made in homicides involving blacks and Latino offenders, compared to those involving whites.[44] While historically clearance rates for homicides were high (e.g., roughly 90 percent in the 1960s), the rate at which offenders have been identified and/or arrested has significantly declined, particularly in the case of black and Latino murder victims.[45] Partly to blame is that homicide involving strangers has been on the rise (related to the illicit drug trade found in most major urban centers[46]), and witnesses are less likely to come forward in police investigations.[47]

However, there is also evidence that police invest more time and resources on high-profile murder cases, which are typically those involving high-socioeconomic status whites that draw media attention.[48] Anyone familiar with "missing white woman syndrome"—wherein police and communities expend tremendous effort investigating the disappearances of young, "attractive," white women while ignoring the similar plight of women of color—understand this example.[49] It is within this critique that arguments about the rights to victimhood and the differing values on individuals' lives as victims are made. Here it is argued that the police are much more likely to investigate, identify, and arrest someone when a white person is murdered, whether it is because of the nature of the homicide, the neighborhood context, or the racial or ethnic identity of the victim.[50] In any case, these early disparities lead to a later cumulative effect that drives disparities in who will be found, arrested, tried, convicted, and executed in the future.

Prosecutorial Discretion and the Right to Charge Death

The unequal racial distribution of those involved in the criminal justice system significantly affects capital cases that involve a minority defendant. This racial discrimination begins with the prosecutor, who arguably holds the most power in the criminal justice system, as there is hardly any over-sight of prosecutorial discretion.[51] Prosecutors are not required to follow a "rule book" that instructs them on how to make decisions about whether and how to charge a defendant. Nor are they bound by the American Bar Association's recommended standards of practice for prosecutors.[52] Thus, if a prosecutor's decision to pursue a capital trial is influenced by his or her own bias, it is not likely to change. This is especially problematic in capital cases, as the prosecutor makes the decision to either obtain a capital trial or to settle with a plea bargain, that is, a sentence that is not death.

The majority of death penalty cases involve a white prosecutor, who is more likely to seek a death sentence if the defendant is black.[53] Pokorak reported findings revealing that 97.6 percent of prosecutors in death pen-alty states are white, 1.2 percent are black, and 1.2 percent are Hispanic.[54] Although having a white prosecutor does not guarantee a death sentence for a minority defendant, the overrepresentation of white prosecutors does have inevitable consequences. Sorensen and Wallace found that in first-degree murder cases involving a black defendant and a white victim, pros-ecutors are 2.5 times more likely to advance to a capital trial than with any other racial grouping.[55] The Baldus Philadelphia study examined five dif-ferent counties in South Carolina and proved "statistically significant race-of-victim effects" in the prosecutor's decision to seek the death pen-alty.[56] Similar studies conducted in Florida, Missouri, Nevada, California, Illinois, and Alabama also found prosecutors are more likely to seek death when the victim is white.[57]

Eberhardt and colleagues note the influence of racial stereotyping on prosecutorial decision making, which increases the likelihood of obtaining a capital trial for cases involving a black defendant.[58] Pokorak uses the racial similarities between prosecutors and victims (who were white in about 80 percent of cases he examined) to explain how a prosecutor's unconscious bias may ultimately influence her or his decision to seek the death penalty, specifically in cases involving a minority defendant.[59] Robinson similarly reasons that because almost 100 percent of prosecutors in death penalty states are white, there may be increased pressure to obtain a capital trial when the victim is white.[60] A prosecutor may be unaware of this unconscious racism, which may influence his or her decision to seek the death penalty in interracial crime cases but not in intraracial cases. Although there is substantial evidence documenting outcomes from cases of racially biased prosecutorial discretion, little effort has been made to expose and change this behavior.

The amount of evidence available to prosecute a case may differ according to the victim's socio-demographics, which also influences a prosecutor's decision to obtain a capital trial.[61] For every death-eligible case, prosecutors must use evidence received from law enforcement officials when deciding whether to seek a death sentence. However, because victimization in white communities is more heavily investigated than in black communities, the strength of evidence may vary among cases.[62] The often favorable treatment of white victims compared to minority victims often results in a "disparity of evidence" that prosecutors can use in the case.[63] One disturbing example of this lack of seriousness paid to black victims comes from Rocky Mount, North Carolina, where a serial killer murdered nine black women over the course of six years before receiving any media coverage or a formal investigation.[64] Although the perpetrator was eventually arrested, his criminal invisibility for six years was ultimately attributed to the victims' demographic characteristics (e.g., race) and geographic location.

Replicating Historical All-White and Majority-White Jury Patterns

Once prosecutors have decided to advance to a capital trial, they have enormous power in assembling the juries they need for convictions. They use a variety of measures to ensure that whites are mainly represented as jurors—a process known as jury bleaching.[65] Jury selection for a capital trial first involves dismissing possible jurors for "cause." Such reasons include having a conflicting schedule or being opposed to the death penalty.[66] The latter reason requires potential jurors to be "death qualified," a requirement in capital trials that ensures jurors are actually capable of sentencing someone to death, no matter their race or ethnicity. However, this process often eliminates more minority jurors than white jurors, as whites are significantly more likely to support the death penalty.[67] Bright suggests that because minority jurors likely recognize the racially discriminatory practices employed in applying death sentences, many express opposition when questioned by the prosecutor during jury selection. Ultimately, jurors perceived to favor the death penalty are chosen to serve on a capital jury.[68]

To eliminate qualified minority jurors, prosecutors might then also use "peremptory strikes," that is, they might remove a potential juror without justification.[69] Despite the ruling that rendered striking a potential juror based on race unconstitutional in *Batson vs. Kentucky* (1986), courts continue to accept unjustified reasons to strike minority jurors.[70] When applying these strikes, many prosecutors target black jurors even though over one-third of black men are already barred from jury participation because they possess a felony record.[71] Ogletree provides examples of Alabama capital trials in which potential black jurors were struck for joblessness, lack of education, or criminality. Although these circumstances were more prevalent in minority communities, the court seemed unperturbed by the disproportionate lack of representation of minorities as jurors.[72] Similarly, a two-year *Dallas Morning News* investigation of noncapital felony trials found that prosecutors were twice as likely to strike black jurors over whites, even when they responded identically to questions posed during the selection process.[73] When the journalists replicated the study 20 years later, they found the same exact pattern.[74] Thus, while a formal prohibition has been enacted to prevent prosecutors from utilizing this discriminatory practice, the courts continue to accept "race-neutral" reasons that actually perpetuate the exclusion of minority members from jury participation.

Studies reveal that utilizing a peremptory striking process (e.g., removing jurors without prejudice) has resulted in racial discrimination, specifically in Alabama, Arkansas, Florida, Georgia, Louisiana, Mississippi, South Carolina, and Tennessee.[75] In Alabama, for example, 75 percent of potential black jurors have been struck from 25 death penalty cases since 1987. In their examination of the prosecutorial jury selection process in 390 trials from the Jefferson Parish District Attorney's Office in Louisiana, the Louisiana Capital Assistance Center found that blacks were struck from juries at a rate three times that of whites.[76] In North Carolina over the past 26 years, prosecutors were 2.5 times more likely to strike eligible black jurors than nonblack jurors.[77] In Philadelphia, this pattern was identical between 1981 and 1997.[78] The elimination of minority jurors through peremptory strikes allows prosecutors to compose a jury that is more inclined to impose a death sentence, especially in cases where the defendant is black and the victim is white.[79]

What these studies also make clear is that the primary reason black Americans even make it onto capital juries is that defense attorneys disproportionately retain them as jury members while disproportionately striking nonblacks.[80] The stakes are high in this struggle: the removal of black jurors through peremptory strikes more than doubles the death sentencing rate for black defendants in comparison to white defendants.[81] As we discuss later in this chapter in greater detail, juries comprised of at least five white men are twice as likely to sentence a defendant to death, particularly in cases involving black defendants and white victims.[82] Bowers and Foglia also found that having at least one black man on a capital jury cuts the chance of a death sentence by half.[83]

As evidenced in the preceding discussion, prosecutors recognize the critical role jury composition has in sentencing decisions.[84] This is why in many death penalty states, defendants of color who faced all-white juries remain on death row.[85] It is apparent that having an all-white jury affects a trial's outcome, especially if the defendant is black. Numerous studies have confirmed this, and still a trial involving a black defendant, a white prosecutor, a white judge, and a majority-white jury remains the most common portrait of a capital case in America.[86]

Race Salience and Racial Biases

The evidence, historically and today, that all-white or majority-white juries are most likely to sentence black defendants to death, particularly in cases involving white victims, is unequivocal. Despite our nation's pretenses of being a "postracial" society, the death penalty is still deeply tied up in racial biases among all actors within the criminal justice system. These actors—police, prosecutors, defense attorneys, judges, and juries—suffer from the same racial biases and prejudices that are consistent with the larger segment of Americans. Whether their racial biases are conscious or not, the outcomes of these actors' collective and cumulative decisions within the capital system are still the same. Defendants of color still remain wildly disadvantaged within the criminal justice system, perhaps particularly so when it involves state killing.

Sixty-three percent of Americans support the death penalty, even though half of Americans feel that the system is unfair and biased.[87] Thus, millions of Americans support a system that kills citizens, even if it is racist. Scholars have wondered if it is precisely because of the death penalty's historical ties to lynching and racism that Americans continue to support such a punitive and clearly racialized policy. For anyone familiar with American racial relations, it should come as no surprise that support of the death penalty in the United States is deeply connected with retribution and racism.

Americans' support of the death penalty is largely emotional and retributive.[88] Increasingly, research on Americans' death penalty views show that Americans support negative racial stereotypes, white racism, and racial animus.[89] In fact, these studies demonstrate that racial animus is the number one predictor of whites' support of the death penalty. This is all to say that while Americans' views on the death penalty are retributive, there are clear ties to suggest that this is a racialized retribution clearly tied up in antiblack views and sentiments. While there is still a need for closer studies examining racial and ethnic bias toward nonblack defendants of color, the pattern is likely the same. This racialized punitiveness has persisted throughout America's death penalty history from lynching to today.

These biases shape every stage of the criminal justice system. From police who do not take crimes against victims of color as seriously as they do crimes against white victims to prosecutors who realize they are most likely to "win" a capital conviction in cases involving defendants of color and white victims, these actors rely not only on their own racial biases, but on those of others to continue these patterns.

Cross-racial misidentification is one of the primary reasons people are wrongfully convicted. That juries are so easily persuaded by incorrect eyewitness evidence against black and brown defendants suggests the all-too-easy link with criminality that has been developed and sustained by a constant stream of media images. White jurors often subconsciously "attribute guilt on the basis of race." Thus, they are unaware of or cannot control this process.[90] Further, in a recent and pioneering study, Eberhardt and colleagues (2006) confirmed that jurors are not influenced by "the knowledge that the defendant is Black, but also [by] the extent to which the defendant appears stereotypically Black."[91] It is likely that these biases prevent governors from granting clemency to defendants of color. We can also place blame on these biases when we seek to understand why black men accused of crimes against whites are disproportionately represented among those who are exonerated after a wrongful conviction.[92] Again, whether these are intentional acts or not, the results remain the same: racism continues to taint the administration of justice—and perhaps when it matters the absolute most, when the state kills.

So it is not just that white individuals hold retributive ideas about punishment, but that this is a form of racialized retributive justice in which individuals' beliefs are shaped by social context. That is, if Americans' views on the death penalty drive its retention, we must understand that these views are tainted by racism that is helping to maintain this racist institution and practice. It is hard to imagine a democratic will of the people when its "evolving standards of decency" are so clearly tied up in racist ideology.

Conclusion

In this chapter, we demonstrated the ways in which race continues to play a significant role in determining the outcomes of capital cases in America. We do not have a colorblind system of justice; rather, race serves as an extralegal and unjust factor that determines who lives and who dies at every stage of the American capital punishment system. Allowing racial bias to enter even a single stage of this system would be unjust. The fact that it remains at every stage is a travesty.

In recent years, scholars and abolitionists have celebrated the decline in American death sentences and executions, as well as decreased public support of the death penalty. While there is perhaps reason to celebrate, it should be noted that states' abolition of their capital statutes or their consideration of such legislation has been largely devoid of any discussion of racial bias as a reason to do away with this practice. In political officials' calls for an end to the death penalty, wrongful convictions and the exorbitant costs of the death penalty are frequently cited, without acknowledgement of the larger costs beyond dollars and cents. How many of these cases and destroyed lives could have been avoided had race not been an acceptable factor in the decisions made at every stage of their cases?

These actions are communicative. Individual actors convey a lack of care about equity and the lives of citizens at every step of the capital system. Police departments and officers devote untold resources searching for suspects in cases involving white victims or those of higher socioeconomic status, and they do not spend sufficient resources to find suspects in homicides involving black and/or Latino victims. Prosecutors are several times more likely to seek death sentences when victims are white, particularly when their killers are black. Juries return death sentences, even though they seem unable to understand or empathize with mitigating evidence related to black defendants. Judges and appellate court members affirm death sentences despite shocking evidence of racial discrimination within defendants' individual cases. Governors' clemency records illustrate a clear favor for pardoning white defendants while defendants of color languish while awaiting death. One must also consider that the individuals identified here who make life and death decisions for persons of color every day are overwhelmingly white. Finally, the U.S. Supreme Court's decisions continue to affirm an active dismissal of claims of racism. That is, the court does not just comment on the so-called inevitability of racial discrimination; rather, it creates that inevitability by it outright refusal to address it in any meaningful way.

The continued use of the death penalty, even though it is in decline, remains a link to a troubling past. While many death penalty proponents argue that contemporary practices look nothing like the perfunctory or sham trials of the past, it is simply wrong to come to such conclusions given the evidence we have outlined in this chapter. That the U.S. Supreme Court has upheld racial discrimination, even calling it "inevitable," serves as a constant reminder to communities of color that slavery, Jim Crow, and lynching have not been fully dismantled.

Notes

1. Please direct correspondence to Danielle Dirks, Assistant Professor at Occidental College in Los Angeles, CA dirks@oxy.edu. The authors wish to thank Kathleen Moriarty and Rebecca Cooper for their assistance and feedback on earlier drafts.

2. Davis, 2005, p. 17.

3. One of the millions of Twitter messages sent around the world about Troy Anthony Davis's execution (as cited in Dirks, 2011).

4. Curry and James, 2011.

5. Fernandez, 2011. The Texas Department of Criminal Justice (TDCJ) terminated the "last meal" part of the execution ritual in response to state senator John Whitmire's outrage at treating Brewer (and other death row prisoners) as "celebrities" during their final hours.

6. A third accomplice, Shawn Berry, was sentenced to life imprisonment.

7. Candiotti, 1999.

8. This factor led to the passage of federal hate crime legislation a decade later. In, 2009, President Barack Obama signed into law the Matthew Shepard and James

Byrd, Jr., Hate Crimes Prevention Act of, 2009, 18 U.S.C. § 249 to assist jurisdictions with investigating and prosecuting hate crimes more effectively. U.S. Department of Justice, accessed August 29, 2012: http://www.justice.gov/crt/about/crm/matthewshepard.php

9. Marquart, Ekland-Olson, and Sorenson, 1994.

10. Banner, 2002.

11. Raper, 1969; Tolnay and Beck, 1995; Zangrando, 1980. "Legal lynchings" were lynchings "whereby officials consented in advance to a sham court trial followed promptly by the prisoner's execution" (Zangrando, 1980, p. 4) or, as Arthur Raper (1969) explains, "In the efforts to prevent a lynching, or to prevent further mob outbreaks after a lynching has occurred, peace officers and leading citizens often make to mob leaders promises which virtually preclude impartial court procedure. It is not incorrect to call a death sentence secured under such circumstance a "legal lynching" (p. 19).

12. Banner, 2002; Bright, 2006.

13. Tolnay and Beck, 1995.

14. Banner, 2003.

15. Banner, 2003, p. 141.

16. Pierce and Radelet, 2005.

17. See Baldus et al., 2003; General Accounting Office, 1990; Phillips, 2008, 2009.

18. Bright, 2006, p. 214.

19. Bowers, 1974; Ekland-Olson and Dirks, 2011; Zimring, 2003.

20. Amnesty International, 2013.

21. Death Penalty Information Center, 2013c.

22. Zimring, 2003.

23. Glaze, 2009.

24. Warren, 2008.

25. Bonczar, 2003.

26. Harrison and Beck, 2001.

27. Death Penalty Information Center, 2013c. Among American death row inmates, 43 percent are white, 42 percent are black, 12 percent as Hispanic, and 3 percent are considered "other."

28. Acker, 1996.

29. Wolfgang and Reidel, 1973.

30. Death Penalty Information Center, 2013a.

31. Newport, 2011. In late, 2011, of Americans polled by Gallup, 52 percent agreed that the death penalty is fairly administered, fewer than the number of people who support the death penalty as a punishment for murder (63 percent).

32. Sharp, 1997.

33. van den Haag, 1998, pp. 151–152.

34. Coulter, 2011, n.p.

35. Sharp, 1997, n.p.

36. Lynch, 2002, p. 225.

37. Death Penalty Information Center, 2013c.

38. Death Penalty Information Center, 2013a.

39. Vargas, 2010.

40. McKinnon, 2003.

41. Bureau of Justice Statistics, 2008.

42. Bureau of Justice Statistics, 2011.

43. Death Penalty Information Center, 2013c.

44. Bureau of Justice Statistics, 2011; Radelet and Pierce, 2008; Russell-Brown, 1999.

45. Litwin, 2004; Radelet and Pierce, 2009.

46. Beckett and Sasson, 2004; Litwin, 2004.

47. Wellford and Cronin, 2000.

48. Corsianos, 2003.

49. Stillman, 2007.

50. Others have argued that it is not the race and/or ethnicity of the murder victim that determines whether the police will arrest a murderer, but the neighborhood where that homicide takes place (see Radelet and Pierce [2009] for a review of such literature).

51. Alexander, 2010; Davis, 1998.

52. Alexander, 2010, p. 112.

53. Bright, 2006; Johnson, 2003; Paternoster, 1984; Pokorak, 1998.

54. Pokorak, 1998.

55. Sorensen and Wallace, 1999.

56. Baldus et al., 1998.

57. Blume et al., 1998; Johnson, 2003, p. 121.

58. Eberhardt et al., 2006.

59. Pokorak, 1998.

60. Robinson, 2011.

61. Bright, 2006.

62. Bright, 2006, p. 221; Radelet and Pierce, 2009.

63. Bright, 2006, p. 222.

64. Draper, 2010.

65. Peffley and Hurwitz, 2007.

66. Equal Justice Initiative, 2010; Parson and McLaughlin, 2013.

67. Unnever and Cullen, 2007a, 2007b.

68. Bowers and Foglia, 2003.

69. Baldus et al., 2000.

70. Price, 2009.

71. Alexander, 2010.

72. Ogletree, 2002, p. 27.

73. McGonigle and Timms, 1986.
74. McGonigle et al., 2005.
75. Dewan, 2010; Equal Justice Initiative, 2010.
76. Bourke et al., 2003.
77. Grosso and O'Brien, 2012.
78. Baldus et al., 2000.
79. Baldus and Woodworth, 2003.
80. Baldus et al., 2000; Grosso and O'Brien, 2012; Price, 2009.
81. Baldus and Woodworth, 2003.
82. Bowers and Foglia, 2003.
83. Bowers and Foglia, 2003.
84. Bowers, Sandys, and Brewer, 2004; Johnson, 1985, 2003.
85. Radelet and Pierce, 2011.
86. Bright, 1994, p. 212.
87. Newport, 2011.
88. Ellsworth and Gross, 2003.
89. Unnever and Cullen, 2007a, 2007b.
90. Johnson, 1985, pp. 1642–1643.
91. Eberhardt et al., 2006, p. 385.
92. Free and Ruesnick, 2012.

References

Acker, James R. "The Death Penalty: A 25-Year Retrospective and a Perspective on the Future." *Criminal Justice Review* 21 (1996): 139–160.

Alexander, Michelle. *The New Jim Crow: Mass Incarceration in the Age of Colorblindness.* New York: New Press, 2010.

Amnesty International. "Countries with the highest rates of executions in 2009," 2009. Accessed on March 19, 2013, http://www.amnesty.org/en/death-penalty/death-sentences-and-executions-in-2009.

Amnesty International. *Death Sentences and Executions.* London: Amnesty International, 2013.

Baldus, David C., and George Woodworth. *Equal Justice and the Death Penalty: A Legal and Empirical Analysis.* Lebanon, NH: Northeastern University Press, 1990.

Baldus, David C., George Woodworth, David Zuckerman, and Neil Alan Weiner. "Use of Peremptory Challenges in Capital Murder Trials: A Legal and Empirical Analysis." *Journal of Constitutional Law* 3, no.1 (2000): 3–170.

Baldus, David C., George Woodworth, David Zuckerman, Neil Alan Weiner, and Barbara Broffitt. "Race Discrimination in the Administration of the Death Penalty: An Overview of the Empirical Evidence with Special Emphasis on the Post-1990 Research." *Criminal Law Bulletin* 39 (2003): 194–226.

Baldus, David C., George Woodworth, David Zuckerman, Neil Alan Weiner, and Barbara Broffitt. "Racial Discrimination and the Death Penalty in the Post-*Furman* Era: An Empirical and Legal Overview, with Recent Findings from Philadelphia." *Cornell Law Review* 83, no. 6 (1998): 1638–1770.

Banner, Stuart. *The Death Penalty: An American History*. Cambridge, MA: Harvard University Press, 2003.

"*Batson v. Kentucky (1984)*." Cornell University Law School, Legal Information Institute. Accessed on September 29, 2013, http://www.law.cornell.edu/supct/html/historics/USSC_CR_0476_0079_ZC1.html.

Baumgartner, Frank, Suzanna De Boef, and Amber Boydstun. *The Decline of the Death Penalty and the Discovery of Innocence*. New York: Cambridge University Press, 2008.

Beckett, Katherine, and Theodore Sasson. *The Politics of Injustice: Crime and Punishment in America*. Thousand Oaks, CA: Sage, 2004.

Bedau, Hugo A., and Michael L. Radelet. "Miscarriages of Justice in Potentially Capital Cases." *Stanford Law Review* 40 (1987): 21–179.

Blume, John H., Theodore Eisenberg, and Sheri Lynn Johnson. "Post-*McCleskey* Racial Discrimination Claims in Capital Cases." *Cornell Law Review* 83, no. 6 (1998): 1771–1810.

Bobo, Lawrence D., and Devon Johnson. "A Taste for Punishment: Black and White Americans' Views on the Death Penalty and the War on Drugs." *Du Bois Review* 1, no.1 (2004): 151–180.

Bonczar, Thomas P. *Prevalence of Imprisonment in the U.S. Population, 1974–2001*. Washington, DC: Bureau of Justice Statistics, 2003.

Bourke, Richard, Joe Hingston, and Joel Devine. *Black Strikes: A Study of the Racially Disparate Use of Peremptory Challenges by the Jefferson Parish District Attorney's Office*. New Orleans: Louisiana Crisis Assistance Center. 2003.

Bowers, William J. *Executions in America*. Lexington, MA: DC Heath, 1974.

Bowers, William J., and Wanda D. Foglia. "Still Singularly Agonizing: Law's Failure to Purge Arbitrariness from Capital Sentencing." *Criminal Law Bulletin* 39 (2003): 51–86.

Bowers, William J., Marla Sandys, and Thomas W. Brewer. "Crossing Racial Boundaries: A Closer Look at the Roots of Racial Bias in Capital Sentencing when the Defendant Is Black and the Victim Is White." *DePaul Law Review* 53 (2004): 1497–1538.

Braman, Donald. *Doing Time on the Outside: Incarceration and Family Life in Urban America*. Ann Arbor: University of Michigan Press, 2004.

Bright, Stephen B. "Counsel for the Poor: The Death Sentence Not for the Worst Crime but for the Worst Lawyer." *Yale Law Journal* 103, no. 7 (1994): 1835–1883.

Bright, Stephen B. "Discrimination, Death and Denial: The Tolerance of Racial Discrimination in Infliction of the Death Penalty." In *From Lynch Mobs to the Killing*

State: Race and the Death Penalty in America, edited by Charles J. Ogletree Jr. and Austin Sarat, pp. 211–259. New York: New York University Press, 2006.

Bureau of Justice Statistics. *Homicide Trends in the United States, 1980–2010*. Washington DC: Bureau of Justice, 2008.

Candiotti, Susan. "Closing Arguments Today in Texas Dragging Death Trial." CNN, February 22, 1999. Accessed on March 21, 2013 from http://www.cnn .com/US/9902/22/dragging.death.03/.

Clarke, James W. "Without Fear or Shame: Lynching, Capital Punishment and the Subculture of Violence in the American South." *British Journal of Political Science* 28 (1998): 269–289.

Cooper, Alexia, and Erica Smith. *Homicide Trends in the United States, 1980–2010*. Washington, DC: Bureau of Justice Statistics, 2008.

Corsianos, Marilyn. "Discretion in Detectives' Decision Making and 'High-Profile' Cases." *Police Practice and Research* 4, no. 3 (2003): 301–314.

Coulter, Ann. "Cop-Killer Is Media's Latest Baby Seal," September 21, 2011. Accessed on December 10, 2013, http://www.anncoulter.com/columns/2011-09-21.html.

Curry, Colleen, and Michael James. "Troy Davis Executed after Stay Denied by Supreme Court." ABCNews, September 21, 2011. http://abcnews.go.com/US/ troy-davis-executed-stay-denied-supreme-court/story?id=14571862, 2011.

Davis, Angela J. "Prosecution and Race: The Power and Privilege of Discretion." *Fordham Law Review* 67, no. 1 (1998): 13–68.

Davis, Angela Y. *Abolition Democracy: Beyond Empire, Prisons, and Torture*. New York: Seven Stories, 2005.

Death Penalty Information Center. "Crimes Punishable by the Death Penalty." Accessed May 20, 2012, http://www.deathpenaltyinfo.org/crimes-punishable -death-penalty#BJS, 2013.

Death Penalty Information Center (DPIC). "Facts about the Death Penalty." Accessed February 1, 2013a. http://www.deathpenaltyinfo.org/documents/ FactSheet.pdf, n.d.

Death Penalty Information Center (DPIC). "Methods of Execution." Accessed March 16, 2013b. http://www.deathpenaltyinfo.org/methods-execution.

Death Penalty Information Center (DPIC). "National Statistics on the Death Penalty and Race." Accessed February 16, 2013c. http://www.deathpenalty info.org/race-death-row-inmates-executed-1976.

Dewan, Shaila. "Study Finds Blacks Blocked from Southern Juries." *New York Times*, June 1, 2010.

Dirks, Danielle. "Saying Goodbye to Troy Anthony Davis." *This Week in Sociology*, September 27, 2011.

Dow, David R. "How the Death Penalty Really Works." In *Machinery of Death: The Reality of America's Death Penalty Regime*, edited by David R. Dow and Mark Dow, pp. 11–36. New York: Routledge, 2002.

Draper, Robert. "The Lost Girls of Rocky Mount." *GQ*, June 2010.

Eberhardt, Jennifer L., Paul G. Davies, Valerie J. Purdie-Vaughns, and Sherri Lynn Johnson. "Looking Deathworthy: Perceived Stereotypicality of Black Defendants Predicts Capital-Sentencing Outcomes." *Psychological Science* 17, no. 5 (2006): 383–386.

Ekland-Olson, Sheldon, and Danielle Dirks. *How Ethical Systems Change: Lynching and Capital Punishment.* New York: Routledge, 2011.

Ellsworth, Phoebe C., and Samuel Gross. "Hardening of the Attitudes: Americans' Views on the Death Penalty." In *The Death Penalty in America: Current Controversies,* edited by Hugo A. Bedau, pp. 90–115. New York: Oxford University Press, 1998.

Equal Justice Initiative. "Illegal Racial Discrimination in Jury Selection: A Continuing Legacy." Montgomery, AL: Equal Justice Initiative, 2010.

Fernandez, Manny. "Texas Death Row Kitchen Cooks Its Last 'Last Meal.'" *New York Times,* September 22, 2011.

Free, Marvin D., Jr., and Mitch Ruesnick. *Race and Justice: Wrongful Convictions of African American Men.* Boulder, CO: Lynne Rienner, 2012.

Furman vs. Georgia. Cornell University Law School, Legal Information Institute. 1972. http://www.law.cornell.edu/supct/html/historics/USSC_CR_0408 _0238_ZO.htm

Glaze, Lauren E. *Correctional Populations in the United States, 2009.* Washington, DC: Bureau of Justice Statistics, 2010.

Grosso, Catherine M., and Barbara O'Brien. "Stubborn Legacy: The Overwhelming Importance of Race in Jury Selection in 173 Post-Batson North Carolina Capital Trials, A." *Iowa Law Review* 97 (2011): 1925.

Harper, Charlie. *Justice Delayed Long Enough for Mark MacPhail.* Tanalach Media LLC, 2011. Accessed August 10, 2013, http://www.peachpundit.com/2011/09/ 15/justice-delayed-long-enough-for-mark-macphail/.

Harrison, Paige M., and Allen J. Beck. *Prisoners in 2001.* Washington, DC: Bureau of Justice Statistics, 2002.

Johnson, Sherri Lynn. "Black Innocence and the White Jury." *Michigan Law Review* 83, no. 7 (1985): 1611–1708.

Johnson, Sherri Lynn. "Race and Capital Punishment." In *Beyond Repair? America's Death Penalty,* edited by Stephen P. Garvey, pp. 121–144. Durham, NC: Duke University Press, 2003.

Litwin, Kenneth J. "A Multilevel Multivariate Analysis of Factors Affecting Homicide Clearances." *Journal of Research in Crime and Delinquency* 41, no. 4 (2004): 327–351.

Lynch, Mona. "Capital Punishment as a Moral Imperative: Pro-Death Penalty Discourse on the Internet." *Punishment and Society* 4, no. 2 (2002): 213–236.

Marquart, James, Sheldon Ekland-Olson, and Jonathan R. Sorensen. *The Rope, the Chair, and the Needle: Capital Punishment in Texas, 1923–1990.* Austin: University of Texas Press, 1994.

Matthew Shepard and James Byrd, Jr. Hate Crimes Prevention Act, Pub. L. No. 111-84, §§4701-13, 123 Stat. 2190, 2835–44, 2009.

McCleskey vs. Kemp. Cornell University Law School, Legal Information Institute. http://www.law.cornell.edu/supct/html/historics/USSC_CR_0481 _0279_ZO.html.

McGonigle, Steve, Holly Becka, Jennifer LaFleur and Tim Wyatt. "Striking Differences." *Dallas Morning News,* 2005. Accessed March 15, 2013 from http:// www.dallasnews.com/s/dws/spe/2005/jury/index jury.html.

McGonigle, Steve, and Ed Timms. "Race Pervades Jury Selection." Dallas Morning News, March 9, 1986. Accessed October 27, 2012 from http://www.apnews archive.com/1986/Racial-Bias-Pervades-Jury-Selection/id-15a4d9c91869b22d b37feb26ba874718.

McKinnon, Jesse. *The Black Populations in the United States, March 2002.* Washington, DC: U.S. Census Bureau, 2003.

Newport, Frank. "In US, Support for the Death Penalty Falls to an All-Time Low." Gallup.com. Accessed October 13, 2011. http://www.gallup.com/poll/150089/ support-death-penalty-falls-year-low.aspx.

Ogletree, Charles J. "Black Man's Burden: Race and the Death Penalty in America." *Oregon Law Review* 81, no. 15 (2002): 15–38.

Parson, Earl E., and McLaughlin, Monique. "Citizenship in Name Only: The Coloring of Democracy while Redefining Rights, Liberties and Self Determination for the 21st Century." *Columbia Journal of Race and Law* 3, no. 1 (2013): 103–118.

Paternoster, Raymond. "Prosecutorial Discretion in Requesting the Death Penalty: A Case of Victim-Based Racial Discrimination." *Law and Society Review* 18, no. 3 (1984): 437–478.

Peffley, Mark, and Jon Hurwitz. "Persuasion and Resistance: Race and the Death Penalty in America." *American Journal of Political Science* 51, no. 4 (2007): 996–1012.

Phillips, Scott. *Racial Disparities in Capital Punishment: Blind Justice Requires a Blindfold.* Washington, DC: American Constitution Society for Law and Policy, 2008.

Phillips, Scott. "Legal Disparities in the Capital of Capital Punishment." *Journal of Criminal Law and Criminology* 99, no. 3 (2009): 717–756.

Pierce, Glenn, and Michael Radelet. "The Impact of Legally Inappropriate Factors on Death Sentencing for California Homicides, 1990–1999." *Santa Clara Law Review* 46 (2005): 1–47.

Pokorak, Jeffrey J. "Probing the Prosecutor's Perspective: Race of the Discretionary Actors." *Cornell Law Review* 83, no. 6 (1998): 1811–1820.

Pokorak, Jeffrey J. "Rape as a Badge of Slavery: The Legal History of, and Remedies for, Prosecutorial Race-of-Victim Charging Disparities." *Nevada Law Journal* 7, no. 1 (2006): 1–54.

Price, Melynda. "Performing Discretion or Performing Discrimination: Race, Ritual, and Peremptory Challenges in Capital Jury Selection." *Michigan Journal of Race and Law* 15, no. 1 (2009): 57–107.

Radelet, Michael L., and Glenn L. Pierce. "Racial and Ethnic Disparities in Resolving Homicides." In *The Future of America's Death Penalty: An Agenda for the Next Generation of Capital Punishment Research*, edited by Charles S. Lanier, William J. Bowers, and James R. Acker, pp. 113–132. Durham, NC: Carolina Academic Press, 2008.

Radelet, Michael L., and Glenn L. Pierce. "Race and Death Sentencing in North Carolina, 1980–2007." *North Carolina Law Review* 89 (2011): 2120–2148.

Raper, Arthur. *The Tragedy of Lynching*. New York: Negro Universities Press, 1969.

Robinson, Matthew. "Is Capital Punishment Just? Assessing the Death Penalty Using Justice Theory." *Journal of Theoretical and Philosophical Criminology* 3, no. 2 (2011): 27–66.

Russell-Brown, Kathryn. *The Color of Crime: Racial Hoaxes, White Fear, Black Protectionism, Police Harassment, and other Macroaggression*. New York: New York University Press, 1999.

Sharp, Dudley. "Race Sentencing and the Death Penalty." *Justice for All*, 1997. Accessed January 9, 2012, http://www.prodeathpenalty.com/dp.html#C.Race.

Sorensen, Jonathan, and Donald H. Wallace. "Prosecutorial Discretion in Seeking Death: An Analysis of Racial Disparity in the Pretrial Stages of Case Processing in a Midwestern County." *Justice Quarterly* 16 (1999): 559–579.

Stillman, Sarah. "The 'Missing White Girl Syndrome': Disappeared Women and Media Activism." *Gender and Development* 15, no. 3 (2007): 491–502.

Tolnay, Stuart E., and E. M. Beck. *Festival of Violence: An Analysis of Southern Lynchings, 1832–1930*. Urbana: University of Illinois Press, 1995.

Unnever, James D., and Francis T. Cullen. "Reassessing the Racial Divide in Support for Capital Punishment: The Continuing Significance of Race." *Journal of Research in Crime and Delinquency* 44 (2007a): 124–158.

Unnever, J. D., and Francis T. Cullen. "The Racial Divide in Death Penalty Support: Does White Racism Matter?" *Social Forces* 85, no. 3 (2007b): 1281–1301.

U.S. General Accounting Office (GAO). *Death Penalty Sentencing: Research Indicates Pattern of Racial Disparities*. Washington, DC: U.S. General Accounting Office, 1990.

van den Haag, Ernest. "Justice, Deterrence and the Death Penalty." In *America's Experiment with Capital Punishment*, edited by James R. Acker, Robert M. Bohm, and Charles S. Lanier, pp. 139–156. Durham, NC: Carolina Academic Press, 1998.

Vargas, Joao H. C. *Never Meant to Survive: Genocide and Utopias in Black Diaspora Communities*. Lanham, MD: Rowman and Littlefield, 2010.

Warren, Jennifer. 2008. *One in 100: Behind Bars in America, 2008*. Washington, DC: PEW Center on the States.

Wellford, Charles, and James Cronin. "Clearing up Homicide Clearance Rates." *National Institute of Justice Journal* 243 (2000): 2–7.

Wolfgang, Marvin E., and Marc Riedel. "Race, Judicial Discretion, and the Death Penalty." *Annals of the American Academy of Political and Social Science* 407 (1973): 119–133.

Woodson v. North Carolina. Cornell University Law School, Legal Information Institute. Accessed April 1, 2012, http://www.law.cornell.edu/supct/html/historics/USSC_CR_0428_0280_ZS.html.

Zangrando, Robert L. *The NAACP Crusade against Lynching, 1909–1950.* Philadelphia: Temple University Press, 1980.

Zimring, Franklin. *The Contradictions of American Capital Punishment.* Oxford: Oxford University Press, 2003.

Chapter 25

Reentry, Revocation, and Recidivism for Racial/ Ethnic Minorities

Nkrumah Lewis

Prisoner reentry, revocation, and recidivism all arguably begin in theory the moment an inmate begins a period of incarceration. The manner in which the period of incarceration is facilitated on the part of the offender can have far-reaching implications upon release. Prisoners are mistakenly under the presumption that rehabilitative and therapeutic programming is abundantly offered and will bolster their successful reentry into society. However, scarce resources and public outrage at the notion of prisons doing anything more than exacting punitive retribution merely adds to the inherent shortcomings of such programs. In essence, the reality of the life that awaits prisoners upon release is largely, if not completely, a subjective and psychological issue. In this chapter, the enumerable challenges to successful reentry, supervision of released ex-offenders, and the likelihood of their return will be examined critically.

Needless to say, a great number of works have been written and funds allocated to the readjustment of the aforementioned populations given the stigma attached to having served time in a correctional facility. A great deal of historical focus has been on how the formerly incarcerated face the challenges of returning to a society that has continued to progress without them and the phenomenon of institutionalization. However, it has instead been society's response to the individual that has proven most difficult to navigate. Bazemore and Stinchcomb proffer that "successful reintegration is not just a matter of whether the offender is prepared to return to the community. It is also a matter of whether the community is prepared to meet the returning offender."[1] To better understand these and the divergent issues, it is first important to look at the incarceration itself, focusing on its stated and intended purposes.

Early thinkers of the classical school became convinced that they might somehow deter crime by making the punitive response to it more severe, public, and prompt. Philosophical thinkers of the time intensely debated whether crime was an act of personal volition or if indeed there were external factors beyond the individual's control that needed to be compensated for. In either instance, it was concluded that individuals who committed criminal acts needed to be identified, labeled, controlled, and/or restrained. Such as it was, a battery of conditions for punishment with the intent to modify the behavior of an individual were thought to be prevalent in deterring further incidences of societal affronts. Moreover, though crime was an individual act, there was a vein of concern that such behaviors and their underlying motivations might spread to others, and it thus became important to make punishment public in an effort to deter others as well as the offender.

It was upon Jeremy Bentham's concept of utilitarianism that the criminal justice system began to debate the notion of premeditation, believing that it was reasonable for one to weigh both the benefits and calculable risks prior to the commission of a crime. If in fact this were the case, then perhaps the risks could be escalated as a mechanism for deterring the facilitation of crime. Ultimately, after decades of adjusting punishments based on severity, duration, promptness, and so on, criminologists began advocating for strategies such as target hardening (e.g., deadbolt locks, the club for auto theft), reductionist strategies, community initiatives (e.g., community watch, crime stoppers), aesthetic deterrents (e.g., broken windows theory). However, researchers reached the conclusion that not much could be done to completely extinguish criminal behavior.

One of the great failures of deterrence doctrine was in the area of homicide, where it was believed that public executions would serve as general deterrence and impede the compulsion by others to commit the act of murder, having witnessed the stern response of society. Actually, it was found that after a well-publicized execution, the rate of homicide increased rather than decreased. When the practice of severe punishment failed to yield replicable or even reliable results, government officials, as well as the criminologists that informed their policies, were forced to rethink the underlying premises.

An undeveloped consideration in deterrence doctrine was whether everyone bought into the notion of the social contract, where it was to be understood that the government/criminal justice system would serve as an intermediary for matters of personal justice. To that degree, terms such as "retaliatory violence," "retributive justice," "specific deterrence," and "just desserts" emerged. In finality, the idea of "just desserts," to each according to that which he deserves, seemed to signal the beginning decline of efforts at rehabilitation by the penal system. It also did not help when, in 1966, the New York State Special Committee on Criminal Offenders commissioned Robert Martinson and other researchers to examine the effect of offender treatment programs, and he concluded that "with few and isolated exceptions, the rehabilitative efforts that have been reported so far have had no appreciable effect on recidivism."[2] Many opponents of such treatment programs seized the opportunity to argue that they were too costly, and even more, a burden to taxpayers who had been harmed by the offender to begin with. In conjunction, the pressure of prison overcrowding in the decades that followed created a new necessity of either housing inmates or processing them for early release, much to the chagrin of those whose platforms called for tougher legislation on criminals.

The ensuing debate in literature and practice would ultimately turn to the conditions of incarceration, where one side contended that the conditions of prison should be neither enjoyable nor comfortable, and the other argued for the humane treatment of the incarcerated, citing harsh conditions that led to duress and declines in both mental and physical health.[3] While it was a foregone conclusion that a high degree of control and routinization were symptomatic of prison function, there still exists no substantive or extensive history in criminological study regarding the conceptualization of institutionalization and its relationship to recidivism. Social learning theorists would argue that the expectation of rehabilitation and subsequent reentry is significantly undermined during a period of isolative correction due to the offender being surrounded by negative and criminalistic behaviors defined as normative or valued. In a sense, incarceration presents itself as a natural and likely continuation of the criminal lifestyle as opposed to a definitive consequence; it becomes a process along the continuum. As well, a process of redefinition within subcultures regards the entrance of one into the penal system as a rite of passage.

In the meantime, incredulous numbers of inmates are being returned to densely populated areas of centralized poverty, where they are placing a strain not only on their nuclear families, but destabilizing the community, threatening the infrastructure of struggling neighborhoods, and causing concern for public safety. As the needs of the returning offender continue to pull on the scarce resources of the community as a whole, systematic impossibilities create stressors for the ex-offender to contribute with all expediency. It is here that strain emerges and as evidenced by statistics, crime resurfaces as a medium for relief; much as it was the medium for doing so during the period of incarceration.

The contradictions of incarceration coupled with the challenges that await an ex-offender create a synergy that ensures they wear the scarlet letter of criminality long after they have served the sentence pronounced by the criminal justice system. Prison now presents itself as a fallacy in ceremony that is a self-perpetuating economic and bureaucratic machine in light of privatization. Moreover, the constant cries of innocence and the reversal of sentences on judicial error, prosecutorial misconduct, DNA evidence, and the like beg the question of the true purpose of incarceration and its relation to the justice of old, whereby the goal was to make whole the citizen who had been harmed. One certainty that becomes more evident is that the by-product of incarceration in the United States as currently employed widens the gap between the "haves" and "have-nots" and does little to dispel the notion that criminality and its subsequent punishment have a color.[4]

Reentry

While reentry continues to be a significant issue within corrections, there continues to be limited research on the subject. During the past decades, sociologists, criminologists, and—to a lesser extent—economists have been devising programs to ease the difficult transition faced by ex-offenders during the period of time between when they are released and when they successfully reenter society. These programs are basically of two types: postrelease programs and in-prison programs. While the former type of program offers assistance after the individual has been released, the latter starts helping individuals while they are in prison. As both experience and literature have accumulated, perhaps the most fundamental goal to a complete reintegration has turned out to be job placement.[5]

While other considerations contained in this discussion serve as functional prerequisites toward holistic treatment, the attainment of stable employment seems to be the culminating experience, given the lingering amount of stigmatization associated with the semantic label of "ex-offender."

According to the Bureau of Justice Statistics, in the United States, close to 1,612,395 million people were in state and federal prisons at the end of 2010. In the middle of 2011, an additional 735,601 were in jail.[6,7] At the end of 2010, about 4,055,500 adults were on probation, and an estimated 840,700 adults were on parole.[8] Considered in another way, a total of 7,244,196 individuals were under the supervision of the U.S. Department of Corrections. Most of these inmates' period of incarceration has likely been occupied by participating in skill or trade programs, formal or informal study, transitional initiatives, and/or making plans for their release. The reality upon release is different than the expected parallel of having entered a facility whose stated purpose was rehabilitation.

Later in this chapter, five important acts of federal legislation that directly impact the quality of life of this population as they seek to again gain reentry to society will be briefly discussed. In addition, a great number of liberties are lost or vacated in large part to confusion, misinformation, self-segregation, and/or defeatist mentalities on the part of ex-offenders. Among the difficulties they are likely to incur, employment is perhaps the most prevalent, given that a large number of them will still be financially responsible to the system for probation or parole fees that have and will continue to accumulate. In addition, a vast amount of criminological literature points to the likelihood of reduction in recidivism rates when an ex-offender is successfully employed.

Employment goes a long way toward diminish the designation of the former offender as an "other" in society. It is, in essence, the gateway that serves as a reintegrative ceremony of sorts. Employment promotes self-esteem, strengthens the bond with society, and truly begins the process of social reintegration by helping the ex-offender become part of a recognized group, thereby creating a sense of belonging as well as providing structure and a measure of discipline.[9,10,11] Antithetically, many sectors of employment are no longer available to the ex-offender, and even more, a number of financial benefits that might otherwise assist in reconstructing their lives find them disqualified for receipt.

Efforts by the Equal Employment Opportunity Commission to attempt to counteract the issue of discriminatory practices in securing gainful employment are ongoing. Title VII of the Civil Rights Act has ruled that employers governed by the act cannot deny people employment based on arrests that did not lead to conviction unless there is a "business justification"; nor can they deny people employment because of a criminal conviction unless there is a "business necessity." Formerly incarcerated individuals are well within their rights to pursue legal action if they believe their record has been used to deny them employment. However, given the subjectivity entailed in hiring practices, blanket company policies regarding the selection of convicted criminals for employment, difficulty in substantiating such claims, and the privatization of a vast number of businesses, enforcement of the statute proves a mountainous undertaking when the immediacy for employment prevails. "Many employers simply do not want to hire former offenders, and in some cases, ex-convicts have problems getting an occupational license or surety bond necessary to employ their skills."[12]

In an effort to reiterate the absence of equal protection under the law for individuals arrested and/or convicted of a crime, a closer look reveals that there are currently inconsistent standards. Twenty-six states have no standards governing the relevance of conviction records of applicants for occupational licenses. Quite simply, this means that they have the ability to deny licenses based on any criminal conviction, regardless of history, circumstance, or business necessity. In addition, 25 states do have standards that require a "direct," "rational," or "reasonable" relationship between the license sought and the applicant's criminal history. Finally, 34 states have no standards governing public employers 43 states have no standards governing private employers; only eight (8) do.[13] Research conducted by Pager goes further in demonstrating the statistical hardship faced by the intersection of race and crime.[14] His research found that race was indeed a mitigating factor when job seekers, even for those who shared a criminal history. The practice of discrimination is found at the outset of the application process vis callback on an application as a proxy for hiring interest. Pager notes that "a white applicant with a criminal record was just as likely to receive a callback as a black applicant without any criminal history (17 vs. 15 percent)." The criminal penalty, then, is arguably just about as strong as the racial penalty (and they do interact, as Pager's results show that only 5 percent of all black applicants with criminal records received job callbacks). The average callback rate for all whites (23.5 percent) was a full 13.5 percent greater than the callback rate for all blacks (10 percent).[15] It is in this instance that employment is identified as being the single most important factor related to the propensity to recidivate and that people of color suffer the greatest challenges during efforts to reenter society.

In a recent effort, some states have drafted proposals to state legislatures asking that for the purposes of equity the question regarding previous criminal acts be completely removed from job applications until such time that it becomes necessary to disclose such information. The advent of new technology, however, threatens to make criminal records a moot point, as they are easily secured online via the Internet, many times for no cost under the premise that they are public information. In response, advocates are seeking mediums through which individuals might have their criminal records sealed, annulled, or expunged strictly for the purposes of securing employment.

It is clear that former prisoners returning to society are met with requirements to disclose their criminal record and subsequent dispositions, and even in the rare cases they are not, they are often penalized for inexplicable gaps in employment. The stigmatization and what many might even characterize as discriminatory practice does not end there; it is pervasive in the attempt at social reacclimation for the individual returning from a stint of incarceration. It is not to be presumed that there are tremendous gender differentiations made related to barriers to reentry, as women are met with the same and sometimes even more exasperating realities, particularly related to social welfare programs such as housing subsidies.

The Federal Five

There are currently five federal laws that not only present challenges to reentry, but more specifically restrict access to the very resources that are regarded as essential to postrelease success. The five federal acts adversely preclude access to public assistance and food stamps (Personal Responsibility and Work Opportunity Reconciliation Act [Public Law 104-193]), housing (Housing Opportunity Program Extension Act [Public Law 104-120] and Quality Housing and Work Responsibility Act [Public Law 105-276]), parenting (the Adoption and Safe Families Act [ASFA] [Public Law 105-89]), and mobility (Department of Transportation and Related Agencies Appropriation Act [Public Law 102-388]) based on prior criminal convictions. These laws frustrate the process of reintegration on the part of the former offender and leave few viable alternatives to "starting over." According to inmates preparing for release, the collaborative impact of such legislation is significantly more than a judicial impediment. It is also, a psychological one in which the inevitability of failure and recidivism become the perceived reality.[16]

Public Assistance and Food Stamps

In 1996, Aid to Families with Dependent Children (AFDC) was modified under the presidency of Bill Clinton and renamed Temporary Assistant to Needy Families (TANF). While many championed the new legislation for seemingly addressing the growing concern over systematic exploitation and complacency, what was overlooked was the Personal Responsibility and Work Opportunity Reconciliation Act that barred mostly women with felony drug convictions in 38 states from receiving the benefits. In addition, 17 states imposed lifetime bans on such individuals, that is, they can never receive cash benefits or food stamps. Further, any probation/parole violations and/or bench warrants precludes one from receiving social security insurance (SSI) as well. Due to a great deal of lobbying, a number of states have opted out of the policy or modified the ban. The states that continue to impose a lifetime ban on the receipts of those benefits are: Alabama, Alaska, Delaware, Georgia, Illinois, Mississippi, Nebraska, South Carolina, South Dakota, Texas, and West Virginia. This loss of benefits makes it increasingly difficult to undertake vocational rehabilitation, provide child-care, seek employment, pay rent, and even provide food, particularly for returning prisoners who are the sole custodial parent.

Housing

Federal law bans individuals convicted of certain sex offenses and the production of methamphetamine from public housing premises. While this mandate seems specific, the same federal statute also gives local public housing agencies discretion to deny eligibility to virtually anyone with a criminal background and to determine the length of that ban. In addition, it is at their sole discretion to define what may qualify as rehabilitation efforts for the purpose of lifting the ban. Also in 1996, Congress presented President Clinton with legislation that has colloquially been referred to as the "one strike eviction policy." This policy mandates the eviction of tenants whose dwelling is the site of any criminal activity. As time progressed, the actuation and enforcement of the policy found tenants evicted for criminal activities that happened outside of the residence as well. While the policy theoretically imposes a lifetime ban, there is language contained therein that allows the tenant to apply for restoration after a period of three years.

Parenting

According to the website "After Prison, Roadblocks to Reentry":

> The federal Adoption and Safe Families Act of 1997 (ASFA) bars people with certain convictions from being foster or adoptive parents. The law mandates that states perform criminal record checks on prospective parents in order to receive federal social security payments for foster care and adoption. It recommends that states bar for life people convicted of child abuse or neglect; spousal abuse; crimes against children, including child pornography; or violent crimes, including rape, sexual assault, or homicide (but not other types of physical assault or battery). It also recommends that states bar anyone convicted of physical assault, battery or drug-related felonies for five years.[17]

As it relates to parents returning from prison, ASFA permanently terminates parental rights if children have been in foster care for 15 of the most recent 22 months, thereby prohibiting contact through any medium. When parental rights are not terminated, to reunite with children, the returning offender (typically a mother) must first secure adequate housing, obtain benefits or employment, and in many cases seek substance abuse treatment. In many parental rights hearings, the inmate's failure to pay child support—even though their earnings are meager—is justification for loss of parental rights.

Mobility

The Department of Transportation and Related Agencies Appropriation Act of 1992 penalizes a state municipality 10 percent of certain federal highway funds unless the state enforces an automatic six-month driver's license ban for an individual convicted of a drug offense. A state can submit an appeal citing that they are opposed to the legislation and have drafted a formal resolution stating this. They may also appeal by proposing that the ban apply only to driving offenses where a drug conviction was secured, such as driving while intoxicated/driving under the influence (DWI/DUI). In addition, they may supersede the federal mandate by imposing an even longer ban. In such cases, it obviously becomes more difficult for ex-offenders to not only secure and maintain employment, but attend treatment, which may be a condition of parole.

The Color of Crime and Disproportionality

African-American men are far more likely than any other racial/ethnic group of men in America to be arrested, convicted, and spend time in prison during their lifetime. Given the statistical data that has emerged the in the past decade, it is also evident that African-American men now have the highest rate of recidivism.[18] While incarceration alone is not a unique phenomenon, the degree at which black men in the United States are incarcerated is. First of all, the United States has the highest overall prison population rate, at 743 per 100,000. We are followed by Rwanda (595 per 100,000).[19] Most inmates are recidivists and disproportionately black men.[20] Gendreau and colleagues concluded in their meta-analysis that gender, age, criminal history, and race were key predictive individual-level risk domains for recidivism.[21]

Given their percentage of the overall population, the rate of incarceration for men of color is historically regarded as a social phenomenon. According to the 2010 census, blacks comprised 12.6 percent of the U.S. population yet accounted for 39.4 percent of the total prison and jail population in 2009.[22] Data from the Bureau of Justice Statistics show that one in six black men had been incarcerated as of 2001. Across the criminal justice system, black males are more likely to be convicted, receive longer and harsher penalties, pay higher trial penalties, and receive pretrial incarceration as opposed to being granted bail/bond in comparison to white defendants.[23] Consistent with these findings, Hispanics comprised 16.3 percent of the total U.S. population according to the 2010 census but made up 20.6 percent of the total jail and prison population in 2009. Census data for 2000, which included a count of the number and race of all individuals incarcerated in the United States, showed for each state that the proportion of blacks in prison populations exceeded the proportion of whites among state residents in every state. In twenty states, the percent of blacks incarcerated was at least five times greater than their share of resident population.[24]

The literature on the disproportionate inclusion of men of color in the criminal justice system is well documented. However, researchers are puzzled about why men of color have exacerbated levels of stigmatization and postrelease discrimination. The concern now is where and how the differences occur between black offenders and their counterparts. A large part of it is attributable to racial profiling by police, but this does not satisfy the breadth of the disparity that occurs at every instance in a systematic process. It is, however, appropriate to point out that the high arrest, conviction, and recidivism rates when paired with the phenomenon of racial profiling creates a self-perpetuating and cyclical affect by continually introducing black males into the proverbial wheel of the criminal justice system.

The clear inequity in the relationship between men of color and the penal system cannot be ignored, nor can the exponential effects. Lyles-Chockley observes that "as compared to their white counterparts, not only do black offenders serve twenty-three percent more time under mandatory release, but this population experiences a nearly doubled recidivism rate. Such disparities in incarceration rates naturally result in a disproportionately negative impact on black families and communities."[25] According to Glaze and Maruschak, approximately 1.7 million children had at least one parent in prison, with approximately half of these children aged 9 or younger.[26] These children are more likely to suffer abuse and neglect, more likely to be among the 40 percent of children raised in poverty or near-poverty, and more likely to go to prison themselves.[27] Thus we can see that the nature of incarceration and its ramifications are cyclical and generational, thereby maintaining the status quo.

A common theme contained in this chapter is that of reintegrative ceremonies and the lack thereof. On a macro level, the message that society does not forgive individuals who have committed felonious crimes resonates no louder than in the realm of suffrage. "Felony disenfranchisement is an obstacle to participation in democratic life which is exacerbated by racial disparities in the criminal justice system, resulting in an estimated 13% of Black men unable to vote."[28] Two states, Virginia and Kentucky, disenfranchise felons for life, unless they are granted clemency. More significant than impacting the outcome of an election, this practice is one of many mediums through which ex-offenders come to understand that they have been actually sentenced to life. More profoundly, black ex-offenders are being faced with the dual stigmatization of ex-convict and nonvoter.

The Female Offender

Because they are the default custodial parent and as previously stated, reentry for women presents a different set of challenges. One such challenge is battling the delicate psychological state that children are most certain to be in, particularly if the incarceration was during their formative years. Reports from 2008 reflect that 64.2 percent of incarcerated mothers in state prisons and 84 percent of the mothers in federal custody reported living with their children either in the month of arrest or just prior to becoming incarcerated. Perhaps even more to the point, 42 percent of mothers in state prison and 52 percent of those in federal prison reported living in a single-parent home with their children. The ability to even attempt reunification is regarded as a gift, as many times child welfare laws prohibit reunification altogether, specifically for women of color.[29] Often children and mates/spouses are angry and resentful, having worked diligently to move on with their lives without the offender, or quite the opposite, having struggled financially to support and visit her during her incarceration. As the psychological reality of lost time becomes ever present, a great amount of stress is incurred because the expectation of those left behind is that the offender should return as a financial contributor to the household, which in many cases is virtually impossible, or at the least, difficult.

Often, the returning offender neglects the process of gradually reentering society. After all, based on the length of incarceration, a great deal may have changed technologically, socially, and so forth. The ex-offender is often exasperated with the demands of immediacy, having to learn and relearn basic functions while at the same time balancing an entirely new reality that suggests at every turn that life has seemingly passed them by. In addition, the financial strains that accompany returning home are an impediment to professional therapy, unless it is court mandated due to substance abuse. It is seldom the case that the family is able to participate in therapy in a meaningful way, thus destabilizing the family unit and increasing the propensity to drug relapse and recidivism. A significant point is that 67.4 percent of all incarcerated parents report substance abuse issues, while 56.5 percent report a mental health problem, 40.6 percent a medical problem, 19.9 percent physical/sexual abuse in their lifetime, and 8.9 percent homelessness. Given the myriad of issues and the small window for a period of readjustment, prison is often regarded as a more favorable alternative to being released.

In addition to the obvious challenged, the news has been littered as of late with more substantiated claims of sexual abuse, rape, and physical abuse by male correctional officers. The American Civil Liberties Union reports that "55% of women in state prisons reported that they had been physically and/or sexually assaulted at some point in their lives."[30] Seventy-nine percent of women in federal and state prisons reported past physical abuse, and over 60 percent reported past sexual abuse only to be incarcerated and revictimized. The allegations have historically been ignored or dealt with wantonly, with the offenders receiving segregation as punishment for having been assaulted or raped and officers seldom being reprimanded at all. In a 2007 survey, the Bureau of Justice Statistics found that 4.5 percent of inmates held in federal and state prisons had been sexually abused in the previous year alone.

In 2003, the Prison Rape Elimination Act (PREA) was passed, and the Bureau of Justice Statistics began administering the National Inmate Survey for the first time. The survey sought to unearth sexual abuse of inmates, and it defined sexual violence as "nonconsensual sexual acts," meaning "giving or receiving sexual gratification and oral, anal or vaginal sex," and "abusive sexual contact," meaning "unwanted touching . . . of specific body parts in a sexual way."[31] Beck and Harrison reported that in one study, 22,700 prisoners reported they "willingly" had sex or sexual contact with staff, while 22,600 reported experiencing "physical force, pressure, or offers of special favors or privileges."[32] In a recent report of systematic female inmate sexual abuse, the inmates revealed that they were often penalized through segregation and even further victimization during investigations, while correctional officers were given little more than paid leave not exceeding two to three days.[33] This does not take into account the countless number of unwarranted and violent strip searches and pat searches enacted against female inmates. Given how the phenomenon has been grossly mishandled and the emerging pregnancies of female inmates, the incidences are likely still underreported.

Many of the usual challenges facing offenders reentering society are more pronounced because they have suffered violence of a physical and/or sexual nature while incarcerated, making readjustment both physiologically and psychologically painstaking. "The few re-entry services and programs that exist are pitifully inadequate to meet the needs of thousands of people returning from prison to face the challenges of re-entry. Most services and programs available for re-entering prisoners are for men—for example, very little transitional or affordable housing exists where women can reunite with their children." A great number of faith-based and nonprofit organizations full of well-intentioned people attempt to assist in the reentry process, but unfortunately many find that they are unable to sustain their programs without grant funds. In addition, too many of these programs receive hostility from returning offenders because of personal and programmatic failures.

Revocation

Revocation of probation or parole occurs when because of technical violations or the commission of a new crime, the court terminates the agreement made to suspend all or part of a sentenced adjudication. These violations do not necessarily consist of illegal activities but may instead be conditions of release set forth during departure. The most common cause of revocation is the commission of a new offense. The U.S. Supreme Court indicates that revocations should be handled in three stages: (1) a *preliminary hearing*, where the facts of the arrest are reviewed to determine if there is probable cause to warrant a violation, (2) an actual *hearing* during which the facts of the allegation(s) are heard and decided, and (3) *sentencing*, at which incarceration is ordered. The probationer is entitled to an attorney at both the hearing and sentencing phases. Once parole is revoked, the parolee is returned to prison.

Marie Pryor suggests, "Far too often, individuals are released from prison with every intention of never returning, only to find themselves trapped by the immobilizing effects of a system with policies that make their re-incarceration for a technical violation more likely than their reintegration into their community."[34] According to a 2010 Department of Justice report, 22 percent of all state prison admissions were individuals returning for violating the conditions of their parole, while another 9 percent were returned for new charges. The issue of when and under what conditions a parolee should be returned to a state of active incarceration rests with each individual state. A more critical observation of the social control to which ex-offenders must adhere sees them placed in a precarious situation, as they may need to maintain employment or consistently pay inordinate fees established prior to their incarceration (e.g., child or spousal support). The once common practice of "forgiving" accumulated balances has largely been abandoned. This accumulated amount due is referred to as arrearage, and the individual is completely responsible for paying it.

Another difficulty referenced by those returning from prison is having to refrain from consorting with other known criminals, or more specifically, felons. Pryor suggests that conditions such as these are "intended to prevent them from negatively influencing one another, also cuts them off from valuable referrals to services, job opportunities, housing, and support networks such as family."[35] Other research, particularly in states such as New York and California, point to municipalities whose population of offenders and ex-offenders is too great to manage, and it continually absorbs inordinate amounts of money that might otherwise be utilized in areas such as social programs.

In their examination of California, Gratter, Petersilla, and Lin determined that "California's 173,312 prisoners constitute the largest prison population of any state. One in seven state prisoners in the United States is incarcerated in California, and between 1980 and 2007, California's prison population increased over sevenfold, compared with a fourfold increase nationally."[36] More to the point, when considering the cost of supervising ex-offenders, one must ask about the quality of supervision and if the public is really being protected. The California Department of Corrections and Rehabilitation reports that in 2011, it supervised 107,667 parolees (this is almost 15 percent of all parolees in the country).[37] In that same year, California's Parole Apprehension Team contributed to a 16-year low in parole absconders. There were 12,882 (12 percent) parolees of "absconder status," that is, they could be neither located nor contacted.[38]

An analysis of frequent revocations indicates little to do with the stated purpose of rehabilitation and supervised transition periods of reentry and more so to do with political platforms of public safety, threat assessment, and scarce resource management. The goal now resembles population control more than reintegration.[39]

In the face of growing concerns for public safety, researchers and politicians alike are seeking answers regarding how best to deal with men and women returning from prison. For decades, states have debated not only the cost of supervision, but the notion of increased supervision and its relationship to deterring crime and assisting in the process of rehabilitation. In fact, much to the chagrin of advocates of this perspective, increased supervision, increased drug testing, and home confinement have merely served to increase the likelihood of technical violations. Moreover, a number of states are both considering and experimenting with Global Positioning System to continually monitor ex-offenders via satellite, and opponents of such increased supervision quickly point out its violation of civil liberties.

Needless to say, as the debate continues, solutions that take into consideration crime and punishment as well as public safety do not appear readily available. One seeming oddity that punctuates the discussion is the idea that whether subconsciously or consciously, a considerable number of offenders would rather be in prison than on probation or parole. In a study conducted on postrelease supervision, the concept of prison tolerance emerged. This is the notion that when faced with the option of lengthy or intensive probation versus active imprisonment, many people chose incarceration. While one might readily conclude that in accordance with perspectives mentioned earlier in this chapter, prison in and of itself is not "harsh enough," this is not what is meant. Instead, there appears to be both psychological trepidation and the perception that probation conditions are intolerable. While the expansion of prison tolerance is often overlooked in criminological study, the more familiar concept of institutionalization is not.

While one might think that upon release, all individuals want to return to the world and against all odds become functioning and contributing members of society, this is simply not the case. Further study of institutionalization must consider length of incarceration and how it relates to recidivism. In addition, psychology will need to be studied as it relates to the alienation felt by someone leaving an incarceration setting that while punitive, was both intimate and social.

Recidivism

Some ambiguity remains even until today over the hotly debated issue of recidivism. There is not even an agreed-upon definition of the term. Criminological literature posits three potential definitions of *recidivism*: rearrest, reconviction, and incarceration subsequent to a prior period of incarceration. Proponents of rehabilitative programming might argue that arrests are not an indication of guilt, and, given the disproportionate arrests of men of color, judging arrests is not the best way to determine whether an individual is making substantial and genuine efforts at reentry.

Langan and David found that 67.5 percent of prisoners were rearrested within three years, and 51.8 percent were reincarcerated.[40] Freeman asserts that after a decade from release, up to 80 percent of prisoners are rearrested.[41] Given the emerging patterns identified in longitudinal studies, researchers have identified 12 additional mitigating factors that affect the propensity to recidivate: gender, age at offense, length of sentence, employment status, level of educational attainment, race and ethnicity, marital status, illicit drug use, guideline applied for instant offense, sentence type, departure status, and type of recidivating event.[42]

A look at the patterns reveals the following findings: men recidivate more than women; younger offenders have a higher rate of recidivism than older offenders; those sentenced to less than six months or probation and those with sentences of *more* than two years have lower rates of recidivism than those sentenced to between six months and two years, as well as those adjudicated to alternative confinement settings; those with stable employment a year prior to incarceration are less likely to recidivate than the unemployed; offenders without a high school diploma had the highest rate of recidivism, followed then by those with a high school diploma only; blacks have higher rates of recidivism than Hispanics, and blacks' rates are more than double those of whites; those who were never married or who were divorced had higher rates of recidivism than those who were still married; overall, persons who used drugs within one year of their offense had higher rates of recidivism than those that did not use illicit drugs; inmates incarcerated for the instant offense of robbery and firearms were more likely to recidivate than those confined for fraud, drug trafficking, and larceny; offenders sentenced to a period of incarceration have the highest rate of recidivism in comparison to those who receive probation and alternative confinement, with those who receive probation only having the lowest rate; offenders that received lesser sentences by cooperating with authorities in the prosecution of another offender (substantial assistance departures) had lower rates of recidivism than offenders sentenced beyond and under the recommended guidelines (upward and downward departures); and finally, the highest rate of recidivism belonged to those who had their probation revoked.

It is important to note that the aforementioned factors that either positively or negatively impact the rate of recidivism can be viewed as mutually exclusive. In theory, given that men of color receive longer prison sentences on average, one could erroneously conclude that the rate of recidivism for their demographic would be lower than their white counterparts, but in fact the converse is true. Hence, in conjunction with the stated patterns, a great deal of intangible subjectivity is at play regarding whether a former offender returns to prison. Moreover, factors such as an individual's criminal history, his or her standing prior to incarceration, familial support, and aptitude for and determination to succeed vary so greatly that the single most debilitating failure of reentry programming becomes believing that there is a template for success.

While there exist enumerable challenges to reentry, quite another issue is discovering what might cause a former offender to give up the criminal lifestyle. A great deal of the literature has examined the quality of life a person had prior to incarceration. It is reasonable to conclude that if challenges existed prior to jail or prison, those issues will only be made more profound once the individual enters a penal institution. Again, the question of whether the notion of rehabilitation during incarceration has been completely abandoned rears its head for consideration.

Sex Offenders

To date, no comprehensive statistical reports exist regarding the recidivism of sex offenders. The most recent report from which substantive information can be gleaned is from 2003 and details a cohort of sex offenders released in

1994. The researchers attempted to conduct a longitudinal study of the three years following the prisoners' release. The 9,691 sex offenders were released from state prisons in Arizona, Maryland, North Carolina, California, Michigan, Ohio, Delaware, Minnesota, Oregon, Florida, New Jersey, Texas, Illinois, New York, and Virginia and were divided according to their offenses. Within these states, there were 3,115 released rapists and 6,576 released sexual assaulters. On average, the offenders served less than half of their adjudicated sentences and were more likely than non–sex offenders released from the same state prisons to recidivate (5.3 percent [517 of 9,691] versus 1.3 percent [3,328 of 262,420], respectively.[43]

One of the focal concerns relative to the release of sex offenders is without question deterrence, given the reality of their rate of recidivism, as well as the immediacy of their reoffense. The 12 months following their release from state prison was when 40 percent of sex crimes were allegedly committed by the released sex offenders. Legislators have responded with a series of acts devised to maintain ongoing postrelease supervision of this population. According to Bonnar-Kidd, the first piece of legislation was the Jacob Wetterling Crimes against Children Act and Sexually Violent Offender Registration Act of 1994, which was created to help law enforcement officials track sex offenders.[44] Bonnar-Kidd further states, "In May 1996, Megan's Law was passed, amending the Wetterling Act by requiring states to establish systems for making registry information available to the public through methods of community notification. In doing so, Megan's Law made the names, addresses and photographs of registered sex offenders available to the public via the Internet and other forms of community notification."[45]

At the end of 2011, there were approximately 700,000 sex offenders on registries in all 50 states and other U.S. jurisdictions (e.g., Puerto Rico and Guam). An unforeseen consequence of this legislative series has been the constant discounting of sex offenders subsequent to their release. This has resulted in significant numbers of sex offenders not being held accountable by states to their whereabouts. For examples, "In 2009, analysts at the Washington State Institute for Public Policy looked at seven studies on recidivism by registered sex offenders that had been conducted since the first registry law was passed. Two studies showed that being on the sex offender registry decreased recidivism, one showed an increase, three indicated no effect, and one didn't measure the effect."[46] Since 1996, many states and municipalities have created safe zones by legally barring registered sex offenders from being present, implemented chemical castration, stripped offenders of their parental rights, branded their forms of identification with the words "sex offender," banned them from using the Internet, and—perhaps most commonly—restricted where they can live based on proximity to schools, daycares, parks, and playgrounds. Human rights activists have raised concerns about these restrictions, and the legislature must also consider whether it has created a situation of "double jeopardy," as many of these measures were imposed upon released sex offenders as the laws were passed.[47]

The previously mentioned life-long monitoring by GPS is akin to the proverbial scarlet letter. Most often in the visible form of a leg bracelet, it becomes apparent to most any observer that there is cause for concern. The utilization of the GPS monitoring is highly controversial and experimental at best. It creates a false sense of security for the public in several ways: (1) much like cell phone reception, there are dead zones where offenders can momentarily be lost; (2) the device indicates the whereabouts of sex offenders but does not reveal what they are doing; (3) typically, the device reports when sex offenders are outside of inclusionary zones and when, yet it fails to map target areas where they cannot go; (4) the device is reactionary, not proactive—at best, once an infraction has been committed, the device can merely verify where the offender was during that time; (5) one can argue that a former inmate should not be monitored following discharge from probation/parole; finally—and perhaps most importantly—(6) based upon discriminatory practices against sex offenders in housing, the likelihood of recidivism is increased rather than decreased because the risk factors of homelessness, transiency and instability are increased.[48]

Further arguments posit that not much reoffending can be predicted or prevented through the measures chronicled herein. Even though most of the legislation seeks to protect children, it is short sighted because it is based on four faulty presuppositions: (1) all sex offenders have a high risk of reoffending, (2) the crimes most often occur in typical areas where children are present, (3) all sex offenders target children, and (4) both children and their families are safe if no registered sex offender resides in their immediate vicinity. These are dangerously fallacious stereotypes that are not supported by statistical evidence. Driven by panic, erroneous prejudices, and even vigilantism, sex offenders find themselves the most stigmatized subgroup of inmates released from prison. There is little confidence in their rehabilitation, and their recidivism becomes a question of when, not if.

It is truly the nature of the crime that alarms the community, rather than how likely it is that such a crime will occur. Several studies on the topic of sex offender recidivism utilize alternative reporting methods, citing the large numbers of offenders that fail to reoffend over longer periods of time, as opposed to focusing on the number that do. When such reports are read in their totality, one is likely to find a disclaimer that a vast number of sexual crimes are underreported because the abuse is made more heinous due to the psychological scarring associated with sexual criminality.[49] "When people ask questions about sexual offender recidivism rates, there often is an inherent assumption that the answer is a fixed, knowable rate that will not change. This supposition is unlikely to be true. The rate of sexual re-offence is quite likely to change over time due to social factors and the effectiveness of strategies for managing this population."

One unique challenge related to sex offenders is harassment as concerned citizens seek to drive them out of their communities, colleges/universities, and places of employment. In 2000, Congress passed the Campus Sex Crimes Prevention Act, which requires institutions of higher learning to provide increased monitoring of sex offenders, as well as take the necessary steps to notify the campus community of their presence. Many campuses screen sex offenders out during the admissions process, while others restrict their access to the full range of the educational experience if they perceive risk. Newspapers and even academic literature chronicle the enumerable acts of violence and even murder by fearful parents turned criminals themselves in an effort to exact more punitive and personal justice in the name of community. Public outcry has been so pronounced that the U.S. Supreme Court intervened in 2008 and struck down death penalty laws that had been passed in five states for the rape of a child. As an indication of how dichotomous the school of thought on sex offenses remains, the decision was carried 5–4.

No matter how well intentioned politicians and legislators are as they seek to quell public outrage over sexually based criminality, they have created legal quagmires that have collateral consequences for both the communities they serve and the targeted population of sex offenders. This is coupled with the exorbitant costs associated with monitoring and tracking these offenders, though it is certain the public would respond that no cost is too great to requite fears that are statistically reiterated in criminological reporting and texts. While those seeking to protect the public have employed advanced technology to supervise released sex offenders, one must keep in mind that such technology is meant to enhance supervision and prevent further victimization, not supplant sound human oversight.

Finally, the legal floodgates have been opened, and not by human rights advocates, as one might suspect. It has in fact been law enforcement that has borne the brunt of the public's disenchantment with instances of both mechanical and human failure, admissibility in court proceedings, and damages associated with preventable victimizations. While there remain numerous potential tools for prevention, calls for evidence-based strategies based on offender risk assessment are increasing.

Conclusion

When considering reentry, revocation, and recidivism, the common theme is deterrence. The ideology of corrections is undermined by the rate of recidivism. In addition, many efforts to thwart criminality and reoffenses have actually yielded opposite results. Reentry programs seem to have the life span of the period of recidivism measures, and more funds are funneled toward "correctional facilities" that hold fast to the ideology of rehabilitation. In actuality, our country is merely facilitating the process of disintegrative shaming. Prison sentences seem endless in the grand scheme of the productive life span. The privatization of prisons insinuates that incarceration is more about business than justice, which in turn perpetuates the notion that the criminal justice system is capitalist and bureaucratic.

As men and women cycle in and out of prisons throughout the country, there is seldom discussion about solving the crime problem, or finding answers to the question of how to prevent individuals from entering penal institutions to begin with. Increasingly, American youth need their own growing system of corrections, and their criminality is of the adult variety. At some juncture, researchers must do significantly more than collect data that simply rearticulates portraits of stigma and inequalities. Evidence-based practice must reduce rates of revocation and recidivism, as well as ease the transition from prison back into society. While the latter is more of an ethical pursuit, much community and offender resistance to reentry is based on statistical projections of failure.

The propensity to fail in these three areas is greatly exacerbated by believing and perpetuating the premise that there are objective solutions to reintegration, postrelease supervision and reoffending. The success of these efforts is heavily reliant on the development of individualized plans of readjustment. Until funds are allocated to treat criminal behavior therapeutically, a great number of the factors that foster criminality will remain undetected, untreated, and likely aggravating in nature. Moreover, while public apprehension is understandable and often warranted, the process of ongoing adjudication must be halted, or there is little motivation for the ex-offender to reengage in the social contract of civility. The reacclimation process should have as its end the ideal of cultural solidarity, whereby definitions of right and wrong are internalized and actuated on a micro level.

Systematically, with the vast amount of resources allocated to corrections, there is little room for overwhelming responsibility, particularly in the arena of probation and parole. Even for sex offenders, data cannot replace evidence-based practice. Careful decisions based on informed forethought must be brought to bear in these three areas. They cannot be reactionary or politically driven. On a deeper level, the philosophy of corrections must be redressed if the initial goals of incarceration are to achieve their end, or we will surely find the inmate worse off than when he first made entry.

Notes

1. Bazemore and Stinchcomb, 2004, p. 22.
2. Martinson, 1974, p. 25.
3. Bierie, 2012, p. 340.
4. Feagin, 1991, p. 102; Harris, 2002; Lundman and Kaufman, 2003; Pager, 2007.
5. Bierens and Carvalho, 2011, p. 2.
6. Harrison and Sabol, 2011.
7. Minton, 2012.
8. Bonczar and Glaze, 2011, p. 1.
9. Harer, 1994.
10. Sampson and Laub, 1997.
11. Uggen, 2000.
12. Pollack, 2008.
13. Legal Action Center, 2009.
14. Pager, 2007.
15. Wehrman, 2011.
16. Howerton, Burnett, Byng, and Campbell, 2009.
17. Legal Action Center, 2009.
18. Department of Justice, Bureau of Justice Statistics, 2003, p. 5.
19. National Institute of Corrections, 2011, p. 1.
20. Department of Justice, Bureau of Justice Statistics Bulletin, June 2007, p. 9.
21. Gendreau, Little, and Goggin, 1996, p. 578.
22. Harrison and Sabol, 2011.
23. Kansal, 2005, pp. 2–12.
24. Mauer and King, 2007, Table 6, 13.
25. Lyles-Chockley, 2009, p. 259.
26. Christian, 2009, p. 2.
27. Department of Justice, Bureau of Justice Statistics, August 2008, p. 1.

28. Sentencing Project, n.d.
29. Evans, 2006.
30. American Civil Liberties Union, 2005, p. 18.
31. Department of Justice, Bureau of Justice Statistics, 2007, p. 2.
32. Beck and Harrison, 2008.
33. Zaitz, 2012.
34. Pryor, 2010, p. 514.
35. Pryor, 2010, p. 515.
36. Grattet, Petersilia, and Lin, 2008, p. 4.
37. California Department of Corrections and Rehabilitation, 2011, p. 12.
38. California Department of Corrections and Rehabilitation, 2011.
39. Simon, 1993, p. 228.
40. Department of Justice, Bureau of Justice Statistics, 2002, p. 1.
41. Freeman, 1999.
42. U.S. Sentencing Commission, May 2004, pp. 11–14.
43. Department of Justice, Bureau of Justice Statistics, November 2011, p. 7.
44. Bonnar-Kidd, 2010.
45. Bonnar-Kidd, 2010, p. 413.
46. Yoder, 2011, p. 30.
47. Bonnar-Kidd, 2010, p. 415.
48. Bishop, 2010, p. 35.
49. Harris and Hanson, 2004, p. 11.

References

American Civil Liberties Union, Brennan Center for Justice. *Caught in the Net: The Impact of Drug Policies on Women and Families.* New York: Brennan Center for Justice, 2005.

Bazemore, Gordon, and Jeanne B. Stinchcomb. "A Civic Engagement Model of Reentry: Involving Community through Service and Restorative Justice." *Federal Probation* 68, no. 2 (2004): 14–24.

Beck Allen, and Paige Harrison. *Sexual Victimization in Local Jails Reported by Inmates, 2007.* Washington, DC: Bureau of Justice Statistics, 2008.

Beck, Allen J., and Bernard Shipley, *Recidivism of Prisoners Released in 1983.* Washington, DC: Bureau of Justice Statistics, 1989.

Bierie, David. "Procedural Justice and Prison Violence: Examining Complaints Among Federal Inmates (2000–2007)." *Psychology, Public Policy, and Law* 19, no. 1, (2012), 15–29.

Bierens, Herman J., and Jose R. Carvalho. "Job Search, Conditional Treatment and Recidivism: The Employment Services for Ex-Offenders Program Reconsidered." *BE Journal of Economic Analysis & Policy* 11, no. 1 (2011): 1–38.

Bishop, Lisa. "The Challenges of GPS and Sex Offender Management." *Federal Probation* 74, no. 2 (2010): 33–35.

Blackmon, Douglas. *Slavery by Another Name: The Re-Enslavement of Black Americans from the Civil War to World War II.* New York: Doubleday, 2008.

Bonczar, Thomas P. *Prevalence of Imprisonment in the U.S. Population, 1974–2001,* Special Report NCJ 197976. Washington, DC: Bureau of Justice Statistics, 2003.

Bonczar, Thomas, and Lauren Glaze. *Probation and Parole in the United States, 2010.* Washington, DC: U.S. Department of Justice, Bureau of Justice, 2011.

Bonnar-Kidd, Kelly K. "Sex Offender Laws and Prevention of Sexual Violence or Recidivism." *American Journal of Public Health* 100, no. 3 (2010): 412–419.

California Department of Corrections and Rehabilitation. "Corrections: Year at a Glance, 2011." Accessed February 18, 2014, http://www.cdcr.ca.gov/News/docs/2011_Annual_Report_FINAL.pdf., 2012.

California Department of Corrections and Rehabilitation. "CDCR's Adult Parole Operations Reduces Number of Parolees-at-Large by More Than 3,000 in Past Year," 2011. Accessed February 18, 2014, http://cdcrtoday.blogspot.com/2011/03/cdcrs-adult-parole-operations-reduces.html.

Christian, Steve. *Children of Incarcerated Parents.* Washington, DC: National Conference of State Legislators, 2009.

Eisner, Alan. *Gates of Injustice: The Crisis in America's Prisons.* New York: Prentice Hall, 2006.

Evans, Linda. "Locked Up, Then Locked Out: Women Coming Out of Prison." *Women and Therapy* 29, no. 3–4 (2006): 285–308.

Feagin, Joe R. "The Continuing Significance of Race: Anti-Black Discrimination in Public Places." *American Sociological Review* 56 (1991): 101–116.

Freeman, Richard. "Economics of Crime." In *The Handbook of Labor Economics,* volume 3C, pp. 3529–3571. Amsterdam: Elsevier, 1999.

Gendreau, Paul, Tracy Little, and Claire Goggin. "A Meta-Analysis of the Predictors of Adult Recidivism: What Works." *Criminology* 34 no. 4 (1996): 575–608.

Glaze, Lauren E., and Thomas P. Bonczar. *Probation and Parole in the United States 2010,* report NCJ236019. Washington, DC: Bureau of Justice Statistics, 2011.

Glaze, Lauren E., and Laura M. Maruschak. *Parents in Prison and Their Minor Children.* Washington, DC: U.S. Department of Justice, 2008.

Grattet, Ryken, Joan Petersilia, and Jeffrey Lin. *Parole Violations and Revocations in California.* Washington, DC: National Institute of Justice, 2008.

Greenfield, Lawrence A., and Tracy Snell. *Women Offenders.* Washington, DC: Bureau of Justice Statistics, 2000.

Harer, Miles D. "Recidivism among Federal Prisoners Released in 1987." *Journal of Correctional Education* 46 (1994): 98–127.

Harris, Andrew, and Karl Hanson. *Public Safety and Emergency Preparedness: Sex Offender Recidivism; A Simple Question, 2004–03*. Ottawa, Ontario: Her Majesty the Queen in Right of Canada, 2004.

Harris, David A. *Profiles in Injustice: Why Police Profiling Cannot Work*. New York: New Press, 2002.

Harrison, Paige M., and William J. Sabol. *Prisoners in 2010*. Revised report NCJ 236096. Washington, DC: Bureau of Justice Statistics, 2011.

Hirsch, Amy, Sharon Dietrich, Rue Landau, Peter Schneider, Irv Arckelsberg, Judith Bernstein-Baker, and Joseph Hohenstein. *Every Door Closed: Barriers Facing Parents with Criminal Records*. Washington, DC, and Philadelphia: Center for Law and Social Policy, 2002.

Howerton, Amanda, Ross Burnett, Richard Byng, and John Campbell. "The Consolations of Going Back to Prison: What 'Revolving Door' Prisoners Think of Their Prospects." *Journal of Offender Rehabilitation* 48 (2009): 439–461.

Kansal, Tushar. *Racial Disparity in Sentencing: A Review of the Literature*. Washington, DC: Sentencing Project, Community Legal Services, 2005.

Langan, Patrick A., and David J. Levin: *Recidivism of Prisoners Released in 1994*. Washington, DC: Bureau of Justice Statistics, 2002.

Langan, Patrick A., Erica L. Schmitt, and Matthew R. Durose. *Recidivism of Sex Offenders Released from Prison in 1994*, NCJ 193427. Washington, DC: Bureau of Justice Statistics, 2011.

Legal Action Center. *After Prison: Roadblocks to Reentry, 2009 Update*. New York: Legal Action Center, 2009.

Lundman, Richard J., and Robert L. Kaufman. "Driving while Black: Effects of Race, Ethnicity, and Gender on Citizen Self-Reports of Traffic Stops and Police Actions." *Criminology* 41 (2003): 195–220.

Lyles-Chockley, Adrienne. "Transitions to Justice: Prisoner Reentry as an Opportunity to Confront and Counteract Racism." *Hastings Race & Poverty Law Journal* 6, no. 2 (2009): 259.

Maltz, Michael D. *Recidivism: Quantitative Studies in Social Sciences*. Orlando, FL: Academic Press, 1984.

Martinson, Robert. "What Works? Questions and Answers about Prison Reform." *National Affairs* 35 (1974): 22–54.

Mauer, Marc, and Ryan S. King. *Uneven Justice: State Rates of Incarceration by Race and Ethnicity*. Washington, DC: Sentencing Project, Community Legal Services 2007.

Minton, Todd. *Jail Inmates at Midyear 2011*. Report NCJ 237961. Washington, DC: U.S. Department of Justice, Bureau of Justice Statistics, 2012.

Mumola, Christopher J. *Incarcerated Parents and Their Children*. Washington, DC: U.S. Department of Justice, Bureau of Justice Statistics, 2000.

National Institute of Corrections. *Report to the Nation: FY 2010*. Washington, DC: U.S. Department of Justice, 2011.

Pager, Devah. "The Mark of a Criminal Record." *American Journal of Sociology* 108 (2003): 937–975.

Pager, Devah. *Marked: Race, Crime, and Finding Work in an Era of Mass Incarceration.* Chicago: University of Chicago Press, 2007.

Pollack, Jocelyn. *Prisons: Today and Tomorrow* (2nd ed.). Sadbury, MA: Jones and Bartlett, 2008.

Pryor, Marie. "The Unintended Effects of Prisoner Reentry Policy and the Marginalization of Urban Communities." *Dialectical Anthropology* 34, no. 4 (2010): 513–517.

Ripley, Amanda. "Outside the Gates: Living on the Outside." *Time*, January 13, 2002.

Sabol, William J., Todd D. Minton, and Paige M. Harrison. *Prison and Jail Inmates at Midyear 2006.* Special Report NCJ 217675. Washington, DC: Bureau of Justice Statistics, 2007.

Sampson, Robert J., and John Laub. "A Life-Course Theory of Cumulative Disadvantage and the Stability of Delinquency." *Advances in Criminological Theory* 7 (1997): 133–161.

Sentencing Project. "Felony Disenfranchisement," n.d. Accessed on July 2, 2012, http://www.sentencingproject.org/template/page.cfm?id=133.

Simon, Jonathan. *Poor Discipline: Parole and the Social Control of the Underclass, 1890–1990.* Chicago: University of Chicago Press, 1993.

Uggen, Christopher. "Work as a Turning Point in the Life Course of Criminals: A Duration Model of Age, Employment and Recidivism." *American Sociological Review* 65 (2000): 529–546.

United States Sentencing Commission. *Measuring Recidivism: The Criminal History Computation of the Federal Sentencing Guidelines.* Washington, DC: United States Sentencing Commission, 2004.

Walmsley, Roy. *World Prison Population List* (9th ed.). London: International Centre for Prison Studies, 2011.

Warren, Jennifer, Adam Gelb, and Jake Horowitz. *One in 100: Behind Bars in America.* Washington, DC: Pew Charitable Trusts, 2008.

Wehrman, Michael M. "Race and Gender Inequality in Recidivism." *Sociology Compass* 5, no. 9 (2011): 846–849.

Wellisch, Jean, M. Douglas Anglin, and Michael L. Prendergast. "Number and Characteristics of Drug-Using Women in the Criminal Justice System: Implications for Treatment." *Journal of Drug Issues* 23, no.1 (1993): 7–30.

Western, Bruce. "Reentry: Reversing Mass Imprisonment." *Boston Review*, July/August 2008, 31–43.

Yoder, Steve. "Life on the List." *American Prospect* 22, no. 4 (2011): 29–32.

Zaitz, Les. "Abuse of Women Inmates at Oregon's Coffee Creek Prison Goes on for Years," April 29, 2012. Accessed January 5, 2013 from http://www.oregonlive.com/politics/index.ssf/2012/04/abuse_of_women_inmates_at_oreg.html.

Chapter 26

Racial/Ethnic Imprisonment and the Larger Community Effects

Eileen M. Ahlin

Incarceration disproportionately affects African Americans and Hispanics, similar to the more commonly studied social disadvantages—such as lower socioeconomic status, lower quality and less advanced education, and residential segregation—experienced by minorities in the United States. This disparity not only impacts the individuals who are sentenced to jail or prison, but it also has larger effects on the community as a whole. In this chapter, I discuss how incarceration became a racial issue and the effects overincarceration has on minority communities and society as a whole. The chapter concludes by summarizing the issues and suggesting methods for addressing the effects of disproportionate racial and ethnic imprisonment on the larger community.

Changing Tides: How Minorities Became the Majority in Jails and Prisons

The corrections system between 1925 and 1975 is often characterized by "stability of punishment." During this period, the incarceration rate was consistently around 100 per 100,000 of the resident population. In the 1920s and 1930s, the percentage of whites incarcerated in state and federal prisons was in the range of 78 to 73, declining over time, and African Americans comprised the balance.[1] At this time, Hispanic ethnicity was not distinguished from race. Between 1942 and 1964, the number of incarcerated whites was about two-thirds, and in the 1970s, the racial gap became narrower until African Americans became the majority of those imprisoned in the late 1980s.[2] Today, these numbers are much larger, particularly for minorities, who are admitted to prison at higher rates than whites. For example, African Americans and Hispanics are incarcerated at 6.7 and 2.7 times the rate of whites, respectively,[3] but only comprise 12.6 percent and 16 percent of the total U.S. population.[4] This surge in the use of incarceration can be traced to several occurrences. Most notable are the war on crime and the war on drugs.

During the post–civil rights era, crime control became a focus of both Republicans and Democrats because crime rates were skyrocketing. Crime was the focus of the 1964 presidential election, and it was used by both Barry Goldwater (the Republican nominee) and Lyndon Johnson (the Democratic nominee) to influence voters. Johnson won the election and as part of his administration, he appointed the Presidential Commission on Law Enforcement to examine the rising crime problem and develop a blueprint for addressing crime in the United States. The final report of this committee, *The Challenge of Crime in a Free Society*, endorsed decreased use of prisons, as well as support for rehabilitation and addressing social welfare policies. This report was presented as President Nixon took office. However, Republicans were more focused on crime control. This tough on crime stance supported the construction of prisons and punitive enforcement of criminals, particularly drug offenders. Simultaneously, the deindustrialization of America's inner cities contributed to the demise of employment for blue collar and working-class skilled laborers that impacted the economic situations of many minorities.[5] To address the demise of inner cities, President Nixon called for a war on crime to control the rising crime rate and contain black radicalism and black power arising from the civil rights movement.

In the 1980s, the focus became drug use. During the Reagan administration, the war on crime transformed to the war on drugs, which intensified the disparity in punishment meted out to whites and African Americans. One example of this is the disparity between sentencing laws for possession of powder cocaine and crack. Until the Fair Sentencing Act of 2010 was signed into law by President Barack Obama, mandatory minimum prison sentences were enacted for possession of crack or cocaine at a ratio of 1 gram of crack versus 100 grams of cocaine (the current ratio is 1:18). This ratio was established by the Anti-Drug Abuse Act of 1986 and 1988, at the peak of the U.S. drug epidemic. The ratio between the two forms of the drug was so large because crack was cheaper and thought to be more addictive than the powered form of the drug, cocaine (though this has since been disputed).[6] Even though the number of whites who have used cocaine or crack is higher than the number of African Americans who have used either substance, and even though the rate of drug use between the two groups is comparable,[7] the war on drugs unfavorably targeted African Americans and led to disproportionate arrest rates. The mandatory minimum sentences associated with possession of crack dramatically increased the incarceration rate of drug offenders, particularly minorities. Incarceration for drugs in the 1980s escalated arrest rates and increased minorities' risk of being sent to jail or prison.[8]

These contextual influences impacted the number of young minorities, particularly men, who were encountering the criminal justice system due to not only increasing participation in the drug trade, but the underlying social disadvantage experienced in their community. Scholars believe that the war on drugs was not really about drugs; rater, it was a mechanism to target minority communities to save them from drug abuse and the associated violence.[9] It led to an increased number of persons of color serving time in jails and prisons, a disparity that continues today.

Current Trends

The practices of the mid- to late 20th century have carried over into the new millennium. As a result, spending time behind bars is not an equal opportunity rite of passage. It affects young African-American males living in large cities and other urban areas more than any other group.[10] Scholar Bruce Western estimates that 60 percent of African-American males who do not finish high school will be incarcerated at some point during their lives.[11] The reality of incarceration also disproportionately affects Hispanics. Despite their gains as a group in a variety of social areas (increasing rates of school attendance and working in the labor market[12]), Hispanics' involvement in the criminal justice system, including incarceration, has also increased in recent years. Currently, Hispanics are the fastest growing group spending time in jail or prison.

While these communities are clearly impacted, often the effects of incarceration are discussed at the micro level. Scholars and policymakers alike contemplate the impact incarceration has on the offender or the victim. These individual-level factors are undoubtedly important topics to consider when evaluating incarceration practices and social service programs. However, Rose and Clear make a compelling argument that incarceration also impacts the community at-large.[13] Social networks and interpersonal relationships are disrupted when someone is incarcerated, which punishes offenders along with the people in their ecological systems, from the microsystem (e.g., family, neighborhood) to the macrosystem (e.g., cultural context).[14] Specifically, incarceration affects communities by reducing family stability, altering parental capacity and oversight, and weakening the economic capacity of its residents.[15] Given the racial disparities of imprisonment, the effects of incarceration are deeply felt in the African-American and Hispanic communities because they are overrepresented in the criminal justice system compared to their proportions in the general population. Further, the effects of imprisonment are often concentrated in certain areas[16] because, even at the beginning of the 21st century, many communities are still racially segregated. While the racial/ethnic disparities of incarceration are evident across the United States as a whole, more nuanced differences can be seen when one examines individual states and various regions of the country where there is a concentration of high incarceration rates among minority populations. For example, Mauer and King note that the highest African American–to-white and Hispanic-to-white ratio of incarceration is in the Northeast and Midwest.[17]

Incarcerating offenders to increase safety and promote community well-being assumes that offenders are a detriment only to the community to which they belong.[18] However, while offenders obviously detract from their community environment in specific ways (e.g., personal threats to safety and property), they may also provide clearly prosocial and positive attributes to their community such as acting as agents of informal social control in their neighborhoods, economically supporting their family, and being partners for their spouse (husband or wife) or significant other (boyfriend or girlfriend).[19] This not to say that all offenders should remain in the community; however, the balance between beneficial and negative contributions criminals make to the community is important to examine because the impact of incarceration is felt not only by the individual, but also the larger community. And these negative effects are disproportionately impacting minority communities.

Incarceration Disproportionately Impacts Minorities

In the previous section, I discussed how the war on crime and war on drugs have resulted in the disproportionate incarceration of minorities since the late 1970s. But how disparate are the numbers? This section addresses that question by examining the number of incarcerated people and their race/ethnicity.

TABLE 26.1   Percentage and Number of Prison Inmates at Year End, 2009

Offense	All Inmates	Male	Female	White[1]	Black[1]	Hispanic
Violent	53.2%	54.4%	35.9%	49.9%	54.9%	55.5%
	726,100	692,600	33,600	265,600	319,700	117,800
Property	19.2%	18.4%	29.6%	24.8%	15.2%	16.2%
	261,900	234,100	27,700	132,000	88,500	34,400
Drug	17.8%	17.2%	25.7%	13.9%	21.1%	19.5%
	242,900	218,800	24,000	73,900	122,600	41,400
Public-order[2]	8.9%	9%	7.2%	10.2%	8%	7.5%
	121,000	114,300	6,800	54,400	46,400	16,000
Other/ unspecified[3]	1%	1%	1.5%	1.1%	0.8%	1.2%
	13,900	12,400	1,400	6,000	4,900	2,500
Total %	100%	100%	100%	100%	100%	100%
Total number	1,365,800	1,272,200	93,600	532,000	582,100	212,100

[1]Excludes Hispanics and persons identifying as two or more races.

[2]Includes weapons, drunk driving, court offenses, commercialized vice, morals and decency offenses, liquor law violations, and other public-order offenses.

[3]Includes juvenile offenses and other unspecified offense categories.

Source: Guerino, Paul, Page M. Harrison, and William J. Sabol. 2011. *Prisoners in 2010*. Washington, DC: Bureau of Justice Statistics.

At the end of 2010, over 1.6 million persons were incarcerated in state or federal prisons and 735,601 were serving time in jails.[20] According to recent estimates, over 60 percent of inmates are minorities.[21] Table 26.1, which was adapted from data reported in the Bureau of Justice Statistics' *Prisoners in 2010*,[22] shows the percentage and corresponding number of persons by gender, race/ethnicity, and offense type, who were serving sentences of 1 year or more at the end of 2009.

Data on persons in jail are not as reliable because of the inherent turn-over among inmates. People serving short sentences, awaiting transfer to prison, or pending trial are released from jail on a regular basis. Estimates are often snapshots of average daily inmate populations.[23] However, data suggest that jail inmates are also primarily from minority groups. Forty-five percent of those serving time in jail are white, 38 percent are African American, and 15 percent are Hispanic.[24]

These percentages demonstrate the number of prison and jail inmates of various racial and ethnic backgrounds. However, the bigger picture of racial/ethnic disparities is cloudy without discussion of the representation of racial/ethnic groups among the U.S. population. One way to examine this issue is to standardize the numbers across a common metric, for example, rate of incarceration for someone of a particular race/ethnicity per 100,000 residents. In doing this, we can see that there are clear discrepancies.

In 2010, the rate of imprisonment was 3,074 per 100,000 U.S. residents for African-American, non-Hispanic males and 1,285 per 100,000 for Hispanic males compared to 459 per 100,000 for white males.[25] This translates to an incarceration rate that is 6.7 times higher for African-American males and 2.7 times higher for Hispanic males than their white male counterparts. There are similar discrepancies for minority females. In 2010, the rate of imprisonment was 133 per 100,000 U.S. residents for African-American, non-Hispanic females and 77 per 100,000 for Hispanic females compared to 47 per 100,000 for white females.[26] While there is seemingly less of a disparity in incarceration rates among females of different racial/ethnic backgrounds compared to males, the numbers show that rates of incarceration among African-American women and Hispanic women are 2.8 times and 1.6 times higher, respectively, than those experienced by white females.

These current rates of imprisonment are striking and highlight racial/ethnic disparities in the criminal justice system. If incarceration rates remain steady at their current levels, Mauer estimates that one in three African-American and one in six Hispanic males born today will serve time in prison at some point in their lives.[27] These high rates are drastic in comparison to the estimate that one in 17 white males will be incarcerated during his lifetime. The disparity for females is not as conspicuous; however, the imparity is still evident when one in 18 African-American and one in 45 Hispanic women can expect to spend time in prison compared to one in 111 white females.

While these are the best data available, adequate data on the number of Hispanics involved in the criminal justice system is limited, and several states do not collect information on this ethnic group at all.[28] Further, measures of race and ethnicity are often not mutually exclusive (e.g., Hispanic white or Hispanic black), and Hispanic ethnicity is not captured because it is confounded with a racial group. With the current data available, Hispanic males are more likely to spend time in jail or prison than whites but are at lower risk than African-American men. Hispanic women are three times more likely than white women to be incarcerated at some point in their lives. However, because of the incongruent methods for collecting

Hispanic ethnicity (if it is collected at all), Mauer and King suggest that current estimates of incarceration among Hispanics may be undercounted.[29]

The extreme number of persons incarcerated from the African-American and Hispanic populations has larger community effects during the periods of incarceration and after release. The remainder of this chapter addresses some of challenges to communities experiencing high rates of incarceration and highlights issues specific to African-American and Hispanic communities.

Larger Community Effects of Incarceration

Incarceration has a variety of effects on the larger community. These include macro level impacts on factors such as reduced informal social control, less civic participation, damage to the local economy and wages earned by ex-offenders residing in the area, and risks to public health. There are also certain barriers facing inmates as they return to the community after a period of incarceration that impact the offenders and their families and are felt more at the individual level but can also be detrimental to the well-being of a neighborhood. For example, ex-offenders have limits on the amount of public funding they can receive such as welfare and public housing, which can affect how well they are able to support their family. These factors are not unique to minority populations, but because African Americans and Hispanics already face a plethora of discrimination and biases, the label of offender (even ex-offender) can significantly add challenges over and above those they already experience. The various effects incarceration can have on the community are discussed in this section, as is scholarly research that explores these ideas.

Effects of Incarceration on Community Social Control

The criminal justice system is in a unique position to play a role in the exercise of both formal and informal social controls in the community. Hunter identified three sources of social control in communities: public, private, and parochial.[30] Public controls are formal, and private and parochial controls are informal. Public controls are experienced at a larger macro level and enacted by agencies like those found the criminal justice system (e.g., police, courts, and corrections). Private controls are exercised at the intimate level, such as family. Parochial controls are less intimate than private controls and are provided by the immediate community and contextual surroundings. While incarceration may seem well in the public sphere, incarceration also is related to private and parochial controls, and these controls compound discrimination.

The criminal justice system is tasked with ensuring that persons who violate the law are handled in a manner that reduces the risk to public safety. This formal (public) control is enacted by the three main criminal justice agencies: law enforcement, courts, and corrections. Police are the front-line representation of the criminal justice system, and their actions as well as the consequences of their actions trickle down to the courts, which hear and decide outcomes of charges against arrestees and the corrections system that is responsible for the custody of offenders sentenced to jail or prison and supervision of offenders serving time in the community. This is important to the topic of the effects of incarceration on the larger community because, for example, the corrections system interacts only with offenders who were arrested by law enforcement and adjudicated by a court, which limits the amount of culpability related to who becomes incarcerated that can be attributed to corrections. The criminal justice system plays a pivotal role in determining who will be arrested, prosecuted, and sentenced to various correctional options,[31] and each step provides an opportunity for racial discrimination.[32] Incarceration is a function of the larger criminal justice system working together, and all parts need to be considered in any serious discussion of the disproportionate incarceration of minorities.

Incarceration, which is a function of public formal controls, can negatively impact private controls such as the immediate family and parochial controls found in the community. These mechanisms of formal social control directly impact community levels of informal social control and can limit a community's ability to control crime at the local neighborhood level and within families.[33] A concentration of incarceration in communities negatively impacts the informal social controls in those areas by weakening the formation of families, reducing participation in the labor force, and altering which people (and how many) are available to engage other members of the community to form informal social controls.[34]

One example of the negative impact of concentrated incarceration is the theory of collective efficacy. Collective efficacy is the shared expectations for informal social control in public spaces, and the mutual trust and willingness among individuals to take action in their neighborhood against social ills such as crime.[35] It pertains to the ability of individuals in a neighborhood to maintain order within the community and a group's shared belief that action can be realized through combined efforts.[36] Collective efficacy is comprised of informal social control and social cohesion. Communities with high levels of collective efficacy can realize their common goals through shared expectations and beliefs and a sense of mutual trust. Incarceration can impact the level of collective efficacy available in the community, which can influence community safety. Incarcerating large numbers of adults in an area reduces the number of people available to provide informal social controls and to engage in collective efficacy in that community.

Additionally, people who live in communities with high levels of incarceration and, consequently, reentry of those returning to their communities, may also feel stigmatized, and living among ex-offenders in their neighborhoods can create a problematic sense of identity for the community members.[37] This disaggregated sense of belonging and shared values can negatively impact levels of informal social control and collective efficacy at the neighborhood level, which in turn, reduces the community's ability to maintain order and informally control crime. A disconnect between an individual and his or her neighborhood can reduce the likelihood that residents will engage in community activities that could provide benefits to other residents. For example, Lynch, Sabol, Planty, and Shelly demonstrate that incarceration rates have a negative effect on attachment to communities and participation in voluntary organizations within communities.[38] The cycle of incarceration and reentry compounds this issue.

Effects of Prisoner Reentry on the Community

Reentry is a process that begins during the period of incarceration and continues in the community. It is a challenging time for offenders, and several barriers exist for inmates once they are released from prison and return to the community. Returning prisoners are in desperate need of programs to prepare them for release and, if they are to succeed as free citizens, many require services such as employment training and general assistance to secure housing, obtain a driver's license, and regain custody of their children or begin paying child support once they return to their communities. While parole/probation is still used for some offenders leaving prison, many inmates reentering society do not experience postrelease supervision because their sentence expired and they are no longer required to be under supervision.[39] With or without postrelease supervision, returning offenders often struggle with a variety of social problems that may have contributed to their incarceration: being unemployable due to a criminal record, particularly among African Americans[40]; barriers to certain jobs[41]; lack of education[42]; limits on federal funds for higher education; lack of treatment for substance dependence or use[43] and lack of treatment for chronic health and/or mental health problems[44]; limited access to public housing (Department of Housing and Urban Development v. Rucker [122 S. Ct. 1230 2002]); limits on the availability of welfare and public assistance; disenfranchisement[45]; and child support and custody issues.[46] All of these prohibitions do not exist in all states, but they are prevalent enough to impact an individual's ability reenter society successfully and can be detrimental to the community as a whole. The high number of offenders (two-thirds) returning to prison for a new offense or technical violation (about one-fourth)[47] indicates a failure to reintegrate offenders back into society,[48] and this failure may be attributable to these barriers of reentry.

As a result of these individual roadblocks to reentry, local communities are also impacted by the release of inmates. Most inmates do not serve life sentences and are released after serving a period of time behind bars. In 2010, there were 708,677 prisoners released from both state and federal prisons,[49] and approximately 230,000 inmates are released from jail each week.[50] People often return to their old communities after release and because there is a clustering of released offenders in a small number of communities,[51] particularly cities,[52] the effects of incarceration can adversely impact those communities.[53] One way incarceration impacts the community is when returning prisoners influence the crime rate. Hipp and Yates found that parolees who were released and returned to neighborhoods in Sacramento, California, increased crime rates in the census tracts in which they were residing.[54] In particular, when there was an increase in the number of violent parolees in an area, there was also an increase in murder and burglary rates.

There is also a reciprocal relationship between communities and ex-offenders. The resources available in a community can influence whether a returning prisoner recidivates. In general, Mears, Wang, Hay, and Bales found that ex-offenders returning to resource-deprived communities (measured as a weighted factor score of median family income, percentage of female-headed household, percentage unemployed, percentage in poverty, and percentage receiving public assistance) were more likely to be reconvicted for violent and drug-related crimes. Further, this finding is moderated by race. Non-white males are at higher risk for recidivism in resource-deprived areas than are whites.[55]

While many barriers exist, ex-offenders have some options following release, and while the criminal justice system may limit their movements (e.g., moving to another state without permission), they are not required to return to the neighborhood or even city where they lived before they were incarcerated. They can choose to relocate to a community with more resources and options for employment that can increase their chances of success and that may also have fewer distractions—such as the crowd they use to hang out with—that could increase their chances of returning to their old criminal ways. Research suggests that those who choose to settle in new places after a period of incarceration may be less likely to recidivate and return to prison, but in doing so, they risk being cut off from their existing family and community support system.[56]

The remaining sections of this chapter will delve deeper into the barriers mentioned at the outset of this section. The discussion revolves around the issues facing individuals during periods of incarceration and upon release. While these barriers apply to all persons facing incarceration, the focus here is on how minorities and their communities are impacted by incarceration. Many of these barriers target persons convicted of drug-related crimes. Thus, the majority of persons affected by these bans are minorities. As was discussed in the introduction to this chapter, the war on drugs and the war on crime disproportionately targeted African Americans at the outset and are currently ensnaring Hispanics in larger numbers as well.

Effects of Incarceration on Public Supports: Public Housing, Welfare, and Funds for Higher Education

There are federal limitations on public housing for those convicted of drug crimes. Section 8 of the Housing Act of 1937 provides federally subsidized rental housing for low-income families. The program includes tenant-based housing (vouchers are given to tenants that they can use to rent from private landlords) and project-based housing (housing units rather than tenants are subsidized). In 1988, Congress amended the U.S. Housing Act and enacted a tough policy for persons residing in Section 8 housing. This amendment stipulates that persons convicted of drug-related crimes are not eligible for federally funded housing. Further, if a drug-related crime occurs in a residence funded by public housing, the family is to be evicted.

This policy is in place to help reduce the amount of drug-related crime occurring in and around public housing. However, many people become homeless because of the indiscretion of one family member or a guest to the household. This impacts African Americans at a disproportionate rate because they inhabit public housing at a greater rate than do whites.[57]

Later, in the 1990s, the federal government expanded public support prohibitions to include limitations on welfare and money for college for convicted drug offenders. First, the 1996 federal welfare reform law creating a lifetime ban on Temporary Assistance for Needy Families (TANF) and food stamp benefits for persons convicted of felony drug offenses. Second, the 1998 reauthorization of Title IV of the Higher Education Act of 1965 included a restriction on federal student loan eligibility and Pell grants for persons convicted of possessing or selling drugs.

These public support prohibitions discriminate against persons, mostly minorities, who have been involved in the criminal justice system as a result of a drug offense. This discrimination comes following release from prisons, when ex-offenders need support more than ever. The effects of these prohibitions are often deeper than was originally intended. In the next section, I will examine the impact these and other barriers to reentry have on the family unit (spouses and children) in general.

Effects of Incarceration on Families and Children

The impact of incarceration on the family and children of those imprisoned unfolds over time. Incarceration is not a discrete event, and therefore, its effects are not static. Experiencing a period of incarceration even reduces the likelihood that men, particularly African American men, will ever marry.[58] Scholar Anthony King predicts that the overuse of incarceration among African Americans will lead to the dissolution of African American families.[59] Also, spending time in prison can also impact a person's capacity to be a successful parent. Inmates are subject to conditions that impact their psychological well-being, such as being overcontrolled by prison staff, which can make them distrustful and emotionally unavailable for their children.[60]

Having a spouse or partner who is incarcerated leaves a hole in the family structure that is ideally be filled by another intimate partner.[61] However, minority women are at a disadvantage if they look to replace a spouse or partner with someone from their community because, statistically speaking, the odds of finding a quality eligible minority male who is not incarcerated are low.[62] In general, overincarceration of minority males also reduces the availability of marriageable men in the community[63] due to their removal from the community and decreased job marketability.[64] Release from prison and reentry to the family can difficult, as the nonincarcerated party (a spouse or significant other) will often have successfully adapted to the situation, perhaps with a new partner serving as parental figure to the children.[65] In other cases, the returning parent may not be welcome to rejoin the family or see his or her children at all, as Sullivan found among unwed African-American fathers who were released from prison.[66]

While the effects of incarceration on the husband, wife, or significant other dynamic are important, the effect of incarceration on a child is undeniable and difficult to justify. About 52 percent of state inmates and 63 percent of federal inmates are parents of children under the age of 18.[67] This means that about 1.7 million children in the United States have one or more parent behind bars (8 percent of incarcerated mothers report that their spouse is also incarcerated, while only 2 percent of incarcerated fathers have an incarcerated spouse).[68] Disparity in offender incarceration trickles down to their children. Approximately half of all imprisoned parents are African American, and about 25 percent are Hispanic.[69] African-American children are 7.5 times and Hispanic children are more than 2.5 times more likely than white children to have a parent incarcerated. African-American and Hispanic male inmates are more likely to report being parents than are their white counterparts. There are fewer differences among women inmates. Overall, about 2 percent of all minors in the United States have an incarcerated parent, but for minorities, the effect of incarceration is much more daunting: 6.7 percent of all African-American and 2.4 percent of all Hispanic minor children live without a parent because that parent is serving time for committing a crime.[70] This number may be even higher when one accounts for jail inmates, whose numbers are not systematically accounted for by corrections officials but are estimated to be in the millions.[71] Johnson estimates that 20 percent of African-American children have a father who has been incarcerated.[72]

Incarceration removes the parent from the child's life and redistributes the workload to provide daily care and financial support to the remaining parent, extended family members, or the public welfare system (e.g., child welfare, foster care).[73] The remaining parent loses financial support (legal and illegal income)[74] and often redirects a part of her income to her loved on in prison via phone calls, letters, deposits in a commissary account, and long trips for in-person visits.[75]

Many parents are able to maintain contact with their children while they are incarcerated, but just over half (55 percent) have in-person visits.[76] A child who visits his or her parent during the period of incarceration may benefit once that parent is released. LaVigne and colleagues found that fathers who experienced more face-to-face visits and letters were more involved with their children following release.[77] However, children may also experience problems after in-person visits, like trouble concentrating in school.[78] Overall, children tend to benefit from staying in touch with their incarcerated parents.[79]

There are many detrimental impacts of growing up with a parent behind bars. These include emotional and psychological developmental delays, development of serious mental health disorders, and poor school performance.[80] The effects vary for each developmental stage, ranging from poor parent-child bonding during infancy to criminality as a young adult.[81] Youth who have a parent behind bars are more likely to engage in delinquency and antisocial behavior.[82] Family members may feel stigmatized by having a loved one in jail or prison, attenuating the already fragile family ties.[83]

Further, many incarcerated parents have family members who have also served time in jail or prison.[84] This underscores the potential for intergenerational transmission of antisocial norms (where serving time in jail or prison becomes normative) and can improve expectations regarding interactions with the criminal justice system as a minority.[85] Serving time is no longer a threat in many communities. Rather, it is just another phase in the life course of a minority male, particularly those with low levels of education. Pettit and Western discovered that the incarceration binge resulting from the war on drugs and general "get tough" attitude toward crime in the 1980s and 1990s resulted in more African-American males serving time than enlisting in the military or graduating from college.[86] Further, 68 percent of African-American male high school dropouts will be incarcerated by the time they are 34.[87] The percentage of African-American offenders arrested for drug-related crimes rose from 21 percent in 1980 to 36 percent in 1992.[88] This is not only disproportionate to the percentage of African Americans in the U.S. population (as of the 2010 Census, 12.6 percent of the U.S. population was African American[89]), but it is contradictory to research indicating they are no more likely to be drug users or drug traffickers than are whites or Hispanics.[90] However, by 2008, 65 percent of drug offenders in state prisons were African American or Hispanic.[91]

Upon reentry, parents are faced with several situations that also impact their children. One potentially devastating problem is that of regaining custody upon release. Many incarcerated mothers were the primary caregivers of their children and were living with their children.[92] Less than a third of these children live with their father during their mother's incarceration.[93] Depending on how long the mother has been incarcerated, her children may have entered the foster care system. The Adoption and Safe Families Act (ASFA), which was signed by President Clinton in 1997, and whose primary purpose was to expedite the placement of foster children into permanent homes, authorizes the termination of parental rights when a child has been living in foster care for 15 of the past 22 months. According to ASFA, permanency hearings must be held within 12 months of a child's entering the foster care system. Moye and Rinker argue that ASFA inherently limits the ability of families to successfully reunite.[94] Foster care in and of itself is a risk factor for future incarceration, unemployment, and dropping out of high school.[95]

Effect of Incarceration on Employment and the Local Economy

After incarceration, offenders return to the community and often need to find work to support themselves. Finding legitimate work can be an intimidating experience for ex-offenders (who may have to disclose their prior conviction history to employers when applying for certain jobs[96]) and may be prohibitive due to life circumstances (e.g., lack of education). In fact, several studies demonstrate that finding a job is more difficult for minorities than whites possibly due to discrimination.[97] However, working postrelease is one of the best predictors of remaining recidivism-free.[98]

Offenders who leave prison and return to disadvantaged neighborhoods face difficulties in finding jobs and earn lower wages if they are employed.[99] Ex-offenders who are not employed are also more likely to recidivate.[100] This is particularly true for violent crimes among African-American inmates returning to areas with high levels of unemployment.[101]

Once a job is secured, two discriminatory factors still remain: job stability and wage earnings. Job stability is less likely and welfare dependence more likely among those who had dealings with the corrections system.[102] It has also been documented that wage earnings are disparate among those who have spent time in prisons/jails, particularly African Americans and Hispanics.[103]

Former inmates who can find steady, gainful employment are less likely to recidivate and return to prison.[104] Those who have strong social ties to their families are better equipped to obtain a job, even if they suffered previous bouts of unemployment.[105] Ex-inmates with jobs can also serve as better parents and spouses by providing financially for their family.[106] However, most employers are not willing to hire ex-inmates, though this may depend on the crime the prospective hire was charged with committing.[107]

Pager examined the issue of employability among ex-offenders by using a randomized experiment to isolate the effects of race and criminal history on being contacted for an interview. She recruited four males (two African American and two white) to apply for entry-level jobs in the Milwaukee area. In each pair, one job seeker was assigned an "ex-offender" status (felony-level drug offense), and each person in the pair applied for the same employment opportunity. The study identified significant racial differences among the "noncriminals" in the two pairs—whites were more likely than African Americans to receive a call from the hiring organization. What was strikingly disturbing was that white "ex-offenders" were slightly more likely than African American "noncriminals" to be contacted again; however, the difference did not reach levels of significance. The finding that white felons were preferred candidates for entry-level jobs over African Americans without a criminal record is a clear message that minorities face serious barriers to employment in general, and adding a criminal record to the mix simply intensifies the despondency of situation. In an updated test of this work, Pager and colleagues found similar results but demonstrated that positive face-to-face interactions with potential employers assist job-seekers, even those with criminal histories, as they can explain their background and provide some reassurance to the hiring agent about their job skills. However, similar to Pager's original work, African Americans were not called for interviews as frequently as whites and therefore had less opportunity to discuss their criminal background and assuage any fears the employer may have about their fit for the position.[108]

The Effects of Incarceration on Civic Participation

Upon turning 18 years old, the age of majority, everyone inherits the right to vote in local and national elections, regardless of race/ethnicity or gender. This basic right, however, can be terminated for offenders temporarily while they serve their sentence (in jail, prison, or the community) or permanently. This loss of voting privileges is called disenfranchisement. A ban on the right to vote is often not the first thought conjured when thinking about the effects of incarceration on the community. The loss of voting privileges may seem to be a small loss in comparison to other losses of freedom such as incarceration and barriers to the process of reentry (e.g., lack of employable skills, job opportunities). However, there are significant social repercussions that are impacted by policies that prevent current or ex-felons from voting.

Currently, over 5 million persons (2.4 percent of the U.S. population) are disenfranchised in the United States, and about 2 million (8.3 percent) African Americans are not allowed to vote.[109] The result of this seemingly arbitrary collateral consequence is that about 13 percent of African-American males are ineligible to vote for their representatives.[110]

Only two states—Maine and Vermont—permit inmates who are serving sentences for felony convictions to vote during their period of incarceration, while the other 48 states and the District of Columbia have laws against voting.[111] Additionally, states prevent offenders from voting while they are supervised in the community under parole ($n = 35$) or during periods of probation ($n = 30$). Florida, Iowa, Kentucky, and Virginia are the harshest states in terms of disenfranchisement, as they prevent felons from ever voting again. The inability to vote may not directly influence deterrence, but it can impact how ex-offenders view themselves as citizens.[112]

On a national level, the practice of disenfranchisement may have impacted the 2000 and 2004 presidential elections, in which Democrats lost close races. Elections are often won by narrow margins, and in these cases, every vote counts. It was estimated that over 4 million persons were prevented from voting in the 2000 presidential election because of a prior felony conviction.[113] In this election, George W. Bush, a Republican, won Florida's Electoral College votes by 537 popular votes over then vice president Al Gore, the Democratic candidate.[114] In their book *Locked Out: Felon Disenfranchisement and American Democracy*, Manza and Uggen detail how barring felons from voting impacted the outcome of the 2000 presidential election, when 614,000 ex-felons were prohibited from voting in Florida.[115] The margin of votes between the lead candidates was wider in the 2004 race. Bush garnered 380,978 more popular votes than Senator John Kerry, the Democratic candidate. However, it is estimated that about 960,000 ex-felons in Florida were disenfranchised during the 2004 presidential election—more than enough to have potentially changed the outcome of the election in favor of John Kerry over the eventual winner

President George W. Bush. Disenfranchisement disproportionately affects African-American citizens (who tend to vote Democratic and are overrepresented in the criminal justice system) and not only limits ex-inmates' reintegration into "normal" society and prohibits full participation in a fundamental part of democratic citizenship, but also significantly impacts the course of history by potentially altering election outcomes.

The basis for current disenfranchisement policies (i.e., linking the loss of voting privileges to any felony conviction rather than for a certain type of crime as was commonplace in colonial times) is linked to the period of Reconstruction after the Civil War when African Americans were first experiencing freedom on a large scale.[116] Uggen and colleagues underscore the fact that disenfranchisement is essentially racially neutral on the surface; however, they also note clear racial links to its development and continued use.[117] Over time, between 1850 and 2002, states were more likely to enact more conservative disenfranchisement policies, removing more voting rights from felons and ex-felons as minority populations in prisons increased.[118]

Effects of Incarceration on Public Health

Inmates face myriad health challenges at disparate rates compared to the general population. These include substance abuse or dependence (68 percent),[119] serious mental health problems (16 percent),[120] and homelessness prior to incarceration (14 percent).[121] Inmates are also at increased risk for public health and medical issues, including contagious infectious diseases. Prisons are institutions of total control that force inmates to reside in close quarters with an ever-changing selection of fellow cellmates and dayroom co-habitants. The risk of transmitting disease between inmates is increased over the general population because prisons are self-contained, and inmates are often into close contact with infected individuals.

One high-profile problem that disproportionately affects inmates is HIV and AIDS. New cases of HIV/AIDS have decreased in recent years but remain a significant health issue in state and federal prisons. The rate of AIDS in prison (0.41 percent) is more than twice that of the general U.S. population (0.17 percent). By the end of 2008, 1.5 percent of inmates in a state or federal prison ($n = 21,987$) were HIV positive or had a confirmed diagnosis of AIDS, and HIV and AIDS disproportionately impact minority populations in prison. In 2007, African-American inmates accounted for 65 percent of AIDS-related deaths. About half of the states ($n = 24$) test inmates for HIV at some point during their prison sentence (upon admission, while in custody, or at the time of release), and all states and the federal prison system test inmates upon request or if they exhibit clinical symptoms of the either disease.[122]

High rates of incarceration can also negatively impact public health among the general population. In terms of HIV/AIDS, all communities are at risk when infected inmates are released if the ex-offender does not take proper precautions to prevent the transmission of the disease (by not sharing needles, practicing safe sex, and preventing others from coming into direct contact with their blood). However, as stated earlier, some communities are more likely to have larger concentrations of former inmates, which increases their risk for contagion due to increased exposure. The number of AIDS cases among prisoners is higher in Florida, New York, and Texas than other states.[123] Assuming these inmates are returning to communities in these states, individuals in those areas would be at higher risk if they had risky contacts (unprotected sex, dirty needle sharing) with infected persons.

Sexually transmitted infections (STIs) are also a health risk in jails and prisons that can translate into a risk to the community once offenders are released. Thomas and Torrone examined rates of imprisonment from 1995 through 2000 in North Carolina and community rates of STIs from 1996 through 2002. Creating a lag variable to account for prison entry and return to the community and establishing causal ordering, they found a strong correlation between the incarceration rate and an increase in common sexually transmitted infections in the community (e.g., chlamydia and gonorrhea).[124]

Conclusion

This chapter reviews many of the challenges facing not only individuals, but the larger community as a result of the disproportionate incarceration of racial and ethnic minorities. These issues include the negative effects on informal social controls among the family and neighborhoods with high rates of incarceration; skewed election results because ex-offenders cannot vote or do not know how and when they can reinstate their voting rights; a lower overall socioeconomic status of offenders and their communities because they will, on average, earn less over their lifetime; and the concern over potential increases in communicable diseases in communities where a large number of prisoners return to live after a period of incarceration.

Other limitations facing offenders and their communities are barriers to public supports such as public housing, welfare, and financial support to attend college. These roadblocks can intensify an already stressful period during reentry to the community after a period of incarceration and further limit the potential for an ex-offender to rebuild his or her life and begin on the path to desistance. There are also prohibitions on the parental rights of ex-felons that can impact the number of single-parent households in an area and negatively affect the number of children who will be retained in foster care or may even be adopted despite the willingness of a parent to retain custody.

What is most discouraging is the effect that incarceration has on innocent people, particularly children. The overreliance upon incarceration is most evident when we step back and realize that 1.7 million children are facing an uncertain future because one or both of their parents are incarcerated. Children of incarcerated parents can have their lives disrupted as they move in with family members or through the child welfare system in foster care if a relative is unavailable or unwilling to care for them. They often are limited in their communications with their incarcerated parent because of the distance between their homes and the correctional facility. These children will face an uphill battle in school and in their general emotional and psychological development, and they are at increased risk for serious mental health disorders and becoming delinquent.

Many of these negative effects of incarceration on the larger community could be avoided or mitigated with adaptations to formal social controls by the police, courts, and corrections systems.[125] In particular, changes could be enacted to ensure better racial/ethnic equality related to policies surrounding patrol and arrest practices; disparities in sentencing could be corrected, as was done with the reformation of the crack-cocaine mandatory sentencing laws; and community supervision or shorter sentences could meet the need to hold offenders accountable but also decrease the magnitude of the effects of incarceration on the offender and the community. Incarcerated parents of minor children are more likely to be serving time for drug, property, or public order offenses rather than violent crimes,[126] and these are offenses that could easily be punished via community corrections. Changing the way formal controls are enacted could permanently alter the life course of a child for the better. At the community level, lowering rates of incarceration may also improve the economic outlook of children. High levels of incarceration, particularly in areas where the majority of residents are racial/ethnic minorities, can increase rates of child poverty.[127] Reducing the use of jail and prison in areas where incarceration has become the norm may begin to reverse the negative effects the incarceration binge has in minority communities.

Notes

1. Langan, 1991.
2. Langan, 1991. See also Tonry, 1995.
3. Guerino, Harrison, and Sabol, 2011; Hartney and Vuong, 2009.
4. Humes, Jones, and Ramirez, 2011.
5. See Wilson, 1987.
6. See Schuster, 2002.
7. Substance Abuse and Mental Health Services Administration, 2010.
8. Tonry, 1995; Tonry and Melewski, 2008.
9. Fellner, 2009; Nunn, 2002.
10. Lynch and Sabol, 1997.
11. Western, 2006.
12. Fry, 2009.
13. Rose and Clear, 1998.
14. Bronfenbrenner, 1979.
15. Clear, 2007.
16. See Clear, 2007.
17. Mauer and King, 2007.
18. Rose and Clear, 1998.
19. Clear, Rose, and Ryder, 2001; Hagan and Coleman, 2001.
20. Guerino, Harrison, and Sabol, 2011; Minton, 2012.
21. Sentencing Project, 2012.
22. Guerino, Harrison, and Sabol, 2011.
23. See Minton, 2012.
24. Minton, 2012.
25. Guerino, Harrison, and Sabol, 2011.
26. Guerino, Harrison, and Sabol, 2011.
27. Mauer, 2011.
28. Mauer and King, 2007.
29. Mauer and King, 2007.
30. Hunter, 1985.
31. See Wilson and Kelling, 1982.
32. See Crutchfield, Bridges, and Pitchford, 1994; Mauer, 2011.
33. See Lynch and Sabol, 2001; Rose and Clear, 1998.
34. See Lynch and Sabol, 2001.
35. Sampson, Raudenbush, and Earls, 1997.
36. Sampson, Raudenbush, and Earls, 1997.

37. Clear, Rose, and Ryder, 2001.

38. Lynch, Sabol, Planty, and Shelly, 2002.

39. Petersilia, 2003.

40. Pager, 2003; Western, Kling, and Weiman, 2001.

41. Matthews and Casarjian, 2002.

42. Harlow, 2003; Petersilia, 2003.

43. Mumola and Karberg, 2006.

44. Travis, 2005.

45. Behrens, Uggen, and Manza, 2003; Uggen and Manza, 2002.

46. Center for Policy Research, 2006.

47. See Langan and Levin, 2002.

48. Lynch and Sabol, 2001.

49. Guerino, Harrison, and Sabol, 2011.

50. Solomon, Osborne, LoBuglio, Mellow, and Mukamal, 2008.

51. See Clear, Rose, Waring, and Scully, 2003.

52. Lynch and Sabol, 2001.

53. Petersilia, 2003.

54. Hipp and Yates, 2009.

55. Mears, Wang, Hay, and Bales, 2008.

56. Kirk, 2012.

57. Carter, Schill, and Wachter, 1998.

58. Thomas, 2012.

59. King, 1993. See also Anderson, 1999.

60. See Haney, 2002.

61. Clear, 2008; Furstenberg, 1995.

62. See Clear, 2008.

63. Rose and Clear, 1998

64. Sabol and Lynch, 2003.

65. See Travis, McBride, and Solomon, 2005.

66. Sullivan, 1993.

67. Glaze and Maruschak, 2010.

68. Glaze and Maruschak, 2010.

69. Mumola, 2000.

70. Glaze and Maruschak, 2010.

71. Western and Wildeman, 2009.

72. Johnson, 2009.

73. Hairston, 2002; Parke and Clarke-Stewart, 2002.

74. Fagan and Freeman, 1999.

75. See Clear, Rose, Waring, and Scully, 2003; Murray, 2005.

76. Glaze and Maruschak, 2010.

77. LaVigne, Naser, Brooks, and Castro, 2005.

78. Dallaire and Wilson, 2010.

79. Poehlmann, Dallaire, Loper, and Shear, 2010.

80. Murray and Farrington, 2008.

81. See Gabel and Johnston, 1997.

82. Aaron and Dallaire, 2010; Murray and Farrington, 2008.

83. Braman, 2002.

84. Glaze and Maruschak, 2010.

85. See Anderson, 1999; Irwin and Austin, 1997.

86. Pettit and Western, 2004.

87. Western and Pettit, 2010.

88. Mauer, 2006.

89. See Humes, Jones, and Ramirez, 2011.

90. See Tonry and Melewski, 2008.

91. West and Sabol, 2010.

92. Glaze and Maruschak, 2010.

93. Johnston, 1995.

94. Moye and Rinker, 2002.

95. Courtney, Piliavin, Grogan-Kaylor, and Nesmith, 2001.

96. See Blumstein and Nakamura, 2009.

97. Pager, 2003; Pager, Western, and Sugie, 2009; Visher, Debus-Sherrill, and Yahner, 2011.

98. See Petersilia, 2003.

99. Morenoff and Harding, 2011.

100. See Kubrin and Stewart, 2006.

101. See Wang, Mears, and Bales, 2010.

102. Sampson and Laub, 1993. See also Bushway, 1998.

103. Western, 2002.

104. Uggen, 2000

105. Berg and Huebner, 2011.

106. See Lopoo and Western, 2005.

107. See Holzer, Raphael, and Stoll, 2003.

108. Pager, 2003.

109. Sentencing Project, 2012; Manza and Uggen, 2006.

110. Sentencing Project, 2012.

111. Sentencing Project, 2012; Uggen, Manza, and Thompson, 2006.

112. Ewald, 2002; Uggen and Manza, 2004a; Uggen and Manza, 2004b.

113. Uggen and Manza, 2002.

114. Federal Election Commission, 2001.

115. Manza and Uggen, 2006.

116. Hench, 1998; Manza and Uggen, 2006.

117. Uggen, Behrens, and Manza, 2005.

118. Behrens, Uggen, and Manza, 2003.

119. Karberg and James, 2005.

120. Ditton, 1999.
121. James, 2004.
122. Maruschak and Beavers, 2010.
123. Maruschak and Beavers, 2010.
124. Thomas and Torrone, 2006.
125. Hunter, 1985.
126. Glaze and Maruschak, 2010.
127. DeFina and Hannon, 2010.

References

Aaron, Lauren, and Danielle H. Dallaire. "Parental Incarceration and Multiple Risk Experiences: Effects on Family Dynamics and Children's Delinquency." *Journal of Youth and Adolescence* 39 (2010): 1471–1484.

Anderson, Elijah. *Code of the Street: Decency, Violence, and the Moral Life of the Inner City.* New York: W.W. Norton & Company, 1999.

Behrens, Angela, Christopher Uggen, and Jeff Manza. "Ballot Manipulation and the 'Menace of Negro Domination': Racial Threat and Felon Disenfranchisement in the United States, 1850–2002." *American Journal of Sociology* 1093 (2003): 559–605.

Berg, Mark T., and Beth M. Huebner. "Reentry and the Ties That Bind: An Examination of Social Ties, Employment, and Recidivism."*Justice Quarterly* 28 (2011): 382–410.

Blumstein, Alfred, and Kiminori Nakamura. "Redemption in the Presence of Widespread Criminal Background Checks." *Criminology* 47 (2009): 327–359.

Bonzcar, Thomas P. *Prevalence of Imprisonment in the U.S. Population, 1974–2001.* Washington, DC: Bureau of Justice Statistics, 2003.

Braman, Donald. "Families and Incarceration." In *Invisible Punishment: The Collateral Consequences of Mass Imprisonment*, edited by Marc Mauer and Meda Chesney-Lind, pp. 117–135. New York: New Press, 2002.

Bronfenbrenner, Urie. *The Ecology of Human Development.* Cambridge, MA: Harvard University Press, 1979.

Bushway, Shawn. "The Impact of an Arrest on the Job Stability of Young White American Men." *Journal of Research in Crime and Delinquency* 35 (1998): 454–479.

Carter, William H., Michael H. Schill, and Susan M. Wachter. "Polarisation, Public Housing and Racial Minorities in U.S. Cities."*Urban Studies* 3510 (1998): 1889–1911.

Center for Policy Research. "Incarceration, Reentry and Child Support Issues: National and State Research Overview." Denver, CO: Department of Health and Human Services, Administration for Children and Families, Office of Child Support Enforcement, 2006.

Clear, Todd R. *Imprisoning Communities: How Mass Incarceration Makes Disadvantaged Neighborhoods Worse*. New York: Oxford University Press, 2007.

Clear, Todd R. "The Effects of High Imprisonment Rates on Communities." In *Crime and Justice: A Review of Research*. Vol. 37, edited by Michael Tonry, pp. 97–132. Chicago: University of Chicago Press, 2008.

Clear, Todd R., Dina Rose, and Judith A. Ryder. "Incarceration and the Community: The Problem of Removing and Returning Offenders."*Crime and Delinquency* 473 (2001): 335–351.

Clear, Todd R., Dina Rose, Elin Waring, and Kristen Scully. "Coercive Mobility and Crime: A Preliminary Examination of Concentrated Incarceration and Social Disorganization." *Justice Quarterly* 20 (2003): 33–64.

Coleman, James S. "Social Capital in the Creation of Human Capital." *American Journal of Sociology* 94 (1988): S95–S120.

Courtney, Mark E., Irving Piliavin, Andrew Grogan-Kaylor, and Ande Nesmith. "Foster Youth Transitions to Adulthood: A Longitudinal View of Youth Leaving Care." *Child Welfare* 80, no. 6 (2001): 685–717.

Crutchfield, Robert D., George S. Bridges, and Susan R. Pitchford. "Analytical and Aggregation Biases in Analyses of Imprisonment: Reconciling Discrepancies in Studies of Racial Disparity." *Journal of Research in Crime and Delinquency* 31 (1994): 166–182.

Dallaire, Danielle H., A. Ciccone, and L. Wilson. "Teachers' Experiences with and Expectations of Children with Incarcerated Parents." *Journal of Applied Developmental Psychology* 31 (2010): 281–290.

Dallaire, Danielle H., and Laura Wilson. "The Impact of Exposure to Parental Criminal Activity, Arrest, and Sentencing on Children's Academic Competence and Externalizing Behavior." *Journal of Child and Family Studies* 19 (2010): 404–418.

DeFina, Robert H., and Lance Hannon. "The Impact of Adult Incarceration on Child Poverty: A County-Level Analysis, 1995–2007."*Prison Journal* 904 (2010): 377–396.

Ditton, Paula. *Mental Health and Treatment of Inmates and Probationers*. Washington, DC: Bureau of Justice Statistics, 1999.

Ewald, Alec C. " 'Civil Death': The Ideological Paradox of Criminal Disenfranchisement Law in the United States." *Wisconsin Law Review* 1045 (2002): 1059–1062.

Fagan, Jeffrey. "Legal and Illegal Work: Crime, Work, and Unemployment." In *The Urban Crises: Linking Research to Action*, edited by Burton A. Weisbrod and James C. Worthy, pp. 33–80. Evanston, IL: Northwestern University Press, 1997.

Fagan, Jeffrey, and Richard B. Freeman. "Crime and Work." In *Crime and Justice: A Review of Research*. Vol. 25, edited by Michael Tonry, pp. 225–290. Chicago: University of Chicago Press, 1999.

Federal Election Commission. "Federal Elections 2000: Election Results for the U.S. President, the U.S. Senate and the U.S. House of Representatives." Washington, DC: Federal Election Commission, 2001.

Fellner, Jaime. "Race, Drugs, and Law Enforcement in the United States." *Stanford Law Review* 20 (2009): 257–292.

Fry, Richard. *The Changing Pathways of Hispanic Youths into Adulthood.* Washington, DC: Pew Hispanic Center, 2009.

Furstenberg, Frank F., Jr. "Fathering in the Inner-City: Paternal Participation and Public Policy." In *Fatherhood: Contemporary Theory, Research, and Social Policy*, edited by William Marsiglio, pp. 119–147. Thousand Oaks, CA: Sage, 1995.

Gabel, Katherine, and Denise Johnston. *Children of Incarcerated Parents.* New York: Lexington Books, 1997.

Glaze, Lauren E., and Laura M. Maruschak. *Parents in Prison and Their Minor Children.* Washington, DC: Bureau of Justice Statistics, 2010.

Guerino, Paul, Page M. Harrison, and William J. Sabol. *Prisoners in 2010.* Washington, DC: Bureau of Justice Statistics, 2011.

Hagan, John, and Juleigh P. Coleman. "Returning Captives of the American War on Drugs: Issues of Community and Family Reentry."*Crime and Delinquency* 473 (2001): 352–367.

Hairston, Creasie F. "Prisoners and Families: Parenting Issues during Incarceration." Paper presented at the National Policy Conference: From Prison to Home: The Effect of Incarceration and Reentry on Children, Families, and Communities, U.S. Department of Health and Human Services, Urban Institute, January 30–31, 2002.

Haney, Craig. "The Psychological Impact of Incarceration: Implications for Post-Prison Adjustment." Paper presented at the National Policy Conference: From Prison to Home: The Effect of Incarceration and Reentry on Children, Families, and Communities, U.S. Department of Health and Human Services, Urban Institute, January 30–31, 2002.

Harlow, Caroline Wolf. *Education and Correctional Populations.* Washington, DC: Bureau of Justice Statistics, 2003.

Hartney, Christopher, and Linh Vuong. *Created Equal: Racial and Ethnic Disparities in the U.S. Criminal Justice System.* Oakland, CA: National Council on Crime and Delinquency, 2009.

Hench, Virginia E. "The Death of Voting Rights: The Legal Disenfranchisement of Minority Voters." *Case Western Reserve Law Review* 48 (1998): 727–789.

Hipp, John R., and Daniel K. Yates. "Do Returning Parolees Affect Neighborhood Crime? A Case Study of Sacramento." *Criminology* 473 (2009): 619–655.

Holzer, Harry J., Steven Raphael, and Michael A. Stoll. "Employer Demand for Ex-Offenders: Recent Evidence from Los Angeles." Discussion Paper 1268-03. Madison, WI: Institute for Research on Poverty, 2003.

Holzer, Harry J., Steven Raphael, and Michael A. Stoll. "Perceived Criminality, Criminal Background Checks, and the Racial Hiring Practices of Employers." *Journal of Law and Economics* 49 (2006): 451–454.

Humes, Karen R., Nicholas A. Jones, and Roberto R. Ramirez. *Overview of Race and Hispanic Origin, 2010: 2010 Census Briefs.* Washington, DC: U.S. Census Bureau, 2011.

Hunter, Albert J. "Private, Parochial and Public School Orders: The Problem of Crime and Incivility in Urban Communities." In *The Challenge of Social Control: Citizenship and Institution Building in Modern Society,* edited by Gerald D. Suttles and Mayer N. Zald, pp. 230–242. Norwood, NJ: Ablex, 1985.

Irwin, John, and James Austin. *It's About Time: America's Imprisonment Binge* (2nd ed.). Belmont, CA: Wadsworth, 1997.

James, Doris. *Profile of Jail Inmates, 2002.* Washington, DC: Bureau of Justice Statistics, 2004.

Johnson, Rucker C. "Ever-Increasing Levels of Parental Incarceration and the Consequences for Children." In *Do Prisons Make Us Safer? The Benefits and Costs of the Prison Boom,* edited by Steven Raphael and Michael A. Stoll, pp. 177–206. New York: Russell Sage, 2009.

Johnston, Denise. "Effects of Parental Incarceration." In *Children of Incarcerated Parents,* edited by Katherine Gabel and Denise Johnston, pp. 59–88. New York: Lexington Books, 1995.

Karberg, Jennifer, and Doris James. *Substance Dependence, Abuse, and Treatment of Jail Inmates, 2002.* Washington, DC: Bureau of Justice Statistics, 2005.

King, Anthony E. O. "The Impact of Incarceration on African American Families: Implications for Practice." *Families in Society: The Journal of Contemporary Human Services* 743 (1993): 145–153.

Kirk, David S. "Residential Change as a Turning Point in the Life Course of Crime: Desistance or Temporary Cessation?" *Criminology* 502 (2012): 1–29.

Kubrin, Charis, and Eric Stewart. "Predicting Who Reoffends: The Neglected Role of Neighborhood Context in Recidivism Studies." *Criminology* 441 (2006): 165–197.

Langan, Patrick A. *Race of Prisoners Admitted to State and Federal Institutions, 1926–86.* Washington, DC: Bureau of Justice Statistics, 1991.

Langan, Patrick A., and David J. Levin. *Recidivism of Prisoners Released in 1994.* Washington, DC: Bureau of Justice Statistics, 2002.

LaVigne, Nancy G., Rebecca L. Naser, Lisa E. Brooks, and Jennifer L. Castro. "Examining the Effect of Incarceration and In-Prison Family Contact on Prisoners' Family Relationships." *Journal of Contemporary Criminal Justice* 21 (2005): 314–355.

Legal Action Center. *After Prison: Roadblocks to Reentry; A Report on State Legal Barriers Facing People with Criminal Records.* Washington, DC: Legal Action Center, 2009.

Lopoo, Leonard M., and Bruce Western. "Incarceration and the Formation and Stability of Marital Unions." *Journal of Marriage and Family* 67 (2005): 721–734.

Lynch, James P., and William J. Sabol. *Did Getting Tough on Crime Pay? Crime Policy Report No. 1*. Washington, DC: Urban Institute, 1997.

Lynch, James P., and William J. Sabol. *Prisoner Reentry in Perspective. Crime Policy Report No. 3*. Washington, DC: Urban Institute, 2001.

Lynch, James P., and William J. Sabol. "Assessing the Effects of Mass Incarceration on Informal Social Control in Communities."*Criminology and Public Policy* 32 (2004): 267–294.

Lynch, James P., William J. Sabol, Michael Planty, and Mary Shelly. *Crime, Coercion and Community: The Effects of Arrest and Incarceration Policies on Informal Social Control in Neighborhoods*. Washington, DC: U.S. Department of Justice, 2002.

Manza, Jeff, and Christopher Uggen. *Locked Out: Felon Disenfranchisement and American Democracy*. Oxford: Oxford University Press, 2006.

Maruschak, Laura M., and Randy Beavers. *HIV in Prison*. Washington, DC: Bureau of Justice Statistics, 2010.

Matthews, Sharron D., and Amanda Casarjian. *Government Personnel Policies Impacting the Hiring of Ex-Offenders. Council of Advisors to Reduce Recidivism through Employment* C.A.R.R.E, Policy Paper #3. Chicago: Safer Foundation, 2002.

Mauer, Marc. "Addressing Racial Disparities in Incarceration." *Prison Journal* 913 (2011): 87S–101S.

Mauer, Marc. *Race to Incarcerate*. New York: New Press, 2006.

Mauer, Marc, and Ryan King. *Uneven Justice: State Rates of Incarceration by Race and Ethnicity*. Washington, DC: Sentencing Project, 2007.

Mears, Daniel P., Xia Wang, Carter Hay, and William D. Bales. "Social Ecology and Recidivism: Implications for Prisoner Reentry."*Criminology* 462 (2008): 301–339.

Minton, Todd D. *Jail Inmates at Midyear 2011: Statistical Tables*. Washington, DC: Bureau of Justice Statistics, 2012.

Morenoff, Jeffrey D., and David J. Harding. *Final Technical Report: Neighborhoods, Recidivism, and Employment among Returning Prisoners*. Washington, DC: National Institute of Justice, 2011.

Moye, Jim, and Roberta Rinker. "It's a Hard Knock Life: Does the Adoption and Safe Families Act of 1997 Adequately Address Problems in the Child Welfare System?" *Harvard Law School Journal on Legislation* 392 (2002): 375–394.

Mumola, Christopher J. *Special Report: Incarcerated Parents and Their Children*. Washington, DC: Bureau of Justice Statistics, 2000.

Mumola, Christopher J., and Jennifer C. Karberg. *Drug Use and Dependence: State and Federal Prisoners, 2004*. Washington, DC: Bureau of Justice Statistics, 2006.

Murray, Joseph. "The Effects of Imprisonment on the Families and Children of Prisoners." In *The Effects of Imprisonment,* edited by Allison Liebling and Shadd Maruna, pp. 442–464. Cullompton, Devon, UK: Willan, 2005.

Murray, Joseph, and David P. Farrington. "The Effects of Parental Imprisonment on Children." In *Crime and Justice: A Review of Research. Vol. 37,* edited by Michael Tonry, pp. 133–206. Chicago: University of Chicago Press, 2008.

Nunn, Kenneth B. "Race, Crime and the Pool of Surplus Criminality: or Why the 'War on Drugs' Was a 'War on Blacks.'" *Journal of Gender, Race and Justice* 6 (2002): 381–427.

Pager, Devah. "The Mark of a Criminal Record." *American Journal of Sociology* 1085 (2003): 937–975.

Pager, Devah, Bruce Western, and Naomi Sugie. "Sequencing Disadvantage: Barriers to Employment Facing Young Black and White Men with Criminal Records." *Annals of the American Academy of Political and Social Science* 623 (2009): 195–213.

Parke, Ross D., and K. Alison Clarke-Stewart. *Effects of Parental Incarceration on Young Children.* National Policy Conference: From Prison to Home: The Effect of Incarceration and Reentry on Children, Families, and Communities. Washington, DC: U.S. Department of Health and Human Services, 2002.

Petersilia, Joan. *When Prisoners Come Home: Parole and Prisoner Reentry.* New York: Oxford University Press, 2003.

Pettit, Becky, and Bruce Western. "Mass Imprisonment and the Life Course: Race and Class Inequality in U.S. Incarceration."*American Sociological Review* 69 (2004): 151–169.

Poehlmann, Julie, Danielle H. Dallaire, Ann Booker Loper, and Leslie D. Shear. "Children's Contact with Their Incarcerated Parents: Research Findings and Recommendations." *American Psychologist* 65 (2010): 575–598.

Rose, Dina, and Todd R. Clear. "Incarceration, Social Capital, and Crime: Implications for Social Disorganization Theory." *Criminology* 36 (1998): 441–479.

Sabol, William J., and James P. Lynch. "Assessing the Longer-Run Consequences of Incarceration: Effects on Families and Employment." In *Crime Control and Social Justice: The Delicate Balance,* edited by Darnell F. Hawkins, Samuel L. Myers Jr., and Randolph N. Stone, pp. 3–26. Westport, CT: Greenwood, 2003.

Sabol, William J., Heather C. West, and Matthew Cooper. *Prisoners in 2008.* Washington, DC: Bureau of Justice Statistics, 2010.

Sampson, Robert J., and John H. Laub. *Crime in the Making: Pathways and Turning Points through Life.* Cambridge, MA: Harvard University Press, 1993.

Sampson, Robert J., Stephen W. Raudenbush, and Felton Earls. "Neighborhoods and Violent Crime: A Multilevel Study of Collective Efficacy." *Science* 277 (1997): 918–924.

Sentencing Project. *Trends in U.S. Corrections.* Washington, DC: Sentencing Project, 2012.

Solomon, Amy L., Jenny W. L. Osborne, Stefan F. LoBuglio, Jeff Mellow, and Debbie Mukamal. *Life after Lockup: Improving Reentry from Jail to the Community.* Washington, DC: Urban Institute, 2008.

Substance Abuse and Mental Health Services Administration (SAMHSA). *National Survey on Drug Use and Health, 2008 and 2009.* Rockville, MD: SAMHSA, 2010.

Sullivan, Mercer L. "Young Fathers and Parenting in Two Inner-City Neighborhoods." In *Young Unwed Fathers: Changing Roles and Emerging Policies,* edited by Robert I. Lerman and Theodora J. Ooms, pp. 52–73. Philadelphia: Temple University Press, 1993.

Testimony of Charles Schuster before the Subcommittee on Crime and Drugs of the Senate Judiciary Committee, May 22, 2002.

Thomas, Adam. "The Old Ball and Chain: Unlocking the Correlation between Incarceration and Marriage." Unpublished manuscript, 2012.

Thomas, James C., and Elizabeth Torrone. "Incarceration as Forced Migration: Effects of Selected Community Health Outcomes." *American Journal of Public Health* 96 (2006): 1762–1765.

Tonry, Michael. *Malign Neglect: Race, Crime, and Punishment in America.* New York: Oxford University Press, 1995.

Tonry, Michael, and Matthew Melewski. "The Malign Effects of Drug and Crime Control Policies on Black Americans." In *Crime and Justice: A Review of Research. Vol. 37,* edited by Michael Tonry, pp. 1–44. Chicago: University of Chicago Press, 2008.

Travis, Jeremy. *But They All Come Back.* Washington, DC: Urban Institute, 2005.

Travis, Jeremy, Elizabeth Cincotta McBride, and Amy L. Solomon. *Families Left Behind: The Hidden Costs of Incarceration and Reentry.* Washington, DC: Urban Institute, 2005.

Uggen, Christopher. "Work as a Turning Point in the Life Course of Criminals: A Duration Model of Age, Employment, and Recidivism."*American Sociological Review* 65 (2000): 529–546.

Uggen, Christopher, Angela Behrens, and Jeff Manza. "Criminal Disenfranchisement." *Annual Review of Law and Social Science* 1 (2005): 307–22.

Uggen, Christopher, and Jeff Manza. "Democratic Contradiction? The Political Consequences of Felon Disenfranchisement in the United States." *American Sociological Review* 67, no. 6 (2002): 777–803.

Uggen, Christopher, and Jeff Manza. "Voting and Subsequent Crime and Arrest: Evidence from a Community Sample." *Columbia Human Rights Law Review* 36 (2004a): 193–215.

Uggen, Christopher, and Jeff Manza. "Lost Voices: The Civic and Political Views of Disenfranchised Felons." In *Imprisoning America: The Social Effects of Mass Incarceration,* edited by Mary Pattillo, D. Weiman, and Bruce Western, pp. 165–204. New York: Russell Sage Foundation, 2004b.

Uggen, Christopher, Jeff Manza, and Melissa Thompson. "Citizenship, Democracy, and the Civic Reintegration of Criminal Offenders."*Annals of the American Academy of Political and Social Science* 605 (2006): 281–310.

Visher, Christy A., Sara A. Debus-Sherrill, and Jennifer Yahner. "Employment after Prison: A Longitudinal Study of Former Prisoners." *Justice Quarterly* 28 (2011): 698–718.

Wang, Xia, Daniel P. Mears, and William D. Bales. "Race-Specific Employment Contexts and Recidivism." *Criminology* 48 (2010): 1171–1211.

West, Heather C., and William J. Sabol. *Prisoners in 2009.* Washington, DC: Bureau of Justice Statistics, 2010.

Western, Bruce. "The Impact of Incarceration on Wage Mobility and Inequality." *American Sociological Review* 674 (2002): 526–546.

Western, Bruce. *Punishment and Inequality in America.* New York: Russell Sage, 2006.

Western, Bruce, Jeffrey R. Kling, and David F. Weiman. "The Labor Market Consequences of Incarceration." *Crime & Delinquency* 47 (2001): 410–427.

Western, Bruce, and Becky Pettit. "Incarceration and Social Inequality." *Daedalus* 139 (2010): 8–19.

Western, Bruce, and Christopher Wildeman. "Law, Reparations and Racial Disparities: Criminal Justice and Racial Disparities: Punishment, Inequality, and the Future of Mass Incarceration." *Kansas Law Review* 57 (2009): 851–877.

Wilson, James Q., and George L. Kelling. "Broken Windows." *Atlantic Monthly* 249 (1982), 29–38.

Wilson, William J. *The Truly Disadvantaged: The Inner City, the Underclass and Public Policy.* Chicago: University of Chicago, 1987.

Chapter 27

Muslims, the War on Terror, and Prisons

Elyshia Aseltine

[Amir] was subjected to religious and sexual humiliation, hooding, sleep deprivation, restraint for hours while naked, and dousing with cold water. In the most horrific incident Amir recalled experiencing, he was placed in a foul-smelling room and forced to lay face down in urine, while he was hit and kicked on his back and side. Amir was then sodomized with a broomstick and forced to howl like a dog while a soldier urinated on him. After a soldier stepped on his genitals, he fainted.[1]

A Muslim inmate alleged that a [Federal Bureau of Prisons] correctional officer sprayed him with chemical agents even though he knew the inmate suffered from chronic asthma. The inmate also alleged he was restrained by his ankles and hands and left in an empty room without a toilet, sink, shower, bed, food, or water for two days. Further, the inmate alleged a BOP correctional officer told him he hated Muslims, forbade him from practicing his religion, and told him if he was hungry that he had a pork chop sandwich for him.[2]

The images of routine and systematic torture occurring within the confines of Abu Ghraib—a U.S. military detention center in Iraq—during the spring of 2003 rightfully triggered public shock and outrage. Generally, however, the response has been to dismiss the abuse as the activities of a "few bad apples" rather than as a reflection of more deeply rooted problems in American ideology and practice. The first excerpt at the start of this chapter describes the experiences of a Muslim detainee in Abu Ghraib; the second describes those of a Muslim prisoner in an unidentified U.S. federal prison. The excerpts were selected to indicate a fundamental premise upon which this chapter is built: American domestic and international policies and practices are rooted in the same ideological and social soil.

This chapter takes the position that rather than an anomaly, the abuse committed in Abu Ghraib (and in other U.S. detention centers around the world) is consistent with a long history of American racism and denial of fundamental human rights both within the country's borders and abroad.

This chapter focuses primarily on the most recent developments with regard to Muslims and prisons—the war on terror, and immigrant and foreign detention centers. In response to the events of September 11, 2001, the American government completed a massive reorganization of military and law enforcement financing and personnel in an effort to combat terrorism. The war on terror has had significant negative ramifications for both foreign and domestic "Muslim-looking" people, a loose collection of groups who are typically cast as perpetually suspicious others in American political and social discourse. As a result, Muslims within the U.S. borders and beyond have been subjected to heightened surveillance, increased immigration control, and denial of civil and human rights.

Though much of the current attention being paid to Muslims is in the context of the war on terror, the history of prisons and Muslims extends back at least until the 1930s when black American prisoners first began converting to Islam in significant numbers. For much of their history, black Muslims have been subjected to discrimination and maltreatment in prison. Though it is rarely acknowledged, black Muslim prisoner advocacy proved to be critical in advancing prison reform during the 1960s and 1970s. Many of the rights prisoners have today were established because of the willingness of black Muslims to challenge the prison administration in court. Similar to other Muslim-looking groups, black Muslims in prison are experiencing the backlash of the contemporary resurgence in anti-Muslim sentiment.

This chapter is organized into four sections. The first section briefly considers the historical and ideological roots of American anti-Muslim sentiment. In this section, the theoretical frame that shapes the remaining sections of the chapter is described. The focus of the second section is on anti-Muslim sentiment in the context of the post-9/11 war on terror. The section illustrates the consequences of the war on terror for immigrants to the United States and Muslims abroad. Third, we consider the experiences of black Muslims in domestic prisons. This section draws parallels between practices in foreign and domestic prisons and demonstrates the consequences of the contemporary war on terror for a group of people who have long been regarded as problematic by prison administration.

Finally, the conclusion considers the long-term consequences of the new paradigm of terrorism for Muslims and non-Muslims alike.

American Exceptionalism and Creating the Muslim "Other"

The abuse at Abu Ghraib, Guantanamo Bay, and an unknown number of other military detention centers around the world are "not isolated aberrations." Rather, this abuse is consistent with a long genealogy of domestic and international discrimination and lawlessness.[3] Counter to those who argue that the United States is a postracial society where social identity matters little in shaping one's life circumstances, anti-Muslim sentiment is a contemporary iteration of long-standing historical practices of racialization and oppression. It is difficult to imagine the torture of Muslim detainees as an irregularity when such abuses are considered against the backdrop of other systematic and state-sanctioned human rights abuses that have occurred both within U.S. borders (e.g., slavery, genocide of Native Americans, segregation, Japanese Internment) as well abroad (e.g., the massacre at Mai Lai, invasion of Grenada, violence related to gas pipeline projects in Nigeria, Burma and elsewhere).

Political leaders have long claimed American exceptionalism—the notion that the United States is unique because of its profound commitment to democracy, justice, and equality. Such an assertion is a "convenient fiction" that contradicts sharply with American practices.[4] Instead, American social processes continue to be marked by racialization, a process that creates and fortifies social, cultural, and economic boundaries between "Americans" and various "others." These boundaries facilitate the systematic geographic, economic, and social exclusion of those dubbed as others through strict immigration control, increased surveillance, and denial of fundamental rights. "Other"-ing also serves the important function of discrediting the experiences and perspectives of others, especially if they are attempting to draw attention to inconsistencies between American ideals and practices.

While the latter part of the chapter focuses on American-born converts to Islam (i.e., black Muslims), the bulk of the chapter considers the looser category of "Muslim-looking" people.[5] Muslim-looking people are those who, because of their national origin, cultural heritage, religious background, or physical appearance are assumed to be Muslim. The category Muslim-looking people captures the popular tendency to collapse the tremendous diversity within Muslim, Middle Eastern, and South Asian (and even African-American and Latino) communities. Those deemed to be Muslim looking are regarded as suspicious or duplicitous, at best, or as terrorists, at worst. Because of their ascribed deviousness, both foreign and native-born Muslim-looking people are regarded as perpetual foreigners whose dubious intentions warrant invasive monitoring by the state.

Demonization and dehumanization processes are crucial in laying the foundation for institutional forms of humiliation and abuse like those described at the beginning of the chapter. Dehumanization expressed and reinforced through violence plays an important role in establishing and reaffirming the boundaries between us and "others."[6] Violence "dramatize[s] the fact that the human community and its ties extend only to a certain limit, and that persons outside are alien and subordinate."[7] Though we typically think of law as a means to regulate violence, law construction and enforcement is frequently used as a means by which the state exercises its power to use violence, especially in the context of prisons.

The War on Terror and Racial Profiling of Muslim-Looking People

Though Europe has a lengthier and more substantial history of terrorist activity, terrorism is not new to the United States. Throughout its history, the nation has faced threats from race-based terror groups (e.g., Ku Klux Klan), as well as antigovernment (e.g., anarchists) and anticapitalist (e.g., socialists and union movements) agitators. Contemporary domestic terrorist groups include right-wing militias and separatists, pro-life activists who bomb abortion clinics and kill abortion providers, and environmental and animal protection groups who engage in economic sabotage and property destruction. Perhaps the most destructive domestic terrorist act was the bombing of the Alfred P. Murrah Federal Building in Oklahoma City, Oklahoma, on April 19, 1995. The bombing killed nearly 170 people and was orchestrated by former army members Timothy McVeigh, Terry Nichols, and Michael Fortier. Prior to his execution, McVeigh, the man who actually carried out the bomb plan, described his motivations for the attack as retaliation for federal law enforcement activities in Ruby Ridge, Idaho, and Waco, Texas. In both events, federal law enforcement engaged in armed confrontations with white separatist groups, resulting in three deaths in Idaho and nearly 80 in Texas.

Foreign groups have also attacked the United States, both abroad and locally. Numerous attacks have occurred abroad, including the hijacking of planes and cruise ships (e.g., TWA flight 847, *Achille Lauro*), bombing of embassies (e.g., Beirut, Kenya, Tanzania), and strikes on U.S. military personnel (e.g., barracks in Beirut, a nightclub in West Berlin). The most significant attack on U.S. soil prior to the events of September 11, 2001, was the bombing of the north tower of the World Trade Center in New York City on February 26, 1993. The bomb and its aftermath killed six people and wounded 1,000 more. Six of the seven planners of the bombing were eventually apprehended. In interviews, participants in the first World Trade Center bombing describe their motivations for the attack—to stop the U.S. interventions in the Middle East and to force the United States to withdraw its financial and military support for Israel.[8]

Though domestic groups, like separatist militias or pro-life groups that bomb abortion clinics, meet the legal definition of terrorism, typically they are not the groups that are referenced in popular and political discourse about terrorism. Much of the discourse about terrorists exemplifies racial profiling—the linking of perceived identity characteristics with specific, problematic beliefs and behaviors. In American discourse, terrorism is perceived primarily as a Muslim phenomenon. A good illustration of the presumed association between Islam and terrorism is the initial reaction to the bombing in Oklahoma City described earlier in this discussion. News outlets covering the bombing drew conclusions about those responsible—Muslim extremists—with "breathtaking speed."[9] Scores of media outlets, being fed information by "unnamed government sources," drew explicit and implicit references to Muslims when discussing the bombing. Even after it was revealed that those responsible for the bombing were "homegrown" and sketches of the suspects were released, media outlets continued with discussions of Muslim extremism.[10]

The association between terrorism and Muslims was solidified in the public mind after the early morning events of September 11, 2001 (9/11). Four planes were hijacked by 19 people and then crashed into New York's World Trade Center, the Pentagon, and a field in rural Pennsylvania (this plane was likely headed to the Capitol). Approximately 3,000 people died, most in the two World Trade Center towers. The events of 9/11 were attributed to Saudi Arabian millionaire Osama bin Laden and al-Qaeda almost immediately. Similar to the first bombing of New York's World Trade Center, motivations for the 9/11 hijackings include forcing the United States to withdraw from the Middle East and to cease its support of Israel. Within a few days of the attacks, Congress authorized use of the military against al-Qaeda. Subsequently, the "war on terror" was formally waged by President George W. Bush.

National responses to September 11 include dramatic increases in federal funding of, and attention to, counterterrorism.[11] Between 1998 and 2005, federal counterterrorism funding increased by over 1,000 percent—from $7.2 billion to $88.1 billion.[12] In addition, the federal government embarked on its largest agency and personnel reorganization effort since World War II when it created the Department of Homeland Security (DHS). According to its website, the "founding purpose" and "highest priority" of the DHS is "protecting the American people from terrorist threats." The massive DHS includes over 20 agencies, including the Coast Guard, the Secret Service, as well as the refashioned Customs and Border Protection and Immigration and Customs Enforcement. Inclusion of the federal immigration control agencies under the federal government's principal counterterrorism organization demonstrates the perceived connection between national threats and immigrants. One could argue that it is in immigration enforcement that we have seen the most pervasive consequences of the war on terror.

The war on terror is often described by its advocates, including President Bush, Secretary of Defense Donald Rumsfeld, his deputy Paul Wolfowitz, and Vice President Dick Cheney, with "an apocalyptic rhetoric of moral absolutism."[13] According to this discourse, the United States was on a mission not only to protect its own interests, but to advance freedom and democracy throughout the world—this mission, if not inspired by God, was sanctioned by Him. In the war on terror, the enemy is a nebulous category comprised of "enemies of freedom" whose goals are "remaking the world and imposing its radical beliefs on people everywhere."[14] In much of the post-9/11 rhetoric, a sharp binary was established between those who love freedom (Christians, Jews, and Americans) and the terrorist evildoers (Muslims). Those who challenged the war on terror or its tactics were warned, "We will direct every resource at our command—every means of diplomacy, every tool of intelligence, every instrument of law enforcement, every financial influence, and every necessary weapon of war—to the destruction and to the defeat of the global terror network. Every nation, in every region, now has a decision to make. Either you are with us, or you are with the terrorists."[15] Anyone who was not on the correct side of this binary—"with us"—was a terrorist and was subject to the full might of the country's diplomatic and enforcement apparatus.

Like other "wars" waged after World War II—for example, the war on poverty, the war on drugs—the war on terror is a "perpetual war ... waged against ever shifting spectral enemies."[16] The reference to terrorists as spectral enemies captures the difficulty of determining just who is and who is not an "enemy of freedom." The enemies in the contemporary war on terror are imagined as a global network of stateless and clandestine groups who fund their activities through complex financing schemes. In much of the federal rhetoric, modern terrorism is described as something new and unique, something that requires innovative strategies to be effectively challenged. This is the new paradigm: the idea that today's terrorist poses a more serious threat than anything ever seen before and, as such, requires different forms of investigation and enforcement.[17] In this new paradigm, many of the characteristics that are said to make the United States exceptional, especially its commitment to the rule of law and its commitment to individual freedoms, are viewed as impediments to effectively combatting terrorism.[18] Counterterrorism "became the rationale for a massively expanded exercise of state power, both domestically and internationally . . . After the September 11 attacks, the only acceptable topic of conversation was terrorism, and the most important speaker was the government."[19] In the new paradigm, the focal purpose of the state is to protect the country from threat rather than to protect its citizens from itself.

Six weeks after 9/11, Congress passed the Uniting and Strengthening America by Providing Appropriate Tools Required to Intercept and Obstruct Terrorism (aka the USA Patriot Act). The passage of this act has dramatically increased the ability of government officials to monitor both foreign nationals and U.S. citizens, to limit immigration and to detain and deport immigrants, and to arrest and detain anyone who could be construed as a threat to "national security."[20] This act is one of the crucial components of the war on terror that served to erode the protections of American citizens from the powerful state.

The following section focuses on the consequences of the war on terror for domestic immigration control and for foreign operations. In the section on domestic control, we consider both interpersonal and state-enacted domestic efforts to control Muslim-looking people and Muslim immigration. Interpersonal efforts to control Muslim-looking people include discrimination and hate crimes. Though these types of control efforts are usually committed by individuals who are not state actors, they are included in this discussion because they form an important part of larger social control efforts of Muslim-looking people. The beliefs and rationales—that Muslim-looking people are perpetually suspicious and do not warrant the protections afforded to other loyal citizens—that undergird interpersonal forms of social control are the same that support state-sponsored control activities. Immigration restriction and detention is the primary form of social control being administered by the state on and within the borders. Though we focus primarily on the effects of post-9/11 immigration control efforts for Muslim-looking people, the consequences of these efforts are felt by other immigrant groups as well as citizens. Finally, we consider foreign operations and the consequences of these operations for those who find themselves caught in the wide net of U.S. antiterrorism efforts.

Domestic Control: Discrimination, Hate Crimes, and Immigration Detention

An important consequence of 9/11, and the federal government's response to it, is heightened anti-Muslim sentiment. Domestically, this sentiment manifests itself in two important ways: (1) discrimination and hate crimes and (2) restrictive immigration policies and practices. Racial profiling in U.S. airports was not unusual prior to September 2001, but after 9/11, non-security personnel (e.g., passengers, flight attendants, pilots) joined in on efforts by informally screening other passengers. News accounts describe at least 30 incidents of Muslim-looking people being removed from Delta, American, and United Airlines flights because they made airline passengers or personnel uncomfortable; in some cases, their removal earned applause from other passengers.[21]

Hate crimes directed at Muslim-looking people also increased dramatically after 9/11. According to Uniform Crime Report data, there was a nearly 1500 percent increase in hate crimes directed toward Muslims between 2000 and 2001. Table 27.1 indicates that even 10 years after 9/11, anti-Muslim hate crimes remain well above their pre-9/11 numbers. Uniform Crime Report data, however, offer a limited picture of the extent to which Muslims have been victims of hate crimes, as many such crimes go unreported by victims or unrecorded as hate crimes by law enforcement personnel. One estimate suggests that over 1,000 hate incidents, including at least 19 murders, and numerous fire bombings, assaults, and incidents of property destruction, occurred in the two months following 9/11 alone. Balbir Singh Sodhi (a Sikh man born in India), Waqar Hasan (a Muslim man born in Pakistan), and Vasudev Patel (a Hindu man born in India) are three of the 19 killed in the post-9/11 anti-Muslim fury. That only one of them was actually Muslim is a good indication of the wide net cast by the category Muslim-looking. When asked about their motivations for

TABLE 27.1   Anti-Muslim Hate Crimes, 1996–2010

Year	Total Muslim Hate Crime Victims	Crimes against Persons*	Crimes against Property[†]
1996	33	26	7
1997	31	22	9
1998	22	14	8
1999	34	15	19
2000	33	18	15
2001	544	389	155
2002	169	100	69
2003	171	83	88
2004	201	114	87
2005	151	99	52
2006	208	133	75
2007	142	84	58
2008	130	83	47
2009	131	89	42
2010	197	132	65

*Crimes against persons: murder/nonnegligent manslaughter, rape, aggravated and simple assault, and intimidation.

[†]Crimes against property: robbery, burglary, larceny-theft, motor vehicle theft, arson, vandalism, and other.

Note: Excludes crimes against society.

Data compiled from FBI's Uniform Crime Reports http://www.fbi.gov/about-us/cjis/ucr/ucr/

killing these men, the perpetrators cited patriotism and their desire for revenge against the terrorists. Though hate crimes are interpersonal and typically committed by nongovernmental actors, they operate in tandem with formal state policies and practices (e.g., immigration enforcement). The justifications for hate crimes and repressive immigration are "different facets of the same social, political, and cultural phenomenon."[22]

Violence as a means of demarcating and reinforcing social boundaries is not limited to private actors; the state also uses violence to "assign meanings of belonging and exclusion, racial worth and worthlessness, to people possessing certain features, ancestries, and nationalities."[23] The form of state violence we will first focus on is restrictive and oppressive immigration enforcement. It is important to note that though the new paradigm of terrorism may shape contemporary immigration enforcement in novel ways, the assumed association between national security and immigration control is not a new. U.S. governmental officials have long touted racist and oppressive immigration control measures as vital to national security. Immigration policies, often borne of racist principals, are integral in producing "new categories of undesirables."[24] A model example of this is Japanese deportation and internment during World War II. Over 100,000 "disloyal" Japanese and Japanese Americans were taken from their communities and interned in military bases or, in some cases, returned to Japan. The evidence of their disloyalty: their Japanese ancestry.[25]

In the context of the war on terror, Muslims have emerged as the contemporary undesirables. For example, in the last decade, Muslim-looking people have been increasingly subjected to both race-specific immigration practices and to selective enforcement of general immigration policies.[26] Within the first year following 9/11, U.S. attorney general John Ashcroft spearheaded two campaigns aimed at 8,000 "voluntary interviews" of U.S. immigrants. Interviewees, largely Muslims and/or people originating from the Middle East, were identified not because of actual criminal or suspicious activity, but because "they fit criteria designed to identify persons who might have knowledge of foreign-based terrorists [and they] might be in the same circles, communities, or social groups as those engaged in terrorist activities."[27] In other words, interviewees were selected not because of actual participation in terrorist or even criminal activity, but because of identity characteristics that they might share with problematic others. Though this interviews were "voluntary," several resulted in arrest or deportation, none of which were for terrorism-related offenses.

In addition, the federal government implemented the National Security Entry and Exit Registration System (NSEERS), a "special registration" program that requires male immigrants from specific countries—a majority of which are Muslim—to register with the government and to be fingerprinted, photographed, and interrogated at regular intervals by immigration agents.[28] Again, registrants were not identified based on individualized suspicion but because they came from countries "where Al-Qaeda or other terrorist organizations have been active or where the United States has other national security concerns."[29] By December 2003, nearly 300,000 people were registered. Similar to the interviews described earlier in this discussion, registration resulted in arrests for some, though none of these arrests were for terrorist-related activities. Finally, under Operation Liberty Shield, those seeking asylum from countries "where al-Qaeda, al-Qaeda sympathizers, and other terrorist groups are known to have operated" (i.e., Muslim countries)[30] were required to submit to detention while being processed, which could take six months or longer.[31]

As will be discussed shortly, conditions in U.S. detention centers are harsh. Muslim asylum-seekers fleeing their home countries because of persecution based on race, religion, nationality, political opinion, and/or social group were subjected to further degradation and abuse in U.S. immigrant detention centers.[32]

After 9/11, immigrants from Arab, Muslim, and South Asian countries faced increased enforcement of general immigration laws. Muslim students who overstayed visas and immigrants who failed to report a change of address within 10 days of moving, for example, found themselves targeted by immigration enforcement officers. In the year following 9/11, the number of immigrants from Muslim countries that were apprehended and removed by immigration officials increased significantly (Pakistan, 228 percent apprehension / 129 percent removal; Saudi Arabia, 239 percent apprehension / 113 percent removal; Algeria, 224 percent apprehension / 111 percent removal; Egypt, 83 percent apprehension / 199 percent removal; Morocco, 76.50 percent apprehension / 229 percent removal).[33] These percentage increases are especially dramatic in light of the fact that the total number of all immigrants that were apprehended/detained that year decreased by 23 percent and 16 percent, respectively.[34]

Post-9/11 immigration policies aimed at Muslims are forms of state violence not only because they "reracialize the communities they target as 'Muslim-looking' foreigners unworthy of membership in the national polity," but also because they result in Muslim immigrants being subjected to prison violence, an equally problematic form of state violence.[35] There are over 80 detention centers in the United States. They are run by local (city, county, and state) and federal government agencies as well as private contractors. Though immigration violations are civil rather than criminal offenses, those who violate immigration policies are subjected to detention in conditions that differ little from those in criminal prisons. In fact, in many cases, people suspected of immigration violations are housed in the same facilities as criminal suspects and offenders. Similar to other prisons, illegal beatings, psychological torment, prolonged detention, racism, and inhumane conditions are serious problems in immigrant detention centers.[36] Unlike those suspected of criminal law violations, however, people suspected of violating immigration policies have few constitutional and procedural protections from the powerful state. Immigrant detainees enjoy no right to counsel, no presumption of innocence, no jury trials, no assurances of speedy trials, no right to release, and lax rules regarding how evidence can be obtained and used during immigration hearings.

"Noncitizenship, in the vehicle of immigrant detention, serves to disappear immigrants from the justice system, leaving them with scant legal or social leverage to contest their criminalization."[37]

Increased attention to immigration in the war on terror has had serious ramifications for all immigrant groups. All immigrants are subjected to heightened immigration enforcement. For example, in government press releases about the NSEERS program discussed previously, government officials state intentions to eventually expand this registration program to all U.S. immigrants.[38] Data from 2007 to 2011 (Table 27.2) demonstrate that the number of people being removed from the United States is increasing. Though heightened enforcement is emphasized as a means for combating terrorism, the majority of those being removed are not being removed for terrorist-related activities. About half are removed for criminal offenses (most of which—92 percent—are drug offenses and driving under the influence), 40 percent are removed for violating immigration laws (i.e., civil offenses rather than criminal offenses), and 10 percent are removed for "other" reasons.[39] On the average, over 30,000 people are housed in these immigrant detention centers per day, and the average length of stay per detainee is about one month.

Contemporary immigration policies have "exploited a national feeling of betrayal to punish immigrants as immigrants, even when no plausible connection to terrorism exists."[40] One non-Muslim group that has suffered increased immigration control under the guise of fighting terrorism and protecting national security is refugees from Haiti. American policy toward Haitian refugees has been one largely of detainment (in both stateside detention centers and abroad, e.g., Guantanamo Bay) and deportation. In court cases where Haitian detainees challenged automatic detention

TABLE 27.2   Immigration and Customs Enforcement (ICE) Removals

Year	Number of Removals	Average Daily Population	Average Detention (Days)
2007	291,060	30,295	37.2
2008	369,221	31,771	30.4
2009	389,834	32,098	31.3
2010	392,862	30,885	31.5
2011	396,906	33,330	29.2

Data compiled from ICE Total Removals through July 22, 2012, http://www.ice.gov/doclib/about/offices/ero/pdf/ero-removals1.pdf

upon arrival into the United States, immigration officials argued that granting bond to Haitians "could threaten national security" because it would "tie up resources that should be committed to homeland security and the war on terrorism" and "send a signal back to Haiti . . . that [would] trigger a mass migration."[41] The implication is that any immigration policy, however remotely related to terrorism or national security, is justified.

U.S. citizens should be wary, as the reverse is also true—U.S. citizens who may be linked to terrorism can see their legal and procedural protections dissolve. The three-year detention of at least two U.S. citizens—Yaser Esam Hamdi (born in Baton Rouge, Louisiana) and Jose Padilla (born in New York City)—without trial demonstrates that "even citizenship proves to be a delicate defense if persons are linked to groups broadly categorized as 'enemies' who do not deserve equal access to due process protections."[42] As a result of the USA Patriot Act, terrorism need not even be the primary suspicion for other invasive state action. The act's provisions allow citizens to be targeted for "sneak and peek" searches or government seizures of personal information (e.g., bank records, library records), often without any knowledge of such activities. Finally, prosecutors in some jurisdictions have attempted to capitalize on concern about terrorism by reinterpreting "traditional" forms of criminal activities (e.g., drug sales, gang activity) in light of the new paradigm of terrorism.[43]

Global Control: Enemy Combatants, Foreign Detention Centers, and Torture

Combatting terrorism was also used as the primary justification for increased activity abroad, including Operation Enduring Freedom in Afghanistan and the invasion of Iraq. In both contexts, outrage over 9/11 was harnessed as a means to solicit public and political support for military operations undertaken as part of the war on terror. "Through the sleight of hand that politicians are so good at, the White House attempted to convince the American public that overthrowing the Iraqi regime was an indispensable part of the war on terrorism."[44] There is little evidence that ties between Iraqi leadership and al-Qaeda existed. Fabricated evidence that Saddam Hussein was developing weapons of mass destruction augmented the weak terrorism links argument and allowed the White House to garner enough national and international support for the invasion of Iraq. In reality, "hawks"—conservative political officials who advocate for increased defense budgets and prioritize the development of a superior U.S. military force—had long been interested in overthrowing the reigning Iraqi regime.[45] Talk of invading Iraq and removing Saddam Hussein from power predated 9/11 by at least a decade.

A growing body of national and international laws, treaties, and conventions (e.g., US War Crimes and US Torture Act, the Geneva Conventions) details how foreign civilians and prisoners of war are to be detained and to be treated once detained. Originating from the legal opinion of key federal legal officials, including Attorney Generals John Ashcroft and Alberto Gonzalez as well as Assistant Attorney General Jay Bybee, we see one of the most disconcerting inventions of the war on terror: the creation of a new legal category of persons, the "enemy combatant."[46] Through a series of legal maneuvers, the U.S. administration pushed aside established human rights law to allow for virtually unfettered control over civilian and military prisoners in foreign detention centers. Now effectively stripped of nearly any modicum of legal protections, enemy combatants were subjected to indefinite detention (without judicial review or legal counsel) and to torture.

There are over 1,000 known U.S. military bases around the world, and nearly all operate some form of detention center or brig. All branches of the military operate prisons, but it is only in the army and the marine corps that one can perform his or her entire military service as a prison guard. The majority of career military prison guards serve in domestic military prisons such as Fort Leavenworth in Kansas. Facing shortages of career prison guards who could be deployed during the operations in Afghanistan and Iraq, the military relied heavily on reservists to run foreign prisons. In the case of the prison in Abu Ghraib, some of the reservists had been prison guards in domestic prisons prior to being deployed.[47] In addition to the known military prisons, there are an unknown number of secret prisons, or "black sites," run by the Central Intelligence Agency (CIA). Sometimes these are separate facilities within known prisons (this is the case in Guantanamo Bay, where the special site was called Secret Squirrel) that are off-limits to regular prison personnel.[48]

During military operations in Iraq, prisoners were often captured en masse. For example, during Operation Iron Hammer, conducted in the city of Fallujah in November 2003, military personnel cordoned off a section of the city, bombed and raided homes, and seized thousands of the city's male residents. Though rejected by the Geneva Conventions and the International Committee of the Red Cross, hundreds of operations like Iron Hammer were conducted in Iraq.[49] These "cordon and sweep" operations were usually conducted in the middle of the night and with wanton violence. Residents were startled awake by heavily armed, masked men yelling orders and destroying their property. Suspects were shoved to the ground, bound with flexi-cuffs (plastic restraint devices similar to zip ties), hooded, and carted away. It was not unusual for arrestees to arrive in prison with injuries, including bruises, cuts, broken bones, or burns that were sustained during their capture.[50] Arrestees were not given time to change their clothes or collect any belongings. Remaining family members were given no information about where their loved ones were being taken or the reason for their apprehension.[51] Detainees had little to no contact with their families or legal representatives once imprisoned. "When entering the military prison, detainees were forced into a legal black hole. They have no access to legal representation or due process, and are treated as having no rights."[52] Because arrests were made indiscriminately, as many as 90 percent of those interned were "arrested by mistake."[53] Few had any tangible ties to al-Qaeda or to terrorism, or had any information that could be valuable to war efforts in Afghanistan or Iraq or to the war against terrorism more broadly.[54]

With a capacity of 4,000, Abu Ghraib was the largest of the 17 detention centers in Iraq. The facility held a mix of criminal offenders, prisoners of war, and newly invented enemy combatants.[55] As a result of massive arrest campaigns, Abu Ghraib prison personnel saw their prison populations expand to as many as 10,000 inmates.[56] Severe overpopulation resulted in overworked prison guards (some units were placed on mandatory 16-hour shifts seven days a week) and serious strains on prison resources, such as food and sanitation. In addition, prisoners and guards had to contend with frequent electrical blackouts, armed attacks from outside the prison, and extreme heat indexes (as high as 130 degrees). Guard misconduct was rampant.[57]

Harsh living conditions for prisoners were exacerbated by abuse from prison guards. Such abuse was condoned, if not sanctioned, by vague directives from top military and government administrators (including Secretary of Defense Donald Rumsfeld). Prison guards were encouraged to take an "aggressive approach" to preparing detainees for interrogation.[58] Though never told explicitly to torture detainees, guards were encouraged to "stress out," to "prepare," to "soften up," or to "loosen up" detainees.[59] Legal leadership in the United States augmented these instructions with a new, and extremely narrow, definition of torture. For an action to constitute torture according to the U.S. attorney general's office, "it must inflict pain that is difficult to endure. Physical pain amounting to torture must be equivalent in intensity to the pain accompanying serious physical injury, such as organ failure, impairment of bodily function, or even death."[60] Such definitions narrowed the range of behaviors that could qualify as torture "almost to a vanishing point."[61]

The excerpt from a Physicians for Human Rights report included at the beginning of this chapter describes some of the most common forms of torture committed by prison guards at Abu Ghraib, which included physical abuse, deprivation (food, water, sleep), humiliation (personal, sexual, religious), subjection to extreme conditions (noise, temperature), and restraint. Restraint is an especially brutal form of torture:

> After being made to stand barefooted on concrete for hours on end, fluids would have begun to flow down to the inmate's legs. The legs would have then swollen, forming lesions that would erupt and separate, possibly leading to hallucinations. Then it is possible that the kidneys would have shut down. As the prisoner tired, he would have slouched forward. The weight of his arms pulling on the chest cavity would have constricted breathing, thereby compromising oxygen flow to the brain and other vital organs. Note that the pain is self-inflicted; it is not coming from the outside in the form of a beating or a cattle prod, but from within—driven by the prisoner's weakness to help himself.[62]

Much of the torture occurring in Abu Ghraib would be unknown by the public if pictures had not been released to the public in April 2004 by CBS's *60 Minutes* and the *New Yorker* magazine.[63] As many as 16,000 pictures and 112 videos were included in the army's internal investigations of the facility, though only about 200 of these were initially seen by the public.[64] In addition to the forms of abuse described earlier in this discussion, these photos include images of dogs being used to terrorize inmates; groups of naked, hooded men laying on top of each other to form pyramids; detainees being led around on leashes; and electrical wires attached to inmates' genitals. Infused in many of the images are violently sexual themes—files from internal investigations indicate that much of the abuse occurring at Abu Ghraib was coupled with American soldiers having sex with prisoners and with each other.[65]

The final consideration with regard to Muslims and imprisonment abroad is the highly secretive "extraordinary renditions" (capture, movement, and detention of suspects outside of the normal legal channels) conducted by the CIA. During an extraordinary rendition, any person from anywhere in the world can be seized and taken to another location for interrogation and indefinite detention. Many of these individuals were brought to Guantanamo Bay in Cuba, but an unknown number were brought to countries known by human rights groups and the U.S. Department of State to practice torture, including Jordan, Syria, Egypt, Morocco, and Uzbekistan.[66] The International Committee for the Red Cross, the international body responsible for ensuring that detainees are treated humanely, has no access to these prisons.[67] Evidence of these kidnappings has come to light from detainees who were wrongly imprisoned and then released. It also comes from "plane spotters"—people whose hobby it is to track airplane activity and log it on the internet—who tracked the activities of the Gulfstream V jet used to transport rendered suspects around the globe.[68] Though the exact number of people subjected to rendition may never be known, at least 150 people were rendered between 2001 and 2010.[69] Most of those rendered simply disappear—their families have no knowledge of their whereabouts, nor do they have access to counsel. In his 2003 State of the Union address, President Bush alludes to the fate of some of those who have been rendered: "All told, more than 3,000 suspected terrorists have been arrested in many countries. And many others have met a different fate. Let's put it this way: They are no longer a problem to the United States and our friends and allies."[70]

Drawing Parallels: Foreign Detention Centers and U.S. Prisons

Though there are exceptions,[71] most American prison literature tends to focus on local or national penal practices, with little attention paid to the undercurrents that resonate with international policies and practices. The growth of detention centers for "terrorists" and the subversion of international human rights law abroad emerge from similar political and social orientations as the mushrooming of American prison populations and hyperpunitive domestic crime policy discussed in other chapters in this collection. Both are built upon the premise that the state's primary responsibility is to control undesirables through aggressive and punitive state action.

There are several ways in which the abusive practices in Abu Ghraib signal problems in domestic prisons. A number of key prison officials in Abu Ghraib had served as corrections officers or administrators in domestic prisons.[72] Many of the Abu Ghraib images released to the public feature, or were taken by, Corporal Charles Graner Jr. Prior to his deployment and upon his return from Iraq, Graner served as a prison guard in Pennsylvania's State Correctional Institute at Greene. SCI-Greene is a maximum security prison built in southwestern Pennsylvania in the 1990s and is not without controversy regarding treatment of prisoners. In 1998, the Pennsylvania Department of Corrections fired four of its guards, demoted or suspended several others, and transferred the superintendent and his deputy because of prisoner abuse.[73] So common were similar forms of abuse used in domestic prisons that one of Graner's lawyer's arguments was that "the human pyramid and other tactics represent routine [domestic] prison-control techniques."[74] The presiding military judge did not allow Graner's lawyer to pursue the argument to its end, so we may never know the extent of the parallels between Abu Ghraib and SCI-Greene.

"The Abu Ghraib photographs exposed the dehumanization that is the modus operandi of the lawful, modern, state-of-the-art prison."[75] The justifications for the treatment of suspected terrorists (or enemy combatants) parallel arguments made for the abusive treatment of domestic prisoners, especially those residing in maximum security prisons. Both are construed as dangerous, violent, and unmanageable and, as such, require exceptional methods of state and institutional control.[76] There are a variety of dehumanizing and physically brutal techniques used in these contexts that mirror the practices of Abu Ghraib, including the use of dogs, forced strip searches, sensory and sleep deprivation, and verbal abuse and assault.[77] "[T]here seems little doubt that what goes on in a number of Supermax facilities would breach the protections enshrined in [international human rights instruments]."[78] As the following section demonstrates, we need not focus exclusively on the most repressive domestic prisons to draw parallels between foreign detention centers and domestic prisons. This discussion will focus primarily on black Muslims—those born in the United States who have converted to Islam—and reveals additional consequences of current anti-Muslim sentiment for the broader category of Muslim-looking people.

Black Muslims in U.S. Prisons

Black Muslims represent various sects of Islam, including Ahamadiyya, Sunni, Moorish Science Temple, and the Nation of Islam. The prison has a long been a central site for black Muslims. The Nation of Islam (NOI) is perhaps the best known of Muslim groups in prisons. It deserves some further elaboration, as some of its tenets are specific to experiences of black Americans rather than Muslims more broadly. NOI was founded in Detroit in the 1930s by Wallace Fard Muhammad, though it did not gain much recognition until it was popularized by Elijah Muhammed and Malcolm X in the mid-20th century. Like a number of its members, each of these NOI leaders served time in prison—Malcolm X for criminal convictions and the others for refusing the military draft. With regard to the draft, NOI leaders point out the contradiction between black Americans being able to die for the country during military service but being unable to enjoy the rights of full citizenship while home. The NOI, especially in the 1960s, emphasized black liberation and pride, and was explicit in its criticisms of racial domination. The religion offered an alternative to Christianity for its largely poor, urban black followers.[79]

Prior to the 1960s, many federal and state penal codes defined prisoners as "civilly dead" or "slaves of the state," and deferred to the authority of prison administrators to develop their own policies and practices for running day-to-day prison operations (*Ruffin vs. Commonwealth*, 1871). Because of the courts' "hands-off" policies, prison guards and administrators enjoyed broad latitude in their (mis)treatment of prisoners. As a series of court cases reveal, prisons conditions were deplorable (see, for example, *Newman vs. Alabama*, 1976). In addition to severe overcrowding, inmates had to contend with lack of access to hygiene supplies (e.g., toilets, showers, soap, toothpaste), insect and rodent infestation, deficient or nonexistent medical care, corruption on the part of corrections officers, and institutionally condoned violence between inmates. These conditions fostered hostilities between inmates and guards, and among inmates themselves, resulting in violent riots in prisons across the country.

Before the courts began to intervene in prison operations, black Muslims were frequently discriminated against in prison employment, in their daily activities, and in disciplinary proceedings. "It is impossible to understand the vehemence and determination with which the prison resisted every Muslim demand, no matter how insignificant."[80] Black Muslims were frequent targets of physical abuse, were not allowed to practice their religion or to possess religious materials, and were subjected to harsh disciplinary action, including lengthy stays in solitary confinement and transfer from institution to institution. A common perception amongst prison administrators was that black Muslim prisoners were manipulative, conspiratorial, and dangerous—if left unregulated, they would provoke violence and unrest in the prison. This sentiment is reiterated as a justification for discriminatory treatment during a number of court proceedings including *In re Ferguson* (1961), where the California prison director argued that black Muslims' "religious principles conflicted with the health, safety, welfare, and morals of the prison."[81] Black Muslim prison groups were considered so threatening in a Washington, DC, prison that a prison administrator placed 38 black Muslims in solitary confinement for three months.[82]

Black Muslim prisoners were active in challenging the conditions of their confinement during the 1960s and 1970s. Though many of their legal battles were unsuccessful, black Muslims prison activism was "the major catalyst" for a number of prison reforms, most significantly in religious freedom and racial discrimination.[83] All prisoners benefited from lawsuits initiated by black Muslim inmates. These suits expanded religious freedoms (i.e., the right to hold religious services, to possess religious materials, and to proselytize);[84] provided protection from arbitrary or discriminatory punishment (*Sewell vs. Pegelow,* 1961; *Walker vs. Blackwell,* 1969); limited prison officials' abilities to interfere with communications between prisoners and their legal representatives (*Sostre vs. McGinnis,* 1964); and allowed prisoners to sue prison officials and to recover monetary damages for the deprivation of their constitutional rights (*Cooper vs. Pate,* 1964). Thousands of prisoners' rights cases were filed and decided upon based upon the courts' decisions in cases filed by black Muslim prisoners. "The Muslim prisoners' cases have had a profound impact upon the entire correction system, both because they helped to change the existing relationships between the 'keeper' and the 'kept' during the 1960s and because they provided the legal vehicles for all incarcerated persons to attempt to vindicate their constitutional rights."[85]

Though conditions may have improved since the 1960s for black Muslim inmates, they, too, are experiencing the consequences of the war on terror and the resurgence of anti-Muslim sentiment in the United States. Between January 1, 2011, and June 30, 2011, the Office of the Inspector General processed 1,065 civil rights or civil liberties complaints filed by Muslim prisoners—the second entry at the beginning of this chapter is one of those complaints. Other issues raised by Muslim inmates include suspension of special diets, unwarranted placement in segregation or in solitary confinement, interference with legal communications, restricted participation in religious activities, delayed or inadequate medical care, threats and abuse from guards to discourage inmates from filing administrative remedy requests, and verbal and physical attacks from guards because of their religion and/or their ethnic background. In a number of cases, Muslims and Middle Eastern inmates describe prison personnel making comments about their presumed participation in terrorist activities. For example, while praying, Muslim inmates were told by a prison guard that they were on the "wrong side" and that "we can smoke you anytime we want"; a prison staff member directed another inmate to stop assisting Islamic inmates "because we don't help terrorists"; and another prison staff member referred to Muslim inmates as "shoe bombers."[86]

The in-prison association between Muslims and terrorism also appears to be a preoccupation of some outside of the prison. In a 2009 article published in the conservative online newspaper *Canadian Free Press*, the author describes prisons as "hothouses for Islam" where an "army of jihadist" African Americans are "being converted by the cellblock, causing FBI officials to speculate that this segment of the population represents the force from which the next 9/11 will originate."[87] The concern about prisons as breeding grounds for future terrorists does not appear to be a preoccupation of just right-wing alarmists. Some federal government officials have expressed similar concerns during several Senate subcommittee meetings that have occurred since 9/11. In reality, there is little evidence to support such an idea. Of the 46 potential cases of "prison-radicalized terrorists" over the last 41 years, 14 might be considered to have become radicalized in prison. "The claim that American prisons spawn terrorism is false—or, at the very least, overstated. U.S. prisons are not systematically generating a large-scale terrorist threat . . . few U.S. prisoners have been radicalized behind bars, and fewer still have engaged in terrorist acts."[88]

Black Muslims have long been perceived as a threatening group in the United States, especially in prisons. In the new paradigm of terrorism, however, old fears of these groups are being expressed in the new language of terrorism. The theme of black Muslims and terrorism in prison is a newly emerging in conservative and political discourse. Time will tell how the state and prison administrators react to the fears this discourse attempts to evoke. Given the poor track record of treatment of black Muslims historically and of Muslim-looking people today, there is cause for concern.

Conclusion: Muslim-Looking People and the Future of the War on Terror

In recent years, a number of significant events have occurred that have impacted the war on terror. Several key court decisions have been handed down that limit the ability of the U.S. government to indefinitely detain foreign nationals without counsel or without trial, that reinforce that the United States is bound by the Geneva Conventions, and that allow enemy combatants access to the U.S. criminal justice system (see, for example, *Rasul vs. Bush*, 2004; *Hamdan vs. Rumsfeld*, 2006; *Al Odah vs. United States*, 2007; *Hamdi vs. Rumsfeld*, 2004). In addition, on his second day of office, President Obama issued an executive order that clarified appropriate interrogation methods and established a policy that commanders can be held criminally culpable for illegal actions of individuals under their charge. The specific forms of interrogation practices include "forced nudity, forced sexual acts, hooding, beatings, electric shock, waterboarding, induced hypothermia, mock executions, and deprivation of necessary food, water, or medical care."[89] During his campaign, Obama promised to shut down Guantanamo Bay and to release its detainees or move them into domestic prisons. To date, Guantanamo Bay is still in operation.

Abu Ghraib was closed as a U.S. detention facility in 2006 but reopened in 2009 under Iraqi government.[90] Sixteen soldiers involved with the abuse that occurred in 2003 at Abu Ghraib have been punished—11 were ordered to serve time in prison, and five others were disciplined through demotion, loss of rank, or loss of pay. Graner received the most severe punishment—a 10-year prison sentence. The response to Abu Ghraib has been criticized as largely symbolic, however, as none of those in leadership positions have been held accountable either domestically or internationally. It is unlikely that international bodies such as the United Nations, the International Court of Justice, or the International Criminal Court will pursue charges against U.S. military or federal leadership. Each of these organizations relies on the UN Security Council for authorization or for enforcement of judicial decisions. As a key player in the UN Security Council, the United States has significant influence to prevent any attempt to hold U.S. leadership accountable.[91]

Though most of these changes are important steps in altering the dynamic of the war on terror, they do little to alter the conditions for the majority of Muslim-looking people within U.S. borders and beyond. The racialization of Muslim-looking people as perpetually suspicious others persists as a dominant perception, and this perception continues to be expressed through discrimination, hate crimes, and selective immigration enforcement. By expanding the surveillance and enforcement authority of the state, policies and practices designed under the guise of dealing with potential terrorist threats also have serious ramifications for other immigrant groups and for U.S. citizens.

Notes

1. Physicians for Human Rights, 2008, p. 3.
2. Office of the Inspector General, 2011, p. 10.
3. Hooks and Mosher, 2005, p. 1635; Gordon, 2006.
4. Scraton and McCulloch, 2008, p. 1.
5. Ahmad, 2004.
6. Ahmad, 2004.
7. Collins, 1974, p. 420.
8. Blin, 2007.
9. Naureckas, 1995, p. 3.
10. Naureckas, 1995.
11. Sidel, 2004.
12. Congressional Budget Office, 2005.
13. Macmaster, 2004, p. 1.
14. "Transcript," 2001, p. 53.
15. "Transcript," 2001, p. 53.
16. Gordon, 2006, p. 53.
17. Mayer, 2010.
18. Macmaster, 2004, p. 5.
19. Ahmad, 2004, p. 1323.
20. Sidel, 2004.
21. Ahmad, 2004.
22. Ahmad, 2004, p. 1277.
23. Haney López, 1996, p. 145.
24. Hernandez, 2005, p. 3.
25. Hernandez, 2005, p. 7.
26. Ahmad, 2004, p. 1269.
27. U.S. Attorney General, 2002, p. 12.
28. Countries include Iran, Iraq, Libya, Sudan, Syria, Afghanistan, Algeria, Bahrain, Eritrea, Lebanon, Morocco, North Korea, Oman, Qatar, Somalia, Tunisia, the United Arab Emirates, Yemen, Pakistan, Saudi Arabia, Bangladesh, Egypt, Indonesia, Jordan, and Kuwait.
29. Department of Homeland Security, 2003, p. 3.
30. Thirty-three countries and two territories were targeted, including Afghanistan, Algeria, Bahrain, Bangladesh, Djibouti, Egypt, Eritrea, Indonesia, Iran, Iraq, Jordan, Kazakhstan, Kuwait, Lebanon, Libya, Malaysia, Morocco, Oman, Pakistan, Philippines, Qatar, Saudi Arabia, Somalia, Sudan, Syria,

Thailand, Tajikistan, Tunisia, Turkey, Turkmenistan, United Arab Emirates, Uzbekistan, Yemen, the Gaza strip and the West Bank.

31. U.S. Department of Defense, n.d.

32. Human Rights First, 2007.

33. Ahmad, 2004, p. 1276.

34. Ahmad, 2004, p. 1277.

35. Ahmad, 2004, p. 1262.

36. Dow, 2005.

37. Hernandez, 2005, p. 18.

38. Department of Homeland Security, 2003.

39. Immigration and Custom Enforcement, n.d.

40. Ahmad, 2004, p. 1316.

41. Bandell, 2002, p. 8.

42. Hernandez, 2005, p. 4.

43. Sidel, 2004, pp. 90–91. A New York gang leader was charged under the antiterrorism statute for the death of a 10-year-old girl; a North Carolina prosecutor charged methamphetamine producers with producing "chemical weapons."

44. Blin, 2007, p. 416.

45. FitzGerald, 2002.

46. Hooks and Mosher, 2005.

47. Gordon, 2006.

48. Doyle, 2010.

49. Macmaster, 2004, p. 11.

50. Ricks, 2006.

51. Danner, 2004.

52. Carlton, 2006, p. 20.

53. Fay and Jones, 2004, p. 37.

54. Hooks and Mosher, 2005.

55. Heurich and Vaughn, 2009.

56. Kennedy, Garbus, and Youngelson, 2006.

57. Hamm, 2007.

58. Smuelers and van Niekerk, 2009.

59. Lankford, 2001, p. 24.

60. Bybee, 2002, p. 2.

61. Hamm, 2007, p. 268.

62. Hamm, 2007, p. 272.

63. Hamm, 2007, p. 265.

64. Additional pictures have been released since. See http://www.wired.com/science/discoveries/multimedia/2008/02/gallery_abu_ghraib/

65. Hamm, 2007, p. 270.

66. Mayer, 2010.

67. Malinowski, 2008, p. 149.

68. Malinoski, 2008.

69. Mayer, 2010, p. 138.

70. Bush, 2003, p. 80.

71. Gordon, 2010; Scraton and McCulloch, 2008.

72. Green, 2004.

73. Bucsko and Dvorchak, 1998.

74. Reid, 2005, p. 14.

75. Gordon, 2006, p. 49.

76. Scraton and Chadwick, 1987; Davis, 2005.

77. Jeffrey, 2007; Rhodes, 2004.

78. King, 1999, p. 164.

79. Curtis, 2001.

80. Jacobs, 1977, pp. 59–60.

81. "Constitutional Law," 1962, p. 837.

82. Smith, 1993.

83. Smith, 1993, p. 132.

84. *Banks vs. Havener*, 1964; *Fulwood vs. Clemmer*, 1962.

85. Smith, 1993, p. 144.

86. Office of the Inspector General, 2011, p. 10.

87. Williams, 2009, p. 10.

88. Useem, 2012, p. 39.

89. Lankford, 2001, p. 25.

90. Doyle, 2010.

91. Rothe, Kramer, and Mullins, 2009.

References

Ahmad, Muneer. "A Rage Shared by Law: Post-September 11 Racial Violence as Crimes of Passion." *California Law Review* 92, no. 5 (2004): 1259–330.

Al Odah vs. United States, 551 US 1161, 2007.

Bandell, Brian. "INS Appeals Bond Issued to Haitians Citing National Security Threat." *St. Augustine Record*, November 8, 2002.

Banks vs. Havener. 234 F.Supp. 27, 1964.

Blin, Arnaud. "The US Confronting Terrorism." In *The History of Terrorism: From Antiquity to Al Qaeda*, edited by Gerard Challand and Arnaud Blin, pp. 398–419. Berkeley: University of California Press, 2007.

Bucsko, Mike, and Bob Dvorchak. "Life in Prison: Firings, Charges Shake up SCI Greene." *Pittsburgh Post-Gazette*, August 9 1998.

Bush, George W. "Text of President Bush's 2003 State of the Union Address." *Washington Post,* January 28, 2003.

Bybee, Jay. *Memorandum for Alberto R. Gonzales, counsel to the president. Re: standards of conduct for interrogation under 18 U.S.C. §§ 2340-2340A*, 2002. http://academics.smcvt.edu/jhughes/Bybee%20Memo.htm.

Carlton, Bree. "From H Division to Abu Ghraib: Regimes of Justification and the Historical Proliferation of State-Inflicted Terror and Violence in Maximum-Security." *Social Justice* 33, no. 4 (2006): 15–36.

Coleman vs. District of Columbia Commissioners, 234 F. Supp. 408 (E.D.Va.1964), 1964.

Collins, Randall. "Three Faces of Cruelty: Towards a Comparative Sociology of Violence." *Theory and Society* 1 (1974): 415–440.

Congressional Budget Office. *The Budget and Economic Outlook: Fiscal Years 2006 to 2015*. Washington, DC: Congress of the United States, 2005.

Constitutional Law. In General. Right to Practice Black Muslim Tenets in State Prisons. *Pierce vs. Lavallee* (2nd Cir. 1961); *in Re Ferguson* (Cal. 1961). *Harvard Law Review* 75, no. 4 (1962): 837–840.

Cooper vs. Pate, 378 US 546 (1964), 1964.

Curtis, Edward. *Islam in Black America: Identity, Liberation and Difference in African American Islamic Thought*. Albany: State University of New York Press, 2001.

Danner, Mark. *Torture and Truth: America, Abu Ghraib, and the War on Terror*. New York: New York Review Books, 2004.

Davis, Angela. *Abolition Democracy: Beyond Empire, Prisons and Torture*. New York: Seven Stories, 2005.

Department of Homeland Security. *Fact Sheet: Changes to National Security Entry Exit Registration System (NSEERS)*. Washington, DC: Department of Homeland Security, 2003.

Dow, Mark. *American Gulag: Inside U.S. Immigration Prisons*. Berkeley: University of California Press, 2005.

Doyle, Robert. *The Enemy in our Hands: America's Treatment of Prisoners of War from the Revolution to the War on Terror*. Lexington: University Press of Kentucky, 2010.

Fay, George, and Anthony Jones. *Investigation of the Abu Ghraib Prison/Detention Facility and 205th Military Brigade*. Washington, DC: Department of Defense, 2004.

FitzGerald, Frances. "How Hawks Captured the White House." *Guardian*, September 23, 2002.

Fulwood vs. Clemmer, 206 F.Supp. 370 (D.D.C. 1962), 1962.

Gordon, Avery. "Abu Ghraib: Imprisonment and the War on Terror." *Race and Class* 48, no. 1 (2006): 42–59.

Gordon, Luk Vervaet. "The Violence of Incarceration: A Response from Mainland Europe." *Race and Class* 51, no. 4 (2010): 27–38.

Green, Judith. "From Abu Ghraib to America." *Ideas for an Open Society* 4, no. 1 (2004): 1–4.

Hamdan vs. Rumsfeld, 548 U.S. 557 (2006), 2006.

Hamdi vs. Rumsfeld, 542 U.S. 507 (2004), 2004.

Hamm, Mark. "'High Crimes and Misdemeanors': George W. Bush and the Sins of Abu Ghraib." *Crime Media Culture* 3, no. 3 (2007): 259–284.

Haney López, Ian. *White by Law: The Legal Construction of Race*. New York: New York University Press, 1996.

Hernandez, David. *Undue Process: Immigrant Detention, Due Process, and Lesser Citizenship*. Berkeley: University of California Press, 2005.

Heurich, Sarah, and Michael Vaughn. "Ill-Treatment and Torture at Abu Ghraib Prison: Irrational Policy Implementation and Administrative Breakdown." *Criminal Justice Studies* 22, no. 2 (2009): 181–201.

Hooks, Gregory, and Clayton Mosher. "Outrages against Personal Dignity: Rationalizing Abuse and Torture in the War on Terror."*Social Forces* 83, no. 4 (2005): 1627–1645.

Human Rights First. *Background Briefing Note: The Detention of Asylum Seekers in the United States: Arbitrary under the ICCPR*. Washington, DC: Human Rights First, 2007.

Immigration and Customs Enforcement. *Removal Statistics*, n.d. Accessed August 7, 2012, http://www.ice.gov/removal-statistics/.

Jacobs, James. *Stateville: The Penitentiary in Mass Society*. Chicago: University of Chicago Press, 1977.

Jeffrey, Ian. "Supermax Prisons." *Society* 44, no. 3 (2007): 60–64.

Kennedy, Rory, Liz Garbus, and Jack Youngelson. *Ghosts of Abu Ghraib*. DVD. Directed by Rory Kennedy, 78 min., HBO, 2006.

King, Roy. "The Rise and Rise of Supermax: An American Solution in Search of a Problem?" *Punishment and Society* 1, no. 2 (1999): 163–186.

Lankford, Adam. "Assessing the Obama Standard for Interrogations: An Analysis of Army Field Manual 2-22.3." *Studies in Conflict & Terrorism* 33, no. 1 (2001): 20–35.

Macmaster, Neil. "Torture: From Algiers to Abu Ghraib." *Race and Class* 46, no. 2 (2004): 1–21.

Malinowski, Tom. "Restoring Moral Authority: Ending Torture, Secret Detention, and the Prison at Guantanamo Bay." *Annals of the American Academy of Political and Social Science* 618 (2008): 148–159.

Mayer, Jane. "Outsourcing Torture: The Secret History of America's 'Extraordinary Rendition' Program." In *The United States and Torture: Interrogation, Incarceration, and Abuse*, edited by Marjorie Cohn, pp. 137–160. New York: New York University Press, 2010.

Naureckas, Jim. "The Oklahoma City Bombing: The Jihad That Wasn't." Accessed July 30, 2012, http://fair.org/extra-online-articles/the-oklahoma-city-bombing/, 1995.

Newman vs. State of Alabama, 503 F.2d 1320 (5th Cir. 1974), 1974.

Office of the Inspector General. *Report to Congress on Implementation of Section 1001 of the USA Patriot Act (as required by Section 1001(3) of Public Law 107-56)*. Washington, DC: U.S. Department of Justice, 2011.

Physicians for Human Rights. *Broken Laws, Broken Lives: Medical Evidence of Torture by US Personnel and its Impacts*. Cambridge, MA: Physicians for Human Rights, 2008.

Pugh vs. Locke, 406 F.Supp. 318 (M.D. Ala. 1976), 1976.

Rasul vs. Bush, 542 U.S. 466 (2004), 2004.

Reid, Thomas. R. "Witness: Graner Ordered to Beat Prisoners." *Washington Post*, January 13, 2005.

Rhodes, Lorna. *Total Confinement: Madness and Reason in the Maximum Security Prison*. Berkeley: University of California Press, 2004.

Ricks, Thomas. *Fiasco: The American Military Adventure in Iraq*. New York: Penguin, 2006.

Rothe, Dawn, Ronald Kramer, and Christopher Mullins. "Torture, Impunity, and Open Legal Spaces: Abu Ghraib and International Controls." *Contemporary Justice Review* 12, no. 1 (2009): 27–43.

Ruffin vs. Commonwealth, 62 Va. 790 (1871), 1871.

Scraton, Phil, and Jude McCulloch. "The Violence of Incarceration: An Introduction." In *The Violence of Incarceration*, edited by Phil Scraton and Jude McCulloch, pp. 1–18. London: Routledge, 2008.

Scraton, Phil, and Kathryn Chadwick. "Speaking Ill of the Dead: Official Responses to Death in Custody." In *Law, Order, and the Authoritarian State: Readings in Critical Criminology*, edited by Phil Scraton, pp. 212–236. Philadelphia: Open University Press, 1987.

Sewell vs. Pegelow, 291 F.2d 196 (4th Cir. 1961), 1961.

Sidel, Mark. *More Secure, Less Free? Antiterrorism Policy and Civil Liberties After September 11*. Ann Arbor: University of Michigan Press, 2004.

Smith, Christopher. "Black Muslims and the Development of Prisoners' Rights." *Journal of Black Studies* 24, no. 2 (1993): 131–146.

Smuelers, Alette, and Sander van Niekerk. "Abu Ghraib and the War on Terror: A Case against Donald Rumsfeld?" *Crime, Law, and Social Change* 51, no. 3 (2009): 327–349.

Sostre vs. McGinnis, 334 F.2d 906 (2d Cir. 1964) cert. denied 379 U.S. 892 (1964), 1964.

Taguba, Antonio. Article 15-6 investigation of the 800th Military Police Brigade. National Public Radio. http://www.npr.org/iraq/2004/prison_abuse_report.pdf (June 18, 2012).

Transcript of President Bush's address to the American people on September 21, 2001. *CNN*. Accessed July 31, 2012, http://articles.cnn.com/2001-09-20/us/gen.bush.transcript_1_joint-session-national-anthem-citizens?_s=PM:US.

U.S. Attorney General. "Transcript from the Eastern District of Virginia/Interview Project Results Announcement." Accessed August 1, 2012, http://www .justice.gov/archive/ag/speeches/2002/032002agnewsconferenceedvainterview projectresultsannouncement.htm, March 20, 2002.

U.S. Department of Defense. "Operation Liberty Shield," n.d. Accessed April 7, 2013, http://www.defense.gov/specials/homeland/liberty.html.

Useem, Bert. "US Prisons and the Myth of Islamic Terrorism." *Contexts* 11, no. 2 (2012): 34–39.

Walker vs. Blackwell, 411 F.2d 23 (5th Cir. 1969), 1969.

Williams, Paul. "American Prisons now Hothouses for Islam." *Chicago Free Press*, August 4, 2009.

Chapter 28

The Ghosts of Slavery: Trying Juveniles as Adults

Christopher Bickel and Janette Diaz

The town of Jena, Louisiana, garnered national attention when District Attorney Reed Walters charged six black youth with attempted murder for what amounted to little more than a schoolyard fight. At the local high school, racial conflict escalated after black students sat under an oak tree usually reserved for white students. The next day, students found three nooses hanging from the tree, reminiscent of the lynching of African Americans during Jim Crow segregation. Fights between black and white students were common. On December 4, 2006, six African-American teenagers confronted Justin Barker, a white student, after he allegedly called a black student a "nigger." Outnumbered six to one, Justin was rushed to the emergency room, where doctors treated him for a concussion and a swollen eye. He attended a school function later that night. Soon after, six African Americans—Mychal Bell, 16; Jesse Ray Beard, 14; Robert Bailey, 17; Carwin Jones, 18; Byrant Purvis, 17; and Theo Shaw, 17—were charged with attempted second-degree murder. Prosecutor Walters identified their shoes as deadly weapons. All youth were charged as adults, except for Jesse Beard, who was charged as a juvenile, and they would become known as the Jena Six. Their case serves as a frightening symbol of a two-tiered system of criminal justice—one for white youth and another far more punitive system for youth of color.

It is sad, but not surprising, that many of the Jena Six were charged as adults in Louisiana, a state described by the *New Orleans Times-Picayune* as the "world's prison capital." Reporter Cindy Chang writes that Louisiana has an incarceration rate "nearly triple Iran's, seven times China's and 10 times Germany's."[1] Louisiana aside, the United States incarcerates black males at a rate of 4,777 per 100,000.[2] This is over five times the black male incarceration rate found under apartheid South Africa in 1993.[3] Not since the rise of slavery has the United States witnessed the growth of an institution that so fundamentally changes the status of the men and women confined within its walls. There are more African-American men behind bars today than were enslaved in 1850.[4] Once free, the former captives of the state are legally discriminated against in terms of voting, housing, employment, and even access to institutions of higher education. In many ways, Jim Crow justice has become American justice once again. This chapter situates the practice of trying children as adults, particularly African-American children, within this context of a two-tiered system of justice that has deep roots in the institution of slavery.

The Ghost of Slavery and the History of Juvenile Justice

Until the late 1800s, it was common practice to confine children alongside adults in jails, prisons, and workhouses.[5] At the time, massive economic disparity between the rich and the poor shaped the landscape. The industrial elite heavily exploited working-class and immigrant laborers in the factories.[6] Riots over working conditions were common. The elite grew ever weary and identified the immigrant working class as a danger to their economic privilege. The wealthy elite was especially concerned with the children of immigrants, who they believed lacked the "proper" Christian values and morals, including a strong "work ethic" and respect for authority. This gave rise to a widespread moral panic about rising juvenile delinquency among poor and working-class youth.

Responding to rising fears of juvenile delinquency, reformers constructed the first House of Refuge in New York City. Established in 1825, the House of Refuge not only held children convicted of crimes, but also those whose only crime was living in poverty. Soon after the opening of the first House of Refuge, similar houses opened in Boston, Philadelphia, and across the Northeast. The Houses of Refuge were designed to reform youth through disciplined activity, prayer, work, and a heavily regimented day. On the one hand, the houses of refuge provided an alternative to the harsh conditions of adult jails and prisons. On the other hand, children were subjected to strict training schools where corporal punishment and harsh working conditions were common.[7]

There has never been an equal system of justice for adults, let alone juveniles, in the United States. Justice has always been doled out more on the basis of race, ethnicity, and class rather than the actual crime committed. While poor white youth were confined to houses of refuge, the children of the elite were never institutionalized in such a manner. The family has always been seen as the proper place to discipline the children of privilege.

While the conditions of the early houses of refuge were harsh for white immigrant youth, there was a far more insidious institution that held African-American youth captive: slavery. Under slavery, there was an entirely different set of rules, the slave codes, which governed the behavior of enslaved human beings. Whippings, beatings, and other forms of torture were commonly used to intimidate and control African Americans on the plantation and were condoned, if not required, by state law. In *Narrative of the Life of Frederick Douglass*, Douglass describes the slave codes as practiced on the plantation:

> A mere look, or motion,—a mistake, accident, or want of power,—are all matters for which a slave must be whipped at any time. Does a slave look dissatisfied? It is said, he has the devil in him, and it must be whipped out. Does he speak loudly when spoken to by his master? Then he is getting high-minded, and should be taken a buttonhole lower. Does he forget to pull off his hat at the approach of a white person? Then he is wanting reverences, and should be whipped for it. Does he ever venture to vindicate his conduct, when censured for it? Then he is guilty of imprudence,—one of the greatest crimes of which a slave can be guilty.[8]

The slave codes made few distinctions between children and adults in the distribution of punishment, leaving African-American youth to suffer the same atrocities as adults. At the same time reformers were arguing that white children should no longer be held in adult jails, the suffering of African-American children confined to slavery went unnoticed and unchanged.

The Thirteenth Amendment officially outlawed slavery and indentured servitude. However, a loophole in the amendment allowed for slavery as punishment for a crime. Not surprisingly, southern states quickly passed laws known as black codes that established a separate and unequal system of justice. Jails and prisons that used to be populated by whites quickly became overwhelmingly black. Sleeping quarters on former plantations, like Angola in Louisiana, were quickly refurbished into prison cells. Within a few years, the shackles of slavery became the bars of the criminal justice system.[9] Unemployment, homelessness, changing employers, and drinking became crimes for which only African Americans were convicted.

These black codes later transformed into Jim Crow laws, which gave rise to what Douglas Blackmon termed "slavery by another name."[10] Local sheriffs rounded up hundreds of thousands of African Americans for petty—often trumped up—infractions, and they were sent to toil, and often die, under brutal working conditions on plantations, mines, roadways, and railways. The convict leasing system, as it was called, became an essential mechanism for reinstating slavery in the South. Much of the southern infrastructure was built by forced convict labor.

Author David Oshinsky describes the convict leasing system as "worse than slavery." In his study of Parchment Farm Penitentiary in Mississippi, Oshinsky estimates that the fatality rate of African Americans there during the 1880s ranged from 9 to 16 percent. He explains that under slavery, at least slave masters had an economic interest in the health of their slaves. But with convict leasing, the criminal justice system could quickly replace those who perished by rounding up even more human bodies. Children were not exempt from the convict leasing system and often worked side by side with men twice their age. Nearly one in four convicts on Parchment Farm were children, some as young as eight years of age.[11]

While African-American children suffered under Jim Crow justice, there were significant improvements in the treatment of white children accused of crimes. In 1899, Illinois established the first juvenile court. The court was founded on the idea of *parens patriae* (Latin for father of the people), which asserts that children are developmentally different than adults.[12] Given this, the state has a vested interest in protecting the welfare of children who cannot protect themselves. Before 1899, there was no formal distinction made between adults and children in the legal system.[13] After the formation of the Illinois juvenile courts, other states soon followed. Juvenile courts sought to protect notions of childhood and control juvenile delinquency through rehabilitation rather than punishment. The courts had the power to remove children from their homes and sentence them to training schools. Although rehabilitation was the goal of training schools, they continued to feel like places of punishment for those confined.

With the rise of the civil rights movement and the weakening of Jim Crow justice, the juvenile justice system saw many progressive reforms in the 1960s. A number of U.S. Supreme Court decisions—*Kent vs. United States* (1966), *In re Gault* (1967)—further protected the rights of juveniles charged with crimes, allowing juveniles many of the same rights afforded adults, such as the right to confront witnesses and protection from self-incrimination.[14] Moreover, popular movements like the Chicano movement, the black power movement, and the feminist movement pushed the juvenile system to focus more on prevention and rehabilitation. This further solidified the distinction between children and adults, as children were considered to be more amenable to rehabilitation. These progressive reforms would be short lived, however, as the "get tough on crime movement" would gain strength and once again blur the distinction between children and adults convicted of crimes.

The 1980s and 1990s saw unprecedented attention to juvenile delinquency in the media. While juvenile crime rates during the 1970s and early 1980s remained fairly constant, there was a substantial increase in juvenile crime from 1987 until 1994, especially crimes involving firearms. For example, teenage homicide rates doubled between 1985 and 1994.[15] Conservative criminologists, academics, commentators, and politicians seized the opportunity to push a get tough on crime agenda that argued for the elimination of rehabilitation and the institutionalization of punishment. John DiIulio, a conservative political scientist at Princeton University, became an academic poster-child for the get tough on crime movement when he coined the racially charged term "super-predator."[16] DiIulio and a cohort of other conservative academics deployed the word term to describe a new kind of juvenile offender that was sociopathic, remorseless, and far more dangerous than earlier criminals had been. Fraught with racial stereotypes and reminiscent of moral panics about immigrant youth in the 1800s, DiIulio's argument was that the new youth offender lacked a moral conscience and values. DiIulio warned that by the year 2010, nearly 270,000 super-predators would be roaming the streets, which would result in an unprecedented crime wave.[17] This stoked the already burning flames of racial and class anxiety, and provided the justification for new laws and penalties for juvenile offenders. Rehabilitation, conservatives argued, would not work with this new "breed" of juvenile offenders. The media ran with the story. Every school shooting, juvenile homicide, and violent crime became a testament to the rise of the Super-Predator, which became a racially imbued code word for children of color in the inner city. By 1994, nearly 40 percent of all print news that covered children was about crime and violence, mostly involving children of color.[18]

Time, however, did not lend much support to DiIulio's thesis of the super-predator. Crime rates began to drop after 1994, and the predicted new crime wave never hit land. In fact, juvenile crime rates have continued to drop well into the new century. Moreover, DiIulio's description of a new kind of juvenile delinquent did not correspond with data on incarcerated children. Of the 106,000 children in secure facilities in 1997, the overwhelming majority was incarcerated for nonviolent offenses. Thirty-six percent of juveniles were incarcerated for crimes against persons. Only 2 percent of incarcerated children had committed homicide, and 6 percent had committed sexual assault. The majority of incarcerated children (approximately 73 percent) had committed nonviolent offenses. Of the 73 percent of nonviolent offenses, property offenses like auto theft and shoplifting accounted for 32 percent, drug offenses accounted for 9 percent (mostly possession), public order violations like being drunk in public accounted for 10 percent, and technical violations of parole accounted for 13 percent.[19]

The portrait of incarcerated children is a far cry from the myth of the violent super-predator. Nonetheless, politicians continued to raise the alarm. By capitalizing on the public's racial anxiety and fear of crime, politicians seized their newly found political capital to win elections.[20] This paved the way to making the United States the number one incarcerator of children in the world.

The 1980s and 1990s saw passage of several punitive laws designed to target youth crime at the federal, state, and local levels. At the federal level, the Violent and Repeat Juvenile Offender Act of 1997 encouraged more prosecution of juvenile offenders, increased penalties for "gang"-related offenses, and increased use of mandatory minimums for juvenile offenders. In addition, an increasing number of states passed laws to lower the age at which juvenile could be tried as adults. Twenty-three states have no minimum age at which children can be charged as adults, while the remaining states set the minimum age anywhere between 10 and 15. There are a number of ways in which children can be tried as adults. There are 13 states, including New York and Louisiana, that charge 16- and 17-year-olds as adults regardless of the infraction. Most states (45) allow for a judicial waiver, so discretion lays in the hands of a judge. Other states (38) have statutory exclusions that waive juveniles to adult court based on their age and offense. Fewer states (15) leave the decision in the hands of the prosecution through direct filing.[21]

The Ghosts of Jim Crow

The reintroduction of trying children, especially children of color, as adults is part of a larger get tough on crime political agenda that appears race neutral but that in practice reflects a rebirth of a two-tiered system of justice that has ushered massive numbers of children of color into a degraded second-class status. As Michelle Alexander notes, "the fact that more than half of the young black men in any large American city are currently under the control of the criminal justice system (or saddled with criminal records) is not—as many argue—just a symptom of poverty or poor choices, but rather is evidence of a new racial caste system àt work."[22] While African Americans represent roughly 13 percent of the population in the United States, they comprise nearly 40 percent of all incarcerated children. And an alarming 60 percent of those children are charged as adults.[23] Of children charged as adults for drug offenses, 95 percent are children of color.

Some may argue that these disproportionate statistics reflect differences in criminal activity. However, there is a growing consensus among researchers that race continues to be a powerful determinate in who is sentenced as an adult. Jordan and Frieburger examined data from 19 of the largest counties in the United States. They found that both black and Latino youth are far more likely to be sentenced to adult jail and prison than their white counterparts, even when controlling for other factors like type of crime and criminal history.[24]

Despite the overwhelming evidence of racial bias in court proceedings, every state has adopted policies to try children as adults, reversing nearly a century of reforms in the juvenile justice system. The United States stands alone in the number of children prosecuted as adults. Amnesty International reported in 1999 that nearly 200,000 children were tried in the adult criminal justice system, most of whom lived in states where 16- and 17-year-olds are automatically tried as adults.[25] It was not until 2005 that the U.S. Supreme Court ruled in *Roper vs. Simmons* that the use of the death penalty for children was "cruel and unusual" and thus unconstitutional. At the time, more than 70 people on death row were there for crimes they committed as children. And the overwhelming majority were African American. Although the death penalty for children was ruled unconstitutional, the United States continues to allow children to be sentenced to life without parole. The National Council on Crime and Delinquency estimates that there are more than 2,200 youth under the age of 18 serving life without parole.[26]

Florida, for example, has a reputation of sentencing juveniles in non-homicide cases to life without parole. According to the Public Interest Law Center at Florida State University, the state sentences juveniles in non-homicide cases to life without parole at 19 times the rate of other states. Juveniles have been sentenced to life without parole for battery, burglary, and carjacking. Nearly 70 percent of all juveniles sentenced to life without parole for nonhomicide cases reside in Florida. The overwhelming majority of these youth, 84 percent, are African American.[27] Given this frightening evidence of a two-tiered system of justice, it is not surprising that Florida was on the losing side of a recent U.S. Supreme Court case, *Graham vs. Florida*, which ruled the courts can sentence children to life in prison only if they commit homicide.

The case was based on the conviction of Terrance Graham, who at the age of 16 tried to rob a local store. His co-defendant hit a store manager with a pipe. At the time of his trial, Graham had no criminal history and was sentenced to three years probation. But at the age of 17, Graham was again accused of committing a robbery, this time with two grown men. Graham denied the accusation, but a trial judge found a preponderance of evidence that Graham had committed the robbery, and he was sentenced to life without parole. Graham was one of hundreds of children sentenced to die in prison for a nonhomicide offense.

Despite recent court decisions, the United States is still the only country in the world that allows children to be sentenced to die in adult prisons for homicide. In doing so, the United States continues to be in violation of a number of international treaties for the protection of the human rights of children, like the Convention on the Rights of the Child, the UN Standard Minimum Rules for the Administration of Juvenile Justice, and the UN Rules for the Protection of Juveniles Deprived of their Liberty. Interestingly, the United States joins only one other nation, Somalia, in refusing to ratify the UN Convention on the Rights of the Child.[28]

When the Uniform Doesn't Fit: Child Abuse inside Adult Institutions

Ian Manuel was condemned to die in prison. At the age of 13, he and two other young men botched a robbery attempt and shot a woman in the face. She survived, but a Florida judge later convicted Manuel as an adult for attempted murder. When he first arrived at the adult prison, none of the uniforms fit. He was too small. Not long after his arrival, guards sent Manuel to solitary confinement, where he has remained since 1992, confined to a closet-like cell for over 23 hours a day. During his time in solitary, Manuel began cutting his arms. In 2006, he attempted suicide five times.[29]

As politicians have made it easier to try children as adults, few know what happens to children once they are inside adult institutions.

Ian Manuel's case is not uncommon. Prison administrators often segregate juveniles "for their own protection" by forcing them to spend 23 hours a day trapped inside a cinderblock cage. The physical and psychological damage caused by solitary confinement is well documented. Sharon Shalev, author of *A Sourcebook for Solitary Confinement*, reviewed the contemporary research on the effects of solitary confinement and found the common physical side effects to be heart palpitations, lethargy, hypersensitivity to noises and smells, and insomnia. The list of psychological effects includes a sense of hopelessness, hostility and anger, poor concentration and memory, social withdrawal, self-mutilation, and suicide.[30]

Aside from solitary confinement, juveniles in adult prisons have limited access to education, exercise, and even family visits. On a much more tragic level, juveniles in adult prisons are exposed to far more violence and abuse than they would experience elsewhere. The state becomes their abuser. Compared to children held in juvenile facilities, children transferred to adult jails and prisons are 7.7 times more likely to commit suicide, five times more likely to be sexually assaulted, twice as likely to be beaten by staff, and 50 percent more likely to be attacked with a weapon.[31] In no other industrialized nation in the world is this kind of child abuse acceptable.

The damage done by confining children with adults serves little purpose. It does not reduce recidivism rates, and it likely makes communities more dangerous. In a report titled "Juvenile Transfer Laws: An Effective Deterrent to Delinquency," Richard Redding of the Office of Juvenile Justice and Delinquency Prevention surveyed the existing research on recidivism rates of juveniles charged as adults. He found that out of the six large-scale studies, every one found recidivism rates to be significantly higher for children tried as adults than for those held in juvenile facilities. Redding explains that "the extant research provides sound evidence that transferring juvenile offenders to criminal court does not engender community protection by reducing recidivism. On the contrary, [it] substantially increases recidivism."[32] In short, the practice of transferring children to adult courts does far more harm than good and more is likely to create crime than reduce it. This is not really surprising. Adult facilities are far less focused on rehabilitation, provide far fewer educational programs, and further stigmatize youth as felons upon their release. People who enter prison as children and are released as adults can be legally discriminated against by the nature of their background. Housing, employment, and even financial aid for education are far more difficult to find when one is marked by a felony record. These legal restrictions only further stigmatize the formerly incarcerated, relegating them to a form of second-class citizenship.

Conclusion

When Mychal Bell of the Jena Six was convicted by an all-white jury of aggravated second-degree battery and conspiracy to commit aggravated second-degree battery, thousands of civil rights activists descended on the streets of Jena to protest what many saw as yet another example of a racist criminal justice system. Bell faced 22 years in adult prison. On the heels of massive protests, Louisiana's Third Circuit Court of Appeals overturned Bell's battery conviction. He later pleaded guilty to simple assault and was released with time served, having spent 18 months in a juvenile detention center. The remaining members of the Jena Six pled guilty to simple assault and were fined. Despite this legal victory, the United States continues to prosecute children as adults at a rate unseen in the international community, raising alarm among human rights activists.

The case of the Jena Six, and the cases of thousands of other children of color tried as adults, stands as a stark reminder of a two-tiered system of justice and the rise of what legal scholar Michelle Alexander terms "the New Jim Crow"—a system of justice that ushers African Americans and Latinos into a permanent undercaste.[33] There has never been an equal system of justice in the United States. Beginning with slavery, continuing through the era of the convict leasing system, and persisting into the contemporary get tough on crime movement, criminal justice in the United States has always been more about controlling communities of color than controlling crime. For far too many of these young men and women who are tried as adults, their time in prison will be marked by solitary confinement, suicide attempts, and physical and sexual abuse. Some will die in prison, and those who are released will forever be marked as felons, forced into a second-class citizenship where legal discrimination is the norm. They will find it difficult, if not impossible, to secure financial aid for education; many will be denied the right to vote; and most will find it difficult to find housing and employment. The story of the Jena Six is not an aberration or some tragic mistake within the system of justice. Rather, it is the inevitable outcome of a criminal justice system that is deeply shaped by racism and the ghosts of slavery.

Notes

1. Chang, 2012.
2. Sabol and West, 2009.
3. Mauer, 1994.
4. Alexander, 2010.
5. Krisberg, 2005.
6. Zinn, 1995.
7. Krisberg, 2005.
8. Douglass, 2001.
9. Wacquant, 2001.
10. Blackmon, 2008.
11. Oshinsky, 1996.
12. Regoli, 2008.
13. Austin and Irwin, 2001.
14. Shelden, 2001.
15. Donziger, 1995.
16. DiIulio, 1996.
17. DiIulio, 1996.
18. Hancock, 2000.
19. Office of Juvenile Justice and Delinquency Prevention, 1999.
20. Parenti, 1999.
21. Hartney, 2006.
22. Alexander, 2010.
23. Rainville and Smith, 1998.
24. Jordan and Freiburger, 2010.
25. Amnesty International, 1999.
26. National Council on Crime and Delinquency, 2006.
27. Annino, Rasmussen, and Rice, 2009.
28. Amnesty International, 1999.
29. Laughlin, 2006.
30. Shalev, 2008.
31. Fagan, Frost, and Vivona, 1989.
32. Redding, 2010.
33. Alexander, 2010.

References

Alexander, Michelle. *The New Jim Crow: Mass Incarceration in the Age of Color-blindness.* New York: New Press, 2010.

Amnesty International. *Betraying the Young.* New York: Amnesty International, 1999.

Annino, Paolo G., David W. Rasmussen, and Chelsea Rice. *Juvenile Life without Parole for Non-Homicide Offense: Florida Compared to Nation.* Tallahassee: Florida State University, Public Interest Law Center, 2009.

Austin, James, and John Irwin. *It's About Time: America's Imprisonment Binge.* Stamford, CT: Wadsworth, 2001.

Blackmon, Douglass. *Slavery by Another Name: The Re-Enslavement of Black People in America from the Civil War to World War II.* New York: Doubleday, 2008.

Chang, Cindy. "Louisiana Is the World's Prison Capital." *Times Picayune* [New Orleans], May 13, 2012.

DiIulio, John. "They're Coming: Florida Youth Crime Bomb." *Impact* 1 (1996): 25–27.

Donziger, Steven. *The Real War on Crime: The Report of the National Criminal Justice Commission.* New York: Harper Perennial, 1995.

Douglass, Frederick. *Narrative of the Life of Frederick Douglass.* New Haven, CT: Yale University Press, 2001.

Fagan, Jeffrey, Martin Frost, and T. Scott Vivona, "Youth in Prisons and Training Schools: Perceptions and Consequences of Treatment-Custody Dichotomy." *Juvenile and Family Court* 40, no. 1 (1989): 1–14.

Hancock, LynNell. "Framing Children in the News: The Face and Color of Youth Crime in America." In *The Public Assault on America's Children: Poverty Violence and Juvenile Injustice,* edited by Valerie Polakow, pp. 78–99. New York: Teachers College Press, 2000.

Hartney, Christopher. *Fact Sheet: Views from the National Council on Crime and Delinquency; Youth under Age 18 in the Adult Criminal Justice System.* Oakland, CA: National Council on Crime and Delinquency 2006.

Jordan, Kareem, and Tina Freiburger, "Examining the Impact of Race and Ethnicity on the Sentencing of Juveniles in Adult Court."*Criminal Justice Policy Review* 21, no. 2 (2010): 185–201

Krisberg, Barry. *Juvenile Justice: Redeeming Our Children.* Thousand Oaks, CA: Sage, 2005.

Laughlin, Meg. "Does Separation Equal Suffering?" *St. Petersburg Times,* December 17, 2006.

Mauer, Marc. *Americans behind Bars: The International Use of Incarceration, 1992–1993.* Washington, DC: Sentencing Project, 1994.

Office of Juvenile Justice and Delinquency Prevention. *Juveniles in Correctional Facilities.* Washington, DC: U.S. Department of Justice, 1999.

Oshinsky, David. *"Worse Than Slavery": Parchman Farm and the Ordeal of Jim Crow Justice.* New York: Free Press, 1996.

Parenti, Christian. *Lockdown America: Police and Prisons in the Age of Crisis.* New York: Verso, 1999.

Rainville, Gerard, and Steven K. Smith. *Juvenile Felony Defendants in Criminal Courts.* Washington, DC: Bureau of Justice Statistics, 1998.

Redding, Richard. "Juvenile Transfer Laws: An Effective Deterrent to Delinquency?" *Juvenile Justice Bulletin,* June 2010.

Regoli, Robert, John Hewitt, and Matt DeLisi. *Delinquency in Society: Youth Crime in the 21st Century.* Boston: McGraw Hill, 2008.

Sabol, William J., and Heather West, *Prison and Jail Inmates at Midyear 2008: Statistical Tables.* Washington, DC: Bureau of Justice Statistics, April 8, 2009, 1–24.

Shalev, Sharon. *A Sourcebook on Solitary Confinement.* London: Manheim Center for Criminology, London School of Economics and Political Science, 2008.

Shelden, Randall. *Controlling the Dangerous Classes: A History of Criminal Justice in America.* Boston: Allyn and Bacon, 2001.

Wacquant, Loic. "Deadly Symbiosis: When Ghetto and Prison Meet and Mesh." *Punishment & Society* 3 (2001): 95–133.

Zinn, Howard. *A People's History of the United States.* New York: Harper Perennial, 1995.

Chapter 29

Privilege and Prison: A Reconstruction of the Race/Crime Paradigm

Scott Wm. Bowman

As of 2009, there were 7.6 million people under some form of correctional supervision in the United States—a number that has increased exponentially since the 1980s.[1] Although the number has increased dramatically for minorities, there has also been substantial growth for women, juveniles, older adults, and most all other groups. However, for black and Latino populations, the growth has been substantial and holds far-reaching effects.[2] Most of the research on the subject of minority overrepresentation has focused on statistical overrepresentations, considerations of whether the statistics are representative of "disparity" or "discrimination,"[3] and the legal and socio-structural factors that influence these disparities.[4] The challenge to this approach is the fundamental assumption that incarceration outcomes, regardless of specific overrepresentations, are inconsistent with a larger social and legal mandate. In other words, there is a basic assumption that the incarceration of Americans, more specifically blacks and Latinos, should not be taking place at the levels that are currently demonstrated. Within this chapter, an alternative approach to black and Latino incarceration rates is presented that is based on three basic postulations. First, there is the assumption that everyone commits crimes. Whether operating a motor vehicle, maneuvering throughout the larger society, or making pragmatic choices that have been labeled as criminal, we are collectively subject to behaviors that are "criminal" in nature. Although the reference is slightly dated, the President's Crime Commission indicated in 1967 that "91 percent of all Americans have violated laws that could have subjected them to a term of imprisonment at one point in their lives."[5] Second, despite the clear increases and overrepresentations that are evident within the criminal justice system, the statistical outcomes that are seen are the result of our collective desire to sharply enforce criminal behavior and punitively incarcerate those that violate the law. From "zero tolerance policing" and "mandatory minimum sentencing" to "truth in sentencing" and limited police and judicial discretion, a contemporary criminal justice system has been established that offers few second chances and few alternatives to incarceration. The result is a system that thrives on increasing punitiveness and is self-sustained through limited discretion and limited alternatives. Therefore (and third), the contention will be made in this chapter that rather than focusing on those that have been incarcerated—although the topic is noteworthy and necessary—an additional focus should be placed upon those that are able to avoid such a punitive criminal justice system.

Based on these postulations, the approach that will be presented is rooted in the concept of *privilege*. Although McIntosh wrote specifically about white and male privilege, her definition describing privilege as "an invisible weightless knapsack of special provisions, assurances, tools, maps, guides, codebooks, passports, visas, clothes, compass, emergency gear, and blank checks" seems universally appropriate.[6] She (and others) describes privilege as an invisible advantage that is either taken for granted or is presumed to be a natural state of social, political, and economic affairs. Regarding the criminal justice system, there are clear privileges held by those that establish the laws, those that help determine the levels and locations of active police enforcement, those that can afford quality legal representation, and those that are presented judicial alternatives to incarceration based on their personal backgrounds and demographics. These, along with other "invisible" privileges, are examples in which privileged individuals are presented the opportunity to elude a criminal justice system that is specifically designed to actively enforce punitive laws and policies. Unmistakably, a careful and thoughtful examination of all privileges held in the criminal justice system would result in a daunting, multivolume text. The goals of this chapter are to slightly "unpack the knapsack of privilege" of the criminal justice system and to consider a *small sample* of the invisible advantages that are presented through "punitive exemption." Because there are far too many privileges to consider for a truly comprehensive examination, a primary focus will be placed upon legal constructions of crime and judicial procedure.

The Power of Legal Constructions

The social construction of "crime" is often taken for granted in the process of examining our social, political, emotional, and moral reaction to the individual and collective interpretation of behaviors and actions. Despite the normalized principle of "harm" being at the forefront of criminological construction, the larger interpretations of "what actions are harmful," "what is the appropriate level of punishment for harmful behavior," and "what social and demographic characteristics can rework our views and labels of 'harmfulness'" are all relevant to the larger construction of laws and implementation of punishments. According to Comack and Brickley, "law can be said to have a distinctly *social basis*; it both shapes—and is shaped by—the society in which it operates."[7] Therefore, as a starting point, legal constructions are formed subjectively through factors that far outweigh simple societal harm and/or social control.

Clearly, not every citizen within a society has the ability to play a fundamental role in the process of legal construction. There is an unmistakable privilege in not only the formation of legal constructions, but also the manner in which the legal construction is narrated and implemented within the larger social structure. While the larger contextualization of legal constructions may be delivered to the larger society as a necessary process for minimizing harm and maintaining social control, there are many individuals that "escape" the enforcement of legal constructions despite their actions—whether as a result of disproportionate enforcement or of the disproportionate legal constructions themselves. According to Domhoff, there is a clear overlap between those that fall in the upper class and the corporate class that shapes the "power elite." As a result, this group holds considerable power in shaping government actions—often within the realm of legal constructions.[8] Although Domhoff does not argue that the upper class holds complete authority over all government-based legal constructions, he does contend that the upper class holds considerably more power (and thus considerably more privilege).[9] Therefore, the primary purpose of legal constructions influenced by the upper class is rooted in the social control of *others*.

Starting with an examination of those directly holding the power of legal construction, it is unambiguously evident that it is an economic privilege to hold political office in the United States. According to Kerbo, all presidents since Jimmy Carter have not only belonged to or been heavily connected with the upper class, but have also appointed cabinet members from socially and economically elite backgrounds.[10] Mintz found that more than 76 percent of cabinet members were associated with corporations either before or after their appointment and that 90 percent came from the upper class or were associated with corporations.[11] In addition, a recent ABC news article indicates that of the 535 members of Congress (100 senators and 435 representatives), 249 are millionaires, including 66 senators and 183 representatives.[12] In addition, another 249 members make more than $250,000 per year. Of the remaining members of Congress, only 46 make less than $100,000 per year. Clearly, being a member of the upper class allows for the social (and cultural) capital necessary to obtain a political office; however, it still costs considerable money to run for office. According to Kerbo, average Senate seat campaign spending in 2006 was $179 million for Republicans and $206 million for Democrats, with the average House of Representatives election campaign costing $600,000 and the average Senate election campaign costing $5.6 million.[13] Although any individual can contribute to a political campaign, those with substantial money or who belong to a political donating corporation (*Citizens United vs. Federal Election Commission*, 2010—"corporations are people too") can significantly influence a political campaign. For example, Kerbo indicates that in 2006, corporate, health care and other business political action committees (PACs) donated $191 million directly to candidates.[14] The underlying suggestion is that individuals and corporations that are privileged to be able to make high-level donations to candidates' campaigns are purchasing particular social, economic, political and criminological leanings. Moreover, it is further suggested that the particular criminological leanings are motivated toward the social control of others.

From a legal construction standpoint, there has been considerable legislation passed that is geared toward harsh laws and punishments. For example, Reiman presents a "sample of . . . proposals" that are indicative of these legal constructions:

> It would be helpful to have laws on the books against drug use, prostitution, and gambling—laws that prohibit acts that have no unwilling victim. This would make many people "criminals" for what they regard as normal behavior and would increase their need to engage in secondary crime . . . It would be good to give police, prosecutors, and/or judges broad discretion to decide who got arrested, who got charged, and who got sentenced to prison. . . . Prisoners should neither be trained in a marketable skill nor provided with a job after release.[15]

In recent years, several legal constructions have been designed to reduce harm and increase social control. A noteworthy example is mandatory minimum drug sentences that were adopted by both Congress and state legislatures to punitively address the drug problems that America faced. According to Tonry, "between 1985 and 1991, Congress enacted at least 20 new mandatory sentencing laws, bringing to more than 100 the number of federal offenses governed by such laws."[16] Although most of these laws addressed drug use, there were also mandatory minimum laws for unregistered firearms, selling drugs in school zones, drunk driving, offenses committed with firearms, and other felonies.[17] While the "law on the books" was designed to formally charge *all* persons that committed offenses within the context of these legal constructions, outcomes suggest that certain privileges were provided to particular offenders. For example, *Boston Globe* reporters found that high-level offenders with significant financial assets managed to evade mandatory minimum sentencing. Specifically, they found that high-level offenders that earned "an average payment of $50,000 in drug profits ... would result in [correlate to] an average sentence reduction of 6.3 years."[18] Moreover, this veiled advantage does not include those holding class- and/or neighborhood-based privilege, where drug enforcement was neither a priority nor an activity. However, for those that did not hold the same privilege(s), the effects of the mandatory minimum sentence remained. According to Beckett and Sasson, the number of drug offenders serving time behind bars increased from 40,000 in 1980 to 453,000 in 1999.[19] In addition to basic drug-related mandatory minimum sentencing, the legal construction of selling drugs in school zones throughout the United States also enhanced punitive outcomes. While most individuals would applaud legal constructions limiting drug sales near schools, there are clear privileges held by some people based on their neighborhoods and other geographic considerations. According to Beckett and Sasson, while inner-city neighborhoods are more densely populated and have more schools within a concentrated area (thus presenting increased opportunities for drug sales near schools), suburban and rural areas provide significantly more space away from schools and school zones.[20] Therefore, despite a large-scale effort to catch drug sellers, dramatic cross-sections of Americans are privileged to evade this type of punitive outcome. Moreover, this does not include the privilege of differential policing in suburban neighborhoods and the privilege to actively use and sell drugs in certain neighborhoods (as opposed to active "open-air" drug use and sales in urban neighborhoods).[21]

Also, in understanding the privilege associated with drug use and drug arrests, it is important to consider the clear disparities between those that are using drugs and those that are policed and prosecuted for drug use. The most recent findings from the National Institutes of Health (2003) indicate that with the exception of Asian populations, the "estimated prevalence of past-month drug use in the United States" is relatively consistent among various racial/ethnic groups (whites, 6.1 percent; blacks, 8.2 percent; Native Americans, 9.3 percent; Asians, 2.8 percent; Hispanics, 6.1 percent). Although there are distinct differences regarding "drug of choice," this ultimately should have no direct bearing on policing and enforcement. Yet research indicates that there are clear disproportionate outcomes regarding prosecution and sentencing for drug offenses. These disparate outcomes are rooted in both race and class-based privilege. For example, the National Institute on Drug Abuse found that white youth between the ages of 12 and 17 were more than one-third more likely to have sold illegal drugs than their black counterparts.[22] Moreover, Walker, Spohn, and Delone found that "the results of Petersillla's study in Los Angeles and Spohn and Spears' study in Detroit provide evidence suggestive of a pattern of *selective prosecution* [italics in original text]—that is, cases involving racial minorities, or certain types of racial minorities, are singled out for prosecution, whereas similar cases involving whites are either screened out very early in the process or never enter the system in the first place."[23] The result of this type of selective prosecution is demonstrated in arrest statistics, where blacks and Latinos are overrepresented. As Alexander suggests, "in seven states, African Americans constitute 80 to 90 percent of all drug offenders sent to prison" and "in at least fifteen states, blacks are admitted to prison on drug charges at a rate from twenty to fifty-seven times greater than that of white men."[24] Moreover, while whites were admitted to prison for drug offenses at eight times the general prison admission rate between 1983 and 2000, black and Latinos were admitted during the same time at a rate of 26 and 22 times respectively. While much of the research has focused on the factors that produce these racial/ethnic overrepresentations, an era of drastic drug enforcement indicates that a better-served examination would incorporate the specific characteristics—whether race/ethnicity, class, or some additional demographic—that allow people to avoid the aforementioned drastic drug enforcement.

Although drug enforcement is arguably the most pronounced example of how privilege-based distinctions are made between legal constructions and legal outcomes, there are countless others. For example, the American

Gaming Association indicates that the 2011 gross revenue gaming totals from *legal* gambling in U.S. commercial casinos totaled approximately $35 billion.[25] This does not include off-track betting on horse and dog racing, single-state and multistate lotteries, and other extralegal gambling. The General Accounting Office estimated that illegal Internet gambling revenues were an additional $4 billion.[26] Aside from the fundamental privilege of being able to afford a computer, an Internet provider, the cultural capital to play poker or understand sports wagering, and the monies necessary to wager, choosing to enter into illegal forms of gambling may be done out of convenience (e.g., sports wagering is legal only in Nevada) and/or preference. Nevertheless, there is ample opportunity to enforce the legal construction of gambling from economic, political, and multinational perspectives.

In examining the enforcement of gambling, the most recent Uniform Crime Report data indicate that African Americans make up 67.5 percent of all gambling arrests in the United States.[27] Although a percentage of these arrests may be the result of Internet gambling, the U.S. Census Bureau's report subsection entitled "Computer and Internet Use in the United States: 2010" intimates that blacks are much less likely to have the privilege of access.[28] While 69.7 percent of whites use a computer at home and 56.1 percent connect to the Internet at home, 56.6 percent of blacks use a computer at home and 41.7 percent connect to the Internet at home. Additionally, 18.1 percent of blacks connect to the Internet at work, 14.0 percent connect to the Internet at school, and 13.6 percent connect at a library, which indicates that neither computers nor Internet access are a privilege widely held by blacks. On the other hand, recent work suggests that the relationship between blacks and gambling is better correlated to "street activity" and more specifically street activity in inner cities.[29] Therefore, while millions of Americans hold the privilege (and run a small risk) of placing offshore sports bets online, playing poker for money in the privacy of their homes, or creating "office pools" for the Super Bowl or during the "March madness" college basketball season, others are relegated to "throwing dice" in alleyways or "running numbers." Consequently, while it could be argued that there are limited resources for the legal enforcement of Internet gambling, "office pool gambling," and "weekend poker tournaments," there are still significant numbers of local police officers that are charged with enforcing "zero tolerance policing," including inner-city gambling enforcement. However, if we have the level of tolerance that is consistent with our political and public opinion–based rhetoric, then the expectation should be to minimize activities that fall under the legal construction of "gambling." Privilege falls to those that are provided invisible exemption within said legal construction.

Overall, the privilege of legal construction not only allows numerous individuals to escape the punishment held within our larger philosophy of crime, but it also preserves the prevalence of these crimes. Reiman indirectly suggests that exclusionary privilege extends the existing criminal justice system when he says, "*most of the system's practices make more sense if we look at them as ingredients in an attempt to maintain rather than reduce crime* [italics in original]" when the legal constructions are fashioned in the spirit of collectiveness yet are enforced in a manner of exclusionary privilege.[30]

Judicial Procedure

The quintessential personification of the American justice system is "lady justice." She is most often depicted with a set of scales in her right hand that signify balanced reasoning, a sword in her left hand signifying swift and powerful justice, and a blindfold over her eyes signifying objective impartiality. However, not only are there distinct racial/ethnic differences in perceptions about the court system, there are also statistical differences that complement these perceptions. According to Hurwitz and Peffley, black and white respondents that were asked to respond to the statements "The justice system in this country treats people fairly and equally" and "The courts in your area can be trusted to give everyone a fair trial" produced racially divergent results.[31] While 67.5 percent of African Americans disagreed ("disagree" or "strongly disagree") with the two statements, only 35.2 percent of whites disagreed. Specifically, Hurwitz and Peffley found that "while 74.0 percent of Blacks do not agree that the justice system treats people fairly and equally, only 44.3 percent of whites express similar sentiments. And the differences are even sharper for the other question, while 61 percent and 26 percent of blacks and whites, respectively, who do not trust the courts to give a fair trial."[32] Walker, Spohn, and DeLone's findings support the notion that "perception is reality," contending that racial minorities face the significant disadvantage of "double jeopardy" due to being both minorities and more likely to be poor.[33] Again, in an era of largely punitive laws and strictly enforced punishments, there should be a fundamental assumption that these differing perceptions between blacks and whites are merely disparities of opinion or of supplemental fact (e.g., blacks face double jeopardy because they are more likely to have prior offenses that would shape their judicial experiences). Yet there are unmistakable and often structural privileges afforded to some, while others experience the full effects of a harsh judicial system. From the initial appearance in a courtroom and the assignment of a public defender (as opposed to having the privilege of retaining a private attorney), to the jury selection and use of peremptory challenges, the greater struggles are faced by most racial/ethnic groups and the majority of lower-class individuals.[34] Reiman explains that "for the same criminal behavior . . . the poor are more likely to be charged; if charged, more likely to be convicted, if convicted, more likely to be sentenced to prison . . ."[35] This section will examine three privileges held within the judicial court system: (1) privileges within the process of an initial court appearance, (2) the privilege of a private attorney, and (3) the privilege of serving on a jury without a particular demographic implicitly warranting a peremptory challenge.

Release on Own Recognizance, Bail, Hold Over for Trial

After arrest, the process of determining what to do with the accused individual is heavily influenced by the prosecuting defense attorneys and is determined by the presiding judge. For reasons that include both an increased likelihood of a guilty verdict and receiving longer sentences after being held prior to trial, as well as the challenges of being "presumed innocent" while simultaneously being held, this decision is an essential element of the larger judicial process.[36] For most judicial procedures in an initial appearance, judges are presented with three options: to release a person on his or her own recognizance, to provide a person with the option of bail with a set amount, or to hold a person over for a criminal trial. Although numerous factors will ultimately determine an individual's fate in an initial appearance, it is worthy of note that comparatively, there is a privilege in being released from jail (regardless of the reasoning or justification) prior to trial compared to being held over for trial. This statement does not take into consideration an individual's prior offenses, the severity of the offense, or other factors that may influence this decision; however, it includes the privilege of "freedom," the privilege of an individual (potentially) maintaining employment, direct family and community ties, and eluding of the stigma and/or perception of guilt by a jury. Nevertheless, the type of offense should be included in the consideration of privilege, as some offenses are viewed differently compared to others. Reiman suggests that this inclusion is important for an examination that is described as "weeding out the wealthy":

> Not only are the poor arrested and charged out of proportion to their numbers for the kinds of crimes poor people generally commit—burglary, robbery, assault, and so forth—but also, when we reach the kinds of crimes poor people almost never have the opportunity to commit, such as antitrust violations, industrial safety violations, embezzlement, and serious tax evasion, the criminal justice system shows an increasingly benign and merciful face. The more likely that a crime is the type committed by middle- and upper-class people, the less likely it is that it will be treated as a criminal offense.[37]

In other words, regardless of the process of the initial court appearance, there are some privileged individuals who will commit crimes that do not fall under the legal construction of crimes that are worthy of fervent investigation, enforcement, and prosecution.

Those released on their own recognizance have ostensibly met the terms of social, personal, emotional stability, and/or connectedness consistent with being released back into society while awaiting trial. For example, an individual's strong ties to the community, demonstrated responsibility to family, and current employment status can significantly influence the likelihood of being released on one's own recognizance. Regarding (nonemployment) ties to the community, the decision-making process is often demonstrated in a manner of volunteerism, community activism, and/or noteworthy forms of social capital. While it is personally and socially admirable to actively participate in the betterment of the community or larger society, there is a fundamental privilege in having the time and financial resources available for involvement. For example, belonging to boards or being a high-ranking member of nonprofit organizations and other social organizations not only requires personal and/or financial investment, but often personal prerequisites such as education or employment. Therefore, it often becomes a structural privilege to hold a high-ranking noteworthy position in a major community organization. For those volunteering on a smaller scale, time becomes a significant factor and is held by those with privilege. Although many events take place during nontraditional work hours, much of the day-to-day work of nonprofit organizations, schools, and similar organizations takes place during working hours. As a result, individuals who are able to volunteer or participate in a similar manner often have the fundamental privilege of doing so. For example, an individual that desires to volunteer at her child's elementary school would presumably have to either have the time available or be able to take time away from work to participate. An individual that is unemployed would presumably be more concerned with finding gainful employment than volunteering. Thus, a judge that renders a decision to release a person on his or her own recognizance produces a judicial decision to a privileged some, while "punishing" those that may not have the time or resources to acquire bail or lack the general social standing to be released on his or her own recognizance. A second factor in the decision-making process is whether a person is gainfully and legally employed. On a basic level, it has been demonstrated that an employed individual holds a measure of privilege that a cross-section of others do not. The most recent Bureau of Labor statistics indicate that while the national unemployment rate is 8.9 percent, whites had an unemployment rate of 7.6 percent, compared to 15.8 percent for blacks, 14.6 percent for Native Americans, and 11.5 percent for Hispanics.[38] From a socioeconomic perspective, it is apparent that those from the working, middle, and upper classes are more likely to enjoy the privilege of employment compared to their lower-class counterparts. Moreover, these statistics do not include people that work illegally in an "undocumented" manner (i.e., "under the table") or acquire income through delinquent means. While a judge's consideration of employment status demonstrates a logical correlation to social stability and can be used to measure other relevant factors such as an individual being a flight risk, it also carries a selective privilege. Not only is it fundamentally challenging for individuals to control for their micro level employment (and it is increasingly challenging for groups such as women, blacks, Hispanics, Native Americans, teenagers), it is also nearly impossible to control for their macro level employment (e.g., layoffs, corporate bankruptcy, job outsourcing).[39] Being unemployed not only affects an individual's ability to be released on his or her own recognizance, it also affects his or her fundamental ability to either make bail or to "bond out." Regarding bail and bonds, it is a privilege for those that are eligible to be released to either have the money to be able to make bail without seeking additional assistance or to have the necessary money or collateral to be bond out of jail. Since the majority of offenders enter the judicial system financially indigent (the median prearrest income for blacks in 1983 [the most recent Bureau of Justice statistics available] was $4,067 and for whites was $6,312) and often unemployed (30 percent of whites and 38 percent of blacks in 1993 reported no full- or part-time employment during the month prior to their arrest), they will be more likely to experience a less tolerant judicial system. On the other hand, financially privileged others will be more likely to experience the benefit of either being released on their own recognizance or through an affordable bail amount.[40] While much focus is placed on those that experience racial/ethnic and socioeconomic struggles at the initial appearance phase, a more careful examination should look at the relatively privileged ease with which others are able to experience the same system.

Private Attorneys versus Public Defenders

The landmark U.S. Supreme Court case *Gideon vs. Wainwright* (1963) ensured that all criminal defendants would have the right to publically provided attorney not only during their trial, but also (potentially) during their arrest and interrogation.[41] During the time, the Supreme Court's decision to ensure the provision of "effective assistance of counsel" was seen as an opportunity to serve a population in need of legal backing. Recent statistics indicate that this provision has been greatly utilized, as "a survey of inmates incarcerated in state and federal prisons in 1997 revealed that about 73 percent of the state inmates and 60 percent of the federal inmates were represented by a public defender or assigned counsel."[42] While the research indicates that utilization of a public defender or assigned counsel is significant, it does not address the actual effectiveness of the counsel. According to Cole, "the Court adopted an 'effective assistance of counsel' standard so low that as a practical matter states need not ensure that defendants are appointed *competent* (italics replicated from original work) attorneys ..."[43] Since public defenders or assigned counsel are often assigned by the court, the individual often receives an attorney based on availability or convenience, rather than ability or experience. Conversely, a person that holds the privilege of affording (literally and figuratively) a private attorney is able to "shop" for the most qualified attorney that can be afforded, one who has specific experience and a proven track record of dealing with a particular offense. Although there is conflicting evidence regarding whether the quality of a public defender or assigned counsel is dramatically worse than that of a private attorney, there are numerous instances of public defenders or assigned counsel "underrepresenting" their clients.[44] According to Cole, "too often, assistance of counsel for the poor can be like getting brain surgery from a podiatrist."[45] Stephen Bright and

Patrick Keenan provide examples of ineffective counsel, including a capital defendant being defended by an attorney that had passed the bar exam six months earlier and had never tried a jury or felony trial, an attorney that referred to his client as "a little old nigger boy," and a Florida attorney that explained, "judge, I am at a loss. I really don't know what to do in this type of proceeding. If I'd been through one, I would, but I've never handled one except this time."[46] While the effectiveness or ineffectiveness of public defenders and assigned counsel can be called into question by the majority of defendants that receive their services, as well as the potentially racial/ethnic and class-based disproportionalities of individuals receiving these services, it is equally noteworthy for those that are privileged to unequivocally afford private, well-paid, well-prepared attorneys. One example of outcomes related to these differences is the likelihood of a guilty verdict. While a private attorney holds the ability to refuse cases, be compensated for the specific amount of time dedicated to a defendant, and be specialized in a particular area of criminal law, it suggests that the ability to fundamentally win a court case favor the privileged. According to Walker, Spohn, and DeLone, individuals at both the state and federal levels were more likely to be incarcerated if they had had a public defender (71.3 percent at the state level and 87.6 percent at the federal level) rather than a private attorney (53.9 percent at the state level and 76.5 percent at the federal level).[47] Overall, despite the best efforts of implementing *Gideon vs. Wainwright*'s charge of providing effective counsel, the greatest courtroom defense privilege is the ability to afford one's own attorney.[48] From the classic trial of O. J. Simpson to the numerous white-collar criminals and corporations that retain their own attorneys, consistently successful outcomes are realized by those with economic privilege.

Jury Selection

Similar to the contemporary staple of "effective use of counsel," an individual's right to a jury trial is a basic judicial right. Philosophically, a jury is supposed to be made up of "one's peers" that are selected through a relatively meticulous and unprejudiced process. Once individual jurors with either direct ties (direct knowledge of the defendant, victim, or witnesses) or indirect ties (a personal experience that is similar to the charged offense) are removed based upon their perceived bias, the remaining jury pool is subjected to a *voir dire*. During the voir dire, to additionally remove them from the jury pool, potential jurors are asked a series of questions regarding any additional biases they may hold. Finally, both the prosecution and the defense are provided several peremptory challenges by which they are able to remove potential jurors without prejudice and without explanation. Despite the procedural fairness of jury selection, there are concerns that the potential for discrimination remains. According to Cole, ". . . racial discrimination in jury selection remains a persistent reality to this day. As it did with the right to counsel, the Court has made strong pronouncements about equality, but has not backed them up with meaningful implementation."[49]

Related to jury selection, the beginnings of privilege are rooted in the ability to simply serve on a jury. It is often said that serving on a jury is a privilege and an obligation within the context of a global comparative perspective, and Americans often do not consider those among them who have been systematically or unknowingly removed from service. For example, it is a privilege to be able to make/have time to be able to serve on a jury, as most all court cases coincide with a typical workday for most Americans. It is also a privilege to have transportation to court, as well as be able to afford to have children or elderly parents cared for in an individual's absence. In addition, approximately 7.6 million people are currently under some form of correctional supervision, with 1.6 million (760 per 100,000 Americans) incarcerated in federal and state prisons and jails.[50] For the remaining 6 million, a significant portion of them will have their ability to serve on a jury duty either temporarily or permanently stripped. This is not to argue that ex-felons or those under suspicion should be able to serve on juries; instead, it is to recognize the largely invisible privilege held by those that are able to serve on juries.

Although there is a clear privilege held by those that can serve on a jury, their ability to do so does not necessarily mean they will be selected to participate in the process of deliberation. Many argue that a principal challenge to this process is application of the peremptory challenge, which is essentially designed to produce equitable juror selection. Yet it produces questionable outcomes.[51] Although most research on the subject of peremptory challenges has focused on the potentially illegal removal of jurors based on race/ethnicity, there is some evidence that both implicit and explicit associations may influence the use of a peremptory challenge. An oft-quoted manual from a 1973 Texas prosecutors' office describes the process of informal exclusion:

"You are not looking for any member of a minority group which may subject him to oppression—they almost always sympathize with the accused . . ."

"I don't like women jurors because I can't trust them . . ."

"Extremely overweight people, especially women and young men, indicate a lack of self-discipline and often time [sic] instability. I like the lean and hungry look."

"People from small towns and rural areas generally make good State's jurors. People from the east or west coasts often make bad jurors."

"Jewish veniremen generally make poor State's jurors. Jews have a history of oppression and generally empathize with the accused."[52]

What is noteworthy in this handbook is that it demonstrates a clear understanding of how "others" (e.g., people classified by race, gender, weight) are expected to perform as jurors. Yet there is no specific description of dominant groups and how they are likely to perform. Therefore, groups such as minorities, women, Jews, and coastal inhabitants are singled out for stereotyped predictions and potentially removed through peremptory challenges, white Christian males from "the heartland" completely avoid being stereotyped and therefore hold the privilege of *automatically* being worthwhile jurors. Moreover, this group of males has the privilege of (potentially) *not* being removed from a jury pool through a peremptory challenge based on some external characteristic such as race, class, or gender. In other words, it is a privilege to know that your jury service will be valued and accepted without reservation. The peremptory challenge potentially allows those that hold privilege to either stand in castigatory judgment of those that do not have it (the demographics and characteristics of those most likely to enter the criminal justice system) or to establish alternatively affable outcomes rooted in a "sacred kinship" with those that seem similar to them.

Conclusion

On some level, it appears that a basic objective of the criminal justice system is to establish equitable, just, and consistent procedures of legal formation, judicial decision making, and incarnation outcomes. There is abundant research on the subject of racial/ethnic[53] and socioeconomic disproportionalities[54] within a particularly harsh and incarceration-friendly criminal justice system.[55] The larger purpose of the research is to better understand and explain why the system works for some groups in a different—often more punitive—manner in comparison to other groups. As our incarceration rates for most offenses continue to climb and our mandatory sentencing schemes endure, this chapter proposes that the lens be shifted to examine how those that operate in and around the system—both as citizens and practitioners—do so with considerable ambiguity. A more comprehensive evaluation ultimately has the potential to move in two policy-based directions: (1) scholars can begin to reassess practices and policies that exclude privileged individuals from a criminal justice system that is designed to incarcerate large numbers of people for a variety of offenses or (2) scholars can begin to elucidate opportunities of privilege within the harsh criminal justice system for groups that have been historically and consistently "protected." In either instance, a privileged perspective not only allows the discourse to move from an autonomous study of "discriminated groups" to a more comprehensive, incorporative examination of "nonprivileged persons."

Notes

1. Walker, Spohn, and DeLone, 2012; Beckett and Sasson, 2000.
2. See Alexander, 2010; Reiman, 2007; Walker, Spohn, and DeLone, 2012.
3. For opposing views, see MacDonald, 2003; Walker, Spohn, and DeLone, 2012.
4. For detailed legal perspectives and socio-cultural outcomes, see Alexander, 2010; Kennedy, 1997.
5. President's Commission on Law Enforcement and Administration of Justice, 1967, p. vi.
6. McIntosh, 2010, p. 148.
7. Brickey and Comack, 1991, p. 15.
8. Domhoff, 2010.
9. Domhoff, 2010.
10. Kerbo, 2012.
11. Mintz, 1975.
12. Bingham, 2011.
13. Kerbo, 2012.
14. Kerbo, 2012.
15. Reiman, 2007, p. 3.
16. Tonry, 1996, p. 146.
17. Beckett and Sasson, 2004.
18. Lehr and Butterfield, 1995.
19. Beckett and Sasson, 2004.
20. Beckett and Sasson, 2004.
21. Stucky, 2005.
22. National Institute on Drug Abuse, 2000.
23. Walker, Spohn, and DeLone, 2012, p. 224.
24. Alexander, 2012, p. 96.
25. American Gaming Association, n.d.

26. U.S. Government Accountability Office, 2002.

27. As cited in Walker, Spohn, and DeLone, 2012.

28. File, 2013.

29. Specifically, Anderson, 2000; Oliver, 2006; and Wilson, 2012 all speak to this issue.

30. Reiman, 2007, p. 4.

31. Hurwitz and Peffley, 2005.

32. Hurwitz and Peffley, 2005.

33. Walker, Spohn, and DeLone, 2012, p. 200.

34. See Kennedy, 1998; Walker, Spohn, and DeLone, 2012.

35. Reiman, 2007, p. 112.

36. Walker, Spohn, and DeLone, 2012.

37. Reiman, 2007, p. 122.

38. Bureau of Labor Statistics, 2012.

39. Kerbo, 2012.

40. Walker, Spohn, and DeLone, 2012.

41. *Gideon vs. Wainwright*, 1963.

42. Walker, Spohn, and DeLone, 2012, p. 201.

43. Cole, 1999, p. 71.

44. For issues associated with public defense, see Weitzer, 1996; Wice, 1985.

45. Cole, 1999, p. 77.

46. Bright and Keenan, 1995, p. 800.

47. Walker, Spohn, and DeLone, 2012.

48. *Gideon vs. Wainwright*, 1963.

49. Cole, 1999, p. 107.

50. See Alexander, 2010; Walker, Spohn, and DeLone, 2012.

51. For issues associated with peremptory challenges, see Cole, 1999; Kennedy, 1997; Walker, Spohn, and DeLone, 2012.

52. Examples come from Alschuler, 1989; Cole, 1999; Walker, Spohn, and DeLone, 2012.

53. Racial/ethnic: Cole, 1999; Gabbidon, 2010; Walker, Spohn, and DeLone, 2012.

54. Socioeconomics: Reiman, 2007; Shelden, 2008; Wilson, 2009.

55. Incarceration-friendly: Alexander, 2010; Beckett and Herbert, 2009; Beckett and Sasson, 2000.

References

Alexander, Michelle. *The New Jim Crow: Mass Incarceration in the Age of Colorblindness.* New York: New Press, 2012.

Alschuler, Albert W. "The Supreme Court and the Jury: Voir Dire, Peremptory Challenges, and the Review of Jury Verdicts." *University of Chicago Law Review* 56, no. 1 (1989): 153–233.

American Gaming Association. "Gaming Revenue: 10-Year Trend," n.d. Accessed, October 1, 2012, from http://www.americangaming.org/industry-resources/research/fact-sheets/gaming-revenue-10-year-trends.

Anderson, Elijah. *Code of the Street: Decency, Violence, and the Moral Life of the Inner City*. New York: W.W. Norton & Company, 2000.

Beckett, Katherine, and Steve Herbert. *Banished: The New Social Control in Urban America* (Studies in Crime and Public Policy). New York: Oxford University Press, 2009.

Beckett, Katherine, and Theodore Sasson. *The Politics of Injustice: Crime and Punishment in America*. Thousand Oaks, CA: Sage, 2000.

Bingham, Amy. "As Americans Get Poorer, Members of Congress Get Richer." ABC News, December 27, 2011. Retrieved December 10, 2013, from http://abcnews.go.com/blogs/politics/2011/12/as-americans-get-poorer-members-of-congress-get-richer/.

Bowman, Scott Wm. "Residential Segregation and the Construction of an Incarcerated Underclass." In *Color Behind Bars: Racism in the U.S. Prison System*, edited by Scott Wm. Bowman, pp. 59–76. Santa Barbara, CA: ABC-CLIO, 2014.

Brickey, Stephen L., and Elizabeth Comack. *The Social Basis of Law: Critical Readings in the Sociology of Law* (2nd ed.). Aurora, ON: Garamond, 1991.

Bright, Stephen B., and Patrick J. Keenan. "Judges and the Politics of Death: Deciding between the Bill of Rights and the Next Election in Capital Cases." *Boston University Law Review* 75 (1995): 759–835.

Bureau of Labor Statistics. *Labor Force Characteristics by Race and Ethnicity, 2011*. Washington, DC: Bureau of Labor Statistics, 2012.

Cole, David. *No Equal Justice: Race and Class in the American Criminal Justice System*. New York: New Press, 1999.

Domhoff, G. William. *Who Rules America? Challenges to Corporate and Class Dominance* (6th ed.). New York: McGraw-Hill, 2010.

File, Thom. *Computer and Internet Use in the United States: Current Population Survey Reports, P20-568*. Washington, DC: U.S. Census Bureau, 2013.

Gabbidon, Shaun L. *Criminological Perspectives on Race and Crime*. New York: Routledge, 2010.

Gideon V. Wainwright, 372 U.S. 335, 1963.

Hurwitz, Jon, and Mark Peffley. "Explaining the Great Racial Divide: Perceptions of Fairness in the US Criminal Justice System." *Journal of Politics* 67, no. 3 (2005): 762–783.

Kennedy, Randall. *Race, Crime, and the Law*. New York: Vintage, 1997.

Kerbo, Harold R. *Social Stratification and Inequality: Class Conflict in Historical, Comparative, and Global Perspective* (8th ed.). New York: McGraw-Hill, 2012.

Lehr, Dick, and Bruce Butterfield. "Small Timers Get Hard Time." *Boston Globe Metro*, September 24, 1995.

MacDonald, Heather. *Are Cops Racist?* Chicago: Ivan R. Dee, 2003.

Massey, Douglas S., and Nancy Denton. *American Apartheid: Segregation and the Making of the Underclass.* Cambridge, MA: Harvard University Press, 1993.

McIntosh, Peggy. "White Privilege and Male Privilege." In *Privilege: A Reader,* edited by Michael Kimmel and Abby Ferber, pp. 147–160. Boulder, CO: Westview, 2010.

Mintz, Beth. "The President's Cabinet, 1891–1912: A Contribution to the Power Structure Debate." *Critical Sociology* 5, no. 3 (1975): 131–148.

National Institute on Drug Abuse. *Monitoring the Future: National Survey Results on Drug Use, 1975–1999. Vol. 1, Secondary School Students.* Washington, DC: National Institute on Drug Abuse, 2000.

Oliver, Melvin L., and Thomas M. Shapiro. *Black Wealth, White Wealth: A New Perspective on Racial Inequality.* New York: Routledge CRC, 2006.

Oliver, William. "'The Streets': An Alternative Black Male Socialization Institution." *Journal of Black Studies* 36, no. 6 (2006): 918–937.

President's Commission on Law Enforcement and Administration of Justice. *The Challenge of Crime in a Free Society.* Washington, DC: U.S. Government Printing Office, 1967.

Reiman, Jeffrey H. *The Rich Get Richer and the Poor Get Prison: Ideology, Class, and Criminal Justice* (8th ed.). Boston: Pearson, 2007.

Sampson, Robert J., and W. Byron Groves. "Community Structure and Crime: Testing Social- Disorganization Theory." *American Journal of Sociology* 94, no. 4 (1989): 774–802.

Sentencing Project. *State-Level Estimates of Felon Disenfranchisement in the United States, 2010.* Washington, DC: Sentencing Project, 2012.

Shapiro, Thomas M. *The Hidden Cost of Being African-American: How Wealth Perpetuates Inequality.* New York: Oxford University Press, 2004.

Shelden, Randall G. *Controlling the Dangerous Classes: A History of Criminal Justice in America.* Boston: Allyn & Bacon, 2008.

Stucky, Thomas Dain. *Urban Politics, Crime Rates, and Police Strength.* New York: LFB Scholarly Publishing, 2005.

Tonry, Michael. *Sentencing Matters.* New York: Oxford University Press, 1996.

U.S. Department of Justice, Federal Bureau of Investigation. "Crime in the United States, 2010," 2011. Accessed May 20, 2012, from http://www.fbi.gov/about -us/cjis/ucr/crime-in-the-u.s/2010/crime-in-the-u.s.-2010/about-cius.

U.S. Government Accountability Office. *Internet Gambling: An Overview of the Issues.* Washington, DC: U.S. Government Accountability Office, 2002.

Walker, Samuel, Cassia Spohn, and Miriam DeLone. *The Color of Justice: Race, Ethnicity, and Crime in America* (5th ed.). Belmont, CA: Wadsworth, 2012.

Weitzer, Ronald. "Racial Discrimination in the Criminal Justice System: Findings and Problems in the Literature." *Journal of Criminal Justice* 24, no. 4 (1996): 309–322.

Wice, Paul. *Chaos in the Courthouse: The Inner Workings of the Urban Municipal Courts.* New York: Praeger, 1985.

Wilson, William Julius. *The Declining Significance of Race: Blacks and Changing American Institutions.* Chicago: University of Chicago Press, 2012.

Wilson, William Julius. *When Work Disappears: The World of the New Urban Poor.* New York: Vintage, 1997.

Wilson, William Julius. *More Than Just Race: Being Black and Poor in the Inner City.* New York: W.W. Norton. 2009.

Bibliography

Abril, Julie C. "Cultural conflict and crime: Violations of Native American Indian cultural values." *International Journal of Criminal Justice Sciences* 2, no. 1 (2007): 44–62.

Abril, Julie C. "Native American Indian women: Implications for prison research." *Southwest Journal of Criminal Justice* 4, no. 2 (2007): 133–144.

Adamson, Christopher R. "Punishment after slavery: Southern state penal systems, 1865–1890." *Social Problems* (1983): 555–569.

Ammar, Nawal H., Robert R. Weaver, and Sam Saxon. "Muslims in prison: A case study from Ohio state prisons." *International Journal of Offender Therapy and Comparative Criminology* 48, no. 4 (2004): 414–428.

Anderson, Elijah. *Against the wall: Poor, young, black, and male.* Philadelphia: University of Pennsylvania Press, 2011.

Archambeault, William G. "The web of steel and the heart of the eagle: The contextual interface of American corrections and Native Americans." *Prison Journal* 83, no. 1 (2003): 3.

Baldus, David C., Charles A. Pulaski Jr., and George Woodworth. "Arbitrariness and discrimination in the administration of the death penalty: A challenge to state supreme courts." *Stetson Law Review* 15 (1985): 133.

Baldus, David C., and George G. Woodworth. *Equal justice and the death penalty: A legal and empirical analysis.* Boston, MA: Northeastern University Press, 1990.

Baldus, David C., George Woodworth, David Zuckerman, Neil Alan Weiner, and Barbara Broffitt. "Racial discrimination and the death penalty in the post-Furman era: An empirical and legal overview, with recent findings from Philadelphia." *Cornell Law Review* 83 (1998): 1638–1821.

Bedi, Sheila A. "Constructed identities of Asian and African Americans: A story of two races and the criminal justice system." *Harvard BlackLetter Law Journal* 19 (2003): 181.

Bosworth, Mary. "Theorizing race and imprisonment: Towards a new penality." *Critical Criminology* 12, no. 2 (2004): 221–242.

Boyd, Graham. "Collateral damage in the war on drugs." *Villanova Law Review* 47 (2002): 839.

Braman, Donald. *Doing time on the outside: Incarceration and family life in urban America*. Ann Arbor: University of Michigan Press, 2004.

Brewer, Rose M., and Nancy A. Heitzeg. "The racialization of crime and punishment: Criminal justice, color-blind racism, and the political economy of the prison industrial complex." *American Behavioral Scientist* 51, no. 5 (2008): 625–644.

Butler, Judith. *Precarious life: The powers of mourning and violence*. New York: Verso, 2004.

Butler, Paul. "One hundred years of race and crime." *Journal of Criminal Law & Criminology* 100 (2010): 1043.

Butterfield, Fox. "Racial disparities seen as pervasive in juvenile justice." In Paula Rothenberg (ed.), *Race, Class, and Gender in the United States: An Integrated Study*, New York: Worth Publishers, 2004, 224.

Cainkar, Louise. 2004. "The impact of the September 11 attacks on Arab and Muslim communities in the United States." In J. Tirman (Ed.), *The maze of fear: Security and migration after 9/11* (pp. 215–240). New York: New Press.

Chesney-Lind, Meda, and Marc Mauer, eds. *Invisible punishment: The collateral consequences of mass imprisonment*. New York: New Press, 2011.

Chilton, Roland J., and Jim Galvin, eds. *Race, crime and criminal justice*. Sage, 1985.

Chiricos, Theodore G., and Charles Crawford. "Race and imprisonment: A contextual assessment of the evidence." *Ethnicity, race, and crime: Perspectives across time and place* 13 (1995): 281–309.

Chiricos, Theodore G., and Miriam A. Delone. "Labor surplus and punishment: A review and assessment of theory and evidence." *Social Problems* (1992): 421–446.

Clear, Todd R. *Imprisoning communities: How mass incarceration makes disadvantaged neighborhoods worse*. Oxford University Press, 2007.

Coker, Donna. "Foreword: Addressing the real world of racial injustice in the criminal justice system." *Journal of Criminal Law and Criminology* 93, no. 4 (2003): 827–880.

Cole, David. *No equal justice: Race and class in the American criminal justice system*. New York: New Press, 1999.

Colvin, Mark. *Penitentiaries, reformatories, and chain gangs: Social theory and the history of punishment in nineteenth-century America*. Macmillan, 1997.

Coyle, Michael J. "Latinos and the Texas criminal justice system." *National Council of La Raza Statistical Brief* 2 (2003): 1.

Daniels, Roger. "Japanese American incarceration revisited, 1941–2010." *Asian American Law Journal* 18 (2011): 133.

Davis, Angela Y. "Race, gender, and prison history: From the convict lease system to the supermax prison." *Prison masculinities* (2001): 35–45.

Davis, Angela Y. *Are prisons obsolete?* Seven Stories, 2011.

De Genova, Nicholas. "The production of culprits: From deportability to detainability in the aftermath of 'homeland security.'" *Citizenship Studies* 11, no. 5 (2007): 421–448.

Ditton, Paula M., and Doris James Wilson. *Truth in sentencing in state prisons.* Washington, DC: U.S. Department of Justice, Office of Justice Programs, Bureau of Justice Statistics, 1999.

Du Bois, W. E. B. "The spawn of slavery: The convict-lease system in the South." *Missionary Review of the World* 14 (1901): 737–745.

Edgar, Kimmett, and Carol Martin. *Perceptions of race and conflict: perspectives of minority ethnic prisoners and of prison officers.* Home Office, Research, Development and Statistics Directorate, 2004.

Enns, Peter K. "The public's increasing punitiveness and its influence on mass incarceration in the United States." In *Annual meeting of the American Political Science Association, Washington, DC,* 2010, 1–37.

Feagin, Joe R. *Racist America: Roots, current realities, and future reparations.* New York: Routledge, 2010.

Forman, James, Jr. "Black poor, black elites, and America's prisons." *Cardozo Law Review* 32 (2010): 791.

Forman, James Jr. "Racial critiques of mass incarceration: Beyond the New Jim Crow." *New York University Law Review* 87 (2012): 21.

Foster, Holly, and John Hagan. "The mass incarceration of parents in America: Issues of race/ethnicity, collateral damage to children, and prisoner reentry." *Annals of the American Academy of Political and Social Science* 623, no. 1 (2009): 179–194.

Franklin, Travis W. "Sentencing Native Americans in US federal courts: An examination of disparity." *Justice Quarterly* 30, no. 2 (2013): 310–339.

French, Laurence ed. *Indians and criminal justice.* Totowa, NJ: Allanheld, Osmun, 1982.

French, Laurence, ed. *Native American justice.* Chicago: Burnham: 2003.

Gabbidon, Shaun L., and Helen Taylor Greene. *Race and crime.* Thousand Oaks, CA: Sage, 2012.

Garcia, Robert. "Latinos and Criminal Justice." *Chicano-Latino Law Review* 14 (1994): 6.

Garland, David. *Punishment and welfare: A history of penal strategies.* Brookfield, VT: Gower, 1985.

Garland, David, ed. *Mass imprisonment: Social causes and consequences.* Thousand Oaks, CA: Sage, 2001.

Goodman, Philip. "'It's Just Black, White, or Hispanic': An Observational Study of Racializing Moves in California's Segregated Prison Reception Centers." *Law & Society Review* 42, no. 4 (2008): 735–770.

Gottschalk, Marie. "The past, present, and future of mass incarceration in the United States." *Criminology & Public Policy* 10, no. 3 (2011): 483–504.

Gray, James. *Why our drug laws have failed: A judicial indictment of the war on drugs.* Philadelphia: Temple University Press, 2010.

Green, Donald E. "The contextual nature of American Indian criminality." *American Indian Culture and Research Journal* 17, no. 2 (1993): 99–119.

Green, Donald E. "American Indian criminality: What do we really know?" *American Indians: Social Justice and Public Policy* (1991): 222–270.

Greene, Helen Taylor, and Shaun L. Gabbidon. *African American criminological thought.* New York: SUNY Press, 2000.

Grobsmith, Elizabeth S. *Indians in prison: Incarcerated Native Americans in Nebraska.* Lincoln: University of Nebraska Press, 1994.

Hallet, Michael A. *Private prisons in America: A critical race perspective.* Urbana: University of Illinois Press, 2006.

Harris, Othello, and R. Robin Miller, eds. *Impacts of incarceration on the African American family.* New Brunswick, NJ: Transaction, 2003.

Hebert, Christopher G. "Sentencing outcomes of black, Hispanic, and white males convicted under federal sentencing guidelines." *Criminal Justice Review* 22, no. 2 (1997): 133–156.

Herivel, Tara, and Paul Wright, eds. *Prison nation: The warehousing of America's poor.* New York: Routledge, 2003.

Hogg, Robert S., Eric F. Druyts, Scott Burris, Ernest Drucker, and Steffanie A. Strathdee. "Years of life lost to prison: Racial and gender gradients in the United States of America." *Harm Reduction Journal* 5, no. 4 (2008): 1–5.

Howard, John. "The politics of dancing under Japanese-American incarceration." In *History Workshop Journal* no. 52 (2001): 123–151.

Howard, John. *Concentration camps on the home front: Japanese Americans in the house of Jim Crow.* Chicago: University of Chicago Press, 2009.

Inverarity, James, and Daniel McCarthy. "Punishment and social structure revisited: Unemployment and imprisonment in the United States, 1948–1984." *Sociological Quarterly* 29, no. 2 (1988): 263–279.

Jackson, Jerome E., and Sue Ammen. "Race and correctional officers' punitive attitudes toward treatment programs for inmates." *Journal of Criminal Justice* 24, no. 2 (1996): 153–166.

Jang, Sung Joon. "Race, ethnicity, and deviance: A study of Asian and non-Asian adolescents in America." In *Sociological Forum* 17, no. 4 (2002): 647–680.

Jensen, Gary F., Joseph H. Stauss, and V. William Harris. "Crime, delinquency, and the American Indian." *Human Organization* 36, no. 3 (1977): 252–257.

Johnson, Brian D., and Sara Betsinger. "Punishing the 'model minority': Asian-American criminal sentencing outcomes in federal district courts." *Criminology* 47, no. 4 (2009): 1045–1090.

Johnson, Jacqueline. "Mass Incarceration: A Contemporary Mechanism of Racialization in the United States." *Gonzaga Law Review* 47 (2011): 301.

Kennedy, Randall. *Race, crime, and the law.* Random House Digital, Inc., 1998.

Klinger, David A., and Dave Grossman. "Who should deal with foreign terrorists on US soil? Socio-legal consequences of September 11 and the ongoing threat of terrorist attacks in America." *Harvard Journal of Law and Public Policy* 25 (2001): 815.

Leiber, Michael J., and Kristan C. Fox. "Race and the impact of detention on juvenile justice decision making." *Crime & Delinquency* 51, no. 4 (2005): 470–497.

Leonard, Karen Isaksen, ed. *Muslims in the United States: The state of research.* New York: Russell Sage Foundation, 2003.

London, Andrew S., and Nancy A. Myers. "Race, incarceration, and health: A life-course approach." *Research on Aging* 28, no. 3 (2006): 409–422.

Lopez, Mark Hugo, and Michael T. Light. *A rising share: Hispanics and federal crime.* Washington, DC: Pew Research Center, 2009.

Lopez, Mark Hugo, and Gretchen Livingston. *Hispanics and the criminal justice system: Low confidence, high exposure.* Washington, DC: Pew Hispanic Center, 2009.

Loury, Glenn C. *Race, incarceration, and American values.* Cambridge, MA: MIT Press, 2008.

Luna-Firebaugh, Eileen M. "Incarcerating ourselves: Tribal jails and corrections." *Prison Journal* 83, no. 1 (2003): 51.

Mann, Coramae R. *Unequal justice: A question of color.* Indiana University Press, 1993.

Massoglia, Michael, and Cody Warner. "The consequences of incarceration." *Criminology & Public Policy* 10, no. 3 (2011): 851–863.

Mauer, Marc. *Race to incarcerate.* New York: New Press, 2006.

Mauer, Marc, and Ryan S. King. *Uneven justice: State rates of incarceration by race and ethnicity.* Washington, DC: Sentencing Project, 2007.

McGovern, Virginia, Stephen Demuth, and Joseph E. Jacoby. "Racial and ethnic recidivism risks: A comparison of postincarceration rearrest, reconviction, and reincarceration among white, black, and Hispanic releasees." *Prison Journal* 89, no. 3 (2009): 309–327.

Meierhoefer, Barbara S. *The general effect of mandatory minimum prison terms.* Washington, DC: Federal Judicial Centre, 1992.

Miller, Jerome G. *Search and destroy: African-American males in the criminal justice system.* New York: Cambridge University Press, 1996.

Minton, Todd D. "Jails in Indian country, 2004." Research Bulletin (NCJ 214257). Washington, DC: Bureau of Justice Statistics, 2005.

Morín, José Luis. *Latino/a rights and justice in the United States: Perspectives and approaches* (2nd ed.). Durham, NC: Carolina Academic Press, 2009.

Murray, Joseph. "The cycle of punishment: Social exclusion of prisoners and their children." *Criminology and Criminal Justice* 7, no. 1 (2007): 55–81.

Myers, Martha A. "Inequality and the punishment of minor offenders in the early 20th century." *Law & Society Review* 27 (1993): 313.

Myers, Martha A. *Race, labor, and punishment in the New South*. Columbus: Ohio State University Press, 1998.

Naber, Nadine. "The rules of forced engagement race, gender, and the culture of fear among Arab immigrants in San Francisco post-9/11." *Cultural Dynamics* 18, no. 3 (2006): 235–267.

Nielsen, Marianne O., and Robert A. Silverman, (eds.) *Native Americans, crime, and justice*. Boulder, CO: Westview, 1996.

Nielsen, Marianne O., and Robert A. Silverman, (eds.) *Criminal justice in Native America*. Tucson: University of Arizona Press, 2009.

Ogletree, Charles J., Jr. "Black man's burden: Race and the death penalty in America." *Oregan Law Review* 81 (2002): 15.

Ogletree, Charles J., Jr., and Austin Sarat, eds. *From lynch mobs to the killing state: Race and the death penalty in America*. New York: NYU Press, 2006.

Owens, Charles E. *Mental health and black offenders*. Boston: Lexington Books, 1980.

Pager, Devah. *Marked: Race, crime, and finding work in an era of mass incarceration*. Chicago: University of Chicago Press, 2008.

Pattillo, Mary E., David F. Weiman, and Bruce Western, eds. *Imprisoning America: The social effects of mass incarceration*. New York: Russell Sage Foundation, 2004.

Petersilia, Joan. *When prisoners come home: Parole and prisoner reentry*. New York: Oxford University Press, 2003.

Pettit, Becky. *Invisible men: Mass incarceration and the myth of black progress*. New York: Russell Sage Foundation, 2012.

Pettit, Becky, and Bruce Western. "Mass imprisonment and the life course: Race and class inequality in US incarceration." *American Sociological Review* 69, no. 2 (2004): 151–169.

Price, Byron Eugene, and John Charles Morris, eds. *Prison privatization: The many facets of a controversial industry*. Santa Barbara, CA: ABC-CLIO, 2012.

Quraishi, Muzammil. *Muslims and crime: A comparative study*. Burlington, VT: Ashgate, 2005.

Radelet, Michael L., and Glenn L. Pierce. "Race and Death Sentencing in North Carolina, 1980–2007." *North Carolina Law Review* 89 (2010): 2119.

Reed, Little Rock, ed. *The American Indian in the white man's prisons: A story of genocide*. Taos, NM: UnCompromising Books, 1993.

Reese, Renford. *American paradox: Young black men*. Durham, NC: Carolina Academic Press, 2004.

Reiman, Jeffrey. *The rich get richer and the poor get prison: Ideology, class and criminal justice* (8th ed.). Boston: Allyn & Bacon, 2010.

Reisig, Michael D., William D. Bales, Carter Hay, and Xia Wang. "The effect of racial inequality on black male recidivism." *Justice Quarterly* 24, no. 3 (2007): 408–434.

Rios, Victor M. "The hyper-criminalization of Black and Latino male youth in the era of mass incarceration." *Souls* 8, no. 2 (2006): 40–54.

Rios, Victor M. "The consequences of the criminal justice pipeline on black and Latino masculinity." *Annals of the American Academy of Political and Social Science* 623, no. 1 (2009): 150–162.

Roberts, Dorothy E. "The social and moral cost of mass incarceration in African American communities." *Stanford Law Review* 56, no. 5 (2004): 1271–1305.

Ross, Luana. *Inventing the savage: The social construction of Native American criminality.* Austin: University of Texas Press, 1998.

Rounds-Bryant, Jennifer L., Mark A. Motivans, and Bernadette Pelissier. "Comparison of background characteristics and behaviors of African-American, Hispanic, and white substance abusers treated in federal prison: Results from the TRIAD Study." *Journal of Psychoactive Drugs* 35, no. 3 (2003): 333–341.

Rowell-Cunsolo, Tawandra L., Roderick J. Harrison, and Rahwa Haile. "Exposure to prison sexual assault among incarcerated black men." *Journal of African American Studies* (2013): 1–9.

Russell-Brown, Katheryn. *Protecting our own: Race, crime, and African Americans.* Lanham, MD: Rowman & Littlefield, 2006.

Salinas, Lupe S. "Latinos and criminal justice in Texas: Has the new millennium brought progress?" *Thurgood Marshall Law Review* 30 (2004): 289.

Sampson, Robert J., and Charles Loeffler. "Punishment's place: The local concentration of mass incarceration." *Daedalus* 139, no. 3 (2010): 20–31.

Schiraldi, Vince, Brenda V. Smith, and J. Zeidenberg. *Reducing racial disparities in juvenile detention.* Annie E. Casey Foundation, 2001.

Selman, Donna, and Paul Leighton. *Punishment for sale: Private prisons, big business, and the incarceration binge.* Lanham, MD: Rowman & Littlefield, 2010.

Smith, Earl, and Angela J. Hattery. "Incarceration: A tool for racial segregation and labor exploitation." *Race, Gender & Class* 15, nos. 1/2 (2008): 79–97.

Spalek, Basia, ed. *Islam, crime and criminal justice.* Portland, OR: Cullompton, 2002.

Spohn, Cassia, and David Holleran. "The imprisonment penalty paid by young, unemployed black and Hispanic male offenders." *Criminology* 38, no. 1 (2000): 281–306.

Steffensmeier, Darrell, and Stephen Demuth. "Ethnicity and sentencing outcomes in US federal courts: Who is punished more harshly?" *American Sociological Review* 65, no. 5 (2000): 705–729.

Tarter, Michele Lise, and Richard Bell, eds. *Buried lives: Incarcerated in early America.* Athens: University of Georgia Press, 2012.

Taylor, Margaret H. "Dangerous by decree: detention without bond in immigration proceedings." *Loyola Law Review* 50 (2004): 149.

Thompson, Anthony C. *Releasing prisoners, redeeming communities: Reentry, race, and politics.* NYU Press, 2008.

Tonry, Michael. *Punishing race: A continuing American dilemma*. Oxford University Press, 2011.

Travis, Jeremy. "Reentry and reintegration: New perspectives on the challenges of mass incarceration." In Mary Patillo, David Weiman, and Bruce Western (eds.), *Imprisoning America: The Social Effects of Mass Incarceration*. New York: Russell Sage Foundation (2004): 247–68.

Travis, Jeremy, and Michelle Waul, eds. *Prisoners once removed: The impact of incarceration and reentry on children, families, and communities*. Urban Insitute, 2003.

Unnever, James D., and Francis T. Cullen. "White perceptions of whether African Americans and Hispanics are prone to violence and support for the death penalty." *Journal of Research in Crime and Delinquency* 49, no. 4 (2012): 519–544.

Unnever, James D., and Shaun L. Gabbidon. *Race, racism, and crime: A theory of African American offending*. New York: Routledge, 2011.

Urbina, Martin Guevara. *Capital punishment and Latino offenders: Racial and ethnic differences in death sentences*. New York: LFB Scholarly Pub., 2003.

Villarruel, Francisco A., Nancy E. Walker, Pamela Minifee, Omara Rivera-Vazquez, Susan Peterson, and Kristen Perry. *Donde esta la justicia? A call to action on behalf of Latino and Latina youth in the US justice system, executive summary*. Washington, DC: Building Blocks for Youth, 2002.

Wacquant, Loïc. "From slavery to mass incarceration: Rethinking the race question in the US." *New Left Review* 13 (2002): 41–60.

Wacquant, Loïc. "America's new 'peculiar institution.'" In Thomas Blomberg and Stanley Cohen (eds.), *Punishment and Social Control*. New York: Aldine de Gruyter, 2003, 471–482.

Wacquant, Loïc. *Punishing the poor: The neoliberal government of social insecurity*. Durham, NC: Duke University Press, 2009.

Wakefield, Sara, and Christopher Wildeman. "Mass imprisonment and racial disparities in childhood behavioral problems." *Criminology & Public Policy* 10, no. 3 (2011): 793–817.

Walker, Nancy E., Francisco Villarruel, J. Michael Senger, and Angela M. Arboleda. *Lost opportunities: The reality of Latinos in the US criminal justice system*. National Council of La Raza, 2004.

Wehr, Kevin, and Elyshia Aseltine. *Beyond the prison industrial complex: Crime and incarceration in the 21st century*. New York: Routledge, 2013.

Weiman, David F. "Christopher Weiss: The origins of mass incarceration in New York State; The Rockefeller drug laws and the local war on drugs." *Do prisons make us safer? The benefits and costs of the prison boom* (2009): 73.

West, Cornel. *Race Matters*, Boston, MA: Beacon, 1993.

Western, Bruce. *Punishment and inequality in America*. New York: Russell Sage Foundation, 2006.

Western, Bruce, and Christopher Wildeman. "The black family and mass incarceration." *Annals of the American Academy of Political and Social Science* 621, no. 1 (2009): 221–242.

Whitford, Andrew B., and Jeff Yates. *Presidential rhetoric and the public agenda: Constructing the war on drugs.* Baltimore, MD: Johns Hopkins University Press, 2009.

Wilson, William J. *More than just race: Being black and poor in the inner city (Issues of our time).* New York: W.W. Norton & Company, 2009.

Wolff, Nancy, Jing Shi, and Cynthia L. Blitz. "Racial and ethnic disparities in types and sources of victimization inside prison." *Prison Journal* 88, no. 4 (2008): 451–472.

Wolfgang, Marvin E., and Marc Riedel. "Rape, race, and the death penalty in Georgia." *American Journal of Orthopsychiatry* 45, no. 4 (1975): 658–668.

Wordes, Madeline, Timothy S. Bynum, and Charles J. Corley. "Locking up youth: The impact of race on detention decisions." *Journal of Research in Crime and Delinquency* 31, no. 2 (1994): 149–165.

Yen, Rhoda J. "Racial stereotyping of Asians and Asian Americans and its effect on criminal justice: A reflection on the Wayne Lo case." *Asian Law Journal* 7 (2000): 1.

About the Editor and Contributors

SCOTT WM. BOWMAN, Ph.D., is an Associate Professor in the School of Criminal Justice at Texas State University. He received a B.A. in Psychology from Arizona State University and his M.A. in Justice Studies from Arizona State University. Dr. Bowman earned his Ph.D. also in Justice Studies from Arizona State University with an emphasis on racial and socioeconomic inequalities. His current teaching and research interests include race and crime, socioeconomic status and crime, hip-hop and positive youth development, and juvenile justice. His recent research appears as various academic journals and books on a variety of criminological and sociological topics. Most important, Dr. Bowman has a beautiful wife Tori and two beautiful daughters, Imani and Qwynci.

About the Contributors

EILEEN M. AHLIN, Ph.D., is an Assistant Professor of Criminal Justice in the School of Public Affairs at Penn State Harrisburg. Dr. Ahlin joined the faculty in 2013 after 15 years with a private corporation, where she conducted research at the federal, state, and local levels. She received a B.A. in Administration of Justice and Sociology (multiple major) from Penn State University and her M.A. in Sociology (focus on crime, delinquency, and corrections) from George Mason University. Dr. Ahlin earned her Ph.D. in Criminology and Criminal Justice from the University of Maryland, College Park. Her teaching and research interests include criminological theory, violence, neighborhood effects, corrections, racial and social justice, and research methods. Her recent research appears in journals such as *Journal of Interpersonal Violence, Journal of Community Psychology,* and *Federal Probation.*

ELYSHIA ASELTINE, Ph.D., is an Assistant Professor in the Department of Sociology, Anthropology, and Criminal Justice at Towson University near Baltimore. She graduated with her Ph.D. in Sociology from the University of Texas at Austin. Her teaching and research focus on punishment and race/ethnicity in the United States and southern Africa.

TONY A. BARRINGER, Ph.D., is Associate Provost for Faculty Affairs at Florida Gulf Coast University (FGCU), where he has also served as Interim Dean, Associate Dean, and Division Chair. Prior to joining FGCU in 1997, he taught at the College of Lake County and Southeast Missouri State University. He has over 20 years of practical experience in criminal justice and has taught in higher education nearly as long. Dr. Barringer has presented nationally and internationally, served as a consultant to the Bulgarian Ministry of Justice, and, because of the impact of his research and practice, served as a guest discussant at the Florida Department of Corrections' Re-entry Summit. He has acted as Principal or Co-Principal Investigator for approximately $1 million in funded state and federal grants in juvenile justice and wraparound services and has published widely on the subject of minorities' experiences with the criminal justice system. Dr. Barringer earned a B.S. in Criminal Justice and an M.S. in Public Administration from Southeast Missouri State University and a doctorate from Northern Illinois University.

CHRISTOPHER BICKEL is an Assistant Professor of Sociology at California Polytechnic State University. As a prison rights activist, he has been researching juvenile detention centers and prisons for over a decade. He is also the Director of the Continuation to College Program, which offers college-level sociology classes to low-income high school students.

NICHOLAS BRADY is an activist-scholar from Baltimore who is currently pursuing his doctorate in Culture and Theory at the University of California–Irvine. At UC-Irvine, he is also the head coach of the James Baldwin Debate Society, the only debate team in the nation housed exclusively in an African-American studies department. He is also a member of Leaders of a Beautiful Struggle, a community-based think tank focused on empowering youth in the political process. Through these organizations, Nicholas has helped produce policy proposals, has supported efforts in Baltimore against the prison industrial complex, has led educational forums on a myriad of community-oriented projects, and has used debate as a critical pedagogical tool to activate the voices of young people from ages 10 to 25.

LAUREN BRINKLEY-RUBINSTEIN is a fourth-year Ph.D. student in the Community Research and Action program at Vanderbilt University and has conducted criminal justice and public health research for seven years. Her primary research interests include investigating the social context of health, the impact of incarceration and drug laws on health, health equity, and health policy. Lauren has an educational background in sociology/criminology and research experience in health research methodology with a focus on health disparities and the social determinants of health. She is also well versed in the needs of the Nashville HIV community, as she collaborated with community members and organizations to conduct and write the Nashville area HIV Needs Assessment from 2008 to 2010. Lauren has also received four research grants to conduct a program evaluation of the efficacy of a community-based program to promote healthy behaviors in at-risk, incarceration-prone youth; conduct an assessment of the impact of health literacy education on the health outcomes of HIV-positive individuals; conduct a qualitative assessment of the role of rural religious leaders in HIV prevention; and investigate the health impact of incarceration and subsequent restrictions via welfare reform on HIV-positive individuals.

BELINDA E. BRUSTER is a BSW Program Director and Assistant Professor at Florida Gulf Coast University (FGCU), College for Health Professions and Social Work. She received her Bachelors of Arts degree in Psychology from Wayne State University (WSU). In 1994, she completed the Masters of Social Work program at Norfolk State University (NSU) and in 2005, she obtained her Ph.D. in Social Work from NSU. She joined the Academy of Certified Social Workers (ACSW) in 1998. She is licensed in Virginia and Florida as a Clinical Social Worker (LCSW). Dr. Bruster received the Ohio State University (OSU) Dissertation Award in 2006. Her dissertation focused on the strengths of African-American female welfare recipients.

MICHAEL J. COYLE, Ph.D., is an Associate Professor in the Department of Political Science at California State University–Chico. In his research, teaching, and activism, he examines language, public policy, and everyday life to expose the social construction of discarded persons, that is, those identified for their difference from promoted norms and who are characterized as "unlike us," "dangerous," or "punishment worthy": the so-called deviant, imprisoned, and excluded.

JANETTE DIAZ is currently a doctoral candidate in the Department of Sociology at the University of California–Santa Barbara. Her research areas include social stratification, race/ethnicity, gender, and class. She is currently working on her dissertation research, which focuses on examining how inequality is created and reproduced in department stores. She also focuses on how department store workers negotiate opportunities for mobility in the retail sector, which tends to be plagued by low pay and few opportunities for advancement.

DANIELLE DIRKS is an Assistant Professor of Sociology at Occidental College, a private, liberal arts college in Los Angeles. Her research and teaching interests, broadly conceived, focus on justice and inequality in America. She recently published *How Ethical Systems Change: Lynching and Capital Punishment* with Sheldon Ekland-Olson (Routledge, 2011). Her work has been published in *Justice Quarterly* and *Qualitative Sociology* and has been featured in more mainstream outlets such as the *New York Times* and National Public Radio. Her current research examines the aftermath of violent victimization, sexual assault survivorship, and punishment in the digital era. She is also the co-founder of the national organization End Rape on Campus (EROC).

RONNIE A. DUNN is an Associate Professor of Urban Studies at the Maxine Goodman Levin College of Urban Affairs at Cleveland State University. He is an urban sociologist whose research and teaching interests primarily address issues related to minorities and the urban poor, with a particularly focus on race, crime, and the criminal justice system. His area of expertise is racial profiling, which is the focus of his 2011 book, *Racial Profiling: Causes & Consequences* (Kendall-Hunt). He has also published research on police oversight and accountability, health disparities, cancer prevention behavior among low-income African Americans, and the evolution of the field of urban studies. He has also provided technical assistance to local law enforcement agencies, public transit authorities, and civil rights organizations and attorneys.

JOE FEAGIN is Ella C. McFadden Professor at Texas A&M University. He has done much research on racism issues and served as Scholar in Residence at the U.S. Commission on Civil Rights. He has published 63 scholarly books and 200-plus scholarly articles and monographs in his research areas. One of his books (*Ghetto Revolts*) was nominated for a Pulitzer Prize. Among his recent books are *Systemic Racism* (Routledge, 2006); *Two-Faced Racism* (Routledge, 2007, with L. Picca); *The White Racial Frame* (2nd ed.; Routledge, 2013); *Racist America* (2nd ed.; Routledge, 2010); *White Party, White Government* (Routledge, 2012); and *Latinos Facing Racism* (Paradigm, 2014, with J. Cobas). He is the recipient of a 2006 Harvard Alumni Lifetime Achievement Award, the 2012 Soka Gakkai International–USA Social Justice Award, the 2013 American Association for Affirmative Action's Arthur Fletcher Lifetime Achievement Award, and the American Sociological Association's 2013 W. E. B. Du Bois Career of Distinguished Scholarship Award. He was the 1999–2000 president of the American Sociological Association.

SUSANA M. FUNES is currently a practicing psychologist in Tijuana, Baja California, México, and has treated diverse clinical and psychiatric populations. She has worked in diverse clinical settings in México, including private practice, prisons, and substance treatment facilities, with a focus on the psychoanalytic and psychosocial treatment of family. She and Roberto Velasquez collaborated on the outreach and treatment of young immigrant women involved in the sex slave industry in San Diego. She has been active in many professional organizations in México and continues to advocate for more mental health services for high-risk populations. She obtained her education at Universidad Autonoma de Queretaro, México.

LAURIE A. GOULD is an Assistant Professor of Criminal Justice and Criminology at Georgia Southern University in Statesboro, Georgia. She has spent the past six years researching comparative penology, and her work has been published in journals such as the *British Journal of Criminology, Women & Criminal Justice,* and *International Criminal Justice Review.* Additionally, she co-authored a book entitled *Corporal Punishment* *around the World* (ABC-CLIO, 2012). She maintains an active research agenda that includes comparative penology, state failure, and gender issues in punishment.

TIMOTHY P. HILTON is an Associate Professor in the School of Social Work at Eastern Washington University. He holds a Master's degree and Ph.D. from the School of Social Service Administration at the University of Chicago. He has several years of social work experience in the areas of welfare and work, homeless services, program evaluation, and policy. His primary areas of research are homelessness, low-wage employment, and prisoner reentry. He has served on several boards, including the Michigan Prison Reentry Initiative Steering Team; Room at the Inn, a homeless shelter in Marquette, Michigan; and Targeted Restart, a service agency for ex-offenders. He lives in Spokane, Washington, with his wife, Samantha, and two daughters, Annabel and Natalie.

DR. NIKITAH IMANI is Professor and Chair of the Department of Black Studies at the University of Nebraska–Omaha. Dr. Imani earned his Bachelor's degree from the Edmund Walsh School of Foreign Service. He subsequently received a Master's in political science and a second Master's and then Ph.D. in sociology from the University of Florida. He is an international political sociologist with a focus on Africana studies and global affairs from an Africana perspective. He has published three major books: *Mbongi, Kinzonzi,* and *Head Games. Mbongi* (Reapalife Press, 2004) is a theoretical formulation of how Africana peoples throughout the diaspora, but particularly in the United States, might go about creating organic, local political institutions that would more effectively represent the communal will and serve as a springboard for domestic development. *Kinzonzi* (Reapalife Press, 2004) is focused on the creation of communitarian mediation institutions for local dispute resolution. *Head Games* (Univeristy Press of America, 2011) was a project on Eurocentric psychotherapy and its neocolonialist implications. Dr. Imani is currently working on a book manuscript involving African classical approaches to mathematics.

DR. RONN JOHNSON is a licensed and board certified clinical psychologist with experience in academic, clinical, and forensic settings.

Dr. Johnson is a Diplomate of the American Board of Professional Psychology. He has served as a staff psychologist in Veterans Affairs health care systems, community mental health clinics, hospitals, schools, and university counseling centers. Alliant International University, the University of Iowa, University of Nebraska–Lincoln, University of Central Oklahoma, San Diego State University, and University of San Diego are among his previous academic appointments. Dr. Johnson is founder and director of the Burn Institute's Juvenile Arson & Explosive Research & Intervention Center. He founded several counseling centers that currently serve racially diverse populations. These sites include the Urban Corp of San Diego County, Southern California American Indian Resource Center, and the Elim Korean Counseling Center. He is also the academic faculty advisor to ASIA (Asian Students in Action). In addition, he established clinical mental health clinics: Korean Mental Health Services and Native American Counseling Services at the Southern California American Indian Resource Center. His forensic, scholarship, and teaching interests include contraterrorism, ethical-legal issues, police psychology, risk assessment, and trauma.

ANNE LI KRINGEN, Ph.D., is currently an Assistant Professor in the Henry Lee College of Criminal Justice and Forensic Sciences at the University of New Haven. With an interest in disparity within the criminal justice system, she has conducted research on a variety of issues concerning both gender and racial inequality in policing, courts, and corrections. Working directly with police agencies, her present research focuses on women entering the policing profession and the challenges they face as minorities within a male-dominated field.

PAT LAUDERDALE, with a Ph.D. from Stanford University, is a Professor of Justice at Arizona State University and has been a visiting scholar at Stanford University in Sociology and the Center for Comparative Studies in Race and Ethnicity. He continues to pursue a research agenda on politics, law, diversity, and nature. He explores the thematic threads of the alternative ways in which marginalized people struggle with dominant concepts of justice and injustice; how such people have fared in utilizing various means to attain justice; and the role of hegemony surrounding conceptions of what is just or unjust. He is author or coauthor of numerous books, including *Lives in the Balance: Perspectives on Global Injustice and Inequality* (Brill, 1997); *Terrorism: A New Testament* (de Sitter, 2005); *Theory and Methodology of World Development: The Writings of Andre*

Gunder Frank (Palgrave MacMillan, 2010); *The Struggle for Control: A Study of Law, Disputes and Deviance* (State University of New York Press, 1993); and *Law and Society: Sociological Perspectives on Criminal Law* (Little, Brown, 1983); *and the third edition of A Political Analysis of Deviance* (de Sitter, 2011).

NKRUMAH LEWIS, Ph.D., is an Assistant Professor of Sociology at Winston Salem State University. He received his Ph.D. in Sociology with an emphasis on race and crime from Virginia Polytechnic Institute and State University. Dr. Lewis's research interests are criminal deviance, criminal justice, interpersonal and domestic violence, masculinities, and psychosocial aggression and religion. He is a Dr. King Building the Dream Award recipient, serves on Institutional Research Boards at both UNC Greensboro and Wake Forest University, and is a mentor for the Real Men Teach Program and Program Evaluator for the University of North Carolina's Minority Male Mentoring Program. He recently released his autobiographical sketch, *Becoming A Butterfly: From Prison to Ph.D.* (Nkrumah Lewis, 2012).

VERA LOPEZ is an Associate Professor in the School of Justice and Social Inquiry at Arizona State University. She received her Ph.D. in School Psychology from the University of Texas at Austin. She also completed a one-year clinical research internship at the Institute for Juvenile Research at the University of Illinois at Chicago, a two-year National Institute of Mental Health (NIMH)–funded research post-doc at Arizona State University's Prevention Research Center, and a clinical internship at the Arizona Department of Juvenile Correction's Black Canyon Correctional School for girls. Lopez's research areas include adolescent delinquency, sexual risk taking, substance use, and prevention research with a major focus on system-involved girls. Her work has been featured in a number of journals, including *Latino Studies*, *Journal of Family Issues*, *Journal of Youth and Adolescence*, *Feminist Criminology*, *Family Relations*, *Journal of Adolescence*, and *Criminal Justice & Behavior*. She and colleagues from ASU also recently published an edited book, *Adolescent Girls' Sexualities and the Media* (Peter Lang, 2013) as part of the Peter Lang Mediated Youth series.

MICHAEL J. LYNCH is a Professor in the Department of Criminology, and Associated Faculty in the Patel School of Global Sustainability at the

University of South Florida. Professor Lynch's primary research areas include green criminology, radical criminology, racial biases in criminal justice processes, and corporate crime.

JOSEPH S. MASTERS was born in Munising, Michigan, and is a member of the Sualt Ste. Marie tribe of Chippewa Indians. He has a 13-year-old daughter named Liliana Loonsfoot Masters. In 2009, Joe returned to school at Northern Michigan University and graduated with his B.S.W. with a minor cluster in Human Behavior and American Indian Studies. During that time, he was the recipient of the Ronald E. McNair Scholarship. As a Masters Student in the George Warren Brown School of Social Work at Washington University in St. Louis,—Joe partnered with Dr. Timothy Hilton and conducted research on American Indians returning to the reservations after being in prison. Joe was also a Kathryn M. Buder scholar at the Brown School of Social Work, with a concentration in Mental Health and administration. He is currently conducting his concentration practicum at the Buder Center under Dr. Tovar on Hunting, Fishing and Gathering, and also on the Two Spirits Project.

TAMARA K. NOPPER has a Ph.D. in sociology and is a lecturer at Temple University and the University of Pennsylvania, where she teaches courses on race and ethnic relations, immigration, economic inequality, and the history and sociology of Asian Americans. Her publications have examined the impact of globalization on racial and economic inequality in the United States, race and immigration enforcement, minority business development and immigrant entrepreneurship, and Black–Asian-American conflict.

LISA PASKO is Associate Professor in the Department of Sociology and Criminology at the University of Denver. She received her Ph.D. from the University of Hawaii at Manoa, and Professor Pasko primarily researches and teaches about gender, sexuality, crime, and punishment. In addition to numerous articles, book chapters, and technical reports, she is co-author of *The Female Offender: Girls, Women, and Crime* (Sage, 2012) and *Girls, Women, and Crime: Selected Readings* (Sage, 2013). Professor Pasko's latest research examines the experiences of sexual minority girls in the justice system, paying particular attention to the correctional attitudes about sexual behaviors and identities as well as reproductive decision making. As a public sociologist, she is also Chair of the Colorado Coalition for Girls and is performing an ongoing evaluation of InterCept, a girl offender intervention program in Colorado Springs.

DR. MATTHEW PATE is a Senior Research Fellow with the Violence Research Group in the School of Criminal Justice at the State University of New York–University at Albany. Pate is a former law enforcement executive who now serves as a certified law enforcement instructor in the state of Arkansas. He has served as a consultant for the U.S. Department of Justice and for the United Nations, and he advises law enforcement agencies around the country. He is the author of two books on criminal justice topics.

PEDRO RODRIGUEZ has a Master's of Science in Justice Studies from Arizona State University's School of Social Transformation, as well as concurrent Bachelor's degrees in History and Political Science. His research interests include wrongful convictions, clemency, capital punishment, colonialism, and the effects of popular activism on political actors. More specifically, his work examines how state-sponsored activists influence pardon and parole decisions. Pedro's role in securing freedom for a wrongfully convicted man was featured in the recent publication *Manifest Injustice* by Barry Siegel. He is a volunteer with the Arizona Justice Project and 2010–2011 ASU Graduate College Fellow. Pedro is a social science and civics teacher in Arizona.

CARL ROOT is an Instructor at Eastern Kentucky University in the School of Justice Studies. His recent research includes work in the realms of police violence, corrections, and national security whistleblowers. When not busy teaching, reading, writing, or otherwise obsessing about justice-related issues, Carl can be found at home in Winchester, Kentucky, with his wonderful wife Danielle and their menagerie of fur babies, including Walter, Bunny, Maude, Che, and Albert.

DOROTHY S. RUIZ is Associate Professor of Africana Studies and Sociology at the University of North Carolina at Charlotte. She has served as

Interim Chair and is presently Director of Undergraduate Studies in the African Studies Department. Her research focuses on ways in which societal patterns and ideologies influence social, economic, and health outcomes of different groups, with specific emphasis on grandparents and incarcerated adults and their children. Her research projects include Contemporary African American Families: Changes in Family Structure and New Roles for Grandmothers; How Incarceration Impacts African American Families; and Contemporary African American Families: Accomplishments, Challenges, and Strategies in the 21st Century. She is author of numerous articles, book chapters, and books, including *The Handbook of Mental Health and Mental Disorder among African Americans* (Greenwood, 1990) *and Amazing Grace: Custodial African American Grandmothers as Caregivers and Conveyers of Traditional Values* (Praeger, 2004).

SARAH SCOTT is currently an Assistant Professor of Criminal Justice and Public Administration at Texas A&M University–Corpus Christi. Her M.S. and Ph.D. are from the School of Criminal Justice at Texas State University. She teaches several courses that focus on correctional practices and also teaches research methods at the graduate and undergraduate levels. Within the area of corrections, she has focused on conducting program evaluations with state and local criminal justice officials.

DR. BRIAN CHAD STARKS is an Assistant Professor in the Sociology and Criminal Justice Department at Delaware State University. B. Chad earned his B.A. in Sociology from Wofford College, an M.A. in Criminal Justice and a Master's Certificate in Alcohol and Drug Studies, both from the University of South Carolina. He completed his Ph.D. in Criminology from the University of Delaware. His current research draws from the law and society tradition and is grounded in a concern for social justice. He focuses broadly on law and inequality and more specifically, uses courtroom and community ethnography to examine the relationship between law, race/ethnicity, crime, and (in)justice.

LEONARD STEVERSON, Ph.D., is a retired Associate Professor of Sociology and Criminal Justice from the University System of Georgia. He is the author of *Policing in America: A Reference Handbook* (ABC-CLIO, 2007) and several book chapters, book reviews, and encyclopedia entries. He is currently an Adjunct Professor of Sociology at Flagler College in St. Augustine, Florida, and at the University of North Florida in Jacksonville.

Dr. RUTH THOMPSON-MILLER is an Assistant Professor at the University of Dayton. For over 15 years, she has conducted research on the Jim Crow South and South African apartheid. She has published in several edited books and journals. She is a McNair Scholar and received the National Institute of Mental Health Fellowship from the American Sociological Association. She has presented her work at national and international conferences.

Dr. ALANA VAN GUNDY is an Assistant Professor and the Criminal Justice Program Coordinator at Miami University in Ohio. Her research and publications focus on the etiology of female criminality, gender-specific theoretical testing, human rights violations within corrections, and policy recommendations for addressing female crime. Additionally, she has published work focused on online pedagogy and the National Inside-Out Prison Exchange Program.

ROBERTO J. VELASQUEZ, Ph.D., is a retired Professor of Psychology and private practitioner. He taught for 21 years at San Diego State University and has worked in diverse settings, including Atascadero State Hospital, a Veterans Affairs hospital in Phoenix, Arizona, and various community-based mental health centers throughout the southwestern United States. He graduated from the University of California–Riverside, Harvard University, and Arizona State University. He also had a postdoctoral fellowship at the University of Michigan that focused on survey methods in the Latino community. He has published one book on Chicano/a psychology and mental health and over 60 articles and book chapters on various aspects of Latino and minority mental health. As a clinician, he has specialized in working with former prison inmates from diverse cultural, economic, and linguistic backgrounds. He has also worked with refugee populations from Cuba, Vietnam, and the Middle East, especially those who were political prisoners. He grew up in a Chicano "barrio" in Riverside, California, and has always been a community activist, especially for the poor and disenfranchised.

EMMA ZACK is an Occidental College student from Boston, Massachusetts, who is majoring in sociology and minoring in music. Her academic interests include criminology, punishment, race and the prison industrial complex, and more recently, perceptions of female offenders. She is currently working on her senior thesis project, which examines public perceptions of female teacher sex offenders.

Index

597; effects of incarceration on families and, 540–43, 596–97; parent behind bars, 541; prison visit, 542; protection of human rights of, 598; recidivism, 599

Children Act and Sexually Violent Offender Registration Act, 520

Child Savers, 191

Chippewa County, 455

The Choice: The Issue of Black Survival in America (Yates), 87

Cholas, 122

CIA (Central Intelligence Agency), 260, 574

Civic Biology, 161

Civic participation and incarceration, 544–46

Civil Liberties Act, 54

Civilly dead prisoners, 579

Civil rights, 251

Civil Rights Act, 392

Civil Rights Congress (CRC), 144–45

Civil rights movement, 85–86

Clark, Kenneth B., 78

Clark, Ramsey, 389

Clinton, Bill, 69, 414–16, 510, 543

COINTELPRO (counterintelligence program), 251, 254

Coker vs. Georgia, 149

Coler, Jack R., 253–54

Coles, Samuel "Redd," 480

Collateral sanctions, 89

Collective efficacy, 536–37

Collective social ideology, 155. *See also* Ideology

Colonial history and Native Americans, 247–49

Colonial ideology, 259. *See also* Ideology

Colonial racism, 247

Colonization, defined, 354

Colonization Program, 54

Colorism, 346

Commissioner of Indian Affairs, 260

A Common Destiny: Blacks and American Society (Jaynes and Williams), 85

Communism, 212, 250

Communities: collective efficacy, 536–37; effects of incarceration, 535–39; effects of prisoner reentry on, 537–39; organizing, and racial profiling, 181; relocation, 539; social control in, 535

Comprehensive Crime Control Act (CCCA), 396–97, 400, 402, 405

Comprehensive Drug Abuse Prevention and Control act, 173

Conflict criminology, 343. *See also* Marxist criminology

Conflict theory, 428

Consent Decree, 258, 261

Conservative political beliefs, 373

Contemporary privatization, 363–65

Controlled Substance Act, 173, 416

Convict leasing: David Oshinsky's views on, 594; described, 362–63; racial disparity in, 363; for reinstating slavery, 594; system, 101–2

Coolidge, Calvin, 45

Cordon and sweep operations, 574–75

Core relational conditions, 324

Cornell Company, 364

Corporal punishments, 347, 348, 592

Corporeal chastisement, 102

Correctional officers: in Abu Ghraib, 377; academy training, 314; in Afghanistan, 574; aggressive approach of, 575; chronic illnesses, 313; in facilities and imprisonment activities, 317–18; forensic psychological realities of, 311–29; in Iraq, 574; job demands, 313; job satisfaction, 378; and juvenile prisons, 322–24; psychological screening for diverse prison facilities, 315–17; stress, 318–20; torture committed by, 576

Corrections Corporation of America (CCA), 104–5, 109–10, 363

Costs: effectiveness of private prisons, 96–97; to monitor sex offenders, 522–23; and three/two strikes laws, 424

Couch surf, 471

Counseling: eurocentric approach, 350; HIV/AIDS, 356; mental health, 354; multicultural, 350–51; substance abuse, 356

Counterterrorism, 313, 566, 567

CPS (Child protection service), 463

Crack baby, 437–38

Crack cocaine: adverse public health, 440; analogous effects on body, 437; and criminal justice system, 444, 446; distribution related violence, 438; and drug trade, 438; emergence of, 436; growth of, 437; and imprisonment, 436; law enforcement, 444, 447; and minorities, 443–44; penalties and drug quantity, 438–40; vs. powder cocaine, 436–37; price, 436; prison abolition from drug war of, 446–48; race implications of, 443; racism, 444; sentencing disparity